Perfect Match

ALSO BY ANISTATIA MILLER AND JARED BROWN

*The Complete Astrological Handbook for the Twenty-first Century:
Understanding and Combining the Wisdom of Chinese, Tibetan, Vedic,
Arabian, Judaic, and Western Astrology*

Anistatia Miller, ISAR CAP, RMAFA, and Jared Brown

Perfect

Match

Discovering Your Soulmate

SCHOCKEN BOOKS, NEW YORK

Photograph/Illustration Credits

Photograph of Jared Brown and Anastasia Miller (page 2), taken by Edward Sun/Sun Photography. · "Scene from Chinese Wedding Ceremony" (page 10), copyright © Bettmann/CORBIS. · "Hindu Marriage Ceremony" (page 90), copyright © Bettmann/ CORBIS. · "Ketubah" (page 178), by Marion Zimmer. Reprinted by permission of the Jessy Judaica Gallery. · "French Bridal Procession" (page 276), copyright © Hulton-Deutsch Collection/CORBIS. · "Michael J. Fox" (page 326), copyright © Hulton-Deutsch Collection/CORBIS. · "Astrological Chart" (page 346), from *Sphaera Mundi* by Johannes de Sacro Busto (1244–1325). Austria, first quarter 15th c. M. 722, f 18v. Copyright © by The Pierpont Morgan Library/Art Resource, NY.

Library of Congress Cataloging-in-Publication Data
Miller, Anistatia R, 1952–
Perfect match : discovering your soulmate / Anistatia R Miller and Jared M. Brown.
p.   cm.
Includes bibliographical references and index.
ISBN 0-8052-1129-2
1. Astrology and marriage.   2. Love.   I. Brown, Jared M., 1964–   II. Title.
BF1729.L6 M55 2002   133.5'83067—dc21   2001042639

www.schocken.com

Book design by Trina Stahl

Printed in the United States of America
First Edition
9 8 7 6 5 4 3 2 1

Contents

Figures and Tables

Figures

Tables

Preface and Acknowledgments

*W*hich way do you turn when "absence makes the heart grow fonder" yet "out of sight is out of mind"? There's no shortage of wisdom out there when it comes to matters of the heart. The problem is that it doesn't always agree with itself. This is the seemingly contradictory nature of advice. Fortunately, when your heart says, "Better safe than sorry," but your head says, "Nothing ventured, nothing gained," the time-tested wisdom of world astrology can help you choose the right path to love and show you how to make it last once you find it.

Even before we wrote *The Complete Astrological Handbook for the Twenty-first Century,* we'd found that most of the questions people ask professional astrologers focus on love and relationships. Yet when we scoured the astrology shelves of bookstores throughout North America, we couldn't find a single book that really answered the question: How can astrology improve relationships? There are stacks of books that identify mutually compatible Sun signs, but Sun signs alone can be extremely misleading. *Perfect Match: Discovering Your Soulmate* goes far beyond the basic zodiac. We cover four major astrological traditions, which include hundreds of planetary compatibilities and incompatibilities, even pairings of birth years. We bring together the astrological information, interpretations, and advice necessary to help you navigate your way through the complex terrain of a relationship. And we make it possible to decipher and compare essential portions of your and your mate's astrological birth charts without using any math.

What kind of lover are you? What does it take to make you happy? What limitations will be tossed in your direction as you take your place on love's playing field? What kind of partner will best suit your particular needs, desires, and personality traits? Can a long-term relationship that has become less than fulfilling be improved? In the pages that follow you'll learn how to use world astrology to answer these questions and many more. The love you crave and seek is achievable and this book will bring you closer to it.

We'd like to thank Nancy Brown, Roberta Chappell, Barbara Renard, Margaret Richardson, Carolyn Steninger, and Jennifer Yewer for taking the time to read and question every bit of the manuscript while it was still in its infancy. Thanks so much to astrologers Maya del Mar and Judi Vitale as well, for their comments on the finished work.

We wish to thank astrologer Susan Miller for inadvertently bringing us together, at a Christmas party we hosted in 1992. Our stars crossed on a very auspicious evening. We also want to express our gratitude to our cousin Daniel Brown who finally got us to meet each other, albeit under more panicked conditions than he'd intended.

Once again, we're indebted to Stephanie Ager for introducing us to yet another thought-provoking source of information. May you never lose your fascination and faith in astrology, Zodiac Lady. We also want to thank George Fertitta for always being the first to see potential and to encourage us to pursue it.

No book is the sole creation of its authors. The enthusiasm and cooperative efforts of many people (forming many interactive relationships) brought these pages to life. Publisher Janice Goldklang instilled faith in this project at the outset, faith that buoyed it every step of the way. Editorial director Susan Ralston's pragmatism, sense, and effervescent spirit kept us straight on course. Editor Cecelia Cancellaro and copyeditor Chuck Antony kept the book's voice alive, making the messages sing through-out. Managing editor Altie Karper kept the river of communication flowing smoothly. Design director

Kristen Bearse, designer Trina Stahl, cover designer Archie Ferguson, and production manager the late Kathy Grasso, who took the finished manuscript and constructed a beautiful visual package. A longtime colleague since 1987, Kathy made the physical quality of books her life. She will be missed. Many thanks also goes to production editor Susan Norton for keeping track of every detail in this book's production. Publicity director Sophie Cottrell introduced it to the world. Our deepest thanks to all of you for seeing this project through to its fruition.

Anistatia Miller, ISAR CAP, RMAFA, and Jared Brown
New York, New York
October 2001

Introduction

So long as lips shall kiss, and eyes shall see,
So long lives This, and This gives life to Thee.
—Sir Richard Burton, from the conclusion to his
1883 translation of *The Kama Sutra*

Everybody wants to love and to be loved. The whole of human behavior and existence has risen up around this simple premise. But before we can discuss love, we have to answer the basic question What is love?

You might fondly recall your first infatuation with a movie star, the local sports hero, a supermodel, a cheerleader, or the neighborhood hunk. You learned to cherish from afar. You adored those qualities that delighted your imagination and sparked your desire: slender or muscular, blond or brunette, heroic or sensitive, comical or serious. You dreamt that he or she was your lover, imagining magical first encounters and intimate moments. Such thoughts swept you off your feet in those formative years. It might've been a wonderful feeling, but it wasn't love. It was infatuation.

As you grew, you began to sense the existence of a more physical form of passion. Think about your first passionate kiss and the excitement you felt when a lover held you close. Those shivers of arousal may have been incredible, but again, that wasn't love. Those were feelings of lust.

If things got serious, you might've wondered how you ever lived before this person entered your life, and you probably believed that you could never be happy without him or her. This sensation has inspired poets, started wars, and built empires. But this isn't love either. It's dependency.

You may also have experienced a sense of pride at being seen with your love, and an instant dislike for anyone who could possibly come between you. That's possessiveness, which rarely exists alone— jealousy, the destructive stepchild of possessiveness, accompanies it wherever it appears.

Real love literally lights up your life. No kidding. According to a 2000 study conducted by Andreas Bartels at London's University College, there are four to twenty parts of the human brain's anterior cingulate cortex, middle insula, putamen, and caudate nucleus that light up on an MRI scan when you're shown a photo of your lover. Three other areas that light up when you're angry or depressed dim when love takes over.

There's nothing wrong with infatuation, lust, or even, at times, a modicum of dependency and possessiveness. In fact, these are all components of virtually every relationship, their importance shifting from time to time when two people are together long enough. They shouldn't, however, be mistaken for love.

So what is love? Love is a commitment you make to trust, respect, admire, and care for yourself or another person. This commitment can be the result of a conscious decision or of a subconscious act, but it's a commitment nonetheless. This may not sound particularly romantic at first, but it is. Love's power is greater than any individual, yet it exists within all of us. Real love begins when you first recognize your own worth. It grows when you realize you've got something to give. It fortifies itself when you find someone with whom you wish to share your love. And finally, it blossoms when someone loves you in return.

However, love isn't always forever. It's a commitment, and "commitment" is just another word for choice. Precious few people make a choice and stick to it without question for life. In Emily Brontë's *Wuthering Heights,* Heathcliff and Cathy did, falling in love when they were young, only to be separated because stark class divisions dictated different destinies. Yet their love never faded, smoldering like embers under ashes until their deaths, when their ghosts reunited along the Yorkshire moors. But most of us are not Heathcliffs and Cathys.

We have enough trouble committing to what we want on our pizza. ("Pepperoni! No, wait . . . sausage! You sure you don't want mushrooms?") We need to realize from the start that even if a relationship lasts the rest of our lives, we'll find ourselves making the choice to maintain the union over and over again. And any relationship can crash to an abrupt end if, just one time, you (or the person who makes up the other half of the pair) waver in your commitment. To endure, even true love requires true effort. As Buddha once said, "He who loves fifty people has fifty woes; he who loves no one has no woes." Of course, every truth can be viewed from two sides, so Buddha's statement can also suggest that a person with fifty loves also has fifty joys.

To further complicate matters, there are nearly as many specific forms of love on this earth as there are couples in love. Although the core elements (respect, trust, and admiration) remain the same, the proportions change endlessly to suit the lovers. And in addition to the three requisites, there are many optional ingredients, including the aforementioned lust, infatuation, and possessiveness, as well as humor, positivity, stability, companionship, appreciation, and support. Each and every one of us writes our own shopping list. You may want a nonstop passion that electrifies every nerve in your body. Perhaps you prefer a confrontational commitment that aggressively races up and down the emotional roller-coaster. Maybe comfortable, unconditional affection that accepts your best and worst characteristics for what they are makes you happiest. Or is a conditional love that molds and changes every inch of your being for the better the thing for you? You may be seeking a spiritual twin who compassionately understands your every thought, desire, and action. You might want a combination of all these things at different times. And someday you may find that you don't want a love commitment at all!

In a day and age when most of us barely have a free evening or two during the week to spend in pursuit of romance, it's no surprise that so many of us are looking for guidance as we search for true love. At its best, astrology can provide vital information and numerous clues to help us navigate these ever-changing waters.

Some people feel that life is easier in cultures where romance and marriage are separated through the tradition and practice of arranged marriage. In these societies, romance is treated as a youthful pastime, occurring before the responsibility of marriage replaces the exuberance of infatuation and passion. If you make a mistake with early romance and fall in love with someone unsuited to you, it doesn't damage the social, financial, and professional status of your and your spouse's families. It doesn't change the way you eat, sleep, live, or react to day-to-day domestic situations.

In many Chinese, Tibetan, Vietnamese, Japanese, Hindu, and Jewish communities, and even in a few European ones, an astrologer isn't normally consulted about frivolous romance matters. His or her arena is the ultimate commitment: marriage. This isn't to say that an astrologer in these cultures can't help you determine if you might have a clandestine, public, prolific, or scant love life, or that he or she can't assist you in discovering if you're a die-hard romantic, a fickle flirt, a sentimentalist, or a onetime, love-for-life type of person. These astrologers just don't dwell on dating and are more inclined to provide insight into the possibilities that exist for you in the area of marriage or similar long-term commitment.

In modern Western societies, however, necessity and demand have directed astrologers to spend their time helping you figure out what type of person you tend to attract and date. They can also help you decide which of your own qualities should be accentuated to attract lovers to whom you are most suited. In countries where family or personal introductions to potential lovers are few, far between, and fruitless for the most part, many people turn to astrologers to help them make important determinations about their potential for long-lasting love.

The real benefit of astrology is the access it provides to your own beliefs about love and your expectations about being loved. Each of the world's astrological traditions can help you discover facets of who you are as a lover or spouse. Armed with this information, you might find out that you can love deeply and securely instead of perpetually sneaking glances at the stranger in the mirror, trying to guess what it is you really want. Or you may discover that brief relationships will ultimately bring you more happiness than a single marriage or lifelong relationship can. You also learn how likely it is that your true desires will be fulfilled and your own limitations in the love department will be revealed. The more you know about yourself, the closer you are to the kind of love we all crave.

In this book we present astrology's intimate role in Chinese, Hindu, Jewish, and Western European love and marriage rituals, offering you an opportunity to try out some of these traditional methods to guide your own love life. If you want to learn more about your aptitude as a potential lover or spouse, or if you want to know if you're destined to find true love, the exercises on these pages will be a great source of insight and wisdom. The four cultures we selected are by no means the only ones that rely on astrology for this purpose. However, these four provide the strongest documented evidence of astrology's use in matters of romance and matrimony from start to finish.

You don't have to be a practicing astrologer, you don't even need a birth chart to use this book. Every chapter has information and insights that don't require a birth chart! If you do have your own or your mate's chart, however, you'll be able to learn even more. We've incorporated worksheets with accompanying examples throughout each chapter to help you organize your own data. We've also provided celebrity examples to help you connect faces to the various planetary influences, and to see what impact those forces have had on some well-known people. Additionally, we've sprinkled in anecdotes about successful relationships, distinctive courtship practices, and regional wedding rituals to enrich your understanding of each culture discussed.

There are numerous free chart services available on the Internet. If you have your and your mate's birth date, birth time, and birthplace, you can easily find a Web site that will let you cast your Western tropical or Hindu chart so that you can use the sections of this book that require a birth chart. On our Web site, http://www.world-astrology.com/, we provide links to Western tropical birth chart sources. This type of chart will be helpful to have for Chapters 4 and 5. We also provide links to Hindu birth chart sources. A Hindu chart will help you get the most out of Chapter 3.

You've no doubt heard the adage "Those who can't do, teach." To allay any concerns you may have in this regard, Chapter 1, "The Sun and the Moon," tells the story of our relationship and illustrates how astrology worked magic for us when we met.

Chapter 2, "Using Chinese Astrology to Find Your Perfect Match," explains how astrology is used to predict compatibility and arrange Chinese marriages. For thousands of years, birth charts called *si zhu* or *ssu chu* (four pillars) have played an integral role in the selection of a mate in this culture. This chapter will teach you how to use the *xing* (planet) that rules your birth year to discover the potential outcome of your relationship with a particular type of person. You'll also learn how to use your Chinese animal sign, along with its year-specific element, to guide you toward your ideal mate. According to Chinese astrology, the Moon plays a critical role in fine-tuning your love life and determining your optimal nuptial date once you've found the right person. We show you how the Moon can help you make decisions about your own relationship and we explain how astrology is used to select both bridal attendants and wedding guests in this ancient civilization. In case you thought Western civilization had a monopoly on wedding superstitions, we close the chapter with a colorful description of the pomp and spectacle of a Chinese wedding ceremony and feast.

Chapter 3, "Using Hindu Astrology to Find Love and Marriage," discusses the astrologer's role in Hindu love and marriage, whether it's arranged or not. You'll learn how a Hindu astrologer would determine your marriageability and the potential geographic location of your ideal mate by consulting your birth chart's seventh house. You'll see how the Moon as well as the planets Venus and Mars can be closely scrutinized for clues about your sexual and romantic inclinations. We then tell you how Hindu astrologers select the prime wedding day and we describe the elaborate and highly romantic Hindu matrimonial ceremony.

Chapter 4, "Using Judaic Astrology to Find Love and Marriage," shows how astrology is used to assist (rather than to completely arrange) many Orthodox Jewish marriages. If you've ever attended a Jewish wedding you've probably heard guests wish the bride and groom a rousing *"Mazal tov!"* The loose translation of this familiar toast is "May Jupiter shower you with abundance!" In this chapter we visit your birth chart's seventh house and we show you how to analyze the placement of the planet Venus in your chart. We also consult the planet of abundance, Jupiter. We explain how a Judaic astrologer would analyze your and your mate's charts, assessing various facets of your union through a comparison of your respective Sun, Moon, Mercury, Mars, Venus, Jupiter, and Saturn placements. We also provide the tools for you to do this yourself. We conclude the chapter with a description of formal Orthodox Jewish nuptials and celebrations.

Chapter 5, "Using Western Astrology to Find Love and Marriage," explains how astrology is used to guide love and relationships in Western cultures. Although its presence is less ingrained in the courtship and marriage process than it is in other societies, astrology serves as a viable source of counsel for a surprising number of marriage-minded Westerners. We detail the Moon's influence on romance from both Celtic and traditional Western perspectives. We also show you how the Sun and Saturn can affect your ability to love and be loved. We finish our international journey with a description of a traditional Celtic handfast ceremony.

What's more important than finding someone who's rich, would make a good parent, or shares your religious beliefs? According to a 2001 Rutgers University survey of single Americans in their twenties, the most important factor in choosing a mate is finding a soulmate. Eighty-eight percent of the people surveyed were certain that somewhere out in the world there is a person who's meant just for them.

Example is always the best teacher. Chapter 6, "Putting It All Together," explores the romantic lives of actors Michael J. Fox and Johnny Depp, who were born the same day two years apart. Using the Chinese, Hindu, Judaic, and Western astrological methods described in this book, we'll explore the similarities and differences in the romantic and marital profiles of these two celebrities and their mates. We strongly believe that the application of more than one astrological method can exponentially expand your insight into yourself and your relationship. To show you how this can be done, we individually examine the love lives of Fox and Depp using each of the four traditions, and we then create a comprehensive astrological profile for each of them that synthesizes the data.

Since we realize that you won't always have the time to go through every planetary placement and interpretation in this book when you're searching for the answer to a specific question, the final chapter, "Entwined As One," provides a checklist of nearly three dozen commonly asked questions, with references to the sections of the book where you can find the answers.

If you're a serious astrology student, you already know that practice is the key to learning this ancient skill. In the Appendix, we've provided you with the birth data for the 209 celebrities mentioned in the pages of this book so you can cast their charts yourself, or simply see who shares your birthday.

A recommended reading list is also provided to direct you on your way if you wish to further your astrological knowledge.

Serious life decisions warrant objective outside assistance. Just as a physician seeks second and third opinions for a diagnosis of his or her own personal illness, and a good psychologist seeks therapy on someone else's couch, even the most experienced astrologer frequently consults another practitioner about his or her own birth chart. (As you'll discover in Chapter 1, even we got a second astrologer's opinion after we first met.) If you are interested in learning everything there is to learn about your love life or relationship, this book will serve as a valuable resource. You may also want to consult a professional astrologer, however, for a more complete astrological profile and the guidance that only a trained and experienced professional can provide. Anyone who tries to be his or her only astrologer cannot gain all that the science of astrology has to offer. And when it comes to matters of the heart, you'll want all the insight you can possibly get.

Perfect Match

CHAPTER ONE

The Sun and the Moon

IT'S BEEN A LIFETIME SINCE WE LAST MET

The sound of a kiss is not so loud as that of a cannon, but its echo lasts a great deal longer.

—Oliver Wendell Holmes

*Y*ou don't find love just because you're looking for it, even if you desperately need it. Love comes into your life only when you're ready to accept it, and this requires a certain amount of self-awareness. Even then, sometimes it takes more than a gut feeling to convince yourself that it's actually happening. Love is a confusing business, so it's always a good idea to look for guidance before the sparks begin to fly. People around the world have been consulting professional astrologers for this very reason for millennia. Name any country and you'll be able to find an astrological practice that's used to determine one's romantic and marital prospects and assess a couple's compatibility. What can happen when two people with extremely compatible astrological profiles meet by chance at a time in both their lives when they're ready for love and well suited to love each other? Here's how it went for us.

Anistatia: It was the seventeenth of December, 1992. I was throwing a Christmas party with another astrologer at my apartment that night. We'd invited loads of people for drinks and a buffet dinner. The trouble was, I couldn't find my caterer anywhere! He hadn't returned my calls for two days. I was completely panicked by noon.

At the time I was editing a book about a New York architect and I was at his Greenwich Village office that day, so I asked my client's chief architect (who's also a good friend) if he had any suggestions as to what I could do. He told me his cousin Jared was a starving hotel school student who cooked professionally. I took Jared's phone number and kept my fingers crossed.

Jared: It was about 2:30 P.M. when Anistatia called me at the midtown club where I made a weekly appearance as guest chef.

Anistatia: I explained that I just needed someone to help me put everything together and serve the food, starting around five-thirty. I'd already spent three days preparing a Southern-style groaning board of Hoppin' John, corn bread, collard greens, and a baked ham.

Jared: I remember the conversation went something like this: How many people? *Fifty-five.* What day? *Today!* I could hear the panic in her voice and told her not to worry. I'd just finished for the day, so I went straight out the door and hopped into a cab. I got about three blocks before I realized I was still wearing my white chef's coat (which wasn't exactly white after a long hot shift in the kitchen). I'd forgotten to change clothes. Anistatia had asked me to wear black, so I had the driver stop at a clothing store. I bought black pants, a black turtleneck, and changed in the cab on the way to her building.

I'd broken my left wrist a few days earlier. When Anistatia opened the door, she didn't even say hello. She just stared at the cast covering my arm from elbow to fingertips.

Anistatia: I said, "You can't even open a bottle of wine, much less carve a ham with that cast on, can you?"

Jared: I told her I'd just cooked lunch for eighty-five people.

Anistatia: When I heard that, I grabbed him by his good arm and dragged him in.

Jared: A bunch of people arrived early. Before long the apartment was full of guests and the party was in full swing. Though I spent most of the evening behind the buffet, I tried to keep an eye on Anistatia, in case she needed anything.

Anistatia: He was scoping me all night.

Jared: I won't deny it. I noticed she was very attractive. Finally, about

1 A.M. we were down to one straggler. I don't know what possessed me, but I threw an arm around his shoulder and said, "Time to go, so we can get this place cleaned up."

After we did the dishes, we sat down in the living room. Anistatia had been barefoot for most of the evening. I figured her feet had to be killing her so I picked one of them up and began rubbing it while we talked. She seemed to enjoy it. After a few minutes I set her foot down and picked up the other. Our conversation ran on as if we'd been together forever. We talked about the guests, which dishes had been most popular, whether the party had been a success, things like that. It was the sort of conversation we've had after every party we've thrown since then.

We realized that we've been together nearly fifty-eight years when we calculated the time we've spent together in comparison to the time the average dual-income American married couple spends together. According to a 1987 survey in the *American Sociological Review*, the average wife spends two hours, five minutes per day (or 8,213.5 hours in nine years) with her husband. During the course of our nine-year marriage, we've spent an average of sixteen waking hours per day together (or 52,560 hours).

Anistatia: I kissed him on the neck. It was such a light kiss. I didn't think he'd even notice. But he did. Then I gave him a shoulder rub. He looked tense after being on his feet all day. That seemed to relax him.

Jared: We talked endlessly, about commitment, previous relationships, monogamy, personal expectations, life goals, marriage. It's funny, we talked more about those things in the first few days than we did in all of the next nine years. I guess once we got them out of the way there was no reason to dwell on them any longer.

Anistatia: I hate relationship conversations. They waste too much time that could be spent on actually having a relationship.

Jared: I knew she was the one for me, not because I was physically attracted to her but because I knew that even without any physical attraction I'd want her as my best friend for life. Within two days we were discussing marriage.

Anistatia: We also talked about astrology. After he mentioned his birth date, I told him *Linda Goodman's Love Signs* said we weren't supposed to get along very well or for very long. According to the book, a Gemini woman and a Virgo man have little in common when it comes to love and commitment. (I'd gone out with three other Virgos in my life, and all three relationships had petered out fairly quickly.)

Jared: "So that's it?" I asked.

Anistatia: I laughed and went upstairs to the computer. I cast Jared's birth chart and pulled up my own. Then I constructed a synastry (the relationship between individual planets found in both charts) of our charts for the day we met. We had seven planetary conjunctions! That meant we had seven points in which a planet in his chart was positioned in the same zodiac sign as a planet in my chart.

The Sun conjuncted the Moon. Many astrologers consider this the most consistent match in the charts of people with successful relationships. It's potentially the most romantic combination and indicates a very strong sexual attraction. The Sun conjuncted Saturn, which has the potential to create a foundation of stability. It's a great aspect for a long-term relationship. The Sun also conjuncted Mars. This indicates that conflicts are inclined to be ego related and filled with fireworks. This usually means some compromises have to be made on both sides.

The Moon conjuncted Jupiter, which instills more than enough trust for any relationship. The Moon also conjuncted Mercury, suggesting communication could be fine if we both resisted the urge to add too many details, which tend to trigger outbursts in the other person.

Venus conjuncted Venus, suggesting an emotionally hot romance, with as much fascination as infatuation. Venus also conjuncted Mars, indicating a lot of potential sexual magnetism.

Jared was also at a point when the planet Saturn was on the verge of returning to the position it held when he was born. It happens to everyone just around their twenty-ninth and fifty-eighth birthdays. Its influence makes you consider and reconsider the direction of your life.

I looked up our Chinese birth charts as well. The one key

phrase that stuck in my mind was that the "relationship would lead to positive change." In Hindu astrology, I was at the end of my Venus *dasa* (time period), which is the optimal marriage time in that culture.

Just to be on the safe side, we went to my astrologer friend's apartment the next night. I brought the charts with us so she could have a quick look. She agreed that we had a lot going for us if we were considering a commitment.

Jared: Still, we both wanted another opinion. The trouble was, Anistatia's best friend was also her soon-to-be ex-husband, and mine was the woman I'd been living with for nearly three years. We got together with each of them separately. After Anistatia's husband met me, he told her that he thought we were absolutely perfect for each other. When my girlfriend met Anistatia, she said the same thing. We've actually remained close to both of them.

Anistatia: A week later I was on the phone with my mother in Chicago, telling her I was getting married and asking if she could line up a minister on short notice. "Is it anyone I know?" she asked. I told her it was someone I'd just met. She was a little surprised, but added, "I'm sure you know what you're doing."

I'd planned to stop off in Chicago on the way back from an upcoming business trip to San Francisco anyway, and I thought it would be nice to get married there so that my ninety-year-old grandfather could attend.

Jared: So we were married five weeks later in below-zero, postblizzard weather at Chicago's Water Tower. I have no idea why church bells all over the neighborhood suddenly rang out as we stepped back out onto the street, but they did.

Anistatia: I'm still trying to figure out why all the stores on Michigan Avenue had wedding gowns and wedding-related stuff in the windows in the middle of winter.

Jared: That was the end of it. But it wasn't the beginning of our story. Over the next few months we found out how many times in the past we'd nearly met.

When I first moved to New York (seven years before we met), I lived on the Lower East Side for six months. At that time Anistatia was living in a brownstone a block away. We both ate in the same neighborhood restaurants: Katz's deli, Ratners, Yonah Shimmel's Knishes Bakery, Veselka. We even bought borsch and matzoh crackers at Streit's matzoh factory, which was the midpoint between our apartments.

We also discovered that we were in Frankfurt, Germany, at the same time in 1986. She was there for the Frankfurt Book Fair. It was my first time in Europe. I'd flown to Zurich, took the train to Paris, then to Frankfurt, and I was wandering aimlessly through the city when I stumbled on a little street fair, the Rhinegau wine festival. Anistatia actually snuck out of the book fair to visit this same festival, which was only one block long. But we didn't meet.

I did see her once, though I didn't know who she was. It was in 1990, about two years before we met. Riders in the Sky, a Texas cowboy band, was playing at the Bottom Line nightclub in Greenwich Village. My sister Laurie and I were both big fans. Laurie knew the lead singer, so after the show we went backstage. Anistatia knew the bass player. That's where I saw her. She was across the room with her back to me, her long black hair cascading down in loose waves over a green Armani suit. I saw her for only a second, and only from behind, but the image was indelibly etched in my memory.

It turns out we'd also been near each other at two benefit concerts without knowing it. At one Anistatia was sitting in the tenth row near the left aisle. I was in the same row, on the other side of the aisle, but we never saw each other. At the other, we both spoke to my cousin Daniel, who was only at the concert for a few minutes. Anistatia had gotten to know him when her editorial work brought her to the architectural firm where he worked.

A month after we finally met, Anistatia was showing me an album of photos she'd taken in various locations around Manhattan. One picture showed the rowing pond in Central Park. It was shot from quite a distance, but when I looked closely, I realized she'd taken a picture of me rowing, three years before our fateful encounter. She didn't believe it was me until I pulled out the awful red, gray, and blue Hawaiian shirt I'd been wearing that day. She said she'd taken the photo because I was the only one who seemed to know how to row a boat. But she made me get rid of the Hawaiian shirt anyway.

Are all well-matched couples destined to meet? We'd like to think so. If not for fate there'd be a lot of people going through life unaware that the perfect person for them lives just down the street or on the other side of town. This might be an unnerving thought, but as you'll learn in the following chapters, you can increase your chances of meeting your true soulmate by using astrology to get to know yourself better. When you understand your strengths and weaknesses, when you're aware of what sort of person and what sort of relationship would be best for you, you'll be more likely to recognize Mr. or Ms. Right when you cross paths. As you'll also find in the coming pages some cultures leave as little of this as possible to chance.

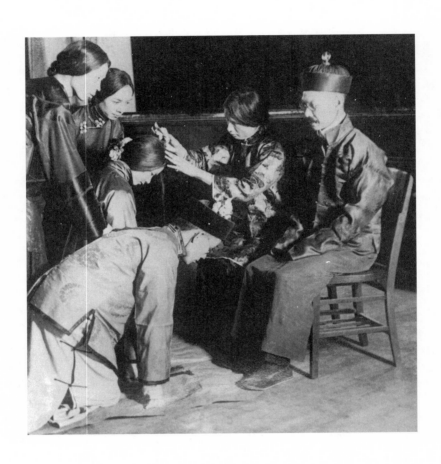

CHAPTER TWO

Using Chinese Astrology to Find Your Perfect Match

THE EXCHANGE OF EIGHT CHARACTERS

Amidst the swirling sea of humanity, I shall seek the only companion of my soul; if I find her, I am lucky; if I find her not, such is my fate, that is all.
—poet Xu Zhimo in a letter to Liang Qichao, 1923

*Y*ou've probably heard the expression that marriages are made in heaven and celebrated right here on Earth. Well, the Chinese certainly contributed to its coinage, with the belief that couples who were united in a previous lifetime join together again in the present as well as in future lives. Chinese myths about Yue Laou (Old Man in the Moon) credit him with connecting predestined couples with a red silk cord so no human or god can prevent their union. Classic Chinese love stories like the 1791 novel *Hong Lou Meng (The Dream of the Red Chamber)* testify to this belief in the strength of transcendent love.

The tale begins with the birth of Bao Yu, who came into the world bearing a jade amulet in his mouth, inscribed with the verse "Lose me not, forget me not; eternal life shall be your lot." His mother placed this heaven-sent talisman on a silk cord that Bao Yu wore around his neck. He grew to be clever, spoiled, and lazy. Destined by birthright to become a government official, Bao Yu occasionally suffered fits of depression over his fate, eschewing his superficial existence. Nevertheless, he was encouraged to study so he could pursue a government appointment when he was grown. Bao Yu refused to read, however, unless he was in the company of two young girls.

Two female cousins, Tai Yu and Bao Chai, were sent to live in his family's household. Tai Yu was beautiful, witty, educated, but frail. Bao Chai was attractive and quiet, but not as intelligent as Tai Yu.

The three teenagers became fast friends. But Bao Yu increasingly idled away the hours in Tai Yu's company, leaving Bao Chai alone. As time passed, it became apparent that Bao Yu and Tai Yu had fallen in love.

Hard times fell upon both families. Tai Yu's mother died and Bao Yu's family fortunes declined when uncles and cousins fell into imperial disfavor. Bao Chai and her mother moved out of the household, leaving Bao Yu and Tai Yu on their own.

Around this time Bao Yu reached the age of eligibility, and his family decided his mate should be either Tai Yu or Bao Chai. Because Tai Yu's health was perennially questionable, Bao Chai was chosen.

The betrothal was settled in secret; not even Bao Yu was told. Tai Yu overheard the servant girls' gossip from her sickbed and her already ill health declined even further. A few days later, Bao Yu lost his jade amulet and he, too, fell ill. Despite these evil omens, the family went ahead with the wedding. Told that he was to be married and believing Tai Yu was to be his bride, Bao Yu quickly recovered.

On his wedding day, as the ceremony came to a close, Bao Yu raised his new bride's veil and screamed in disbelief. "I want Tai Yu!" he babbled until he passed out in grief. That same night, Tai Yu died alone in her room, calling out Bao Yu's name.

Things went from bad to worse as the months passed. Bao Yu's father's appointment failed and several family members died. One day a Buddhist priest appeared at the gate, bearing Bao Yu's lost jade talisman. But rather than leaping up from his sickbed, Bao Yu seemed to be struck dead when he clasped the amulet in his hands. At that moment he entered the spirit world, where a stranger told him that he could be with his departed love, Tai Yu, in the Place of the Serene, if he promised to fulfill his duties and nourish his soul when he returned to the physical world. For a fleeting moment he saw Tai Yu behind a veil of mist. When he regained consciousness he was a changed man, and he was determined to take the government examinations.

Bao Yu took the arduous tests along with thousands of other aspirants, but on his return home he disappeared. Days later, the posted results showed that Bao Yu had earned the seventh-highest score. It was such an impressive accomplishment that the emperor granted Bao Yu's family clemency from any past wrongdoings, and ordered an audience with Bao Yu. But he was nowhere to be found. Simultaneously, Bao Chai announced that she was pregnant, guaranteeing Bao Yu's family an heir. His father was overjoyed about the restoration of his family's fortunes and the news of an imminent heir but devastated by the disappearance of his only son.

A few months later, three Buddhist monks visited Bao Yu's father. One monk knelt down and touched his head to the ground four times at the surprised man's feet. Before he could utter a word, the three monks vanished. Only then did the man realize that the monk was his son, Bao Yu.

As this story demonstrates, in the realm of Chinese thought a lot of onus rides on the union of a bride and groom. Not only can the couple's health and fortunes be turned for better or worse; their families and friends may also experience the same fate as a result of this singular decision.

Are you willing to bet your marriage will last forty years? In an effort to reward couples who stay together for life, the People's Insurance Company of China offers mainland Chinese citizens "marriage insurance." People can purchase twenty-five-, forty-, or fifty-year policies. If they stay together they get their principal back, plus a hefty dividend.

Because of this, arranged marriage has a long history in Chinese communities and still survives in the People's Republic of China, even though the government passed a 1955 law banning it in an attempt to encourage young people to seek their own mates. Most young people do prefer to choose whom they marry without parental intervention, but many families continue to engineer this critical portion of their children's lives in order to preserve family fortunes as well as social and business interests. Even the most lenient families often apply various forms of pressure in the realm of courtship and marriage in an attempt to weave traditional customs into the fabric of otherwise modern rituals.

Destiny's Pillars:
Are Your Ruling Planets Harmonious?

The practitioners of these time-honored rituals are called *mei* (matchmakers). Usually an elderly woman or midwife, the *mei* is hired by the family of the future groom. In order to go about her work, she is given certain tools, namely a *cao ba zi* (eight characters draft) inscribed with the ancestral family name and the groom's *si zhu* (four pillars) astrological chart, which has been cast by the family astrologer.

A *si zhu* consists of four individual *zhu* (pillars) that govern your personality traits and direct your destiny. The first *zhu* is derived from your Chinese year of birth. The second *zhu* is determined by the lunar month in which your birth occurred. The third *zhu* is extracted from your birthday. And the fourth *zhu* is derived from the hour of your birth.

Each of these four *zhu* is assigned two *zi* (characters). A single *zi* consists of a *xing* (planet) and a gender specifier, which is either *yang* (male) or *yin* (female). In Chinese astrology there are five *xing:* Mars, represented by fire; Saturn, represented by earth; Mercury, represented by water; Jupiter, represented by wood; and Venus, represented by metal. The astrologer reads a *si zhu* in terms of these eight *zi.* In fact, the *si zhu* is sometimes called the *ba zi,* or eight characters. By comparing the positive or negative effect the *zi* of one partner has on the *zi* of the other, it is possible to determine whether the couple's traits produce mutually productive or chaotic behaviors.

Fully assessing a couple's *si zhu* is very complicated; it takes years of study and practice to properly construct and interpret it. But take heart. In this chapter, we'll show you how to effectively apply four of the key steps used by Chinese astrologers to assess relationships. We'll explain how to read the ruling *xing* for your birth-year *zhu* to determine the potential outcome of your relationship with your mate. We'll illustrate how the lunar-driven *zhu* of your birth month allows you to delve further in your relationship's potential by defining your and your mate's emotional needs. You'll also learn how to use your Chinese birth-year *ming shu* (animal sign) as a guide as you search for your ideal mate and as you select the optimal month for your wedding. And finally, we'll show you how astrologers use the Chinese almanac and the Moon's orbit to determine the perfect day for a wedding ceremony.

Reading the Ruling *Xing*

There's a simple procedure that you can use if your curiosity about a relationship's potential gets the best of you. This method does not provide the in-depth assessment of a professional consultation, but it is a good kickoff point. As astrologer Jean-Michel Huon de Kermadec showed in his book *The Way to Chinese Astrology*, some practitioners compare the ruling *xing* (planets) of a couple's birth years to determine their relationship's outcome. Here's how the system works.

You don't need *si zhu* birth charts to use this particular section. Enter your (and/or your mate's) birth date onto Worksheet 1. Then look at Table 1, which contains a list of Chinese years and their corresponding elements. Unlike the Western calendar, which follows the Sun's path and always begins on January 1, the Chinese calendar follows the Moon's movements and starts on a different day each year. First, locate your birth year in the left-hand column. Then read across to the middle column to check that it's truly your birth year. If you were born in January or February of a given Western calendar year, your birth date could be in the previous Chinese calendar year. (Someone born 19 January 1952, for example, was born in the Chinese year 1951, because the Chinese year didn't begin until 27 January 1952.) Once you've found your Chinese birth year, read across to the right-hand column to find the ruling *xing* for your birth year's *zhu* (pillar). Enter that *xing* in the space provided on the worksheet. Gender plays a critical role in this astrological tradition, so there is a space on the worksheet in which your gender should be entered. Follow the same procedure for your mate. Once you've completed the worksheet, locate your pair of ruling *xing* in the following text to read about how your combined birth years might influence your relationship's outcome. For example, in the case of Kurt Cobain and Courtney Love,

whose information already appears in the worksheet, you'd look for
the pairing *male water with female fire*.

WORKSHEET 1. RULING *XING*

	Example 1:	Example 2:	Name A:	Name B:
	Kurt Cobain	Courtney Love		
Birthdate	20 Feb 1967	09 Jul 1964		
Gender	male	female		
Ruling *xing*	water	fire		

TABLE 1. RULING *XING* FOR THE CHINESE YEARS 1927–1987

Year	New Year's Day	Ruling *Xing*
1927	02 Feb	fire
1928	23 Jan	wood
1929	10 Feb	wood
1930	30 Jan	earth
1931	17 Feb	earth
1932	06 Feb	metal
1933	26 Jan	metal
1934	14 Feb	fire
1935	04 Feb	fire
1936	24 Jan	water
1937	11 Feb	water
1938	31 Jan	earth
1939	19 Feb	earth
1940	08 Feb	metal
1941	27 Jan	metal
1942	15 Feb	wood
1943	05 Feb	wood
1944	25 Jan	water
1945	13 Feb	water
1946	02 Feb	earth

Year	New Year's Day	Ruling *Xing*
1947	22 Jan	earth
1948	10 Feb	fire
1949	29 Jan	fire
1950	17 Feb	wood
1951	06 Feb	wood
1952	27 Jan	water
1953	14 Feb	water
1954	03 Feb	metal
1955	24 Jan	metal
1956	12 Feb	fire
1957	31 Jan	fire
1958	18 Feb	wood
1959	08 Feb	wood
1960	28 Jan	earth
1961	15 Feb	earth
1962	05 Feb	metal
1963	25 Jan	metal
1964	13 Feb	fire
1965	02 Feb	fire
1966	21 Jan	water
1967	09 Feb	water
1968	30 Jan	earth
1969	17 Feb	earth
1970	06 Feb	metal
1971	27 Jan	metal
1972	15 Feb	wood
1973	03 Feb	wood
1974	23 Jan	water
1975	11 Feb	water
1976	31 Jan	earth
1977	18 Feb	earth
1978	07 Feb	fire

Year	New Year's Day	Ruling *Xing*
1979	28 Jan	fire
1980	16 Feb	wood
1981	05 Feb	wood
1982	25 Jan	water
1983	13 Feb	water
1984	02 Feb	metal
1985	20 Feb	metal
1986	09 Feb	fire
1987	29 Jan	fire

This data is taken from *The Complete Astrological Handbook for the Twenty-first Century* (New York: Schocken Books, 1999).

We'd like to add a word of caution to those of you who are accustomed to Western-style interpretations. Chinese astrological delineations can sound pretty abrupt and sometimes frighteningly certain. Please keep in mind that this tradition is based on predeterminism, the belief that we are fated to our destinies. These interpretations exemplify particular cultures' beliefs about love and marriage, and they may well vary from your own culturally based viewpoint. Also, a professional consultation can disclose a more refined interpretation of a relationship, using the *zi* (characters) derived not only from your and your mate's birth year, but from the month, day, and hour as well. In many cases this kind of detailed reading can point to greatly improved or diminished chances for a happy relationship.

Male earth with female earth. Despite an easy start, later years will bring much hard work to your relationship. It may feel as though life is turned upside down during this period. This doesn't mean that these years will be unpleasant. After all, the only difference between work and play is that one is done by necessity, the other by choice. Don't settle for unenjoyable work when you're young. The experience you accumulate will allow you to excel when times get rough. If work is in an area you enjoy, life will be a lot more fun. Devotion and compassion will help you out, especially during times of sickness and distress. (*Famous examples:* Michael J. Fox and Tracy Pollan, John F. Kennedy Jr. and Daryl Hannah, Bill Clinton and Hillary Rodham Clinton, Anthony Armstrong-Jones and Princess Margaret Windsor, Richard Benjamin and Paula Prentiss, Mikhail Gorbachev and Raisa Gorbachev.)

Male earth with female fire. This has the makings of a tender relationship. But you'll need true tolerance and compassion to maintain harmony. Tolerance is the acknowledgment and acceptance of beliefs and philosophies that might differ from yours. Compassion is a heartfelt recognition of anguish coupled with the will to relieve it. (*Famous examples:* Antonio Banderas and Melanie Griffith, John F. Kennedy Jr. and Carolyn Bessette Kennedy, Donald Trump and Ivana Trump, Hugh Grant and Elizabeth Hurley.)

Male earth with female metal. The two of you will find wealth and prosperity arriving in abundance because your mutual luck and loving natures are a strong draw. Good luck doesn't just happen. It is a product of kindness. Be good to people and they'll wish success upon both of you. Kind people triumph because others willingly give them aid when it's most needed. This is the moral of just about every fairy tale ever written. (*Famous examples:* Arnold Schwarzenegger and Maria Shriver, Donald Trump and Marla Maples, Will Smith and Jada Pinkett Smith, David Bowie and Iman Abdul Majid.)

Male earth with female water. The wife in this relationship must not be too influenced by her husband. If she doesn't maintain her independence within the union, what starts out well becomes miserable in later years. Sometimes it's actually the differences between people that attract and keep them together. If two people allow themselves to be too heavily influenced by each other these contrasts and their benefits might disappear. (*Famous examples:* Ted Turner and Jane Fonda, Steven Spielberg and Kate Capshaw, Steven Spielberg and Amy Irving, Mike Nichols and Diane Sawyer, Marilyn Manson and Rose McGowan, David Duchovny and Téa Leoni, Edward Norton and Salma Hayek, Kenneth Branagh and Helena Bonham Carter.)

Male earth with female wood. Disharmony emerges from the lies and estrangements you both create, unless your other *zi* readings (month, day, and hour) improve your chances for a happy union. Money dwindles rather than accumulates throughout your relationship. The beginning of this relationship is as good as it gets. If you allow trust to develop gradually between you and let the walls that protect you come down just as slowly, there's less chance that the relationship will blow up in both your faces. (*Famous examples:* Elliot Gould and Barbra Streisand, Kenneth Branagh and Emma Thompson, Sean Penn and Madonna, O. J. Simpson and Nicole Brown Simpson, Lukas Haas and Natalie Portman.)

Male fire with female earth. Happiness and long life are yours in this luck-filled relationship. You appear to be the classic husband-and-wife team, planning and pursuing your goals while simultaneously building a solid home life. Children and possessions come in abundance. (*Famous examples:* John Derek and Linda Evans, Ellen DeGeneres and Anne Heche, Prince Charles Windsor and Princess Diana Spencer Windsor, Sonny Bono and Cher.)

Male fire with female fire. Concessions will have to be made on both sides of this union to avoid violent arguments. When lovers fight, there are no winners. Victory inevitably pales in comparison to the love lost in the process. Find more peaceful ways to settle disputes, and let the little things go. Some things really aren't worth fighting about. Détente will also improve the quality of your children's upbringing. (*Famous examples:* Al Gore and Tipper Gore, Don Johnson and Melanie Griffith, John Derek and Bo Derek, Ben Stiller and Calista Flockhart, Ozzy Osbourne and Sharon Osbourne, Dwight Yoakam and Bridget Fonda.)

Male fire with female metal. Disputes lead to an inharmonious existence, unless one of you willingly concedes. As the Chinese military strategist Sun Tzu wrote thousands of years ago: "There is no instance of a country having benefited from prolonged warfare." This also applies to relationships. The choice is painful but simple: concede the fights or concede the relationship. Guard against potential loss of savings during your later years. Jewelry isn't a good asset. It may cost a fortune, but it can never be sold for more than a fraction of its purchase price. Try a conventional savings plan and a written agreement as to who gets what in case the relationship ends. (*Famous examples:* Daniel Day-Lewis and Isabelle Adjani, Nicky Hilton and Elizabeth Taylor, John W. Warner and Elizabeth Taylor, Humphrey Bogart and Lauren Bacall.)

Male fire with female water. Mutual jealousy and diminished finances loom in the shadows of this union if concessions aren't made and goals aren't set to preserve your future together. There's a point in every successful relationship when the courtship ends and the empire building begins. The dinners out, dancing, and movies rob your bank account and, more disastrously, your productive time. Let these things steal a little, but not too much. Also, it's a desire to be together that makes a relationship. If either of you begins to spend excessive social time elsewhere, why be in the relationship at all? (*Famous examples:* Woody Allen and Mia Farrow, Woody Allen and Diane Keaton, John Derek and Ursula Andress, Elvis Presley and Priscilla Beaulieu Presley, Lenny Kravitz and Lisa Bonet.)

Male fire with female wood. If you can learn to confide in each other, your relationship will be very intimate. Together you can achieve fame and prosperity, if you share the same goals. Otherwise, the wife in this union risks the loss of her self-esteem. We play many roles in any alliance, but most of them come down to being either the star or the pep squad. No man or woman on earth is so self-assured that they aren't uplifted by praise. The trouble is, unless you're working with your mate or at least included in your mate's professional life, you may never receive the recognition you deserve.

Male metal with female earth. You'll need a good accountant to keep this relationship from financial ruin. The wife must act as the household head in all domestic matters, maintaining needed stability. Some men (and women) never outgrow the need to have an allowance. If they have money in their pockets, they'll spend it. This ostensible irresponsibility isn't as bad as it sounds. Some people are great at making money, others are great at saving it. It takes one of each to accumulate wealth. If you decide to have children, they'll have a prosperous future because your example has taught them how to make and hold on to money. (*Famous examples:* André Agassi and Steffi Graf, Ringo Starr and Barbara Bach, Sir Michael Caine and Shakira Caine, Quincy Jones and Nastassja Kinski, Dennis Quaid and Meg Ryan, Louis Malle and Candice Bergen, Brad Pitt and Jennifer Aniston, Nicolas Cage and Patricia Arquette, Tommy Lee and Heather Locklear, Eddie Van Halen and Valerie Bertinelli.)

Male metal with female fire. Ill health and domestic problems might plague this relationship, depending on your other *zi* readings (month, day, and hour). Our surroundings affect our health. There's no question about it. If a spouse dies after a happy couple has been together for decades, quite often the other person will die within a year, but stress kills far more people than heartbreak. Fighting at home can really take its toll on more than your relationship. Compassion and tolerance are the keys to your union's survival and your health while you're together. (*Famous examples:* André Agassi and Brooke Shields, David Arquette and Courteney Cox Arquette, Matthew Broderick and Sarah Jessica Parker.)

Male metal with female metal. This relationship may start out on easy street. But constant struggles eventually erode what little harmony truly existed, unless your other *zi* readings (month, day, and hour) improve your chances for marital bliss. Ill health and prejudices on the wife's part might also instigate marital difficulties. Expressions like "The best is yet to come" don't always apply. There are rare occasions when the best portion of a relationship is the early part. Without a lot of effort and some luck, this is likely to be one of those unions. Enjoy it for what it has to offer, then decide if you really want to live up to the "in sickness" part of the basic vow, and remember that it also includes emotional imbalance. (*Famous examples:* Bruce Willis and Demi Moore, Richard Burton and Elizabeth Taylor, John

Travolta and Kelly Preston, Ethan Hawke and Uma Thurman, John Lennon and Yoko Ono, Johnny Depp and Winona Ryder, Sean "Puffy" Combs and Jennifer Lopez.)

Male metal with female water. This is an extremely prosperous relationship. Longevity and wealth are at hand. Dreams can be fulfilled on both sides. Unless your *zi* readings (month, day, and hour) diminish your marital bliss, this is a match made in the heavens. Plan for a long and happy life together, and don't let momentary setbacks and occasional arguments derail this train as it heads down the tracks to long-term happiness. (*Famous examples:* Tom Cruise and Nicole Kidman, Tommy Lee and Pamela Anderson Lee, Benjamin Bratt and Julia Roberts, Billy Bob Thornton and Angelina Jolie, Tom Green and Drew Barrymore.)

Male metal with female wood. This union may get off to a difficult start, but your lives together should improve gradually with age. Also, remember that great relationships don't just happen; they are constructed. The essential building blocks are communication, respect, and trust. Talk to each other. But don't try to have serious relationship-analysis conversations. Read jokes out loud, tell each other all the things you'd really like to do in this lifetime. Be friends as well as lovers. (*Famous examples:* Johnny Depp and Vanessa Paradis, Brad Pitt and Gwyneth Paltrow, James Brolin and Barbra Streisand, Johnny Depp and Kate Moss, Peter Sellers and Britt Ekland, Brad Pitt and Juliette Lewis.)

Male water with female earth. Ill health and constant need may create disputes. It'll take hard work to keep this relationship afloat. Does your mate need attention because he or she is sick? Or is your mate sick because he or she needs attention? Everyone has times of need, but they shouldn't be constant and a marriage can't be based on them. There's a critical difference between need and desire. Need says, "I can't live without you." Desire says, "I'm just fine on my own, but life is better when I'm with you." Also, constant arguments aren't an indication of a robust union, nor are they good for your health.

Your other *zi* readings (month, day, and hour) may improve your chances for marital bliss. (*Famous examples:* Michael Douglas and Catherine Zeta-Jones.)

Male water with female fire. This union is destructive for both of you, unless your other *zi* readings (month, day, and hour) improve your chances for marital bliss. Never settle for an abusive relationship. Mental and emotional trauma can be just as awful as physical abuse. If someone is cruel to you, don't try to get them to change. Just change mates. Life is too short and too valuable to waste it in a bad situation. Your other *zi* readings (month, day, and hour) may improve your chances for marital bliss. (*Famous examples:* Kurt Cobain and Courtney Love.)

Male water with female metal. Money and friends are abundant. If you place your confidence in the right people, you'll continue to prosper in later years. Otherwise, misplaced trust will deteriorate your relationship. Hold your friends to a high ethical standard. People who lie, cheat, and steal don't make great friends. It doesn't matter if they never rob you. If they're ever caught, their reputation pulls you down by association. It even affects your mate by association with you. (*Famous examples:* Warren Beatty and Julie Christie.)

Male water with female water. You rarely ever agree on any topic. Although you're both smart, you're not necessarily successful on any level, unless your *zi* readings (month, day, and hour) improve your chances for marital bliss. Differences of opinion can definitely reduce your chances for success. How can you move forward in life if you can't agree on where you should be headed, much less how to get there? There are as many points of view as there are people in this world. Relationships work better between people with similar visions. (*Famous examples:* Eric Clapton and Patti Boyd, Eric Benét and Halle Berry, Warren Beatty and Diane Keaton.)

Male water with female wood. Money flows like water for you. If you don't permit your good fortune to spoil your practicality, you'll enjoy peace and long lives together. For every story of a fortune that's made,

there's another story of a fortune that's lost: lost through bad investments or extravagance. Be thrifty with wealth today and you'll still be
rich tomorrow. (*Famous examples:* Peter Horton and Michelle Pfeiffer,
Jack Nicholson and Anjelica Huston, Ray Davies and Chrissie Hynde,
Warren Beatty and Annette Bening.)

Male wood with female earth. There's great mutual comprehension
between the two of you. Together you'll accumulate wealth and possessions. You may not, however, have many children. Once considered to be a partial curse, this facet is now regarded as a potentially
positive element. You share the blessings of communication and
material success with each other. Money would drain right out the
window with loads of children. Few offspring is a third blessing in
disguise. Also, remember always that you are in this relationship to
love each other. The presence or absence of a child doesn't mark the
success or failure of the match. Your happiness together does. (*Famous
examples:* Richie Sambora and Heather Locklear, Tim Robbins and
Susan Sarandon, Burt Bacharach and Angie Dickinson.)

Male wood with female fire. It'll take time and patience to establish a
harmonic coexistence. If you avoid controversial subjects, happiness
will ultimately ensue. There's a reason they put curtains on voting
booths. We're entitled to private, personal opinions on important
issues. There's no need to spend time at home on subjects that create
friction when there are so many other things to talk about. (*Famous
examples:* Roger Vadim and Brigitte Bardot, Kevin Bacon and Kyra
Sedgwick, the Reverend Dr. Martin Luther King Jr. and Coretta Scott
King, Simon LeBon and Yasmin Parvaneh LeBon, Mick Jagger and
Jerry Hall.)

Male wood with female metal. One of you will be on the road for business more times than not. If you plan your life together carefully,
you'll prosper. Otherwise, this relationship will deteriorate from
separation. The expression "Distance lends enchantment" misses the
point. It isn't the distance, it's the good times in between the separa-
tions that make it all worthwhile. Make these times together as special and intimate as possible, preserving what you've got. (*Famous*

examples: Eddie Fisher and Elizabeth Taylor, Larry Fortensky and Elizabeth Taylor, Sir Paul McCartney and Linda Eastman McCartney, Eddie Fisher and Debbie Reynolds.)

Male wood with female water. You'll have to share the same goals and work hard together to achieve prosperity. Properly nurtured, yours will become a strong partnership. As a team you are still just two against the world, but the odds are tipped decidedly in your favor when you focus on common goals, unless your other *zi* readings (month, day, and hour) diminish your chances for marital bliss. (*Famous examples:* Kurt Russell and Goldie Hawn, Roger Vadim and Jane Fonda, Alec Baldwin and Kim Basinger, George Harrison and Patti Boyd, Prince and Mayte Garcia.)

Male wood with female wood. A lack of harmony between the two of you instigates perpetual disputes, unless your other *zi* readings (month, day, and hour) improve your chances for marital bliss. A house at war with itself cannot nurture life. When you allow bad patterns of communication—shouts and accusations—to creep into your relationship, it's very difficult to get rid of them. As time passes, smaller and smaller offenses will serve as catalysts for blowout fights. Your children will be unruly, learning from your behavior. (*Famous examples:* Roger Vadim and Catherine Deneuve, Macaulay Culkin and Rachel Miner Culkin, Prince and Vanity, Ben Affleck and Gwyneth Paltrow, Harrison Ford and Melissa Mathison, Britney Spears and Justin Timberlake.)

Contrary to Western perceptions, not all attractive Chinese women are petite and fragile. Emperor Kublai Khan's cousin Aijaruc was described by the explorer Marco Polo as an Amazonian beauty who was "so tall and brawny that she outdid all the men in her father's realm in feats of strength." The daughter of the Tatar king Caidu, she was also willful, vowing never to marry until she found a man who could vanquish her in a wrestling match. Each zealous suitor had to pay the princess one hundred horses to enter the competition. Aijaruc accumulated a massive herd, consisting of a few thousand steeds, before she settled down with a strong and valiant warrior.

As you can see, no relationship works by the same expectations or rules as another. In the case of a couple like Kurt Cobain and Courtney Love, the astrologer would've suggested further exploration of the couple's month, day, and hour *zi* to determine if the union's outcome was likely to be truly as destructive as their male water with female fire reading implied. There's always a chance of improvement or variation.

A Match Made in Heaven: Your *Ming Shu* Compatibility

After a family astrologer assesses the "exchange of eight characters" between a future bride and groom, the couple's *ming shu* (reckoned fates) are reviewed for compatibility. This particular method is based solely on your birth year and its affinity to surrounding years.

Surely, some of you already know the *ming shu* of your birth year: Rat, Ox, Tiger, Hare, Dragon, Snake, Horse, Ram, Monkey, Rooster, Dog, and Pig. Some of you may have even discounted Chinese astrology because you've read that a relationship between two people born six years apart is always bad. It's important to remember that even the classic Chinese astrology texts insist that we don't use the six-year difference to destroy what might be a good marriage.

Unlike the generic descriptions assigned to each of the animal signs in many modern books written on the subject or on the paper placemats in Chinese restaurants, the classic *ming shu* narrows the interpretation of your general personality by assigning a subordinate *xing* (planet) to each year. So rather than reading about the compatibility between a Dragon and a Dog, you're better served by learning how well a Wood Dragon gets along with a Water Dog or a Fire Dog. This qualifier can change the picture quite radically in some instances. In the next few pages we'll describe a few hundred of these matches, covering people born between 1927 and 1987, to let you determine your *ming shu* compatibility for yourself.

You don't need a *si zhu* birth chart to use this particular section. Enter your (and/or your mate's) birth date onto Worksheet 2. Then look at

Table 2, which contains a list of Chinese years. Locate your birth year in the first column. Read across to the second column to check that it's truly your Chinese birth year. You may be surprised to discover that you're not the *ming shu* you thought you were. Be careful. As we mentioned in the last section, if your birthday is in January or February, you could be born in the previous year according to the Chinese calendar. Once you've found your correct Chinese birth year, read across to the third and fourth columns, which contain your *xing* and *ming shu*. Then locate your Chinese birth year in the text following the table and read about its compatibility with a variety of other birth years. If you're curious about a year you don't see listed under your particular sign, that's okay. Those are considered to be neutral years. People born in years that aren't listed under your Chinese birth year have neither a beneficial nor a negative impact on your love life. Chinese astrologers believe that although neutral-year matches are not the best or the worst situations, these relationships can work if their emotional makeups are harmonious or if other *zhu* (pillars) in their *si zhu* (four pillars) exhibit strong compatibility.

It's also worthwhile when you check your own birth year to check your mate's birth year as well. Not every *ming shu* is mutually compatible. In other words, your life may be enhanced by a person with a particular *ming shu,* but you may not have as beneficial an influence on that person's life. Similarly, you may be strongly attracted to a particular *ming shu,* but your own personality may be too strong for that person to handle. Also, even if your mate's *ming shu* isn't the best for your year, you might be an ideal person for your mate.

WORKSHEET 2. MING SHU

	Example 1:	Example 2:	Name A:	Name B:
	Kurt Cobain	Courtney Love		
Birthdate	20 Feb 1967	09 Jul 1964		
Xing	fire	wood		
Ming shu	ram	dragon		

TABLE 2. *MING SHU* FOR THE CHINESE YEARS 1927–1987

Year	New Year's Day	*Xing*	*Ming Shu*
1927	02 Feb	fire	hare
1928	23 Jan	earth	dragon
1929	10 Feb	earth	snake
1930	30 Jan	metal	horse
1931	17 Feb	metal	ram
1932	06 Feb	water	monkey
1933	26 Jan	water	rooster
1934	14 Feb	wood	dog
1935	04 Feb	wood	pig
1936	24 Jan	fire	rat
1937	11 Feb	fire	ox
1938	31 Jan	earth	tiger
1939	19 Feb	earth	hare
1940	08 Feb	metal	dragon
1941	27 Jan	metal	snake
1942	15 Feb	water	horse
1943	05 Feb	water	ram
1944	25 Jan	wood	monkey
1945	13 Feb	wood	rooster
1946	02 Feb	fire	dog
1947	22 Jan	fire	pig
1948	10 Feb	earth	rat
1949	29 Jan	earth	ox
1950	17 Feb	metal	tiger
1951	06 Feb	metal	hare
1952	27 Jan	water	dragon
1953	14 Feb	water	snake
1954	03 Feb	wood	horse
1955	24 Jan	wood	ram
1956	12 Feb	fire	monkey
1957	31 Jan	fire	rooster

Year	New Year's Day	*Xing*	*Ming Shu*
1958	18 Feb	earth	dog
1959	08 Feb	earth	pig
1960	28 Jan	metal	rat
1961	15 Feb	metal	ox
1962	05 Feb	water	tiger
1963	25 Jan	water	hare
1964	13 Feb	wood	dragon
1965	02 Feb	wood	snake
1966	21 Jan	fire	horse
1967	09 Feb	fire	ram
1968	30 Jan	earth	monkey
1969	17 Feb	earth	rooster
1970	06 Feb	metal	dog
1971	27 Jan	metal	pig
1972	15 Feb	water	rat
1973	03 Feb	water	ox
1974	23 Jan	wood	tiger
1975	11 Feb	wood	hare
1976	31 Jan	fire	dragon
1977	18 Feb	fire	snake
1978	07 Feb	earth	horse
1979	28 Jan	earth	ram
1980	16 Feb	metal	monkey
1981	05 Feb	metal	rooster
1982	25 Jan	water	dog
1983	13 Feb	water	pig
1984	02 Feb	wood	rat
1985	20 Feb	wood	ox
1986	09 Feb	fire	tiger
1987	29 Jan	fire	hare

This data is taken from *The Complete Astrological Handbook for the Twenty-first Century* (New York: Schocken Books, 1999).

1927 (Fire Hare). A Metal Ram (1931) may encourage mutual extravagance and carelessness, while a Water Ram (1943) dampens your spirits. A Wood Dog (1934), however, is positively inspirational. A Wood Pig (1935) invites good behavior. Another Fire Hare (1927) might be a little too temperamental a match. A modicum of agreement can be reached with a Wood Rat (1924), Earth Tiger (1938), and Earth Dragon (1928) if your lunar month signs are compatible (see next section). There's a lack of communication with a Water Rooster (1933) and Fire Rat (1936). Avoid the Metal Dragon (1940) and Water Dragon (1952) altogether, because you might be on the same planet but you're in totally separate worlds. (*Famous examples:* Coretta Scott King, John W. Warner.)

1928 (Earth Dragon). The Wood Rat (1924) loves you, but causes you some trouble. The Fire Rat (1936) ignites your determination. The Water Monkey (1932), Wood Monkey (1944), Wood Rooster (1945), and Water Rooster (1933) cause some disappointment. Another Earth Dragon (1928) could be too dominant, but a Fire Dragon (1940) is an exhilaration. Mutual comprehension is possible with a Fire Tiger (1926), Metal Tiger (1950), or Fire Ox (1937) if you've got compatible lunar month signs (see next section). There's a lack of communication with an Earth Tiger (1938), Wood Ox (1925), and Wood Dog (1934). (*Famous examples:* Eddie Fisher, the Reverend Dr. Martin Luther King Jr. [birth year 1929 in a Western calendar], Roger Vadim.)

1929 (Earth Snake). You may be happy in the arms of a Water Rooster (1933), if you can accept delays and disappointment. If you let a Fire Ox (1937) take the lead in a relationship, you'll be loved for life. There's some potential for good communication with a Fire Tiger (1926), Fire Pig (1947), or a Metal Tiger (1950) if your lunar month signs are compatible (see next section). You can't find agreement or compassion with an Earth Tiger (1938) or a Wood Pig (1935). Avoid living with another Earth Snake (1929) or a Metal Snake (1941). It's not destined to work. (*Famous example:* Burt Bacharach.)

1930 (Metal Horse). A Metal Ram (1931) or a Water Ram (1943) always stands by you. An Earth Tiger (1938) or Metal Tiger (1950) protects you. A Fire Tiger (1926) or a Wood Dog (1934) might create some disappointment. A modicum of comprehension is possible with a Water Monkey (1932) or a Fire Monkey (1956) if your lunar month signs are compatible (see next section). Stay away from a Wood Rat (1924), Fire Rat (1936), Wood Monkey (1944), or Fire Ox (1937); you'll never comprehend each other. Avoid another Metal Horse (1930) or a Water Horse (1942); the two of you can't live together. (*Famous examples:* Anthony Armstrong-Jones, Prince Margaret Windsor, Debbie Reynolds.)

The Manchus of Liaoning, Jilin, and Heilongjiang Provinces arrange marriages for their children after their sixteenth or seventeenth birthday. Just like their cousins to the south, they hire a *mei* (matchmaker) to negotiate the betrothal and nuptials. After the prospective couple's birth charts are compared, the *mei* visits the young woman's family three times before a betrothal is considered. Each time, the *mei* presents a bottle of wine (wine is very expensive to produce in the region) and asks if it's all right to pursue the idea of a match between the daughter and the suitor. Then the *mei* asks the family if their daughter is worth three bottles of wine! If they agree, they request betrothal gifts on their daughter's behalf: pigs, wine, money, clothes, and ornaments that the bride keeps for herself after the marriage.

1931 (Metal Ram). The Earth Hare (1939), Water Horse (1942), and Metal Horse (1930) love you just as you are. You might have some trouble with a Fire Hare (1927) or a Wood Pig (1935). You exasperate the Fire Ox (1937), Wood Ox (1925), and Wood Dog (1934). Another Metal Ram (1931) or Water Ram (1943) might lead to excessive codependency if you're not careful. Avoid the Fire Rat (1936) and the Wood Rat (1924) because there's no hope for mutual agreement. (*Famous examples:* Angie Dickinson, Mikhail Gorbachev, Raisa Gorbachev [birth year 1932 in a Western calendar], Mike Nichols.)

1932 (Water Monkey). You can reach a mutual agreement with a Metal Dragon (1940), Water Dragon (1952), or Wood Rat (1924). But it's touch and go with an Earth Dragon (1928) or a Fire Rat (1936). There's no communication with an Earth Tiger (1938) or Fire Tiger (1926). However, there's potential compatibility with a Metal Horse (1930), Wood Horse (1954), or Water Horse (1942) if your lunar month signs agree (see next section). It's too difficult for you to deal with another Water Monkey (1932) or a Wood Monkey (1944). (*Famous examples:* Louis Malle, Elizabeth Taylor.)

1933 (Water Rooster). Elated with a Metal Dragon (1940), a Water Dragon (1952), or a Wood Dragon (1964), you're also happy with a Wood Ox (1925) or a Metal Snake (1941). You'd be ill advised to seek out the Earth Dragon (1928) or the Earth Snake (1929) because either one can only cause you trouble. You've nothing in common with the Earth Hare (1939), Fire Hare (1927), Fire Dog (1946), or an Earth Dog (1958). Moderate comprehension could occur with a Wood Dog (1934) if your lunar month signs are compatible (see next section). Another Water Rooster (1933) or Wood Rooster (1945) under the same roof never works, because each of you is too internally focused to give sufficient attention to the other. (*Famous examples:* Sir Michael Caine, Quincy Jones, Yoko Ono.)

1934 (Wood Dog). You'll find happiness with the supportive Water Horse (1942), Wood Horse (1954), or Fire Tiger (1926). Bliss may not be a smooth road with a Metal Horse (1930), Metal Tiger (1950), or Earth Tiger (1938). Peace is yours with a Fire Hare (1927), but less so with an Earth Hare (1939). Commitment might be difficult with another Wood Dog (1934), a Water Dog (1922), or Fire Dog (1946). Some mutual agreement can be had with a Water Rooster (1933) or a Fire Ox (1937) if you share compatible lunar month signs (see next section). The Earth Dragon (1928), Metal Dragon (1940), Wood Ox (1925), and Wood Rooster (1945) are off limits if you wish to keep your sanity. (*Famous examples:* Brigitte Bardot, Elvis Presley [birth year 1935 in a Western calendar].)

1935 (Wood Pig). The Fire Hare (1927) understands you. A Water Ram (1943) or Wood Ram (1955) knows how to lead you. Your life is relatively pleasant with an Earth Hare (1939) or a Metal Ram (1931), but not quite as blissful. You'll need trusted advisers to avoid deceptive outsiders if you commit to a relationship with another Wood

Pig (1935) or a Fire Pig (1947). There's possible agreement with a Water Monkey (1932), Wood Monkey (1944), or Water Snake (1953) if you've got compatible lunar month signs (see next section). The Earth Snake (1929) and Metal Snake (1941) aren't good for your well-being. (*Famous examples:* Woody Allen, Sonny Bono.)

1936 (Fire Rat). Success is yours with an Earth Dragon (1928) or Wood Dragon (1964) by your side. A Metal Dragon (1940) might invite extravagance and carelessness, and a Water Dragon (1952) will dampen your spirits. There's too much independence between you and another Fire Rat (1936) or an Earth Rat (1948). A Wood Monkey (1944) may be a source of inspiration, but don't expect to be the same in return. A Water Monkey (1932) might spur too much sarcasm or boredom in you. There's no agreement or compassion in the arms of a Water Horse (1942), a Metal Horse (1930), or a Wood Horse (1954). There's a chance that mutual determination could win the day with an Earth Hare (1939), especially if you have compatible lunar month signs (see next section). A Metal Ram (1931) might instigate carelessness and extravagance, and a Water Ram (1943) may dampen your dynamic spirit. (*Famous example:* Ursula Andress.)

1937 (Fire Ox). The Water Rooster (1933) might create some opposition, but the Wood Rooster (1945) instills inspiration. There might be too much drive between you and another Fire Ox (1937) or a Fire Rooster (1957); if you're not headed in the same direction, there's a head-on collision. A Metal Snake (1941) may lead to carelessness. An Earth Snake (1929) fires up your determination. Moderate comprehension is possible with an Earth Tiger (1938) if you have compatible lunar month signs (see next section). Avoidance is the best relationship with a Fire Tiger (1926), Water Ram (1943), Metal Ram (1931), Metal Horse (1930), or Water Horse (1942). (*Famous examples:* Warren Beatty, Jane Fonda, Jack Nicholson.)

1938 (Earth Tiger). Potential success exists with a Metal Horse (1930), although a Water Horse (1942) or Wood Horse (1954) may lead to some disappointment. A Fire Dog (1946) provides the determination you need, while a Wood Dog (1934) may be the harbinger of obstacles. An Earth Dog (1958) will stand by you. Life is stormy but successful with a Metal Dragon (1940). Compatibility can occur with a Metal Snake (1941), Fire Ox (1937), or Earth Ox (1949) if your lunar month signs agree (see next section). An Earth Dragon (1928) may make for rough but influential seas. Avoid another Earth Tiger (1938) as well as a Fire Tiger (1926), Metal Tiger (1950), Earth Snake (1929), Earth Ox (1949), Water Monkey (1932), or Wood Monkey (1944) because any of them will only bring you trouble. (*Famous examples:* Richard Benjamin, Elliot Gould, Ted Turner.)

1939 (Earth Hare). A Water Ram (1943) or Wood Ram (1955) may cause some disappointment, but a Metal Ram (1931) brings success. A Fire Dog (1946) ignites your determination, while a Wood Dog (1934) causes some trouble. A Wood Pig (1935) might be too moralistic, while a Fire Pig (1947) inspires determination and ethical behavior. Another Earth Hare (1939) might be the perfect ally. A Fire Hare (1927) ignites your resolve. Agreement can be reached with a Fire Rat (1936) or Metal Tiger (1950) if you've got compatible lunar month signs (see next section). There's a lack of communication with a Wood Rooster (1945), Water Rooster (1933), Earth Rat (1948), or Earth Tiger (1938). Avoid the Metal Dragon (1940), Water Dragon (1952), and the Earth Dragon (1928) altogether. (*Famous example:* Paula Prentiss.)

1940 (Metal Dragon). The Fire Rat (1936) loves you but is too extravagant. The Water Rooster (1933) finds you attractive, but the Wood Rooster (1945) wants to dominate you. The Earth Rat (1948) encourages your success, becoming your cheerleader. The Wood Monkey (1944) makes it hard to save money, while the Water Monkey (1932) is a strong and positive attraction. Another Metal Dragon (1940) or a Wood Dragon (1964) is too strong-willed to coexist with you, but a Water Dragon (1952) is a beneficial ally. Compatibility is possible with an Earth Tiger (1938), Earth Dog (1958), or Earth Ox (1949) if your lunar month signs agree (see next section). There's a lack of communication with a Metal Tiger (1950), Fire Ox (1937), and Wood Dog (1934). (*Famous examples:* John Lennon, Ringo Starr.)

1941 (Metal Snake). Happiness is yours in the arms of a Water Rooster (1933). With a Wood Rooster (1945) or Fire Rooster (1957), however, you may not be able to financially afford your desires. If you let a Fire Ox (1937) or Earth Ox (1949) take the lead, you'll be loved for life, as long as you hire an accountant to handle your mutual finances. There's some compatibility with an Earth Tiger (1938) or Water Tiger (1962) if your lunar month signs agree (see next section). You can't communicate with a Fire Pig (1947) or Wood Pig (1935). Avoid living with another Metal Snake (1941), an Earth Snake (1929), or a Water Snake (1953); it's not destined to work. (*Famous examples:* James Brolin, Julie Christie, Linda Eastman McCartney.)

1942 (Water Horse). A Water Ram (1943) or a Metal Ram (1931) will stick by you. A Metal Tiger (1950) or a Wood Dog (1934) protects you. An Earth Tiger (1938) or a Fire Dog (1946) might create disappointment. Mutual agreement is possible with a Wood Monkey (1944) if you've got compatible lunar month signs (see next section). Stay away from a Fire Rat (1936), Earth Rat (1948), Water Monkey (1932), or Fire Ox (1937); you'll never comprehend each other. Avoid another Water Horse (1942), Metal Horse (1930), or a Wood Horse (1954); the two of you can't live together. (*Famous examples:* Britt Ekland, Harrison Ford, Sir Paul McCartney, Barbra Streisand.)

1943 (Water Ram). A Metal Hare (1951), Wood Pig (1935), Water Horse (1942), or Wood Horse (1954) will love you just as you are. You might have some trouble with an Earth Hare (1939) or a Fire Pig (1947). You might find a small level of agreement with a Wood Dog (1934) if your lunar month signs are compatible (see next section). You exasperate the Fire Ox (1937), Earth Ox (1949), and Fire Dog (1946). Another Water Ram (1943), Metal Ram (1931), or Wood Ram (1955) might lead to unhealthy codependency if you're not careful. Avoid the Fire Rat (1936) and the Earth Rat (1948) because there's no hope for mutual agreement. (*Famous examples:* Catherine Deneuve, George Harrison, Mick Jagger.)

1944 (Wood Monkey). You can reach an agreement with a Water Dragon (1952) or a Fire Rat (1936), but it's nip and tuck with a Metal

Dragon (1940) or an Earth Rat (1948). There's no communication with a Metal Tiger (1950), Earth Tiger (1938), or Wood Horse (1954), but there's potential compatibility with a Water Horse (1942) if your lunar month signs are agreeable (see next section). It's too difficult for you to deal with another Wood Monkey (1944) or a Fire Monkey (1956) or Water Monkey (1932). (*Famous examples:* Ray Davies, Michael Douglas, Mia Farrow [birth year 1945 in a Western calendar].)

1945 (Wood Rooster). You're elated with a Water Dragon (1952) or a Fire Dragon (1940). You're also happy with the Fire Ox (1937), Fire Snake (1941), and Water Snake (1953). You'd be ill advised to seek out the Earth Ox (1949) or Metal Ox (1961), because either one will only cause you trouble. You've got nothing in common with the Earth Hare (1939), Metal Hare (1951), or Wood Dog (1934). Some communication occurs with an Earth Dog (1946) if you've got compatible lunar month signs (see next section). Another Wood Rooster (1945) or a Fire Rooster (1957) under the same roof would never work, because each of you is too internally focused to give sufficient attention to the other. You'd never be able to give enough of yourselves to keep each other happy. (*Famous examples:* Patti Boyd, Eric Clapton, Goldie Hawn, Diane Keaton [birth year 1946 in a Western calendar], Priscilla Beaulieu Presley, Diane Sawyer.)

> Love was the subject of many poems found in the classic Chinese text *Shi ching (Book of Poetry)*, which was published around 1100 B.C. In one poem, a group of weary soldiers lament, "For life or death, however separated, to our wives we pledged our word. We held their hands. We were to grow old together with them. Alas or our separation! We have no prospect of life."

1946 (Fire Dog). You'll find happiness with the supportive Wood Horse (1954) or Earth Tiger (1938). Marital bliss may not be a smooth road with a Water Horse (1942) or Metal Tiger (1950). Peace is yours with an Earth Hare (1939), but less so with a Metal Hare (1951). Commitment might be difficult with another Fire Dog (1946) or a Wood Dog (1932), but it's not insurmountable with an Earth Dog (1958). Some mutual agreement could be had with Wood Rooster (1945) or Wood Dragon (1964) if you share compatible lunar month signs (see next section). The Water Dragon (1952), Metal Dragon (1940), Earth Ox (1949), Fire Ox (1937), and Fire Rooster (1957) are off limits if you wish to keep your sanity. (*Famous examples:* Candice Bergen, David Bowie [birth year 1947 in a Western calendar], George W. Bush, Cher, Bill Clinton, Susan Sarandon, Steven Spielberg, Donald Trump.)

1947 (Fire Pig). The Earth Hare (1939) understands you and the Wood Ram (1955) knows how to lead you. Your life is pleasant with a Metal Hare (1951) or a Water Ram (1943), but not quite as blissful. There's possible compatibility with a Wood Monkey (1944) if your lunar month signs agree (see next section). You'll need trusted advisers to keep outsiders from deceiving both of you if you commit to a relationship with a Wood Pig (1935), another Fire Pig (1947), or an Earth Pig (1959). The Metal Snake (1941), Water Snake (1953), and Fire Monkey (1956) aren't good for your well-being. (*Famous examples:* Barbara Bach, Shakira Caine, Hillary Rodham Clinton, Linda Evans, Arnold Schwarzenegger, O. J. Simpson.)

1948 (Earth Rat). A Metal Dragon (1940) is your best match. Although there may be delays or disappointments, a Water Dragon (1952) is a fair match. A relationship with another Earth Rat (1948) may mean the loss of opportunities because neither of you is willing to risk the unknown. A Fire Monkey (1956) might be an enticement, but don't expect reciprocal love or attraction. There's nothing but instability and losses with a Wood Horse (1954) or a Water Horse (1942). Frustration occurs with an Earth Hare (1939) or a Metal Hare (1951). Delays and struggles take place with a Water Ram (1943). With a Wood Ram (1955) there may be troubles, but none are insurmountable. (*Famous examples:* Al Gore, Tipper Gore, Ozzy Osbourne, Prince Charles Windsor.)

1949 (Earth Ox). A Wood Rooster (1945) may cause troubles, but you can't resist the temptation. A Fire Rooster (1957), on the other hand, is a source of inspiration. Another Earth Ox (1949) makes the world a very serious place, with few moments of excitement and even less play. A Water Snake (1953) may cause some disappointment and give oodles of compassion. But a Metal Snake (1941) could lead the way to success. Some compatibility is possible with a Metal Tiger (1950) if your lunar month signs agree (see next section). You might find a Water Ram (1943), Wood Ram (1955), Wood Horse (1954), or Water Horse (1942) attractive, but avoidance is the ideal course of action. (*Famous examples:* Don Johnson, Ivana Trump.)

1950 (Metal Tiger). On the financial level, your desires will be hard to afford with a Wood Horse (1954). A Fire Dog (1946) brings nothing but extravagance. The strong attraction to a Water Horse (1942) provides benefits, and an Earth Dog (1958) instigates success. The relationship with a Water Dragon (1952) or a Metal Dragon (1940) might be too stormy to handle. But a Wood Dragon (1964) provides inspiration. Compatibility is possible with a Water Snake (1953) or Earth Ox (1949) if your lunar month signs agree (see next section). Avoid a Wood Snake (1965), Metal Ox (1961), Wood Monkey (1944), Fire Monkey (1956), Metal Hare (1951), Earth Tiger (1938), Water Tiger (1962), or another Metal Tiger (1950) because they will divert your energy from your goals. (*Famous example:* Melissa Mathison.)

1951 (Metal Hare). There's a strong attraction and mutual benefits with a Water Ram (1943). However, a Wood Ram (1955) might be a little rough on the finances. A Fire Dog (1946) may put an equally large crimp on the pocketbook. An Earth Dog (1958), on the other hand, leads the way to achievement. An Earth Pig (1959) also guides the way to sensible success, while a Fire Pig (1947) causes some carelessness. Another Metal Hare (1951) might be a little too preoccupied with self-fulfillment to establish a viable relationship. Compatibility is possible with an Earth Rat (1948) if your lunar month signs agree (see next section). There's a lack of communication with a Wood Rooster (1945), Metal Rat (1960), or Metal Tiger (1950). Avoid the Water Dragon (1952) and the Metal Dragon (1940) altogether; their personalities are far stronger than yours. (*Famous examples:* Larry Fortensky [birth year 1952 in a Western calendar], Anjelica Huston, Chrissie Hynde, Kurt Russell.)

1952 (Water Dragon). The Earth Rat (1948) loves you but creates disappointment. A Metal Rat (1960) is a strong and beneficial attraction. The Fire Monkey (1956) or a Fire Rooster (1957) ultimately instigates opposition, while the Wood Monkey (1944) or Wood Rooster (1945) is a harbinger of positive change. Another Water Dragon (1952) is too strong willed to coexist with you, but a Wood Dragon (1964) brings about positive change, and a Metal Dragon (1940) understands your idiosyncrasies. Compatibility is possible with a Metal Tiger (1950) or a Metal Ox (1962) if your lunar month signs agree (see next section). There's a lack of communication with a Water Tiger (1962), Earth Ox (1949), Fire Dog (1946), or Earth Dog (1958). (*Famous examples:* Grace Jones, Isabella Rossellini.)

1953 (Water Snake). Happiness is yours in the arms of a Wood Rooster (1945). With a Fire Rooster (1957), however, there might be some opposition. If you let a Metal Ox (1961) take the lead, you'll be loved for life. An Earth Ox (1949) may be a little too cautious for your tastes, but loves you all the same. There's some compatibility with a Metal Tiger (1950) if your lunar month signs agree (see next section). You can't reach an agreement with a Water Tiger (1962) or Earth Pig (1959). Avoid living with another Water Snake (1953) or a Wood Snake (1965); it's not destined to work. (*Famous examples:* Kim Basinger, Kate Capshaw, Peter Horton, Amy Irving.)

1954 (Wood Horse). A Wood Ram (1955) or a Water Ram (1943) stands by you. A Water Tiger (1962) or a Fire Dog (1946) protects you. A Metal Tiger (1950) or an Earth Dog (1958) might create some trouble or financial loss. Compatibility is possible with a Fire Monkey (1956) if your lunar month signs agree (see next section). Stay away from an Earth Rat (1948), Metal Rat (1960), Wood Monkey (1944), Earth Monkey (1968), or Metal Ox (1961); you'll never understand each other. Avoid another Wood Horse (1954), Water Horse (1942), or a Fire Horse (1966); the two of you can't live together. (*Famous examples:* Dennis Quaid, John Travolta, Oprah Winfrey.)

1955 (Wood Ram). A Water Hare (1963), Fire Pig (1947), Wood Horse (1954), or Fire Horse (1966) loves you just as you are. You might have some trouble with a Metal Hare (1951) or an Earth Pig (1959). Some compatibility exists with a Fire Dog (1946) if your lunar month signs agree (see next section). You exasperate the Earth Ox (1949), Metal Ox (1961), and Earth Dog (1958). Another Wood Ram (1955) or a Water Ram (1943) or Fire Ram (1967) might lead to too much codependency if you're not careful. Avoid the Earth Rat (1948) and the Metal Rat (1960) because there's no hope for mutual agreement. (*Famous examples:* Isabelle Adjani, Bill Gates, Iman Abdul Majid, Maria Shriver, Billy Bob Thornton, Eddie Van Halen, Bruce Willis.)

1956 (Fire Monkey). You can reach a high degree of compatibility with a Wood Dragon (1964) or an Earth Rat (1948). But it comes and goes with a Water Dragon (1952) or a Metal Rat (1960). There's no communication with a Metal Tiger (1950), Water Tiger (1962), or Fire Horse (1966), but there's potential communication with a Wood Horse (1954) if your lunar month signs agree (see next section). It's too difficult for you to deal with another Fire Monkey (1956) or an Earth Monkey (1968). (*Famous examples:* Bo Derek, Carrie Fisher, Jerry Hall, Sharon Osbourne, Dwight Yoakam.)

1957 (Fire Rooster). Elated with the Wood Dragon (1964), you're also happy with the Earth Ox (1949) and the Wood Snake (1965). You'd be ill advised to seek out the Water Dragon (1952), Metal Ox (1961), or Water Snake (1953) because they'll only cause you trouble. You've got nothing in common with the Water Hare (1963) or Fire Dog (1946), although compatibility could occur with a Metal Hare (1951) or Earth Dog (1958) if your lunar month signs agree (see next section). Another Fire Rooster (1957), Earth Rooster (1969), or Wood Rooster (1945) under the same roof would never work, because each of you is too internally focused to give sufficient attention to the other. (*Famous examples:* Daniel Day-Lewis, Ellen DeGeneres [birth year 1958 in a Western calendar], Melanie Griffith.)

1958 (Earth Dog). You'll find happiness with the supportive Fire Horse (1966) or Metal Tiger (1950). Bliss may not be a smooth road with a Wood Horse (1954) or Water Tiger (1962). Peace is yours with a Metal Hare (1951), but less so with a Water Hare (1963). Commitment

Even in arranged marriages, a husband and wife can fall in love with each other and celebrate tender moments. In his nineteenth-century autobiographical novel, *Six Chapters of a Floating Life*, the author Shen Fu described such an occasion with his wife, Yun, which took place on the Chinese equivalent of Valentine's Day: the seventh night of the seventh Moon. He had carved two small stone seals for the occasion, each with the inscription "That we remain husband and wife from incarnation to incarnation." The seals were made to fit together: the inscription on one was carved into its stone, and the inscription on the other was carved in relief. He gave her the one with negative characters, while he kept the one with positive characters, so they could sign their love letters to each other with this attractive sentiment. Yun set up a cozy spot by a window of their home with candles and incense, where on that night they could contemplate the nighttime sky in each other's arms. There they snuggled together, watching the stars Altair and Vega, which are also called the Cowherd and the Spinster. These stellar entities encounter each other only on this one night every year, set against the backdrop of the Milky Way.

might be difficult with a Fire Dog (1946). But it's not insurmountable with another Earth Dog (1958) or Metal Dog (1970). Some compatibility exists with a Metal Ox (1961) or Fire Rooster (1957) if your lunar month signs agree (see next section). The Water Dragon (1952), Wood Dragon (1964), Earth Ox (1949), and Earth Rooster (1969) are off limits if you wish to keep your sanity. (*Famous examples:* Kevin Bacon, Alec Baldwin, Annette Bening, Simon LeBon, Madonna, Michelle Pfeiffer, Prince, Tim Robbins, Vanity [birth year 1959 in a Western calendar].)

1959 (Earth Pig). The Metal Hare (1951) understands you and the Fire Ram (1967) knows how to lead you. Your life is potentially pleasant with a Water Hare (1963) or a Wood Ram (1955), but not quite as blissful. You'll need trusted advisers to avoid deceptive outsiders if you commit to a relationship with a Fire Pig (1947), another Earth Pig (1959), or a Metal Pig (1971). The Wood Snake (1965), Water Snake (1953), Earth Monkey (1968), and Fire Monkey (1956) aren't good for your well-being. (*Famous examples:* Richie Sambora, Nicole Brown Simpson, Emma Thompson.)

1960 (Metal Rat). A Water Dragon (1952) is your perfect match. But you may not be able to financially afford your desires with a Wood Dragon (1964). True feelings may never surface between you and another Metal Rat (1960). It'll be hard to save for the future with a Fire Monkey (1956). However, you'll find a measure of success with an Earth Monkey (1968), Metal Hare (1951), or Water Hare (1963). Just don't expect to be repaid in kind. Your jealous nature is tested to the hilt with a Wood Horse (1954) or a Fire Horse (1966). A Wood Ram (1955) might run off even before you say hello, and a Fire Ram (1967) may instigate extravagance or carelessness. (*Famous examples:* Antonio Banderas, Valerie Bertinelli, Kenneth Branagh, David Duchovny, Hugh Grant, Daryl Hannah, John F. Kennedy Jr., Nastassja Kinski, Sean Penn, Tracy Pollan, Michael Stipe.)

1961 (Metal Ox). Life with an Earth Rooster (1969) has the potential to be heavenly. But with a Fire Rooster (1957), love could lead to extravagance and more than a few quarrels. Another Metal Ox (1961) might make too forceful a match because neither of you accepts failure or defeat as an option. There's a strong attraction and many benefits found with a Water Snake (1953). Get a good accountant to handle mutual finances with a Wood Snake (1965). Compatibility is possible with an Earth Monkey (1958) or Water Tiger (1962) if your lunar month signs agree (see next section). The Fire Monkey (1956), Fire Ram (1967), Wood Ram (1955), Metal Tiger (1950), Wood Horse (1954), and Fire Horse (1966) are off limits if you wish to avoid failure. (*Famous examples:* Michael J. Fox, Heather Locklear, Meg Ryan, Princess Diana Spencer Windsor.)

1962 (Water Tiger). Life with a Wood Horse (1954) or Metal Dog (1970) brings about positive changes, but a Fire Horse (1966) might create too much opposition. An Earth Dog (1958), on the other hand, may instigate disappointment. A stormy life with a Wood Dragon (1964) can bring about significant changes. There are calmer seas with a Water Dragon (1952), but little mutual agreement. Compatibility is possible with a Wood Snake (1965), Metal Ox (1961), or Metal Hare (1951) if your lunar month signs agree (see next section). Avoid a Water Snake (1953), Water Ox (1973), Earth Monkey (1968), Fire Monkey (1956), Water Hare (1963), Metal Tiger (1950), Wood

Tiger (1974), or another Water Tiger (1962) because you'll lose your composure and your ability to assess situations. (*Famous examples:* Matthew Broderick, Garth Brooks, Tom Cruise, Tommy Lee, Demi Moore, Kelly Preston.)

1963 (Water Hare). A Fire Ram (1967) might find you a little dull, but a Wood Ram (1955) will discover that you're a positive influence. An Earth Dog (1958) might create too many delays, but a Metal Dog (1970) is a strong and beneficial attraction. An Earth Pig (1959) may be a little too moral and sensible, but you benefit from an ethical Metal Pig (1971). Another Water Hare (1963) might dwell too much on the past or be too cautious about the future to promote progress. Compatibility can be reached with a Metal Rat (1960) if your lunar month signs agree (see next section). There's a lack of communication with a Fire Rooster (1957), Water Rat (1972), or Water Tiger (1962). Avoid the Wood Dragon (1964) and the Water Dragon (1952) altogether; their personalities are far stronger than yours. (*Famous examples:* Benjamin Bratt, Nicolas Cage [birth year 1964 in a Western calendar], Johnny Depp, Bridget Fonda [1964, Western calendar], Marla Maples, Brad Pitt.)

1964 (Wood Dragon). The Water Rat (1972) loves you, creating positive change. The Metal Rat (1960) makes it hard for you to afford your desires. The Earth Monkey (1968) and Earth Rooster (1969) cause losses, while the Fire Monkey (1956) and Fire Rooster (1957) ignite inspiration. Another Wood Dragon (1964) is too dominant and outspoken, but a Water Dragon (1952) incites positive change. Moderate compatibility is possible with a Water Tiger (1962) or Water Ox (1973) if your lunar month signs agree (see next section). There's a lack of communication with a Metal Tiger (1950), Metal Ox (1961), Earth Dog (1958), and Metal Dog (1970). (*Famous examples:* Courteney Cox Arquette, Calista Flockhart, Lenny Kravitz, Yasmin Parvaneh LeBon, Courtney Love.)

1965 (Wood Snake). Happiness is yours in the arms of a Fire Rooster (1957). With an Earth Rooster (1969), however, there's bound to be some trouble. If you let a Water Ox (1973) take the lead, you'll be loved for life. A Metal Ox (1961) might prevent the financial fulfillment of your desires. There's good communication with a Water Tiger (1962) if your lunar month signs agree (see next section). You can't find common ground for compatibility with a Wood Tiger (1974), Earth Pig (1959), or Metal Pig (1971). Avoid living with another Wood Snake (1965), Water Snake (1953), or a Fire Snake (1977); it's not destined to work. (*Famous examples:* Elizabeth Hurley, Carolyn Bessette Kennedy [birth year 1966 in a Western calendar], Sarah Jessica Parker, Kyra Sedgwick, Brooke Shields, Ben Stiller.)

1966 (Fire Horse). A Wood Ram (1955) or a Fire Ram (1967) stands by you. A Wood Tiger (1974) or an Earth Dog (1958) protects you. A Water Tiger (1962) or a Metal Dog (1970) might create some disappointment. Compatibility is possible with an Earth Monkey (1968) if your lunar month signs agree (see next section). Stay away from a Water Rat (1972), Metal Rat (1960), Fire Monkey (1956), Metal Ox (1961), or Water Ox (1973); you'll never communicate on level ground with each other. Avoid another Fire Horse (1966), a Wood Horse (1954), or an Earth Horse (1978); the two of you can't live together. (*Famous examples:* Eric Benét, Halle Berry, Helena Bonham Carter, Salma Hayek, Téa Leoni.)

1967 (Fire Ram). The Wood Hare (1975), Earth Pig (1959), Fire Horse (1966), and Wood Horse (1954) love you just as you are. Some trouble might well up with a Water Hare (1963) or a Metal Pig (1971). You could communicate adequately with an Earth Dog (1958) if your lunar month signs agree (see next section). You exasperate the Water Ox (1973), Metal Ox (1961), and Metal Dog (1970). Another Fire Ram (1967) or a Wood Ram (1955) might lead to too much codependency if you're not careful. Avoid the Metal Rat (1960) and the Water Rat (1972) because there's no hope for mutual agreement. (*Famous examples:* Lisa Bonet, Kurt Cobain, Nicole Kidman, Pamela Anderson Lee, Julia Roberts.)

1968 (Earth Monkey). You can be compatible with a Fire Dragon (1976) or a Metal Rat (1960), but it's a questionable match with a Wood Dragon (1964) or a Water Rat (1972). There's no communication with a Water Tiger (1962) or an Earth Horse (1978). But there's potential compatibility with a Fire Horse (1966) if your lunar month signs agree (see next section). It's too difficult for you to deal with another Earth Monkey (1968) or a Metal Monkey (1980). (*Famous examples:* Jennifer Aniston [birth year 1969 in a Western calendar], Patricia Arquette, Marilyn Manson [1969, Western calendar], Will Smith.)

1969 (Earth Rooster). Elated with the Fire Dragon (1976), you're more happy with the Metal Ox (1961) and the Fire Snake (1977). You'd be ill advised to seek out the Wood Dragon (1964) or the Wood Snake (1965) because either one only causes you trouble. You've nothing in common with the Wood Hare (1975), Water Hare (1963), Earth Dog (1958), or Water Dog (1982), although mutual agreement could occur with a Metal Dog (1970) if your lunar month signs agree (see next section). Another Earth Rooster (1969), a Fire Rooster (1957), or a Metal Rooster (1981) under the same roof would never work, because each of you is too internally focused to give sufficient attention to the other. (*Famous examples:* Steffi Graf, Anne Heche, Edward Norton, Catherine Zeta-Jones.)

1970 (Metal Dog). You'll find happiness with the supportive Earth Horse (1978). There's no smooth road to bliss, however, with a Fire Horse (1966) or Wood Tiger (1974). Peace is yours with a Water Hare (1963), but less so with a Wood Hare (1975). Mutual agreement can be had with an Earth Rooster (1969), Water Ox (1973), or Earth Dragon (1988) if you have compatible lunar month signs (see next section). Commitment might be difficult with a Wood Dog (1934) or a Fire Dog (1946), but it's not insurmountable with an Earth Dog (1958), a Water Dog (1982), or another Metal Dog (1970). The Fire Dragon (1976), Wood Dragon (1964), Metal Ox (1961), and Metal Rooster (1981) are off limits if you wish to keep your sanity. (*Famous examples:* André Agassi, Sean "Puffy" Combs, Ethan Hawke, Jennifer Lopez, Uma Thurman.)

1971 (Metal Pig). The Water Hare (1963) understands you and the Earth Ram (1979) knows how to lead you. Your life is pleasant with a

Wood Hare (1975) or a Fire Ram (1967), but not quite as blissful. There's potential compatibility with an Earth Monkey (1968) or a Fire Snake (1977) if your lunar month signs agree (see next section). You'll need trusted advisers to keep outsiders from deceiving both of you if you commit to a relationship with a Fire Pig (1947), an Earth Pig (1959), a Water Pig (1983), or another Metal Pig (1971). The Wood Snake (1965) and Metal Monkey (1980) aren't good for your well-being. (*Famous examples:* David Arquette, Tom Green, Winona Ryder, Jada Pinkett Smith.)

1972 (Water Rat). Only positive changes occur in the arms of a Wood Dragon (1964), who's your perfect match. You might become too sarcastic in the company of a Fire Dragon (1976). Another Water Rat (1972) might lead you to become too shrewd and opportunistic for your own good. An Earth Monkey (1968) could slow you down, while a Metal Monkey (1980) may be too emotionally intense. A Fire Horse (1966) or a Fire Ram (1967) creates too much opposition, while an Earth Horse (1978) or an Earth Ram (1979) places obstacles in the way at every turn. A Water Hare (1963) and a Wood Hare (1975) don't understand you. (*Famous examples:* Ben Affleck, Gwyneth Paltrow, Vanessa Paradis.)

1973 (Water Ox). Your best bet is a Metal Rooster (1981). An Earth Rooster (1969) might instigate too many delays or place obstacles in your path. Unless another Water Ox (1973) shares your same personal values, there's little chance of détente, since neither of you relinquishes your position easily. A Wood Snake (1965) potentially makes positive changes to your life, but a Fire Snake (1977) causes too much opposition. A Water Rat (1972) or a Metal Rat (1960) may try to understand you. Mutual agreement is possible with the very seductive Metal Monkey (1980) or enigmatic Wood Tiger (1974) if you have compatible lunar month signs (see next section). It's best to avoid an Earth Monkey (1968), Fire Ram (1967), Earth Ram (1979), Water Tiger (1962), Earth Horse (1978), or Fire Horse (1966). (*Famous examples:* Juliette Lewis, Kate Moss [birth year 1974 in a Western calendar].)

1974 (Wood Tiger). A Fire Horse (1966) is an ideal mate, but an Earth Horse (1978) may instigate trouble. A Metal Dog (1970) reeks havoc on the bank account, while an Earth Dog (1958) heralds even greater loss. A Wood Dragon (1964) might be a little too outspoken, but a Fire Dragon (1976) is an inspiration. Compatibility is possible with a Fire Snake (1977) or Water Ox (1973) if your lunar month signs agree (see next section). A relationship with a Wood Snake (1965), Wood Ox (1985), Metal Monkey (1980), Earth Monkey (1968), Wood Hare (1975), Fire Hare (1987), Water Tiger (1962), or Wood Tiger (1974) should be avoided. (*Famous examples:* Leonardo DiCaprio, Mayte Garcia.)

1975 (Wood Hare). Inspiration comes in abundance with a Fire Ram (1967), but an Earth Ram (1979) instigates trouble. A Water Dog (1982) creates positive changes, whereas a Metal Dog (1970) or Metal Pig (1971) is bad for your financial security. Another Wood Hare (1975) might not be able to curb your generosity or defend you when you feel intimidated. Compatibility can be reached with a Water Rat (1972) if your lunar month signs agree (see next section). There's a lack of communication with an Earth Rooster (1969), Wood Rat (1984), or Wood Tiger (1974). Avoid the Fire Dragon (1976) and the Wood Dragon (1964) altogether; their personalities are far stronger than yours. (*Famous examples:* Drew Barrymore, Angelina Jolie, Rose McGowan.)

1976 (Fire Dragon). The Water Rat (1972) loves you but ultimately creates opposition. The Wood Rat (1984) ignites inspiration. The Earth Monkey (1968) strikes up your determination, while the Metal Monkey (1980) instigates extravagance or carelessness. Another Fire Dragon (1976) would create too dramatic an atmosphere; a Wood Dragon (1964), however, could provide loads of inspiration. Compatibility is possible with a Wood Tiger (1974) or Wood Ox (1985) if your lunar month signs agree (see next section). There's a lack of communication with a Fire Tiger (1986), Water Ox (1973), or Metal Dog (1970). (*Famous example:* Lukas Haas.)

1977 (Fire Snake). You'll be happy with an Earth Rooster (1969). You could be content in the arms of a Metal Rooster (1981) if someone else watches the expenses. If you let a Wood Ox (1985) take the lead, you'll be loved for life. A Water Ox (1973) might cause some opposition. There's compatibility with a Wood Tiger (1974) if your lunar month signs agree (see next section). You can't communicate with a Fire Tiger (1986) or Water Pig (1983). Avoid living with another Fire Snake (1977) or a Wood Snake (1965); it's not destined to work. (*Famous example:* Liv Tyler.)

1978 (Earth Horse). An Earth Ram (1979) or a Fire Ram (1967) stands by you. A Fire Tiger (1986) or a Metal Dog (1970) protects you. A Wood Tiger (1974) or a Water Dog (1982) might create some disappointment. Compatibility is possible with a Metal Monkey (1980) if your lunar month signs agree (see next section). Stay away from a Water Rat (1972), Wood Rat (1984), Earth Monkey (1968), or Water Ox (1973). Avoid another Earth Horse (1978) or a Fire Horse (1966) because the two of you can't live together. (*Famous example:* Amy Chow.)

Westernized society has slowly overtaken tradition in Japan. In 1973, 40 percent of all Japanese marriages were arranged. The 1988 Asia Society's *Video Letter from Japan* estimated 25 to 50 percent of marriages were arranged through assisted correspondence or through formal introductions made by a go-between or introduction service. According to the 1996 *Japan Almanac*, however, only 12 percent of all marriages performed in 1991 were arranged by the couples' families. But this figure didn't include the number of introductions that had been formally contracted by the prospective bride or groom without their families' intervention.

1979 (Earth Ram). A Fire Hare (1987), Metal Pig (1971), Fire Horse (1966), or Earth Horse (1978) loves you just as you are. You might have some trouble with a Wood Hare (1975) or a Water Pig (1983). You'll potentially be compatible with a Metal Dog (1970) if your lunar month signs agree (see next section). You exasperate a Water Ox (1973), Wood Ox (1985), or Water Dog (1982). Another Earth Ram

(1979) or a Fire Ram (1967) might lead to extreme codependency if you're not careful. Avoid the Water Rat (1972) and the Wood Rat (1984) because there's no hope for mutual agreement. (*Famous example:* Claire Danes.)

1980 (Metal Monkey). You're compatible with an Earth Dragon (1988) or a Water Rat (1972). But it's going to be a challenge with a Fire Dragon (1976) or a Wood Rat (1984). There's no communication with a Wood Tiger (1974), Fire Tiger (1986), or Metal Horse (1990), but there's potential agreement with an Earth Horse (1978) if your lunar month signs agree (see next section). It's too difficult for you to deal with another Metal Monkey (1980) or an Earth Monkey (1968) for long periods. (*Famous examples:* Christina Aguilera, Macaulay Culkin, Rachel Miner Culkin.)

1981 (Metal Rooster). Elated with the Earth Dragon (1988), you're also happy with the Water Ox (1973) and the Earth Snake (1989). You'd be ill advised to seek out the Fire Dragon (1976) or the Fire Snake (1977) because they'll only cause you trouble. You've nothing in common with the Wood Hare (1975), Fire Hare (1987), or Water Dog (1982), although you can be compatible with a Metal Dog (1970) if your lunar month signs agree (see next section). Another Metal Rooster (1981) or an Earth Rooster (1969) under the same roof would never work because each of you is too internally focused to give sufficient attention to the other. (*Famous examples:* Natalie Portman, Britney Spears, Justin Timberlake.)

1982 (Water Dog). You'll find happiness and support with a Metal Horse (1990) or Wood Tiger (1974). Bliss may not be a smooth road with an Earth Horse (1978) or Fire Tiger (1986). Peace is yours with a Wood Hare (1975), but less so with a Fire Hare (1987). Commitment might be difficult with another Water Dog (1982). But it's not insurmountable with a Metal Dog (1970). A measure of compatibility could be had with a Metal Rooster (1981) or Wood Ox (1985) if your lunar month signs agree (see next section). The Fire Dragon (1976), Earth Dragon (1988), Water Ox (1973), and Earth Rooster (1969) are off-limits if you wish to keep your sanity. (*Famous example:* Prince William Windsor.)

1983 (Water Pig). The Wood Hare (1975) understands you and the Metal Ram (1991) knows how to lead you. Your life is pleasant with an Earth Ram (1979), but not quite as blissful. You'll need trusted advisers to keep outsiders from deceiving both of you if you commit to a relationship with another Water Pig (1983) or a Metal Pig (1971). There's potential compatibility with a Metal Monkey (1980) and a Wood Snake (1965) if your lunar month signs agree (see next section). The Fire Snake (1977) and Earth Monkey (1968) aren't good for your well-being. (*Famous examples:* Kim Smith, Taylor Hanson.)

1984 (Wood Rat). A Fire Dragon (1976) incites inspiration, while an Earth Dragon (1988) may create a hindrance to your ego and your creative nature. There's too much ego and calculation between you and another Wood Rat (1984). A Metal Monkey (1980) drains your pocketbook without leaving you so much as an IOU. An Earth Horse (1978) tramples your ego into the ground, while an Earth Ram (1979) only creates losses for both of you. (*Famous examples:* Prince Henry Windsor, Dave Moffatt, Clint Moffatt, Bob Moffatt.)

1985 (Wood Ox). A Metal Rooster (1981) may not help your dreams come true. But a Water Rooster (1993) or Water Rat (1972) could bring about positive changes. So long as you and another Wood Ox (1985) or Wood Rat (1984) are directed toward the same goals, you'll compassionately lead each other toward success. An Earth Snake (1989) creates troubles for you, but a Fire Snake (1977) instigates inspiration. A measure of compatibility is possible with a Fire Tiger (1986) if your lunar month signs agree (see next section). The Metal Monkey (1980), Earth Ram (1979), Wood Tiger (1974), Earth Horse (1978), and Metal Horse (1990) should be avoided at all costs. (*Famous examples:* Zac Hanson, Athina Onassis Roussel.)

1986 (Fire Tiger). Determination is in abundance in the arms of an Earth Horse (1978). Extravagance is the order of the day with a Metal

Horse (1990) or a Metal Dog (1970). Your spirits might get damp-
ened with a Water Dog (1982). Although the relationship is stormy,
determination rules the day with an Earth Dragon (1988). Arguments
might get a little heated with a Fire Dragon (1976). There's some
compatibility with an Earth Snake (1989), Wood Ox (1985), Wood
Hare (1975), or Wood Tiger (1974) if your lunar month signs agree
(see next section). Don't think about a lengthy commitment if a Fire
Snake (1977), Water Ox (1973), Metal Monkey (1980), Fire Hare
(1987), or another Fire Tiger (1986) crosses your path, because the
relationship eventually becomes a disaster. (*Famous examples:* Ashley
Olsen, Mary-Kate Olsen.)

1987 (Fire Hare). A Metal Ram (1991) may instigate mutual extravagance, but an Earth Ram (1979) or Wood Dog (1994) is inspirational.
A Water Dog (1982) or Water Pig (1983) causes problems. A Wood
Pig (1995) encourages good behavior. Another Fire Hare (1987)
might be a little too temperamental a match. A modicum of communication can be reached with a Wood Rat (1984) if your lunar month
signs agree (see next section). There's a lack of comprehension with a
Water Rooster (1993), Metal Rooster (1981), Fire Tiger (1986), and
Earth Tiger (1998). Avoid the Metal Dragon (2000) and the Earth
Dragon (1988) altogether; their personalities are far stronger than
yours. (*Famous examples:* Naya Rivera, Jamie Renée Smith.)

In the eyes of a Chinese astrologer, a couple like Kurt Cobain (1967,
Fire Ram) and Courtney Love (1964, Wood Dragon) would've been
advised to wed with some caution. A dominant and outspoken Wood
Dragon like Love would've been recommended to seek the dynamic
company of a Water Rat (1972), Fire Monkey (1956), or Water
Dragon (1952), or at least a Water Tiger (1962). A more dependent
and dramatic Fire Ram like Cobain would've been unconditionally
loved by a Wood Hare (1975), Earth Pig (1959), Fire Horse (1966), or
Wood Horse (1954), or at least an Earth Dog (1958). Neither was
married, however, to someone who was considered truly detrimental
to their emotional, physical, or spiritual health. This was a neutral
pairing, because neither person created positive or negative influences on the outcome of the relationship.

The age differences in some of the above pairings may seem wide by conventional standards. Marriages and long-term unions between people who differ in age more than two or three years weren't very prevalent in the United States two decades ago. But in the past five to ten years, more people have grown to ignore those boundaries. Tim Robbins and Susan Sarandon (twelve years apart), Michael Douglas and Catherine Zeta-Jones (twenty-five years apart), and Johnny Depp and Vanessa Paradis (nine years apart) are but a handful of couples in which age hasn't been a barrier to love. Even in modern-day China, the age gap widened from five or six years during the 1980s to an average of ten years in 2000, according to Professor Wang Zhenyu from the Marriage and Family Research Office of the Chinese Academy of Social Sciences.

As the Moon Rises: What Your Lunar Month Sign Can Tell You

After the couple's *si zhu* are assessed and their *ming shu* compatibility is considered by their family astrologers, an almanac is consulted to determine the best date for the first face-to-face meeting of the families. (We'll detail how the astrologer figures out an optimal date later in this chapter.) The bride's family then sends a *ding jin tie* (definite offer card) via the *mei* (matchmaker) to the groom's home that fixes the day when a formal betrothal can take place.

The official betrothal ceremony revolves around the creation of the *chuan geng tie* (literally, string-together cards). A gilded card with a golden dragon imprinted on its front is placed on the groom's family altar, where it's inscribed with the groom's full name, his father's full name, the groom's *si zhu*, the *mei*'s full name, and a few other details. The ends of two red silk threads are threaded onto two needles and then sewn into the card in one stitch, symbolizing Yue Laou's (the Old Man in the Moon's) decision to unite the pair. A blank gilded card imprinted with a golden phoenix on the front along with another pair of threads and needles is also bundled up.

The *mei* takes the package with both gilded cards and threaded needles along with *guo li* (profit parcels) to the bride's home. Gifts of cash, small cakes decorated with a dragon and a phoenix, tea, sweets, sugar, tobacco, ancestral offerings, pairs of poultry, and a few other valuable items are sent along with a formal letter, listing the description and quantity of gifts sent. (The cakes are distributed among family members according to a rigid protocol in recognition of their standing within the household.)

The bride's family fills out the blank card imprinted with a golden phoenix, sews the threaded needles into the card, and returns it along with a few gifts for the groom's family via the *mei*. They keep the groom's card, imprinted with the golden dragon. The betrothal presents traditionally sent to the groom's family include a chamber pot filled with fruit and strings of coins. There might also be other gifts of food, clothing, and sometimes servants. This allows the bride's family to publicly display their wealth and status as well as their love for their daughter.

If the family astrologers agree that the couple's *si zhu* are a good match, the families deliberate for three days, checking traditional omens. The bride's card is placed on the groom's family altar surrounded by incense and candles. The same thing happens with the groom's card at the bride's family altar. If they're truly in love, the young couple pray that no member of either household gets into a quarrel, loses something, or breaks a rice bowl. If any unlucky incident like that occurs, the engagement's called off. If the three days pass smoothly, the betrothal's confirmed. The *chuan geng tie* (string-together cards) are kept by the respective families as legal proof of the engagement, which can last a year or two while wedding preparations are made. It's a grave affront to break off a betrothal once the three-day period has passed.

Call them superstitious, but the Chinese are picky about when their children get married. A news service in Penang reported that more couples registered to be married during the Ox year 1997 than during the Rat year, 1996. According to reporter Choong Kwee Kim, "a staff member of the Goddess of Mercy Temple here, who chooses auspicious days for wedding couples, said he anticipated a thirty percent drop in marriage registration in the next [Tiger] year." Lots of weddings are also booked during Dragon years because good fortune and optimism are said to accompany those periods.

The Chinese consult their family astrologers to determine the best day for nuptials as well, since they won't risk having weddings on a bad day even if it's in a popular marriage month or year. The bride's family is responsible for the selection of the appropriate lunar month, but the groom's family chooses the day. Fortunately, this isn't as complicated a task as matching up the lucky couple.

If you'd like to choose your wedding date according to Chinese tradition, you must determine the lunar month of the bride's birth year. First, look up the bride's birth year in Table 2 to figure out the *ming shu* for that year. For example, in the case of Courtney Love, she was born in 1964, which was a Dragon year. Then consult the list below to determine which month the wedding should take place.

> Tibetan astrologers match animal signs in an identical manner to the Chinese. The most ideal relationships occur between *thun-sun* (friend animals) such as a Horse and a Tiger or a Horse and a Dog. A union between enemy animals or with neutral animals can be improved if the *xing* (planets) that rule the couple's birth year are in harmony with each other. In the same manner, an inharmonious pair of elements can diminish the happiness of a union. Vietnamese and Japanese astrologers follow the same procedure.

Hare year: first lunar month
Tiger year: second lunar month
Pig year: third lunar month
Dragon year: fourth lunar month
Ox year: fifth lunar month
Rat year: sixth lunar month
Rooster year: seventh lunar month
Monkey year: eighth lunar month
Snake year: ninth lunar month
Dog year: tenth lunar month
Ram year: eleventh lunar month
Horse year: twelfth lunar month

Courtney Love's family would have sent Kurt Cobain's family a note, telling them that the wedding would take place in the fourth lunar month, since she was born in a Dragon year. The groom's family would then choose the day of that month on which the wedding should take place (see "Choosing the Most Auspicious Day," later in this chapter).

As we mentioned earlier, unlike the calendar used in the Western hemisphere, which marks the Sun's visible movements along the Earth's horizon, the Chinese calendar follows the Moon's phases from New Moon to New Moon. Every twenty-eight to thirty days, a New Moon heralds the start of a new lunar month. Consequently, each lunar month starts on a different day each year. Table 3 below shows how this works. So if Courtney Love and Kurt Cobain were to be married in the fourth lunar month of the year 2002, Table 3 tells us that this particular month begins on May 12 that year.

The Chinese lunar month calendar serves yet another important purpose for the betrothed couple. Their Chinese birth year interpretations (*ming shu* compatibility) can be usefully enhanced with an analysis of the bride's and groom's lunar birth months. This is how it's done.

You don't need a *si zhu* to use this section. Enter your (and/or your mate's) birth date onto Worksheet 3. Look for the period in which you were born in Table 3 by locating your birth year in the far left column and then looking across to the columns on the right. The dates listed are the starting dates for each lunar month. Your birthdate should fall on or after a chosen starting date in a particular column and definitely before the starting date that appears in the next column to your right. Enter the lunar month indicated at the top of that column in the worksheet space provided. Do the same for your mate. Then, look for the lunar month in the text following and read how this influences your ability to love and be loved by another person.

WORKSHEET 3. LUNAR MONTH

	Example 1:	Example 2:	Name A:	Name B:
	Kurt Cobain	Courtney Love		
Birth date	20 Feb 1967	09 Jul 1964		
Lunar month	first	sixth		

First lunar month. You're an enigmatic character even to yourself, tantalizing and infuriating a potential mate because you can't be categorized or pigeonholed in any way. Just when you become understandable, you might find that you've changed or matured, developed new tastes and interests, and questioned your own long-held beliefs in the face of new evidence. You're protective of your reputation at all costs. Love and life, however, will always be a fascination in your presence. You're intelligent, well read, romantic, tender, and self-sacrificing on many levels. (*Famous examples:* Drew Barrymore, Sonny Bono, Garth Brooks, Kurt Cobain, Mikhail Gorbachev, George Harrison, Yoko Ono, Paula Prentiss, Elizabeth Taylor, John Travolta, Ivana Trump, Roger Vadim, Eddie Van Halen, John W. Warner.)

Second lunar month. A highly sensitive person, you detest change of any kind. Yet, as a mate, you aren't necessarily faithful and possess very little comprehension of domestic bliss. Although you display immense compassion for others, you are secretly egotistical. A life in contradiction continues, since you tend to choose an unsuitable mate and frequently appear to have unlucky romances. There's an old Pogo newspaper cartoon that reads, "We have met the enemy and he is us." No one has more domain over our lives than we do. So why do we put ourselves into uncomfortable situations? It is always easier to revert to that which we know than to venture into the unknown, even if the known path is an unpleasant one. There's a morbid comfort in familiarity, even familiar pain. Seek to educate yourself about people. If you can reveal more of the world to yourself, you'll have more of a selection. (*Famous examples:* Ursula Andress, Anthony Armstrong-Jones, Alec Baldwin, Warren Beatty, Patti Boyd, Matthew Broderick, Sir Michael Caine, Shakira Caine, Eric Clapton, Al Gore, Quincy Jones, Téa Leoni, Sarah Jessica Parker, Debbie Reynolds, Kurt Russell, Bruce Willis.)

Third lunar month. Since you're a natural-born leader, it takes a special person to cope with you on an intimate, day-to-day basis. Although you're very protective of your mate, offering a constant stream of advice, it's only the rarest of souls who realizes that beneath your hard exterior is a warm, softhearted human being. One of the world's

TABLE 3. CHINESE LUNAR MONTHS FOR THE YEARS 1927–2005

Year	Month 1	Month 2	Month 3	Month 4	Month 5	Month 6
1927	02 Feb	04 Mar	02 Apr	01 May	31 May	29 Jun
1928	23 Jan	21 Feb	20 Apr	19 May	18 Jun	17 Jul
1929	10 Feb	11 Mar	10 Apr	09 May	07 Jun	07 Jul
1930	30 Jan	28 Feb	30 Mar	29 Apr	28 May	26 Jun
1931	17 Feb	19 Mar	18 Apr	17 May	16 Jun	15 Jul
1932	06 Feb	07 Mar	06 Apr	06 May	04 Jun	04 Jul
1933	26 Jan	24 Feb	26 Mar	25 Apr	24 May	22 Jul
1934	14 Feb	15 Mar	14 Apr	13 May	12 Jun	12 Jul
1935	04 Feb	05 Mar	03 Apr	03 May	01 Jun	01 Jul
1936	24 Jan	23 Feb	23 Mar	21 May	19 Jun	18 Jul
1937	11 Feb	13 Mar	11 Apr	10 May	09 Jun	08 Jul
1938	31 Jan	02 Mar	01 Apr	30 Apr	29 May	28 Jun
1939	19 Feb	21 Mar	20 Apr	19 May	17 Jun	17 Jul
1940	08 Feb	09 Mar	08 Apr	07 May	06 Jun	05 Jul
1941	27 Jan	26 Feb	28 Mar	26 Apr	26 May	25 Jun
1942	15 Feb	17 Mar	15 Apr	15 May	14 Jun	13 Jul
1943	05 Feb	06 Mar	05 Apr	04 May	03 Jun	02 Jul
1944	25 Jan	24 Feb	24 Mar	23 Apr	21 Jun	20 Jul
1945	13 Feb	14 Mar	12 Apr	12 May	10 Jun	09 Jul
1946	02 Feb	04 Mar	02 Apr	01 May	31 May	29 Jun
1947	22 Jan	21 Feb	21 Apr	20 May	19 Jun	18 Jul
1948	10 Feb	11 Mar	09 Apr	09 May	07 Jun	07 Jul
1949	29 Jan	28 Feb	29 Mar	28 Apr	28 May	26 Jun
1950	17 Feb	18 Mar	17 Apr	17 May	15 Jun	15 Jul
1951	06 Feb	08 Mar	06 Apr	06 May	05 Jun	04 Jul
1952	27 Jan	25 Feb	26 Mar	24 Apr	24 May	22 Jul
1953	14 Feb	15 Mar	14 Apr	13 May	11 Jun	11 Jul
1954	03 Feb	05 Mar	03 Apr	03 May	01 Jun	30 Jun
1955	24 Jan	22 Feb	24 Mar	22 May	20 Jun	19 Jul
1956	12 Feb	12 Mar	11 Apr	10 May	06 Jun	08 Jul
1957	31 Jan	02 Mar	31 Mar	30 Apr	29 May	28 Jun

Year	Month 7	Month 8	Month 9	Month 10	Month 11	Month 12
1927	29 Jul	27 Aug	26 Sep	25 Oct	24 Nov	24 Dec
1928	15 Aug	14 Sep	13 Oct	12 Nov	12 Dec	11 Jan 1929
1929	05 Aug	03 Sep	03 Oct	01 Nov	01 Dec	31 Dec
1930	24 Aug	22 Sep	22 Oct	20 Nov	20 Dec	19 Jan 1931
1931	14 Aug	12 Sep	11 Oct	10 Nov	09 Dec	08 Jan 1932
1932	02 Aug	01 Sep	30 Sep	29 Oct	28 Nov	27 Dec
1933	21 Aug	20 Sep	19 Oct	18 Nov	17 Dec	15 Jan 1934
1934	10 Aug	09 Sep	08 Oct	07 Nov	07 Dec	05 Jan 1935
1935	30 Jul	29 Aug	28 Sep	27 Oct	26 Nov	26 Dec
1936	17 Aug	16 Sep	15 Oct	14 Nov	14 Dec	13 Jan 1937
1937	06 Aug	05 Sep	04 Oct	03 Nov	03 Dec	02 Jan 1938
1938	27 Jul	24 Sep	23 Oct	22 Nov	22 Dec	20 Jan 1939
1939	15 Aug	13 Sep	13 Oct	11 Nov	11 Dec	09 Jan 1940
1940	04 Aug	02 Sep	01 Oct	31 Oct	29 Nov	29 Dec
1941	23 Aug	21 Sep	29 Oct	19 Nov	18 Dec	17 Jan 1942
1942	12 Aug	10 Sep	10 Oct	08 Nov	08 Dec	06 Jan 1943
1943	01 Aug	31 Aug	29 Sep	29 Oct	27 Nov	27 Dec
1944	19 Aug	17 Sep	17 Oct	16 Nov	15 Dec	14 Jan 1944
1945	08 Aug	06 Sep	06 Oct	05 Nov	05 Dec	03 Jan 1946
1946	28 Jul	27 Aug	25 Sep	25 Oct	24 Nov	23 Dec
1947	16 Aug	15 Sep	14 Oct	13 Nov	12 Dec	11 Jan 1948
1948	05 Aug	03 Sep	03 Oct	01 Nov	01 Dec	30 Dec
1949	26 Jul	22 Sep	22 Oct	20 Nov	20 Dec	18 Jan 1950
1950	14 Aug	12 Sep	11 Oct	10 Nov	09 Dec	08 Jan 1951
1951	03 Aug	01 Sep	01 Oct	30 Oct	29 Nov	28 Dec
1952	20 Aug	19 Sep	19 Oct	17 Nov	17 Dec	15 Jan 1953
1953	09 Aug	08 Sep	08 Oct	07 Nov	06 Dec	05 Jan 1954
1954	30 Jul	28 Aug	27 Sep	27 Oct	25 Nov	25 Dec
1955	18 Aug	16 Sep	16 Oct	14 Nov	14 Dec	13 Jan 1955
1956	06 Aug	05 Sep	04 Oct	03 Nov	02 Dec	01 Jan 1957
1957	27 Jul	25 Aug	23 Oct	22 Nov	21 Dec	20 Jan 1958

Year	Month 1	Month 2	Month 3	Month 4	Month 5	Month 6
1958	18 Feb	20 Mar	19 Apr	19 May	17 Jun	17 Jul
1959	08 Feb	09 Mar	08 Apr	08 May	06 Jun	06 Jul
1960	28 Jan	27 Feb	27 Mar	26 Apr	25 May	24 Jun
1961	15 Feb	17 Mar	15 Apr	15 May	13 Jun	13 Jul
1962	05 Feb	06 Mar	05 Apr	04 May	02 Jun	02 Jul
1963	25 Jan	24 Feb	25 Mar	24 Apr	21 Jun	21 Jul
1964	13 Feb	14 Mar	12 Apr	12 May	10 Jun	09 Jul
1965	02 Feb	03 Mar	02 Apr	01 May	31 May	29 Jun
1966	21 Jan	20 Feb	22 Mar	20 May	19 Jun	18 Jul
1967	09 Feb	11 Mar	10 Apr	09 May	08 Jun	08 Jul
1968	30 Jan	28 Feb	29 Mar	27 Apr	27 May	26 Jun
1969	17 Feb	18 Mar	17 Apr	16 May	15 Jun	14 Jul
1970	06 Feb	08 Mar	06 Apr	05 May	04 Jun	03 Jul
1971	27 Jan	25 Feb	27 Mar	25 Apr	24 May	22 Jul
1972	15 Feb	15 Mar	14 Apr	13 May	11 Jun	11 Jul
1973	03 Feb	05 Mar	03 Apr	03 May	01 Jun	30 Jun
1974	23 Jan	22 Feb	24 Mar	22 Apr	20 Jun	19 Jul
1975	11 Feb	13 Mar	12 Apr	11 May	10 Jun	09 Jul
1976	31 Jan	01 Mar	31 Mar	29 Apr	29 May	27 Jun
1977	18 Feb	20 Mar	18 Apr	18 May	17 Jun	16 Jul
1978	07 Feb	09 Mar	07 Apr	07 May	06 Jun	05 Jul
1979	28 Jan	27 Feb	28 Mar	26 Apr	26 May	24 Jun
1980	16 Feb	17 Mar	15 Apr	14 May	13 Jun	12 Jul
1981	05 Feb	06 Mar	05 Apr	04 May	02 Jun	02 Jul
1982	25 Jan	24 Feb	25 Mar	24 Apr	21 Jun	21 Jul
1983	13 Feb	15 Mar	13 Apr	13 May	11 Jun	10 Jul
1984	02 Feb	03 Mar	01 Apr	01 May	31 May	29 Jun
1985	20 Feb	21 Mar	20 Apr	20 May	18 Jun	18 Jul
1986	09 Feb	10 Mar	09 Apr	09 May	07 Jun	07 Jul
1987	29 Jan	28 Feb	29 Mar	28 Apr	27 May	26 Jun
1988	17 Feb	18 Mar	16 Apr	16 May	14 Jun	14 Jul
1989	06 Feb	08 Mar	06 Apr	05 May	04 Jun	03 Jul

Year	Month 7	Month 8	Month 9	Month 10	Month 11	Month 12
1958	15 Aug	13 Sep	13 Oct	11 Nov	11 Dec	09 Jan 1959
1959	04 Aug	03 Sep	02 Oct	01 Nov	30 Nov	30 Dec
1960	22 Aug	21 Sep	20 Oct	19 Nov	18 Dec	17 Jan 1960
1961	11 Aug	10 Sep	10 Oct	02 Nov	08 Dec	06 Jan 1962
1962	31 Jul	30 Aug	29 Sep	28 Oct	27 Nov	27 Dec
1963	19 Aug	18 Sep	17 Oct	16 Nov	16 Dec	15 Jan 1964
1964	08 Aug	06 Sep	06 Oct	04 Nov	04 Dec	03 Jan 1965
1965	28 Jul	28 Aug	25 Sep	24 Oct	23 Nov	23 Dec
1966	16 Aug	15 Sep	14 Oct	12 Nov	12 Dec	11 Jan 1967
1967	06 Aug	04 Sep	04 Oct	02 Nov	02 Dec	31 Dec
1968	25 Jul	22 Sep	22 Oct	20 Nov	20 Dec	18 Jan 1969
1969	13 Aug	12 Sep	11 Oct	10 Nov	09 Dec	08 Jan 1970
1970	02 Aug	01 Sep	30 Sep	30 Oct	29 Nov	28 Dec
1971	21 Aug	19 Sep	19 Oct	18 Nov	18 Dec	16 Jan 1972
1972	09 Aug	08 Sep	07 Oct	06 Nov	06 Dec	04 Jan 1973
1973	30 Jul	28 Aug	26 Sep	26 Oct	25 Nov	24 Dec
1974	18 Aug	16 Sep	15 Oct	14 Nov	14 Dec	12 Jan 1975
1975	07 Aug	06 Sep	05 Oct	03 Nov	03 Dec	01 Jan 1976
1976	27 Jul	25 Aug	23 Oct	21 Nov	21 Dec	19 Jan 1977
1977	15 Aug	13 Sep	13 Oct	11 Nov	11 Dec	09 Jan 1978
1978	04 Aug	02 Sep	02 Oct	01 Nov	30 Nov	30 Dec
1979	23 Aug	21 Sep	21 Oct	20 Nov	19 Dec	18 Jan 1980
1980	11 Aug	09 Sep	09 Oct	08 Nov	07 Dec	06 Jan 1981
1981	31 Jul	29 Aug	28 Sep	28 Oct	26 Nov	26 Dec
1982	19 Aug	17 Sep	17 Oct	15 Nov	15 Dec	14 Jan 1983
1983	09 Aug	07 Sep	06 Oct	05 Nov	04 Dec	03 Jan 1984
1984	28 Jul	27 Aug	25 Sep	24 Oct	22 Dec	21 Jan 1985
1985	16 Aug	15 Sep	14 Oct	12 Nov	12 Dec	10 Jan 1986
1986	06 Aug	04 Sep	04 Oct	02 Nov	02 Dec	31 Dec
1987	24 Aug	23 Sep	23 Oct	21 Nov	21 Dec	19 Jan 1988
1988	12 Aug	11 Sep	11 Oct	09 Nov	09 Dec	08 Jan 1989
1989	01 Aug	31 Aug	30 Sep	29 Oct	28 Nov	28 Dec

Year	Month 1	Month 2	Month 3	Month 4	Month 5	Month 6
1990	27 Jan	25 Feb	27 Mar	25 Apr	24 May	22 Jul
1991	15 Feb	16 Mar	15 Apr	14 May	12 Jun	12 Jul
1992	04 Feb	04 Mar	03 Apr	03 May	01 Jun	30 Jun
1993	23 Jan	21 Feb	23 Mar	21 May	20 Jun	19 Jul
1994	10 Feb	12 Mar	11 Apr	11 May	09 Jun	09 Jul
1995	31 Jan	01 Mar	31 Mar	30 Apr	29 May	28 Jun
1996	19 Feb	19 Mar	18 Apr	17 May	16 Jun	16 Jul
1997	07 Feb	09 Mar	07 Apr	07 May	05 Jun	05 Jul
1998	28 Jan	27 Feb	28 Mar	26 Apr	26 May	23 Jul
1999	16 Feb	18 Mar	16 Apr	15 May	14 Jun	13 Jul
2000	05 Feb	06 Mar	05 Apr	04 May	02 Jun	02 Jul
2001	24 Jan	23 Feb	25 Mar	23 Apr	21 Jun	21 Jul
2002	12 Feb	14 Mar	13 Apr	12 May	11 Jun	10 Jul
2003	01 Feb	03 Mar	02 Apr	01 May	31 May	30 Jun
2004	22 Jan	20 Feb	19 Apr	19 May	18 Jun	17 Jul
2005	09 Feb	10 Mar	09 Apr	08 May	07 Jun	06 Jul

This data is taken from *The Complete Astrological Handbook for the Twenty-first Century* (New York: Schocken Books, 1999).

most successful breadwinners, you tend to give love and support from the deepest financial and spiritual pockets. Remember, expensive gifts bring joy to those you love. Gestures of affection that cost nothing are truly priceless. (*Famous examples:* André Agassi, Patricia Arquette, Valerie Bertinelli, Julie Christie, Lukas Haas, Daniel Day-Lewis, Coretta Scott King, Jack Nicholson, Michelle Pfeiffer, Dennis Quaid, Barbra Streisand, Emma Thompson, Uma Thurman, Dwight Yoakam.)

Fourth lunar month. A very lovable and compassionate person, you publicly demonstrate your affections and maintain an extremely laid-back demeanor. You speak and listen well. You're also supportive of your mate's dreams and ideas. You're also more likely to give in to persuasion than pressure. Like a tree with solid roots, you can't be

Year	Month 7	Month 8	Month 9	Month 10	Month 11	Month 12
1990	20 Aug	19 Sep	18 Oct	17 Nov	17 Dec	16 Jan 1991
1991	10 Aug	08 Sep	08 Oct	06 Nov	06 Dec	05 Jan 1992
1992	30 Jul	28 Aug	26 Sep	26 Oct	24 Nov	24 Dec
1993	18 Aug	16 Sep	15 Oct	14 Nov	13 Dec	12 Jan 1994
1994	07 Aug	06 Sep	05 Oct	03 Nov	03 Dec	01 Jan 1995
1995	27 Jul	26 Aug	24 Oct	22 Nov	22 Dec	20 Jan 1996
1996	14 Aug	13 Sep	12 Oct	11 Nov	11 Dec	09 Jan 1997
1997	03 Aug	02 Sep	02 Oct	31 Oct	30 Nov	30 Dec
1998	22 Aug	21 Sep	20 Oct	19 Nov	19 Dec	17 Jan 1999
1999	11 Aug	10 Sep	09 Oct	08 Nov	08 Dec	07 Jan 2000
2000	31 Jul	29 Aug	28 Sep	27 Oct	26 Nov	26 Dec
2001	19 Aug	17 Sep	17 Oct	15 Nov	15 Dec	13 Jan 2002
2002	09 Aug	07 Sep	06 Oct	05 Nov	04 Dec	03 Jan 2003
2003	29 Jul	28 Aug	26 Sep	25 Oct	24 Nov	23 Dec
2004	16 Aug	14 Sep	14 Oct	12 Nov	12 Dec	10 Jan 2005
2005	05 Aug	04 Sep	03 Oct	02 Nov	01 Dec	31 Dec

pushed over but you can be swayed. (*Famous examples:* Burt Bacharach, Annette Bening, Richard Benjamin, Candice Bergen, Helena Bonham Carter, Cher, Johnny Depp, Michael J. Fox, Steffi Graf, Anne Heche, Lenny Kravitz, Priscilla Beaulieu Presley, Prince, Nicole Brown Simpson.)

Fifth lunar month. You love to travel and conquer the world. You're never deliberately unfaithful, but if you're not busy enough, happy at home, or feeling truly fulfilled, you might find yourself drawn toward temptation, if only for a moment. If you do, you might find it difficult to locate the compassion within your heart to forgive yourself. You actually hold very high personal values, rarely tolerating less than the best in life and love. There's nothing wrong with high standards. There is no surer method for getting the best out of life than to resist opportunities to settle for less. (*Famous examples:* Isabelle Adjani, Courteney Cox Arquette, Kevin Bacon, Jerry Hall, Elizabeth Hurley, Angelica Jolie, Pamela Anderson Lee, Juliette Lewis, Sir Paul McCartney, Tracy Pollan, Natalie Portman, Brooke Shields, O. J. Simpson, Donald Trump, Princess Diana Spencer Windsor.)

To the Chinese, the fifteenth day of the seventh lunar month kicks off the Da Jui (Hungry Ghost festival). Like Halloween and the Día de los Muertos (Day of the Dead, in Mexico), Da Jui is the time to pacify the spirits of the unsettled dead. Unlike the more serious spring festival, Ching Ming, in which families honor venerable ancestors at their graves, the point of Da Jui is to coax wandering ghosts away from you and your loved ones, luring them with lit paper lanterns floated on a pond or river or leaving sacrifices of fruit and incense far away from the house. The two weeks that follow aren't considered to be a good time for marriage unless you want a ghost to attend or, worse, carry the bride or groom off to the afterworld.

Sixth lunar month. You possess remarkable integrity and a very warm heart. You're a dyed-in-the wool homebody, caring for home and family above all else. You may not willingly face the truth of a situation, however, preferring self-denial to realistic news. Rejection of the truth and of reality is a highly efficient, very unhealthy way to cope with life. You can't solve a problem until you admit it exists. Every family, no matter how white their picket fence and how manicured their hedge, has a skeleton in the closet. You don't have to drag yours out, just accept that they're part of human life. (*Famous examples:* Antonio Banderas, Halle Berry, James Brolin, George W. Bush, Tom Cruise, Rachel Miner Culkin, Ray Davies, David Duchovny, Harrison Ford, Tom Green, Anjelica Huston, Mick Jagger, Nicole Kidman, Jennifer Lopez, Courtney Love, Iman Abdul Majid, Sean Penn, Richie Sambora, Arnold Schwarzenegger, Ringo Starr, Billy Bob Thornton, Prince William Windsor.)

Seventh lunar month. You're extremely loyal, generous, and warm when it suits you. Otherwise, you're touchy and distant. This rift in your personality can make you appear to be self-serving. It may gain you many things in life, but it'll cost you valuable friendships. You have high expectations of yourself and your mate, which sometimes makes for difficult daily coexistence. While it's true that determination and drive are admirable qualities, so are warmth, humor, and compassion. Real success comes from a balance of all of them. (*Famous examples:* Ben Affleck, David Arquette, Barbara Bach, Bill Clinton, Macaulay Culkin, Eddie Fisher, Tipper Gore, Elliot Gould, Hugh Grant, Melanie Griffith, Salma Hayek, Peter Horton, Madonna, Rose McGowan, Edward Norton, Kyra Sedgwick, Jada Pinkett Smith.)

Eighth lunar month. You are excessively fastidious and very domestic. Your routine may be too tedious for most potential mates to handle. However, this doesn't mean you should try to change. Be yourself and you'll be loved for who you are. Put up a front and you'll never know if it's you that's loved or the person you pretend to be. Also, your ability to do more than one task at a time will be appreciated by anyone worth knowing who gets to know you. (*Famous examples:* Brigitte Bardot, Angie Dickinson, Michael Douglas, Britt Ekland, Chrissie Hynde, Amy Irving, Heather Locklear, Linda Eastman McCartney, Gwyneth Paltrow, Will Smith, Catherine Zeta-Jones.)

Ninth lunar month. You're a considerate and amiable person. However, you can be extremely indecisive and may do anything to maintain a peaceful existence. You'll bend over backward to please your mate, your family, your friends, and everyone at work all at the same time. It's a little unrealistic of you. When you ask yourself why you do it, the answer might be that it's because what you really want in life is for those around you to be happy. The truth is you work so hard to make everyone else happy because it's a lot easier than figuring out exactly what you could do for your own happiness. What do you really want? Take some time. Be selfish. Figure out what you want out of life before life passes you by. (*Famous examples:* Eric Benét, Hillary Rodham Clinton, Catherine Deneuve, Leonardo DiCaprio, Carrie Fisher, Bill Gates, Simon LeBon, Yasmin Parvaneh LeBon, Tommy Lee, John Lennon, Marla Maples, Mike Nichols, Kelly Preston, Tim Robbins, Julia Roberts, Winona Ryder, Susan Sarandon, Maria Shriver, Ted Turner.)

Tenth lunar month. You're a sensuous person who's hell-bent for creature comforts. You make your mate's life unbearable until you get them. But in return for the massive kitchen, a spacious bathroom, and a master bedroom suite, you'll follow your mate to the ends of the earth and back again, and you'll defend that person with every ounce of your strength. You must warn this special someone, however, that your jealous side should never be taken lightly. Because you offer extra commitment beyond what's expected, it's not unreasonable for you to demand extra comforts and commitment in return. However, it'll take a special sort of person to live up to this, so don't settle for less. (*Famous examples:* Lisa Bonet, Kate Capshaw, Sean "Puffy" Combs, Bo Derek, Linda Evans, Calista Flockhart, Daryl Hannah, Ethan Hawke, Goldie Hawn, Don Johnson, John F. Kennedy Jr., Louis Malle, Demi Moore, Meg Ryan, Prince Charles Windsor.)

Eleventh lunar month. Nothing keeps you down long enough that you're reluctant to rise again and start from ground zero. Even when you've had the darkest day, you're always able to turn on your love light for your mate. Think of this as the phoenix month. The phoenix, which in many myths rises from the ashes, bringing only happiness and doing no harm, is said in Chinese legends to have emerged directly from the Sun. The phoenix is also a symbol of happiness and success, especially in marriage. (*Famous examples:* Christina Aguilera, Woody Allen, Kim Basinger, Kenneth Branagh, Benjamin Bratt, Jane Fonda, Marilyn Manson, Vanessa Paradis, Brad Pitt, Diane Sawyer, Britney Spears, Steven Spielberg, Ben Stiller.)

Twelfth lunar moon. Your mate needs loads of patience to coexist with you. Even so, you always manage to do what you promised, give what you guaranteed, and be as supportive as your mate needs you to be. Steady as a rock and steadfast as cement, you're also deeply romantic, remembering every sentimental occasion. But you're the last person to bring excitement or spontaneity into someone's life. Some lives are carefree and adventurous, without a single thought about tomorrow. Yours is an exceedingly structured existence, and like a tree that doesn't bend in the wind, it's potentially more breakable. The right person will appreciate your qualities and shortcomings alike, as these are all positive facets to that person. (*Famous examples:* Jennifer Aniston, David Bowie, Nicolas Cage, Ellen DeGeneres, Mia Farrow, Bridget Fonda, Larry Fortensky, Raisa Gorbachev, Diane Keaton, Carolyn Bessette Kennedy, the Reverend Dr. Martin Luther King Jr., Nastassja Kinski, Kate Moss, Elvis Presley, Michael Stipe, Justin Timberlake, Vanity, Princess Margaret Windsor, Oprah Winfrey.)

After careful consideration of the lunar month signs, the astrologer might say that musician Kurt Cobain was an enigmatic character even to himself. He protected his reputation at all costs. Romance and life were never dull around him: intelligent, well read, sentimental, tender, and self-sacrificing on many levels, he stimulated every waking moment for his mate. His wife, Courtney Love, possesses remarkable integrity and a very warm heart. She's a dyed-in-the-wool homebody, caring for home and family above all else. She may not willingly face the truth of a situation, however, preferring self-denial to realistic news. It's this one fact that kept Cobain and Love together until his death. She never faced the truth. Their only attractions were Cobain's lunar month charisma and Love's dynamic birth year personality. But that's not enough to establish a sound union. Based on a reading of their ruling *xing*, their *ming shu* compatibility, and their lunar birth months, Chinese astrologers would have said their relationship was never meant to last.

Choosing the Most Auspicious Day

Once the bride's family names the marriage month, the groom's family consults their astrologer to select the most fortunate day within that month for the wedding ceremony. There's only one time that's traditionally ruled out of the selection process, based on ancient superstitions: the two-week period that begins on the fifteenth day of the seventh lunar month (mid-to-late August). It's called Da Jui (Hungry Ghost festival) and is believed to be an unlucky fortnight, when the gates of hell open and lost spirits wander the earth. Otherwise, the basic ingredient used by the astrologer to set this critical appointment is found in any Chinese almanac.

The Moon's orbit around the Earth is seen as a pathway marked by twenty-eight fixed stars that it passes along over the course of a Chinese lunar month. Each star is called a *sieu* (lunar mansion). Documented in an almanac, the daily *sieu* are used by astrologers and laypeople in the same way daily horoscopes are read by millions of people in the Western hemisphere. The major difference is that the predictions apply to everyone (not just a particular zodiac sign) and relate mainly to the outcome of projects started or ended, namely marriages, funerals, contracts, plantings, and harvests.

So let's say you've decided on your big day. To find out if this is a good day for a wedding, all you have to do is find the day and its associated *sieu* in the Chinese almanac. Then look at the wedding prediction for that *sieu*. Unfortunately, the daily *sieu* (and the entire Chinese almanac) is published only in Chinese. But we've re-created some of this data here for your reference. First, enter your potential date onto Worksheet 4. Then look at Table 4, which contains the daily *sieu* for the years 2002 through 2005. Simply locate your intended date in the first column and note the *sieu* in the year column, entering it onto the worksheet space provided. Then find the particular *sieu* in the text that follows. This will allow you to read about the auspicious or inauspicious nature of your chosen wedding day. If you want to check a wedding date that occurred between 1950 and 2000, go to http://www.world-astrology.com, where we've listed further wedding data.

WORKSHEET 4. WEDDING DATE

	Example:	Date Choice A:	Date Choice B:
Wedding date	18 Jun 2001		
Sieu	19		

TABLE 4. DAILY *SIEU* FOR THE CHINESE YEARS 2001–2005

Day	2001 Sieu	2002 Sieu	2003 Sieu	2004 Sieu	2005 Sieu
01 Jan	19	20	21	22	24
02 Jan	20	21	22	23	25
03 Jan	21	22	23	24	26
04 Jan	22	23	24	25	27
05 Jan	23	24	25	26	28
06 Jan	24	25	26	27	1
07 Jan	25	26	27	28	2
08 Jan	26	27	28	1	3
09 Jan	27	28	1	2	4
10 Jan	28	1	2	3	5
11 Jan	1	2	3	4	6
12 Jan	2	3	4	5	7
13 Jan	3	4	5	6	8
14 Jan	4	5	6	7	9
15 Jan	5	6	7	8	10
16 Jan	6	7	8	9	11
17 Jan	7	8	9	10	12
18 Jan	8	9	10	11	13
19 Jan	9	10	11	12	14
20 Jan	10	11	12	13	15
21 Jan	11	12	13	14	16
22 Jan	12	13	14	15	17
23 Jan	13	14	15	16	18
24 Jan	14	15	16	17	19
25 Jan	15	16	17	18	20
26 Jan	16	17	18	19	21
27 Jan	17	18	19	20	22
28 Jan	18	19	20	21	23
29 Jan	19	20	21	22	24

Day	2001 Sieu	2002 Sieu	2003 Sieu	2004 Sieu	2005 Sieu
30 Jan	20	21	22	23	25
31 Jan	21	22	23	24	26
01 Feb	22	23	24	25	27
02 Feb	23	24	25	26	28
03 Feb	24	25	26	27	1
04 Feb	25	26	27	28	2
05 Feb	26	27	28	1	3
06 Feb	27	28	1	2	4
07 Feb	28	1	2	3	5
08 Feb	1	2	3	4	6
09 Feb	2	3	4	5	7
10 Feb	3	4	5	6	8
11 Feb	4	5	6	7	9
12 Feb	5	6	7	8	10
13 Feb	6	7	8	9	11
14 Feb	7	8	9	10	12
15 Feb	8	9	10	11	13
16 Feb	9	10	11	12	14
17 Feb	10	11	12	13	15
18 Feb	11	12	13	14	16
19 Feb	12	13	14	15	17
20 Feb	13	14	15	16	18
21 Feb	14	15	16	17	19
22 Feb	15	16	17	18	20
23 Feb	16	17	18	19	21
24 Feb	17	18	19	20	22
25 Feb	18	19	20	21	23
26 Feb	19	20	21	22	24
27 Feb	20	21	22	23	25
28 Feb	21	22	23	24	26

Day	2001 Sieu	2002 Sieu	2003 Sieu	2004 Sieu	2005 Sieu
29 Feb	—	—	—	25	—
01 Mar	22	23	24	26	27
02 Mar	23	24	25	27	28
03 Mar	24	25	26	28	1
04 Mar	25	26	27	1	2
05 Mar	26	27	28	2	3
06 Mar	27	28	1	3	4
07 Mar	28	1	2	4	5
08 Mar	1	2	3	5	6
09 Mar	2	3	4	6	7
10 Mar	3	4	5	7	8
11 Mar	4	5	6	8	9
12 Mar	5	6	7	9	10
13 Mar	6	7	8	10	11
14 Mar	7	8	9	11	12
15 Mar	8	9	10	12	13
16 Mar	9	10	11	13	14
17 Mar	10	11	12	14	15
18 Mar	11	12	13	15	16
19 Mar	12	13	14	16	17
20 Mar	13	14	15	17	18
21 Mar	14	15	16	18	19
22 Mar	15	16	17	19	20
23 Mar	16	17	18	20	21
24 Mar	17	18	19	21	22
25 Mar	18	19	20	22	23
26 Mar	19	20	21	23	24
27 Mar	20	21	22	24	25
28 Mar	21	22	23	25	26
29 Mar	22	23	24	26	27

Day	2001 Sieu	2002 Sieu	2003 Sieu	2004 Sieu	2005 Sieu
30 Mar	23	24	25	27	28
31 Mar	24	25	26	28	1
01 Apr	25	26	27	1	2
02 Apr	26	27	28	2	3
03 Apr	27	28	1	3	4
04 Apr	28	1	2	4	5
05 Apr	1	2	3	5	6
06 Apr	2	3	4	6	7
07 Apr	3	4	5	7	8
08 Apr	4	5	6	8	9
09 Apr	5	6	7	9	10
10 Apr	6	7	8	10	11
11 Apr	7	8	9	11	12
12 Apr	8	9	10	12	13
13 Apr	9	10	11	13	14
14 Apr	10	11	12	14	15
15 Apr	11	12	13	15	16
16 Apr	12	13	14	16	17
17 Apr	13	14	15	17	18
18 Apr	14	15	16	18	19
19 Apr	15	16	17	19	20
20 Apr	16	17	18	20	21
21 Apr	17	18	19	21	22
22 Apr	18	19	20	22	23
23 Apr	19	20	21	23	24
24 Apr	20	21	22	24	25
25 Apr	21	22	23	25	26
26 Apr	22	23	24	26	27
27 Apr	23	24	25	27	28
28 Apr	24	25	26	28	1

Day	2001 Sieu	2002 Sieu	2003 Sieu	2004 Sieu	2005 Sieu
29 Apr	25	26	27	1	2
30 Apr	26	27	28	2	3
01 May	27	28	1	3	4
02 May	28	1	2	4	5
03 May	1	2	3	5	6
04 May	2	3	4	6	7
05 May	3	4	5	7	8
06 May	4	5	6	8	9
07 May	5	6	7	9	10
08 May	6	7	8	10	11
09 May	7	8	9	11	12
10 May	8	9	10	12	13
11 May	9	10	11	13	14
12 May	10	11	12	14	15
13 May	11	12	13	15	16
14 May	12	13	14	16	17
15 May	13	14	15	17	18
16 May	14	15	16	18	19
17 May	15	16	17	19	20
18 May	16	17	18	20	21
19 May	17	18	19	21	22
20 May	18	19	20	22	23
21 May	19	20	21	23	24
22 May	20	21	22	24	25
23 May	21	22	23	25	26
24 May	22	23	24	26	27
25 May	23	24	25	27	28
26 May	24	25	26	28	1
27 May	25	26	27	1	2
28 May	26	27	28	2	3

Day	2001 Sieu	2002 Sieu	2003 Sieu	2004 Sieu	2005 Sieu
29 May	27	28	1	3	4
30 May	28	1	2	4	5
31 May	1	2	3	5	6
01 Jun	2	3	4	6	7
02 Jun	3	4	5	7	8
03 Jun	4	5	6	8	9
04 Jun	5	6	7	9	10
05 Jun	6	7	8	10	11
06 Jun	7	8	9	11	12
07 Jun	8	9	10	12	13
08 Jun	9	10	11	13	14
09 Jun	10	11	12	14	15
10 Jun	11	12	13	15	16
11 Jun	12	13	14	16	17
12 Jun	13	14	15	17	18
13 Jun	14	15	16	18	19
14 Jun	15	16	17	19	20
15 Jun	16	17	18	20	21
16 Jun	17	18	19	21	22
17 Jun	18	19	20	22	23
18 Jun	19	20	21	23	24
19 Jun	20	21	22	24	25
20 Jun	21	22	23	25	26
21 Jun	22	23	24	26	27
22 Jun	23	24	25	27	28
23 Jun	24	25	26	28	1
24 Jun	25	26	27	1	2
25 Jun	26	27	28	2	3
26 Jun	27	28	1	3	4
27 Jun	28	1	2	4	5

Day	2001 Sieu	2002 Sieu	2003 Sieu	2004 Sieu	2005 Sieu
28 Jun	1	2	3	5	6
29 Jun	2	3	4	6	7
30 Jun	3	4	5	7	8
01 Jul	4	5	6	8	9
02 Jul	5	6	7	9	10
03 Jul	6	7	8	10	11
04 Jul	7	8	9	11	12
05 Jul	8	9	10	12	13
06 Jul	9	10	11	13	14
07 Jul	10	11	12	14	15
08 Jul	11	12	13	15	16
09 Jul	12	13	14	16	17
10 Jul	13	14	15	17	18
11 Jul	14	15	16	18	19
12 Jul	15	16	17	19	20
13 Jul	16	17	18	20	21
14 Jul	17	18	19	21	22
15 Jul	18	19	20	22	23
16 Jul	19	20	21	23	24
17 Jul	20	21	22	24	25
18 Jul	21	22	23	25	26
19 Jul	22	23	24	26	27
20 Jul	23	24	25	27	28
21 Jul	24	25	26	28	1
22 Jul	25	26	27	1	2
23 Jul	26	27	28	2	3
24 Jul	27	28	1	3	4
25 Jul	28	1	2	4	5
26 Jul	1	2	3	5	6
27 Jul	2	3	4	6	7

Day	2001 Sieu	2002 Sieu	2003 Sieu	2004 Sieu	2005 Sieu
28 Jul	3	4	5	7	8
29 Jul	4	5	6	8	9
30 Jul	5	6	7	9	10
31 Jul	6	7	8	10	11
01 Aug	7	8	9	11	12
02 Aug	8	9	10	12	13
03 Aug	9	10	11	13	14
04 Aug	10	11	12	14	15
05 Aug	11	12	13	15	16
06 Aug	12	13	14	16	17
07 Aug	13	14	15	17	18
08 Aug	14	15	16	18	19
09 Aug	15	16	17	19	20
10 Aug	16	17	18	20	21
11 Aug	17	18	19	21	22
12 Aug	18	19	20	22	23
13 Aug	19	20	21	23	24
14 Aug	20	21	22	24	25
15 Aug	21	22	23	25	26
16 Aug	22	23	24	26	27
17 Aug	23	24	25	27	28
18 Aug	24	25	26	28	1
19 Aug	25	26	27	1	2
20 Aug	26	27	28	2	3
21 Aug	27	28	1	3	4
22 Aug	28	1	2	4	5
23 Aug	1	2	3	5	6
24 Aug	2	3	4	6	7
25 Aug	3	4	5	7	8
26 Aug	4	5	6	8	9

Day	2001 Sieu	2002 Sieu	2003 Sieu	2004 Sieu	2005 Sieu
27 Aug	5	6	7	9	10
28 Aug	6	7	8	10	11
29 Aug	7	8	9	11	12
30 Aug	8	9	10	12	13
31 Aug	9	10	11	13	14
01 Sep	10	11	12	14	15
02 Sep	11	12	13	15	16
03 Sep	12	13	14	16	17
04 Sep	13	14	15	17	18
05 Sep	14	15	16	18	19
06 Sep	15	16	17	19	20
07 Sep	16	17	18	20	21
08 Sep	17	18	19	21	22
09 Sep	18	19	20	22	23
10 Sep	19	20	21	23	24
11 Sep	20	21	22	24	25
12 Sep	21	22	23	25	26
13 Sep	22	23	24	26	27
14 Sep	23	24	25	27	28
15 Sep	24	25	26	28	1
16 Sep	25	26	27	1	2
17 Sep	26	27	28	2	3
18 Sep	27	28	1	3	4
19 Sep	28	1	2	4	5
20 Sep	1	2	3	5	6
21 Sep	2	3	4	6	7
22 Sep	3	4	5	7	8
23 Sep	4	5	6	8	9
24 Sep	5	6	7	9	10
25 Sep	6	7	8	10	11

Day	2001 Sieu	2002 Sieu	2003 Sieu	2004 Sieu	2005 Sieu
26 Sep	7	8	9	11	12
27 Sep	8	9	10	12	13
28 Sep	9	10	11	13	14
29 Sep	10	11	12	14	15
30 Sep	11	12	13	15	16
01 Oct	12	13	14	16	17
02 Oct	13	14	15	17	18
03 Oct	14	15	16	18	19
04 Oct	15	16	17	19	20
05 Oct	16	17	18	20	21
06 Oct	17	18	19	21	22
07 Oct	18	19	20	22	23
08 Oct	19	20	21	23	24
09 Oct	20	21	22	24	25
10 Oct	21	22	23	25	26
11 Oct	22	23	24	26	27
12 Oct	23	24	25	27	28
13 Oct	24	25	26	28	1
14 Oct	25	26	27	1	2
15 Oct	26	27	28	2	3
16 Oct	27	28	1	3	4
17 Oct	28	1	2	4	5
18 Oct	1	2	3	5	6
19 Oct	2	3	4	6	7
20 Oct	3	4	5	7	8
21 Oct	4	5	6	8	9
22 Oct	5	6	7	9	10
23 Oct	6	7	8	10	11
24 Oct	7	8	9	11	12
25 Oct	8	9	10	12	13

Day	2001 Sieu	2002 Sieu	2003 Sieu	2004 Sieu	2005 Sieu
26 Oct	9	10	11	13	14
27 Oct	10	11	12	14	15
28 Oct	11	12	13	15	16
29 Oct	12	13	14	16	17
30 Oct	13	14	15	17	18
31 Oct	14	15	16	18	19
01 Nov	15	16	17	19	20
02 Nov	16	17	18	20	21
03 Nov	17	18	19	21	22
04 Nov	18	19	20	22	23
05 Nov	19	20	21	23	24
06 Nov	20	21	22	24	25
07 Nov	21	22	23	25	26
08 Nov	22	23	24	26	27
09 Nov	23	24	25	27	28
10 Nov	24	25	26	28	1
11 Nov	25	26	27	1	2
12 Nov	26	27	28	2	3
13 Nov	27	28	1	3	4
14 Nov	28	1	2	4	5
15 Nov	1	2	3	5	6
16 Nov	2	3	4	6	7
17 Nov	3	4	5	7	8
18 Nov	4	5	6	8	9
19 Nov	5	6	7	9	10
20 Nov	6	7	8	10	11
21 Nov	7	8	9	11	12
22 Nov	8	9	10	12	13
23 Nov	9	10	11	13	14
24 Nov	10	11	12	14	15

Day	2001 Sieu	2002 Sieu	2003 Sieu	2004 Sieu	2005 Sieu
25 Nov	11	12	13	15	16
26 Nov	12	13	14	16	17
27 Nov	13	14	15	17	18
28 Nov	14	15	16	18	19
29 Nov	15	16	17	19	20
30 Nov	16	17	18	20	21
01 Dec	17	18	19	21	22
02 Dec	18	19	20	22	23
03 Dec	19	20	21	23	24
04 Dec	20	21	22	24	25
05 Dec	21	22	23	25	26
06 Dec	22	23	24	26	27
07 Dec	23	24	25	27	28
08 Dec	24	25	26	28	1
09 Dec	25	26	27	1	2
10 Dec	26	27	28	2	3
11 Dec	27	28	1	3	4
12 Dec	28	1	2	4	5
13 Dec	1	2	3	5	6
14 Dec	2	3	4	6	7
15 Dec	3	4	5	7	8
16 Dec	4	5	6	8	9
17 Dec	5	6	7	9	10
18 Dec	6	7	8	10	11
19 Dec	7	8	9	11	12
20 Dec	8	9	10	12	13
21 Dec	9	10	11	13	14
22 Dec	10	11	12	14	15
23 Dec	11	12	13	15	16
24 Dec	12	13	14	16	17

Day	2001 Sieu	2002 Sieu	2003 Sieu	2004 Sieu	2005 Sieu
25 Dec	13	14	15	17	18
26 Dec	14	15	16	18	19
27 Dec	15	16	17	19	20
28 Dec	16	17	18	20	21
29 Dec	17	18	19	21	22
30 Dec	18	19	20	22	23
31 Dec	19	20	21	23	24

This data is taken from *The Complete Astrological Handbook for the Twenty-first Century* (New York: Schocken Books, 1999).

Sieu 1 (sieu chio). A wedding on this day results in promotion and honors. It's ideal if one of you aspires to a political career.

Sieu 2 (sieu kang). The marriage ceremony causes an untimely demise for some family member, the groom, or a wedding guest, "leaving widows in the house."

Sieu 3 (sieu di). A wedding ceremony (or the signing of engagement documents) attracts evil people to both households. Your children will be poor and unable to express themselves.

Sieu 4 (sieu fang). Happiness, longevity, and riches will come to a marriage that takes place on this day.

Sieu 5 (sieu xin). The union is viewed as disastrous by others and assures three years of calamities for both households. This day causes your children to be sickly.

Sieu 6 (sieu wei). A wedding on this day leads to honor, distinction, and dignity for both families, and may also produce numerous children.

Sieu 7 (sieu chi). A wedding on this day is beneficial for both house-holds.

Sieu 8 (sieu dou). The union is guaranteed many overlapping hap-pinesses.

Sieu 9 (sieu niu). The marriage becomes a sea of troubles, causes a loss of interest in the union itself, and causes livestock to suffer.

Sieu 10 (sieu nü). A wedding on this day causes luck to disappear, obliging the couple to move to another country. It can also create sud-den removals for both households.

Sieu 11 (sieu xu). The marriage will be plagued with chaos and troubles as well as delinquent children. It's also said that "a wind of debauch-ery will blow through the family from a lack of rites."

Sieu 12 (sieu wei). Great losses occur to both families if a wedding takes place on this day.

Sieu 13 (sieu shi). Cares go away forever if a wedding occurs on a day that falls under this *sieu.*

Sieu 14 (sieu pi). Peace and joy as well as talented children come to those who marry on this day.

Sieu 15 (sieu kui). A mysterious and unfortunate end occurs. This can indicate a death or divorce (the death of a marriage) and may affect either the couple or a family member from either household.

Sieu 16 (sieu lou). A wedding on this day produces fruitful results, including children who'll become rich.

Sieu 17 (sieu wei). The marriage ushers in growth and lush harmony as well as children who are destined to encounter heads of state.

Sieu* 18 *(sieu mao). Those who marry under this *sieu* will soon separate. The marriage might also bring misery to both families.

Sieu* 19 *(sieu pi). Double longevity comes to this union because both you and your children will live long lives.

Sieu* 20 *(sieu zui). A wedding on this day depletes reserves and causes calamities in both households. All guests and members of the wedding party must be extremely careful in their conduct. An argument or lapse of basic etiquette could spark much larger problems.

Sieu* 21 *(sieu shen). A marriage ceremony (or the creation of engagement documents) on this day shatters both families' domestic order and leads to the betrothed couple's separation.

Sieu* 22 *(sieu jing). The union brings prosperity to both households as well as numerous heirs.

Sieu* 23 *(sieu gui). This marriage "sees a woman lonely in the nuptial chamber." It's also said that "Women who marry on a ghosts' day will be widows longer than wives."

Sieu* 24 *(sieu liu). The wedding ceremony is a prelude to many miseries for both households.

Sieu* 25 *(sieu xing). The marriage causes prosperity for you and your families. You will be noticed by those in authority and will gain advancement. It's also cautioned that "The woman who marries on this day falls prey to a ravisher."

Sieu* 26 *(sieu zhang). The wedding is the cause of ceaseless happiness and joy in your personal relationship.

Sieu* 27 *(sieu yi). The marriage doesn't bring prosperity and portends that you'll suffer from chronic illness.

Sieu 28 (sieu zhen). The union receives the blessing of those in authority. The couple "will find their own children developing rare talents."

Let's use Courtney Love's 1964 birth year to illustrate how Table 4 will help determine an optimal date for a 2002 wedding. We already figured out that since she was born in a Dragon year, the wedding must take place during the fourth lunar month, which begins on 12 May 2002 and ends on 10 June 2002 (Table 3). The best *sieu* for matrimony, as we have just seen, are 1, 4, 6, 7, 8, 13, 14, 16, 17, 19, 22, 25, 26, 28. Therefore, May 14, 15, 17, 18, 20, 23, 26, 27, 29, 30, as well as June 2, 4, 5, 6, are the days in the fourth lunar month that would be selected as optimal dates, based on the data in Table 4. For example, if 20 May 2002 was the choice, *sieu* 19 suggests that double longevity comes to this union because both the couple and their children will live long lives.

Within the Chinese community, however, the final choice depends on the bride's, groom's, and parents' compatibility with a particular date. If the ruling *xing* (planet) of the day's characters exerts a positive influence on the ruling *xing* of each person's birth year characters, then it's an optimal day to conduct such a life-altering occasion. Protocol dictates that a professional astrologer chooses the date: in China, it's considered bad form to select it yourself.

Believe it or not, the astrologer's job isn't over when the match is approved, the engagement is confirmed, and the wedding date is selected. In fact, this is when the astrologer's largest task begins. He or she must then compare the ruling *xing* of the birth year for each of the bride's female attendants, every member of the wedding party, and every potential wedding guest to the ruling *xing* of the bridal couple's birth years, especially the groom's. People are tactfully uninvited if they don't pass this critical test, because it's believed that one counterproductive influence could change the tide of destiny. This practice also exists for funerals and other important family gatherings.

Putting It All Together:
A Traditional Chinese Wedding

The ceremony that takes place after this elaborate process is truly grand. Although regional variations do exist and there's always the matter of economics to consider, the traditional nuptial rites we're about to describe are still performed in many Chinese communities. Even modern families (whose children often choose a Christian church wedding) will include portions of these time-honored observances in their plans. As you'll see, some elements can be easily incorporated into your own nuptials, while others might be more challenging to arrange.

The most important people to undergo the astrological wedding process described earlier are the man and woman held responsible for decorating the bridal chamber and the woman designated to comb the bride's hair on her wedding eve. Their tasks include positioning the newlyweds' bed in the bridal chamber, making the bed with linens provided by the bride's family, and placing bowls of pomegranates, jujube dates, chestnuts, pears, peaches, and pumpkin seeds on it. (In some regions, children are invited to sit on the bed and eat the fruits and seeds before the bed is made.)

In the meantime, the bride retreats to a separate part of her parents' house with her closest friends and ceases her normal household routines. It's not uncommon for her to sing laments about her impending separation from her home, cursing the *mei* and even her parents and future in-laws, during this time.

It's customary for the family and guests to give the bride *hong bao* during the wedding feast. Placed in a bright red paper envelope imprinted with gold characters, *hong bao* is both a blessing and a curse. The couple may enjoy the extra funds as they establish their home together. But if they're ever invited to the nuptials of a former wedding guest or family member, they're required by etiquette to reciprocate with a *hong bao* of an equal or greater amount. Smart couples actually set aside all of the *hong bao* in a special account reserved for attending weddings.

A few days before the ceremony, the bride's dowry arrives at the groom's house. Jewelry, kitchen utensils, clothes, additional bed linens, and good luck items such as peonies, artemesia, water lilies, sunflowers, chestnuts, peaches, pears, and litchis are sent along with money, appliances, and anything else the bride's family thinks the newlyweds might need to start their new life.

The night before the ceremony, the bride bathes in water infused with pomelo (a type of grapefruit) to rinse away any evil influences she might possess, changes into fresh undergarments, lights incense and candles decorated with dragons and phoenixes, and sits next to a window where she can watch the Moon. Her hair is combed four times. The first combing signifies the start and finish of life; the second combing symbolizes harmony from present to old age; the third combing wishes for numerous sons; and the fourth combing wishes for wealth and a long marriage. If the bride has been married before, this particular ceremony is frequently skipped since it also represents a rite of passage from girlhood to womanhood.

On the big day, the bride's and groom's households as well as the bridal chamber are decorated in red and gold. The bride is carried to the main hall on the back of her eldest sister-in-law or the woman who has prepared the bridal chamber. (In fact, until she enters the groom's house, her feet will not touch bare earth.) She's then dressed in an elaborately embroidered red jacket, red skirt, and red shoes while standing in the center of a flat bamboo sieve that's placed on the floor. A red silk veil or a beaded curtain suspended from a bridal phoenix crown is positioned so that it covers her face. She bows to her parents and the ancestral altar as she awaits the groom's entourage.

A similar ritual takes place at the grooms' home. There, dressed in a red gown, a red sash with a silk ball pinned to it, and red shoes, the groom kneels before his ancestral altar while his father places a cap decorated with small cypress boughs on his head. After he's bowed to his parents, the ancestral tablets, and family members, his father takes the ball from his sash and places it at the top of the bridal sedan chair. The family astrologer consults the almanac to determine which direction the sedan chair's opening must face on that day so that the bride enters it with the *xi shen* (genius of joy) overlooking her entry into a new life.

A procession of servants, musicians, and costumed "lion" or "unicorn" dancers accompanies the sedan chair, which is carried by four servants, to retrieve the bride. Firecrackers, drums, and gongs herald the entourage's passage, which is led by the groom and a young boy. When they arrive at the bride's house, her friends meet the party, refusing to surrender the bride unless they receive *hong bao* (red envelopes filled with money) from the groom's agents. In some regions, the groom dines with his in-laws on sweet longan tea, a pair of hardboiled eggs topped with sweet syrup, and cellophane noodles. He then receives a pair of chopsticks and two wine goblets wrapped in red paper as a symbol that he's taking away the family's joy.

As the bride is carried to the sedan chair she is protected with a parasol from the uncooked rice that's being thrown at her. A flat bamboo sieve, an almanac, and a metal mirror are suspended from the chair to protect the bride from evil spirits. The bride also affixes another mirror to the buttonhole of her jacket with a red silk cord, which she won't remove until she's seated on the bridal bed. Firecrackers are lit to scare off demons as she departs from her home. The sedan chair is heavily curtained so the bride doesn't see any-

A Chinese wedding banquet must contain eight specific types of dishes, not including the dessert. This is because the word *xin* (eight) sounds like *xing* (good luck). Lobster and chicken are typical appetizer ingredients because they symbolize the dragon and the phoenix as well as the male and female roles in marriage. Shark's fin soup follows, signifying wealth. Entrée items also carry symbolic references. Roast suckling pig suggests virginity, fish represents abundance, a whole Peking duck or red chicken implies the union's completeness, and a whole lobster suggests good fortune (as all red-colored foods do). Sautéed vegetables served with sea cucumber are a wish to the couple for a life without conflict. A noodle dish finishes the main course, symbolizing the marriage's longevity. Sweet red bean soup with lotus seeds or fresh peaches is a dessert that wishes a hundred years of happiness to the newlyweds. An alternate dessert dish of steamed buns filled with sweet lotus paste offers a wish for fertility.

thing inauspicious during her journey, such as a widow, a water well, or a cat. Her attendants toss beans and rice in the procession's path, symbolizing her future fertility.

Riddle:

Two people are two. When they marry they are three. What are they?

Can you answer the riddles on pages 99, 218, and 308? Then visit www.world-astrology.com.

When they arrive at the groom's house, firecrackers welcome the procession and a red carpet is laid out before the sedan chair so the bride's feet don't touch the bare earth when she exits. Once she's entered the groom's house, the groom lifts her veil or curtain so he can finally view his bride.

The actual marriage ceremony begins when the bride and groom pay their respects to the heavens, the Earth, the groom's ancestors, and the kitchen god Tsao Chün, while standing before the groom's family's ancestral altar. They then serve tea, garnished with two lotus seeds or two red dates, to the groom's parents. In Manchuria and other northern regions, the couple drink wine from the same glass and eat a piece of sugar molded into the shape of a rooster to conclude the ceremony. Then the groom's parents and family members give the newlyweds *hong bao* and wish them good luck. A wedding banquet held by the groom's family follows. The *mei* (matchmaker) instigates toasts to the couple throughout the elaborate meal.

After the banquet, the couple retires to the bridal chamber, followed by family and friends, who tease them for a while. Alone at last, the couple drink honey-laced wine from glasses tied together with a red silk thread while the *mei* toasts them with a third glass. Then they eat sweets and fruits before ending their eventful day.

♥ ♥ ♥

In China, the auspicious union of two people represents fortunate growth and continued longevity for the couple and for both of their families. It's believed that the wrong decision can have disastrous effects on the health, happiness, and fortune of a large group of people. For this reason, marriage decisions aren't taken lightly in this culture; arranged unions or, at least, formal introductions are quite desirable. But not all arranged marriages carry such a heavy burden. In the next chapter we move to neighboring India, where families approach marriage a bit differently.

CHAPTER THREE

Using Hindu Astrology to Find Love and Marriage

THE SUTRAS OF LOVE

An instant love in a new land,
And a happy wedding there,
I am now courting a new lady,
And building a new house,
In which to stay with her.

—from a Hindu folktale,
translated by Dulal Chaudhuri

One folktale from the northern Indian state of Uttar Pradesh tells the story of a king who had seven sons and a daughter named Maya. Even after she'd grown and married, Maya was her father and brothers' pride and joy. In October, soon after her marriage, it was time for the annual Krishna Chaturthi of Kartika festival—which honors Princess Savitri for restoring the life of her husband, Prince Satyavan, by pleading with Yama, the god of death. Maya, like all dutiful wives, began a ceremonial fast to ensure that her husband would be protected from an untimely death throughout the coming year.

Immediately after her morning bath, she took the fasting vow. She cupped fresh water into one hand and sprinkled a few drops to the east, then to the north, then to the west, then to the south. While she did this, she prayed to the gods Siva, Parvati, Karttikeya, Ganesha, and Candrama to bless her fast. She placed rice, black pulse

The Krishna Chaturthi of Kartika is celebrated on the day that it's believed Princess Savitri restored Prince Satyavan's life. He'd died while the couple gathered firewood in the forest. As the god of death, Yama, arrived to escort Satyavan to the next world, Savitri pleaded to remain by Satyavan's side. Yama refused to restore his life but promised to grant her a wish in exchange for her loyalty. She asked for the restoration of her father-in-law's kingdom and his sight. Yama granted her wish and continued on his way. She pleaded with him that he was robbing her of happiness. So the god promised to grant her a wish in exchange for her devotion, just not Satyavan's life. She asked for her father to be blessed with more children, and the god granted her wish and continued on his way. She climbed steep mountains in her bare feet and torn clothes to keep up. Dismayed, Yama ordered her to return home. Admiring her courage, he offered her one more wish, anything except for Satyavan's life. She asked to have children by Satyavan. Amused by her wit, he granted her wish because she hadn't asked for Satyavan's return.

(another type of grain), a comb, a mirror, powdered vermilion, and a silver bangle decorated with bright ribbons on a copper plate surrounded with fresh fruits. Then she set this festive platter aside to give to her mother-in-law after the Moon rose that night. During the fast, Maya was not supposed to eat or drink anything, not even a drop of water. As the day wore on, she became so weak and pale that her brothers grew worried.

When they felt certain she wouldn't survive the ordeal, they devised a plan to trick her into believing that the fast time was over. One brother climbed a tall tree and held a lit lantern behind a round drum top. The other brothers ran to their sister, saying, "Come, see how the Moon rises behind the tamarind tree. Give your thanks to the gods and end your fast." The young woman believed them. An hour before the Moon was due to rise, she dressed in her wedding garments and jewelry, thanked the gods for seeing her through her ordeal, and bowed down at her husband's feet. Just before the Moon emerged above the treetops, Maya placed the platter of fruits and gifts before her mother-in-law. Then she ate her dinner.

The next day, Maya's husband fell ill, growing weaker as days passed. No medication could cure him. The worried woman called on the priests, who told her that she had ended her fast before the Moon had actually risen. Like the Moon itself, they explained, her husband was waning. There was only one cure: she had to vow to fast next year during the Krishna Chaturthi until she was certain the Moon had risen. Maya did as she was told. The next year, as the Moon rose, she dressed in her wedding clothes, bowed at her dying husband's feet, and presented a decorative platter of fruits and gifts to her mother-in-law. The next morning, her husband completely recovered.

Like every fable, this tale is built around an essential truth. Awareness of reciprocity (give-and-take) and causality (cause and effect) are essential if you choose to make the commitment to share your life with another person. The bonds of marriage and love run deeper than you'd think. What one spouse does has a profound effect on the other, even if it's unintended.

The Hindus of India believe matrimony is a means to personal enlightenment. In fact, marriage is viewed as one of the four stages of existence that must be achieved during one's lifetime. In this tradition, you spend the first quarter of life getting an education, the second quarter being married, the third quarter exploring the world, and the fourth quarter renouncing all earthly things. By following this course, you can achieve the four *purusarthas* (purposes of human life): *dharma* (righteousness), *artha* (wealth), *kama* (desire), and *moksa* (liberation from the physical world). In Hindu culture marriage clearly ranks in importance with eating, sleeping, and breathing.

The ancient Hindu text *Manusmrti (Laws of Manu)* names the *brahma* rite as the best of the eight potential marriage ceremonies. A *brahma* marriage is a well-chosen union between a man and a woman in which a father freely gives away his daughter, "after decking her with costly garments and honoring her with presents of jewels," to a husband without the lure of money, the use of physical force, or imposed conditions.

Naturally, *brahma* marriages don't occur easily. There are, after all, important questions to be addressed when searching for such a match. Where was the bride born in relation to the groom's birthplace? What are their social castes, their educational and professional status, and their ages? Then there are secondary concerns: the bride's dowry, the couple's ability to bear children, and, in many cases, the potential for the families to gain business or political advantage from the union. Thankfully, there's also the question of love. If either person expresses extreme disinterest, the bride's parents cannot consider the groom's proposal. Finally, the time of the *vivaha* (wedding ceremony) must be carefully plotted.

For all of these concerns, the family astrologer is called upon to provide guidance and direction. However, the astrologer's work doesn't begin with a marriage proposal. He or she would have been hard at work when the bride and groom in question were just children, analyzing their marriage potential and the possible outcomes. This practice has existed for at least a thousand years and is still quite common today in Hindu communities. But unlike Chinese astrology, where eight elements tell the whole story to an adept practitioner, Hindu astrology has a far more complicated system of defining matrimonial prospects. A *jataka* (personality profile) must be constructed, which itself involves the calculation of at least three different astrological charts. In addition, one's *naksatra* (Moon sign) must be determined and a *vimsottari dasa* (timeline) of one's life must be configured.

The *bhavacakra* (house chart) is the primary device in the *jataka* that is used to determine one's ability to wed. (In southern India, the *rasicakra*, or sign chart, is frequently used in place of the *bhavacakra* for this purpose.) Segmented into twelve houses just like a Western birth chart, the *bhavacakra* is cast using the sidereal zodiac, which means that the Sun, Moon, and planets are situated against a visible backdrop of constantly moving constellations. This is unlike most Western birth charts, which use the tropical zodiac and place the Sun, Moon, and planets on a stationary and imaginary path called the ecliptic.

The Hindu astrologer uses the *bhavacakra* to determine the Moon's location as well as the placement of the planet Venus and the lunar node Ketu (the Moon's South Node); the zodiac sign that's associated with the seventh house (which is the marriage house); and the marriage *yoga*, which is a pattern of planetary placements that suggests whether you'll encounter an early or a late marriage; an arranged marriage or a marriage born from love; or more than one marriage.

In this chapter we'll show you how to locate and interpret some of these same elements without going through the arduous chart construction process.[1] You'll learn how to read your *bhavacakra*'s seventh house to see if you're destined to wed and the type of mate you might encounter. You'll see how the placement of the planet Venus in your chart and the zodiac sign with which it's associated determine your sex appeal and your ability to be romantic. We'll explain how the planet Mars's placement in your chart, as well as its zodiac sign association, influences your sex drive and determines what sort of external stress might thwart your physical intimacy with your mate. We'll also show you how the placement of the Moon's South Node, or Ketu, in your chart may instigate matrimonial strife. Then we'll show you how the Moon's placement in your chart determines your emotional needs. We'll also explain how Hindu astrologers follow a procedure similar to their Chinese counterparts' to find the optimal date for a wedding ceremony.

To those of you who are accustomed to Western-style interpretations, Hindu astrological explanations can sound abrupt and sometimes frighteningly certain, like the Chinese delineations you encountered in the previous chapter. It is important to remember that the Hindu tradition, like the Chinese, is based on predeterminism, insinuating that we are fated to our destinies. The following commentaries exemplify how one particular culture perceives love and marriage, and this may very well differ from your own culturally based viewpoint.

Will You Ever Marry?: The Seventh House's Zodiac Sign

The zodiac sign that governs your chart's seventh house tells the astrologer if you're destined to marry, what type of spouse you'll encounter, and the influence matrimony will have on your life. It can also give a hint as to where your future mate was born. Each zodiac sign rules specific compass directions, and the sign associated with

---

1. The general calculation and interpretation of the numerous *jataka* charts is too complex to present in this book. If you're interested in learning more about the procedures, we detail much of the process in our book *The Complete Astrological Handbook for the Twenty-first Century*.

your seventh house oversees the location of your true love's birthplace in relation to your own birth location.

This particular section requires that you already have a *bhavacakra*. If you don't have one, visit our Web site at http://www.world-astrology.com and click on to the linked site that lets you cast and print out your *bhavacakra* free of charge. Enter your (and/or your mate's) birth date onto Worksheet 5. Then consult your *bhavacakra* and look for the zodiac sign associated with your seventh house. (Fig. #1, which is Brad Pitt's *bhavacakra*, highlights the seventh house's location.) For reference, here's a list of the numbers used to represent the zodiac signs in Hindu astrology:

Zodiac sign	Hindu number
Aries	1
Taurus	2
Gemini	3
Cancer	4
Leo	5
Virgo	6
Libra	7
Scorpio	8
Sagittarius	9
Capricorn	10
Aquarius	11
Pisces	12

You'll find the number that represents the zodiac sign in the diamond that represents a particular house. For example, in Brad Pitt's *bhavacakra*, you'll see the number 2 in his seventh house, which is highlighted. According to the list above, 2 represents Taurus, making Taurus the zodiac sign that rules Pitt's seventh house. Enter the number and corresponding zodiac sign from your *bhavacakra*'s seventh house on Worksheet 5. Do the same for your mate. Then find the sign's interpretation in the text following to determine your marital prospects.

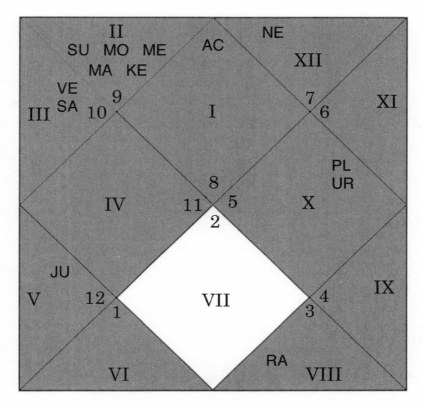

Figure 1. Brad Pitt's Seventh House in a *Bhavacakra*.

WORKSHEET 5. SEVENTH HOUSE'S HINDU ZODIAC SIGN

	Example:	Name A:	Name B:
	Brad Pitt		
Birth date	18 Dec 1963		
Seventh house's Hindu zodiac sign	2 (Taurus)		

Aries in your chart's seventh house. You're potentially attracted to open confrontation with an exciting mate who doesn't mind an occasional shouting match. You might marry a dominant person who was born east of your birthplace. There's an enormous difference between arguments and fights. When a couple argues, it's because they have a difference of opinion and each tries to convince the other— on the strength of reason—that their opinion is the correct one. There's no shame in concession; there is only shame in continuing an argument when it's clear the other person is right. A fight, on the other hand, is what happens when someone is tired, hungry, or under extreme stress. Fights and bouts of name-calling are never healthy for a relationship and should always be avoided. Eat or get some sleep if you don't want an argument to transform into a fight. Keep your confrontations constructive to build a great relationship. We're all humbled enough by life outside the home. (*Famous examples:* Michael Douglas, George Harrison, Katharine Hepburn, Diane Keaton, Courtney Love, Prince, Elizabeth Taylor, Justin Timberlake.)

Some couples are meant to do everything together. Book dealers Basant and Anita Jain are such a pair. Residents of Madhya Pradesh, the couple work together in their shop, travel together, eat together, sleep together, and wear exactly the same-colored clothes at all times. According to a 2000 Reuters news report, they've sported the same-color attire for fourteen years, turning heads wherever they go. If Anita dons a pink sari with green trim, Basant wears pink trousers and a green shirt. It's made local tailors very happy. Textile merchants have been bringing special fabrics to them from big city markets, hoping the couple will have outfits made from the selections, because they've become such good advertising.

Taurus in your chart's seventh house. You might have a stable, long-lasting, happy marriage with someone born south of your birthplace. Life's greatest challenge can sometimes be the gracious acceptance of happiness. Don't excessively question a good relationship; just enjoy it. In the words of American entrepreneur Franklin P. Jones: "Love doesn't make the world go round. Love is what makes the ride worthwhile." (*Famous examples:* Brigitte Bardot, Candice Bergen, John Derek, Bridget Fonda, Bill Gates, Brad Pitt, Elvis Presley, Princess Diana Spencer Windsor.)

Gemini in your chart's seventh house. You're inclined to marry more than once or not at all. Throughout childhood, we heard stories about couples who live "happily ever after." The truth is that when those stories were written, people lived to the ripe old age of thirty-five or forty. We now live a couple of lifetimes by comparison. Our marriages may follow a similar path. If you do take that big step, your mate might be an educator or a writer, or work in the communications, publishing, or advertising world. This person may be born west of your birthplace. (*Famous examples:* Catherine Deneuve, Michael J. Fox, Goldie Hawn, Spencer Tracy, Ted Turner, Prince William Windsor.)

Cancer in your chart's seventh house. You're inclined to maintain a close, caring relationship with a mate who was born north of your birthplace. If you're a man, you might marry someone who strongly resembles your mother or is much younger than yourself. If you're a woman, you'll most likely maintain a strong emotional connection with a dominant mate. The healthiest partnerships aren't necessarily between similar people. Qualities or character found in a spouse can complete us, whether it's maturity and experience or youthful enthusiasm. (*Famous examples:* Carrie Fisher, Carolyn Bessette Kennedy.)

Riddle:

The more you give away, the more you have. What is it?

Can you answer the riddles on pages 88, 218, and 308? Then visit www.world-astrology.com.

Leo in your chart's seventh house. Marriage to a person who's born east of your birthplace potentially satisfies your ego's needs on a positive level. The greatest mystery we face in life is ourselves. We are the great unknown. How can you judge what you're worth in this world? Look at the wonderful person who has chosen to love you. But this person doesn't simply reflect your own self-worth, which exists before, during, and after any relationship; this person also adds to it. When you truly enjoy being loved by someone it shows. (*Famous examples:* Richard Burton, Mikhail Gorbachev, Heather Locklear.)

Virgo in your chart's seventh house. You're inclined to marry more than once. You tend to ladle out constructive criticism to your mate, who may be born south of your birthplace. Sometimes you can offer your spouse a more accurate reflection than a mirror, which only scans the surface. If a situation requires a comment, make sure you address the problem and not the person. A human can do something stupid without being stupid. If this is the case, don't tell your mate he or she is foolish; don't even say he or she did something absurd. Offer a solution and ask if it might be a better alternative. Then let your beloved make the obvious choice. And remember, the marital mirror has a two-way reflection. If you're not observant, you might overlook your mate telling you subtly if you've gone too far. (*Famous examples:* Ray Davies, Bo Derek, the Reverend Dr. Martin Luther King Jr., John Lennon, Barbra Streisand.)

Libra in your chart's seventh house. You may find it difficult to settle down or to form a permanent relationship. You enjoy the concept of marriage but may equate romance and charm with emotional commitment. Infatuation—that divine sensation you get when you start falling for a new person—should not be mistaken for true love. That first sparkle always fades as new discovery is replaced with familiarity. But it doesn't always mean the relationship has soured. Think of love as a fermentation process. With time and attention the sweetness of the juice is transformed into fine wine. If you treat pets and new friends better than you treat your spouse, that wine will quickly turn to sour grapes. Your mate will quite possibly be born west of your birthplace. (*Famous examples:* Antonio Banderas, Mia Farrow, Melanie Griffith.)

Scorpio in your chart's seventh house. You tend to attract an intellectual or powerful mate who's born north of your birthplace. Why are we attracted to power? Why are we mesmerized by fire, from candlelight to fireplace? It's not the fire itself. It's our ability to be close to it, to direct it, to influence it. There's also some secrecy or mystery attached to your relationship. There's nothing wrong with privacy, provided your secrets don't harm anyone outside the relationship.

(*Famous examples:* Drew Barrymore, Humphrey Bogart, Pamela Anderson Lee, Michelle Pfeiffer, Richie Sambora, John Travolta.)

Sagittarius in your chart's seventh house. You tend to demand personal freedom within your marriage. You're attracted to a mate who lives on a grand scale and was born east of your birthplace. Sometimes when we're enticed by someone who has their own goals and ambitions, it's not because we share them, it's because we know that person is preoccupied enough with their own life to allow us to lead ours. A perfect relationship isn't necessarily one where two people are inseparable, it's simply one that satisfies the needs of both individuals, allowing them to grow. French author Antoine de Saint-Exupéry wrote, in *The Little Prince,* "Life has taught us that love does not consist in gazing at each other but in looking outward together in the same direction." (*Famous examples:* Ben Affleck, Sir Michael Caine, Cher, Julie Christie, Hillary Rodham Clinton, Al Gore, Tipper Gore, Steffi Graf, Jack Nicholson, Kurt Russell, Arnold Schwarzenegger.)

Capricorn in your chart's seventh house. If you wait until your twenty-seventh birthday, you've got a chance to attain a stable and enduring marriage with someone who's born south of your birthplace. Romance is fun. Infatuation is wonderful. Enjoy them early and you won't have regrets later about what might have been. Wedlock is work—delightful work, but work nonetheless. It comes with a lot of responsibilities. As with any endeavor, if you bring more skills to the job, you increase your chances of success. Interaction, compassion, empathy, respect, patience, and self-awareness improve with age. (*Famous examples:* Lauren Bacall, George W. Bush, Johnny Depp, Jane Fonda, Julia Roberts, Steven Spielberg, Donald Trump, Prince Charles Windsor.)

Aquarius in your chart's seventh house. You're inclined to marry more than once or not at all. If you do make that giant leap, you're likely to wed an unconventional mate born west of your birthplace and lead a nonconformist existence. Relationships have been around for as long as Homo sapiens has walked the Earth (and longer). There've been a few million books written on the subject, but not one carves out a definitive set of relationship rules. Why? Because every couple writes the rules for themselves. There are guidelines, but ultimately every pair of lovers blazes their own trail to happiness, which may or may not include 2.5 children, a dog, a cat, a minivan, and weekends at the mall. (*Famous examples:* Woody Allen, Kim Basinger, Bill Clinton, Kurt Cobain, John F. Kennedy Jr., Madonna, Brooke Shields, O. J. Simpson, Britney Spears, Oprah Winfrey, Dwight Yoakam.)

Pisces in your chart's seventh house. You're inclined to have unrealistic expectations about marriage. You may wed someone who is very artistic, or from a minority group, or addicted to drugs or alcohol. Matrimony as it's painted in movies and novels is far removed from reality. A person who's incredibly exciting at first might lack stability in the long run. Depending on who we choose, life can be a stroll in suburbia or a roller-coaster ride around the world. You know your tastes; just make sure your seat belt's fastened, and avoid people with self-destructive habits (however you might be tempted to overlook them). The person in question's birthplace is probably west of your own. (*Famous examples:* Warren Beatty, David Bowie, Eric Clapton, Harrison Ford, Debbie Reynolds, Maria Shriver.)

To give you an idea of how this information's used, we'll employ actor Brad Pitt's seventh house position (Worksheet 5) as an example. In a personal consultation, the Hindu astrologer might tell Pitt that because Taurus governs his chart's seventh house, he potentially has a stable, enduring, happy marriage with someone born south of his birthplace.

Where's the Romance?: Venus's Sidereal Placement in Your Chart

Traditionally, the planet Venus represents the bride in a man's chart and the planet Jupiter represents the groom in a woman's chart. Many modern astrologers such as Ronnie Gale Dreyer, however, use Venus as the love and romance indicator for both men and women. The planet's house placement in your chart and its association with a zodiac sign are combined by the astrologer into a synthesized interpretation, determining your sex appeal, your ability to ignite romantic flames around you, and your ability to fan the matrimonial fires.

The Indian epic *Mahabharata* tells how Arjuna won the hand of Princess Draupadi of Panchala, competing in a *svayamivara*. In a true test of skill, Arjuna and other suitors had to shoot five arrows through a revolving wheel and hit a target that lay beyond with each try. The winner took home the princess and her dowry.

You don't need a *bhavacakra* to use this section. Simply enter your (and/or your mate's) birth date onto Worksheet 6. Using Table 5, look in the first column for the period in which your birth date falls, and in the second column find the zodiac sign associated with that period. (The dates listed are the starting dates for each period: your birth date should fall on or after the appropriate date, and before the date in the row below.) Enter that sign in the space provided on the worksheet. Do the same with your mate's Venus placement. Then locate the zodiac sign in the following text and read how your tendency toward romance, your overall sexual appeal, and your ability to give love might influence your love life. Naturally, if you have a *bhavacakra,* you need only look for Venus's symbol (VE) and note the zodiac sign associated with that planet on the worksheet. (Fig. 2 highlights Venus's placement in Brad Pitt's *bhavacakra,* showing it to be in the third house and associated with the zodiac sign Capricorn, number 10). A list of zodiac signs and their numbers appears on page 96.)

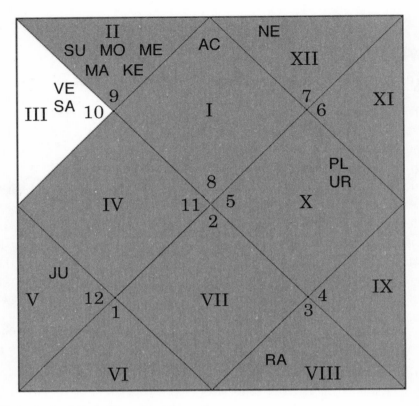

Figure 2. Brad Pitt's Venus in a *Bhavacakra*.

Worksheet 6. Venus's *Bhavacakra* Placement

	Example:	Name A:	Name B:
	Brad Pitt		
Birth date	18 Dec 1963		
Venus's *bhavacakra* placement	10 (Capricorn)		

TABLE 5. SIDEREAL PLACEMENTS FOR VENUS, 1927–1987

Starting Date	Zodiac Sign	Starting Date	Zodiac Sign
01 Jan 1927	Sagittarius (♐)	27 Feb 1929	Aries (♈)
04 Jan 1927	Capricorn (♑)	05 May 1929	Pisces (♓)
28 Jan 1927	Aquarius (♒)	20 May 1929	Aries (♈)
21 Feb 1927	Pisces (♓)	01 Jul 1929	Taurus (♉)
17 Mar 1927	Aries (♈)	30 Jul 1929	Gemini (♊)
11 Apr 1927	Taurus (♉)	25 Aug 1929	Cancer (♋)
06 May 1927	Gemini (♊)	20 Sep 1929	Leo (♌)
02 Jun 1927	Cancer (♋)	15 Oct 1929	Virgo (♍)
30 Jun 1927	Leo (♌)	08 Nov 1929	Libra (♎)
10 Aug 1927	Virgo (♍)	02 Dec 1929	Scorpio (♏)
31 Aug 1927	Leo (♌)	26 Dec 1929	Sagittarius (♐)
01 Nov 1927	Virgo (♍)	18 Jan 1930	Capricorn (♑)
02 Dec 1927	Libra (♎)	11 Feb 1930	Aquarius (♒)
29 Dec 1927	Scorpio (♏)	07 Mar 1930	Pisces (♓)
23 Jan 1928	Sagittarius (♐)	31 Mar 1930	Aries (♈)
17 Feb 1928	Capricorn (♑)	25 Apr 1930	Taurus (♉)
12 Mar 1928	Aquarius (♒)	19 May 1930	Gemini (♊)
06 Apr 1928	Pisces (♓)	13 Jun 1930	Cancer (♋)
30 Apr 1928	Aries (♈)	09 Jul 1930	Leo (♌)
25 May 1928	Taurus (♉)	04 Aug 1930	Virgo (♍)
18 Jun 1928	Gemini (♊)	31 Aug 1930	Libra (♎)
13 Jul 1928	Cancer (♋)	02 Oct 1930	Scorpio (♏)
06 Aug 1928	Leo (♌)	31 Jan 1931	Sagittarius (♐)
30 Aug 1928	Virgo (♍)	28 Feb 1931	Capricorn (♑)
24 Sep 1928	Libra (♎)	26 Mar 1931	Aquarius (♒)
18 Oct 1928	Scorpio (♏)	20 Apr 1931	Pisces (♓)
12 Nov 1928	Sagittarius (♐)	15 May 1931	Aries (♈)
06 Dec 1928	Capricorn (♑)	09 Jun 1931	Taurus (♉)
31 Dec 1928	Aquarius (♒)	04 Jul 1931	Gemini (♊)
27 Jan 1929	Pisces (♓)	28 Jul 1931	Cancer (♋)

Starting Date	Zodiac Sign	Starting Date	Zodiac Sign
22 Aug 1931	Leo (♌)	1 Jan 1934	Capricorn (♑)
15 Sep 1931	Virgo (♍)	29 Mar 1934	Aquarius (♒)
09 Oct 1931	Libra (♎)	30 Apr 1934	Pisces (♓)
02 Nov 1931	Scorpio (♏)	27 May 1934	Aries (♈)
26 Nov 1931	Sagittarius (♐)	22 Jun 1934	Taurus (♉)
20 Dec 1931	Capricorn (♑)	18 Jul 1934	Gemini (♊)
13 Jan 1932	Aquarius (♒)	12 Aug 1934	Cancer (♋)
07 Feb 1932	Pisces (♓)	05 Sep 1934	Leo (♌)
03 Mar 1932	Aries (♈)	30 Sep 1934	Virgo (♍)
30 Mar 1932	Taurus (♉)	24 Oct 1934	Libra (♎)
28 Apr 1932	Gemini (♊)	17 Nov 1934	Scorpio (♏)
01 Sep 1932	Cancer (♋)	11 Dec 1934	Sagittarius (♐)
01 Oct 1932	Leo (♌)	03 Jan 1935	Capricorn (♑)
27 Oct 1932	Virgo (♍)	27 Jan 1935	Aquarius (♒)
21 Nov 1932	Libra (♎)	20 Feb 1935	Pisces (♓)
16 Dec 1932	Scorpio (♏)	17 Mar 1935	Aries (♈)
09 Jan 1933	Sagittarius (♐)	10 Apr 1935	Taurus (♉)
02 Feb 1933	Capricorn (♑)	06 May 1935	Gemini (♊)
26 Feb 1933	Aquarius (♒)	01 Jun 1935	Cancer (♋)
22 Mar 1933	Pisces (♓)	30 Jun 1935	Leo (♌)
15 Apr 1933	Aries (♈)	2 Nov 1935	Virgo (♍)
09 May 1933	Taurus (♉)	02 Dec 1935	Libra (♎)
03 Jun 1933	Gemini (♊)	29 Dec 1935	Scorpio (♏)
27 Jun 1933	Cancer (♋)	23 Jan 1936	Sagittarius (♐)
22 Jul 1933	Leo (♌)	16 Feb 1936	Capricorn (♑)
16 Aug 1933	Virgo (♍)	12 Mar 1936	Aquarius (♒)
10 Sep 1933	Libra (♎)	05 Apr 1936	Pisces (♓)
05 Oct 1933	Scorpio (♏)	30 Apr 1936	Aries (♈)
31 Oct 1933	Sagittarius (♐)	24 May 1936	Taurus (♉)
28 Nov 1933	Capricorn (♑)	18 Jun 1936	Gemini (♊)
10 Jan 1934	Aquarius (♒)	12 Jul 1936	Cancer (♋)

Starting Date	Zodiac Sign	Starting Date	Zodiac Sign
05 Aug 1936	Leo (♌)	27 Feb 1939	Capricorn (♑)
30 Aug 1936	Virgo (♍)	25 Mar 1939	Aquarius (♒)
23 Sep 1936	Libra (♎)	20 Apr 1939	Pisces (♓)
17 Oct 1936	Scorpio (♏)	15 May 1939	Aries (♈)
11 Nov 1936	Sagittarius (♐)	09 Jun 1939	Taurus (♉)
06 Dec 1936	Capricorn (♑)	03 Jul 1939	Gemini (♊)
31 Dec 1936	Aquarius (♒)	28 Jul 1939	Cancer (♋)
27 Jan 1937	Pisces (♓)	21 Aug 1939	Leo (♌)
27 Feb 1937	Aries (♈)	14 Sep 1939	Virgo (♍)
26 Apr 1937	Pisces (♓)	09 Oct 1939	Libra (♎)
24 May 1937	Aries (♈)	02 Nov 1939	Scorpio (♏)
01 Jul 1937	Taurus (♉)	26 Nov 1939	Sagittarius (♐)
30 Jul 1937	Gemini (♊)	20 Dec 1939	Capricorn (♑)
25 Aug 1937	Cancer (♋)	13 Jan 1940	Aquarius (♒)
19 Sep 1937	Leo (♌)	06 Feb 1940	Pisces (♓)
14 Oct 1937	Virgo (♍)	03 Mar 1940	Aries (♈)
07 Nov 1937	Libra (♎)	29 Mar 1940	Taurus (♉)
01 Dec 1937	Scorpio (♏)	28 Apr 1940	Gemini (♊)
25 Dec 1937	Sagittarius (♐)	01 Sep 1940	Cancer (♋)
18 Jan 1938	Capricorn (♑)	01 Oct 1940	Leo (♌)
11 Feb 1938	Aquarius (♒)	27 Oct 1940	Virgo (♍)
07 Mar 1938	Pisces (♓)	21 Nov 1940	Libra (♎)
31 Mar 1938	Aries (♈)	15 Dec 1940	Scorpio (♏)
24 Apr 1938	Taurus (♉)	08 Jan 1941	Sagittarius (♐)
19 May 1938	Gemini (♊)	01 Feb 1941	Capricorn (♑)
13 Jun 1938	Cancer (♋)	25 Feb 1941	Aquarius (♒)
08 Jul 1938	Leo (♌)	21 Mar 1941	Pisces (♓)
03 Aug 1938	Virgo (♍)	15 Apr 1941	Aries (♈)
31 Aug 1938	Libra (♎)	09 May 1941	Taurus (♉)
03 Oct 1938	Scorpio (♏)	02 Jun 1941	Gemini (♊)
31 Jan 1939	Sagittarius (♐)	27 Jun 1941	Cancer (♋)

Starting Date	Zodiac Sign	Starting Date	Zodiac Sign
21 Jul 1941	Leo (♌)	05 Apr 1944	Pisces (♓)
15 Aug 1941	Virgo (♍)	29 Apr 1944	Aries (♈)
09 Sep 1941	Libra (♎)	24 May 1944	Taurus (♉)
05 Oct 1941	Scorpio (♏)	17 Jun 1944	Gemini (♊)
31 Oct 1941	Sagittarius (♐)	12 Jul 1944	Cancer (♋)
29 Nov 1941	Capricorn (♑)	05 Aug 1944	Leo (♌)
30 Mar 1942	Aquarius (♒)	29 Aug 1944	Virgo (♍)
30 Apr 1942	Pisces (♓)	23 Sep 1944	Libra (♎)
27 May 1942	Aries (♈)	17 Oct 1944	Scorpio (♏)
22 Jun 1942	Taurus (♉)	11 Nov 1944	Sagittarius (♐)
17 Jul 1942	Gemini (♊)	05 Dec 1944	Capricorn (♑)
11 Aug 1942	Cancer (♋)	31 Dec 1944	Aquarius (♒)
05 Sep 1942	Leo (♌)	27 Jan 1945	Pisces (♓)
29 Sep 1942	Virgo (♍)	28 Feb 1945	Aries (♈)
23 Oct 1942	Libra (♎)	19 Apr 1945	Pisces (♓)
16 Nov 1942	Scorpio (♏)	25 May 1945	Aries (♈)
10 Dec 1942	Sagittarius (♐)	01 Jul 1945	Taurus (♉)
03 Jan 1943	Capricorn (♑)	29 Jul 1945	Gemini (♊)
27 Jan 1943	Aquarius (♒)	25 Aug 1945	Cancer (♋)
20 Feb 1943	Pisces (♓)	19 Sep 1945	Leo (♌)
16 Mar 1943	Aries (♈)	13 Oct 1945	Virgo (♍)
10 Apr 1943	Taurus (♉)	07 Nov 1945	Libra (♎)
05 May 1943	Gemini (♊)	01 Dec 1945	Scorpio (♏)
01 Jun 1943	Cancer (♋)	25 Dec 1945	Sagittarius (♐)
30 Jun 1943	Leo (♌)	17 Jan 1946	Capricorn (♑)
02 Nov 1943	Virgo (♍)	10 Feb 1946	Aquarius (♒)
02 Dec 1943	Libra (♎)	06 Mar 1946	Pisces (♓)
28 Dec 1943	Scorpio (♏)	30 Mar 1946	Aries (♈)
22 Jan 1944	Sagittarius (♐)	24 Apr 1946	Taurus (♉)
16 Feb 1944	Capricorn (♑)	18 May 1946	Gemini (♊)
11 Mar 1944	Aquarius (♒)	12 Jun 1946	Cancer (♋)

Starting Date	Zodiac Sign	Starting Date	Zodiac Sign
08 Jul 1946	Leo (♌)	21 Mar 1949	Pisces (♓)
03 Aug 1946	Virgo (♍)	14 Apr 1949	Aries (♈)
31 Aug 1946	Libra (♎)	08 May 1949	Taurus (♉)
04 Oct 1946	Scorpio (♏)	02 Jun 1949	Gemini (♊)
31 Jan 1947	Sagittarius (♐)	26 Jun 1949	Cancer (♋)
27 Feb 1947	Capricorn (♑)	21 Jul 1949	Leo (♌)
25 Mar 1947	Aquarius (♒)	15 Aug 1949	Virgo (♍)
19 Apr 1947	Pisces (♓)	09 Sep 1949	Libra (♎)
14 May 1947	Aries (♈)	04 Oct 1949	Scorpio (♏)
08 Jun 1947	Taurus (♉)	31 Oct 1949	Sagittarius (♐)
03 Jul 1947	Gemini (♊)	29 Nov 1949	Capricorn (♑)
27 Jul 1947	Cancer (♋)	30 Mar 1950	Aquarius (♒)
21 Aug 1947	Leo (♌)	29 Apr 1950	Pisces (♓)
14 Sep 1947	Virgo (♍)	26 May 1950	Aries (♈)
08 Oct 1947	Libra (♎)	21 Jun 1950	Taurus (♉)
01 Nov 1947	Scorpio (♏)	17 Jul 1950	Gemini (♊)
25 Nov 1947	Sagittarius (♐)	11 Aug 1950	Cancer (♋)
19 Dec 1947	Capricorn (♑)	04 Sep 1950	Leo (♌)
12 Jan 1948	Aquarius (♒)	29 Sep 1950	Virgo (♍)
06 Feb 1948	Pisces (♓)	23 Oct 1950	Libra (♎)
02 Mar 1948	Aries (♈)	16 Nov 1950	Scorpio (♏)
29 Mar 1948	Taurus (♉)	09 Dec 1950	Sagittarius (♐)
29 Apr 1948	Gemini (♊)	02 Jan 1951	Capricorn (♑)
01 Sep 1948	Cancer (♋)	26 Jan 1951	Aquarius (♒)
30 Sep 1948	Leo (♌)	19 Feb 1951	Pisces (♓)
26 Oct 1948	Virgo (♍)	16 Mar 1951	Aries (♈)
20 Nov 1948	Libra (♎)	09 Apr 1951	Taurus (♉)
15 Dec 1948	Scorpio (♏)	05 May 1951	Gemini (♊)
08 Jan 1949	Sagittarius (♐)	01 Jun 1951	Cancer (♋)
01 Feb 1949	Capricorn (♑)	30 Jun 1951	Leo (♌)
25 Feb 1949	Aquarius (♒)	02 Nov 1951	Virgo (♍)

Starting Date	Zodiac Sign	Starting Date	Zodiac Sign
02 Dec 1951	Libra (♎)	06 Mar 1954	Pisces (♓)
28 Dec 1951	Scorpio (♏)	30 Mar 1954	Aries (♈)
22 Jan 1952	Sagittarius (♐)	23 Apr 1954	Taurus (♉)
15 Feb 1952	Capricorn (♑)	18 May 1954	Gemini (♊)
11 Mar 1952	Aquarius (♒)	12 Jun 1954	Cancer (♋)
04 Apr 1952	Pisces (♓)	07 Jul 1954	Leo (♌)
29 Apr 1952	Aries (♈)	03 Aug 1954	Virgo (♍)
23 May 1952	Taurus (♉)	31 Aug 1954	Libra (♎)
17 Jun 1952	Gemini (♊)	05 Oct 1954	Scorpio (♏)
11 Jul 1952	Cancer (♋)	30 Jan 1955	Sagittarius (♐)
04 Aug 1952	Leo (♌)	27 Feb 1955	Capricorn (♑)
29 Aug 1952	Virgo (♍)	25 Mar 1955	Aquarius (♒)
22 Sep 1952	Libra (♎)	19 Apr 1955	Pisces (♓)
16 Oct 1952	Scorpio (♏)	14 May 1955	Aries (♈)
10 Nov 1952	Sagittarius (♐)	08 Jun 1955	Taurus (♉)
05 Dec 1952	Capricorn (♑)	02 Jul 1955	Gemini (♊)
30 Dec 1952	Aquarius (♒)	27 Jul 1955	Cancer (♋)
26 Jan 1953	Pisces (♓)	20 Aug 1955	Leo (♌)
01 Mar 1953	Aries (♈)	13 Sep 1955	Virgo (♍)
14 Apr 1953	Pisces (♓)	07 Oct 1955	Libra (♎)
27 May 1953	Aries (♈)	31 Oct 1955	Scorpio (♏)
01 Jul 1953	Taurus (♉)	25 Nov 1955	Sagittarius (♐)
29 Jul 1953	Gemini (♊)	19 Dec 1955	Capricorn (♑)
24 Aug 1953	Cancer (♋)	12 Jan 1956	Aquarius (♒)
18 Sep 1953	Leo (♌)	06 Feb 1956	Pisces (♓)
13 Oct 1953	Virgo (♍)	02 Mar 1956	Aries (♈)
06 Nov 1953	Libra (♎)	29 Mar 1956	Taurus (♉)
30 Nov 1953	Scorpio (♏)	29 Apr 1956	Gemini (♊)
24 Dec 1953	Sagittarius (♐)	09 Jul 1956	Taurus (♉)
17 Jan 1954	Capricorn (♑)	20 Jul 1956	Gemini (♊)
10 Feb 1954	Aquarius (♒)	01 Sep 1956	Cancer (♋)

Starting Date	Zodiac Sign	Starting Date	Zodiac Sign
30 Sep 1956	Leo (♌)	19 Feb 1959	Pisces (♓)
26 Oct 1956	Virgo (♍)	15 Mar 1959	Aries (♈)
20 Nov 1956	Libra (♎)	09 Apr 1959	Taurus (♉)
14 Dec 1956	Scorpio (♏)	05 May 1959	Gemini (♊)
07 Jan 1957	Sagittarius (♐)	31 May 1959	Cancer (♋)
31 Jan 1957	Capricorn (♑)	30 Jun 1959	Leo (♌)
24 Feb 1957	Aquarius (♒)	03 Nov 1959	Virgo (♍)
20 Mar 1957	Pisces (♓)	02 Dec 1959	Libra (♎)
13 Apr 1957	Aries (♈)	28 Dec 1959	Scorpio (♏)
08 May 1957	Taurus (♉)	21 Jan 1960	Sagittarius (♐)
01 Jun 1957	Gemini (♊)	15 Feb 1960	Capricorn (♑)
26 Jun 1957	Cancer (♋)	10 Mar 1960	Aquarius (♒)
20 Jul 1957	Leo (♌)	04 Apr 1960	Pisces (♓)
14 Aug 1957	Virgo (♍)	28 Apr 1960	Aries (♈)
08 Sep 1957	Libra (♎)	23 May 1960	Taurus (♉)
04 Oct 1957	Scorpio (♏)	16 Jun 1960	Gemini (♊)
31 Oct 1957	Sagittarius (♐)	10 Jul 1960	Cancer (♋)
29 Nov 1957	Capricorn (♑)	04 Aug 1960	Leo (♌)
30 Mar 1958	Aquarius (♒)	28 Aug 1960	Virgo (♍)
29 Apr 1958	Pisces (♓)	22 Sep 1960	Libra (♎)
26 May 1958	Aries (♈)	16 Oct 1960	Scorpio (♏)
21 Jun 1958	Taurus (♉)	10 Nov 1960	Sagittarius (♐)
16 Jul 1958	Gemini (♊)	05 Dec 1960	Capricorn (♑)
10 Aug 1958	Cancer (♋)	30 Dec 1960	Aquarius (♒)
04 Sep 1958	Leo (♌)	26 Jan 1961	Pisces (♓)
28 Sep 1958	Virgo (♍)	02 Mar 1961	Aries (♈)
22 Oct 1958	Libra (♎)	07 Apr 1961	Pisces (♓)
15 Nov 1958	Scorpio (♏)	28 May 1961	Aries (♈)
09 Dec 1958	Sagittarius (♐)	01 Jul 1961	Taurus (♉)
02 Jan 1959	Capricorn (♑)	28 Jul 1961	Gemini (♊)
26 Jan 1959	Aquarius (♒)	24 Aug 1961	Cancer (♋)

Starting Date	Zodiac Sign	Starting Date	Zodiac Sign
18 Sep 1961	Leo (♌)	18 Dec 1963	Capricorn (♑)
13 Oct 1961	Virgo (♍)	11 Jan 1964	Aquarius (♒)
06 Nov 1961	Libra (♎)	05 Feb 1964	Pisces (♓)
30 Nov 1961	Scorpio (♏)	02 Mar 1964	Aries (♈)
23 Dec 1961	Sagittarius (♐)	29 Mar 1964	Taurus (♉)
16 Jan 1962	Capricorn (♑)	29 Apr 1964	Gemini (♊)
09 Feb 1962	Aquarius (♒)	30 Jun 1964	Taurus (♉)
05 Mar 1962	Pisces (♓)	25 Jul 1964	Gemini (♊)
29 Mar 1962	Aries (♈)	01 Sep 1964	Cancer (♋)
23 Apr 1962	Taurus (♉)	30 Sep 1964	Leo (♌)
17 May 1962	Gemini (♊)	26 Oct 1964	Virgo (♍)
11 Jun 1962	Cancer (♋)	19 Nov 1964	Libra (♎)
07 Jul 1962	Leo (♌)	14 Dec 1964	Scorpio (♏)
02 Aug 1962	Virgo (♍)	07 Jan 1965	Sagittarius (♐)
31 Aug 1962	Libra (♎)	31 Jan 1965	Capricorn (♑)
07 Oct 1962	Scorpio (♏)	24 Feb 1965	Aquarius (♒)
08 Nov 1962	Libra (♎)	20 Mar 1965	Pisces (♓)
29 Dec 1962	Scorpio (♏)	13 Apr 1965	Aries (♈)
30 Jan 1963	Sagittarius (♐)	07 May 1965	Taurus (♉)
26 Feb 1963	Capricorn (♑)	01 Jun 1965	Gemini (♊)
24 Mar 1963	Aquarius (♒)	25 Jun 1965	Cancer (♋)
18 Apr 1963	Pisces (♓)	20 Jul 1965	Leo (♌)
13 May 1963	Aries (♈)	14 Aug 1965	Virgo (♍)
07 Jun 1963	Taurus (♉)	08 Sep 1965	Libra (♎)
02 Jul 1963	Gemini (♊)	04 Oct 1965	Scorpio (♏)
26 Jul 1963	Cancer (♋)	30 Oct 1965	Sagittarius (♐)
20 Aug 1963	Leo (♌)	29 Nov 1965	Capricorn (♑)
13 Sep 1963	Virgo (♍)	31 Mar 1966	Aquarius (♒)
07 Oct 1963	Libra (♎)	29 Apr 1966	Pisces (♓)
31 Oct 1963	Scorpio (♏)	26 May 1966	Aries (♈)
24 Nov 1963	Sagittarius (♐)	21 Jun 1966	Taurus (♉)

Starting Date	Zodiac Sign	Starting Date	Zodiac Sign
16 Jul 1966	Gemini (♊)	04 Dec 1968	Capricorn (♑)
10 Aug 1966	Cancer (♋)	30 Dec 1968	Aquarius (♒)
03 Sep 1966	Leo (♌)	26 Jan 1969	Pisces (♓)
28 Sep 1966	Virgo (♍)	05 Mar 1969	Aries (♈)
22 Oct 1966	Libra (♎)	30 Jun 1969	Taurus (♉)
15 Nov 1966	Scorpio (♏)	28 Jul 1969	Gemini (♊)
08 Dec 1966	Sagittarius (♐)	23 Aug 1969	Cancer (♋)
01 Jan 1967	Capricorn (♑)	18 Sep 1969	Leo (♌)
25 Jan 1967	Aquarius (♒)	12 Oct 1969	Virgo (♍)
18 Feb 1967	Pisces (♓)	05 Nov 1969	Libra (♎)
15 Mar 1967	Aries (♈)	29 Nov 1969	Scorpio (♏)
09 Apr 1967	Taurus (♉)	23 Dec 1969	Sagittarius (♐)
04 May 1967	Gemini (♊)	16 Jan 1970	Capricorn (♑)
31 May 1967	Cancer (♋)	09 Feb 1970	Aquarius (♒)
01 Jul 1967	Leo (♌)	05 Mar 1970	Pisces (♓)
03 Nov 1967	Virgo (♍)	29 Mar 1970	Aries (♈)
01 Dec 1967	Libra (♎)	22 Apr 1970	Taurus (♉)
27 Dec 1967	Scorpio (♏)	17 May 1970	Gemini (♊)
21 Jan 1968	Sagittarius (♐)	11 Jun 1970	Cancer (♋)
15 Feb 1968	Capricorn (♑)	07 Jul 1970	Leo (♌)
10 Mar 1968	Aquarius (♒)	02 Aug 1970	Virgo (♍)
03 Apr 1968	Pisces (♓)	31 Aug 1970	Libra (♎)
28 Apr 1968	Aries (♈)	10 Oct 1970	Scorpio (♏)
22 May 1968	Taurus (♉)	31 Oct 1970	Libra (♎)
16 Jun 1968	Gemini (♊)	30 Dec 1970	Scorpio (♏)
10 Jul 1968	Cancer (♋)	30 Jan 1971	Sagittarius (♐)
03 Aug 1968	Leo (♌)	26 Feb 1971	Capricorn (♑)
28 Aug 1968	Virgo (♍)	24 Mar 1971	Aquarius (♒)
21 Sep 1968	Libra (♎)	18 Apr 1971	Pisces (♓)
16 Oct 1968	Scorpio (♏)	13 May 1971	Aries (♈)
09 Nov 1968	Sagittarius (♐)	07 Jun 1971	Taurus (♉)

Starting Date	Zodiac Sign	Starting Date	Zodiac Sign
01 Jul 1971	Gemini (♊)	03 Oct 1973	Scorpio (♏)
26 Jul 1971	Cancer (♋)	30 Oct 1973	Sagittarius (♐)
19 Aug 1971	Leo (♌)	30 Nov 1973	Capricorn (♑)
12 Sep 1971	Virgo (♍)	31 Mar 1974	Aquarius (♒)
06 Oct 1971	Libra (♎)	29 Apr 1974	Pisces (♓)
31 Oct 1971	Scorpio (♏)	25 May 1974	Aries (♈)
24 Nov 1971	Sagittarius (♐)	20 Jun 1974	Taurus (♉)
18 Dec 1971	Capricorn (♑)	16 Jul 1974	Gemini (♊)
11 Jan 1972	Aquarius (♒)	09 Aug 1974	Cancer (♋)
05 Feb 1972	Pisces (♓)	03 Sep 1974	Leo (♌)
01 Mar 1972	Aries (♈)	27 Sep 1974	Virgo (♍)
28 Mar 1972	Taurus (♉)	21 Oct 1974	Libra (♎)
30 Apr 1972	Gemini (♊)	14 Nov 1974	Scorpio (♏)
23 Jun 1972	Taurus (♉)	08 Dec 1974	Sagittarius (♐)
27 Jul 1972	Gemini (♊)	01 Jan 1975	Capricorn (♑)
01 Sep 1972	Cancer (♋)	25 Jan 1975	Aquarius (♒)
29 Sep 1972	Leo (♌)	18 Feb 1975	Pisces (♓)
25 Oct 1972	Virgo (♍)	14 Mar 1975	Aries (♈)
19 Nov 1972	Libra (♎)	08 Apr 1975	Taurus (♉)
13 Dec 1972	Scorpio (♏)	04 May 1975	Gemini (♊)
06 Jan 1973	Sagittarius (♐)	31 May 1975	Cancer (♋)
30 Jan 1973	Capricorn (♑)	01 Jul 1975	Leo (♌)
23 Feb 1973	Aquarius (♒)	03 Nov 1975	Virgo (♍)
19 Mar 1973	Pisces (♓)	01 Dec 1975	Libra (♎)
13 Apr 1973	Aries (♈)	27 Dec 1975	Scorpio (♏)
07 May 1973	Taurus (♉)	21 Jan 1976	Sagittarius (♐)
31 May 1973	Gemini (♊)	14 Feb 1976	Capricorn (♑)
25 Jun 1973	Cancer (♋)	10 Mar 1976	Aquarius (♒)
20 Jul 1973	Leo (♌)	03 Apr 1976	Pisces (♓)
14 Aug 1973	Virgo (♍)	27 Apr 1976	Aries (♈)
08 Sep 1973	Libra (♎)	22 May 1976	Taurus (♉)

Starting Date	Zodiac Sign	Starting Date	Zodiac Sign
15 Jun 1976	Gemini (♊)	31 Dec 1978	Scorpio (♏)
10 Jul 1976	Cancer (♋)	30 Jan 1979	Sagittarius (♐)
03 Aug 1976	Leo (♌)	26 Feb 1979	Capricorn (♑)
27 Aug 1976	Virgo (♍)	24 Mar 1979	Aquarius (♒)
20 Sep 1976	Libra (♎)	18 Apr 1979	Pisces (♓)
15 Oct 1976	Scorpio (♏)	12 May 1979	Aries (♈)
09 Nov 1976	Sagittarius (♐)	06 Jun 1979	Taurus (♉)
04 Dec 1976	Capricorn (♑)	01 Jul 1979	Gemini (♊)
29 Dec 1976	Aquarius (♒)	25 Jul 1979	Cancer (♋)
26 Jan 1977	Pisces (♓)	19 Aug 1979	Leo (♌)
09 Mar 1977	Aries (♈)	12 Sep 1979	Virgo (♍)
25 Mar 1977	Pisces (♓)	06 Oct 1979	Libra (♎)
29 May 1977	Aries (♈)	30 Oct 1979	Scorpio (♏)
30 Jun 1977	Taurus (♉)	23 Nov 1979	Sagittarius (♐)
28 Jul 1977	Gemini (♊)	17 Dec 1979	Capricorn (♑)
23 Aug 1977	Cancer (♋)	11 Jan 1980	Aquarius (♒)
17 Sep 1977	Leo (♌)	04 Feb 1980	Pisces (♓)
12 Oct 1977	Virgo (♍)	01 Mar 1980	Aries (♈)
05 Nov 1977	Libra (♎)	28 Mar 1980	Taurus (♉)
29 Nov 1977	Scorpio (♏)	01 May 1980	Gemini (♊)
23 Dec 1977	Sagittarius (♐)	17 Jun 1980	Taurus (♉)
15 Jan 1978	Capricorn (♑)	28 Jul 1980	Gemini (♊)
08 Feb 1978	Aquarius (♒)	01 Sep 1980	Cancer (♋)
04 Mar 1978	Pisces (♓)	29 Sep 1980	Leo (♌)
28 Mar 1978	Aries (♈)	25 Oct 1980	Virgo (♍)
22 Apr 1978	Taurus (♉)	19 Nov 1980	Libra (♎)
17 May 1978	Gemini (♊)	13 Dec 1980	Scorpio (♏)
11 Jun 1978	Cancer (♋)	06 Jan 1981	Sagittarius (♐)
06 Jul 1978	Leo (♌)	30 Jan 1981	Capricorn (♑)
02 Aug 1978	Virgo (♍)	23 Feb 1981	Aquarius (♒)
31 Aug 1978	Libra (♎)	19 Mar 1981	Pisces (♓)

Starting Date	Zodiac Sign
12 Apr 1981	Aries (♈)
06 May 1981	Taurus (♉)
31 May 1981	Gemini (♊)
24 Jun 1981	Cancer (♋)
19 Jul 1981	Leo (♌)
13 Aug 1981	Virgo (♍)
07 Sep 1981	Libra (♎)
03 Oct 1981	Scorpio (♏)
30 Oct 1981	Sagittarius (♐)
30 Nov 1981	Capricorn (♑)
31 Mar 1982	Aquarius (♒)
29 Apr 1982	Pisces (♓)
25 May 1982	Aries (♈)
20 Jun 1982	Taurus (♉)
15 Jul 1982	Gemini (♊)
09 Aug 1982	Cancer (♋)
03 Sep 1982	Leo (♌)
27 Sep 1982	Virgo (I)
21 Oct 1982	Libra (♎)
14 Nov 1982	Scorpio (♏)
08 Dec 1982	Sagittarius (♐)
31 Dec 1982	Capricorn (♑)
24 Jan 1983	Aquarius (♒)
18 Feb 1983	Pisces (♓)
14 Mar 1983	Aries (♈)
08 Apr 1983	Taurus (♉)
04 May 1983	Gemini (♊)
31 May 1983	Cancer (♋)
01 Jul 1983	Leo (♌)
03 Nov 1983	Virgo (♍)
01 Dec 1983	Libra (♎)

Starting Date	Zodiac Sign
27 Dec 1983	Scorpio (♏)
20 Jan 1984	Sagittarius (♐)
14 Feb 1984	Capricorn (♑)
09 Mar 1984	Aquarius (♒)
02 Apr 1984	Pisces (♓)
27 Apr 1984	Aries (♈)
21 May 1984	Taurus (♉)
15 Jun 1984	Gemini (♊)
09 Jul 1984	Cancer (♋)
02 Aug 1984	Leo (♌)
27 Aug 1984	Virgo (♍)
20 Sep 1984	Libra (♎)
15 Oct 1984	Scorpio (♏)
09 Nov 1984	Sagittarius (♐)
04 Dec 1984	Capricorn (♑)
29 Dec 1984	Aquarius (♒)
26 Jan 1985	Pisces (♓)
29 May 1985	Aries (♈)
30 Jun 1985	Taurus (♉)
28 Jul 1985	Gemini (♊)
22 Aug 1985	Cancer (♋)
17 Sep 1985	Leo (♌)
11 Oct 1985	Virgo (♍)
04 Nov 1985	Libra (♎)
28 Nov 1985	Scorpio (♏)
22 Dec 1985	Sagittarius (♐)
15 Jan 1986	Capricorn (♑)
08 Feb 1986	Aquarius (♒)
04 Mar 1986	Pisces (♓)
28 Mar 1986	Aries (♈)
21 Apr 1986	Taurus (♉)

Starting Date	Zodiac Sign	Starting Date	Zodiac Sign
16 May 1986	Gemini (♊)	12 May 1987	Aries (♈)
10 Jun 1986	Cancer (♋)	06 Jun 1987	Taurus (♉)
06 Jul 1986	Leo (♌)	30 Jun 1987	Gemini (♊)
02 Aug 1986	Virgo (♍)	25 Jul 1987	Cancer (♋)
31 Aug 1986	Libra (♎)	18 Aug 1987	Leo (♌)
31 Dec 1986	Scorpio (♏)	11 Sep 1987	Virgo (♍)
30 Jan 1987	Sagittarius (♐)	06 Oct 1987	Libra (♎)
26 Feb 1987	Capricorn (♑)	30 Oct 1987	Scorpio (♏)
23 Mar 1987	Aquarius (♒)	23 Nov 1987	Sagittarius (♐)
17 Apr 1987	Pisces (♓)	17 Dec 1987	Capricorn (♑)

These dates are derived from calculations using *The American Ephemeris for the Twentieth Century* (San Diego: ACS Publications, 1980–1996) and the latitude and longitude for New York City at noon, and applying the Lahiri *ayanamsa* for each year to its placement.

Venus in Aries. You're inclined to appreciate the opposite sex. Consequently, you may marry very early or hastily. You may also encounter an inharmonious relationship because of your own impulsiveness. Your libido is activated before you're twenty-four years old, which in Hindu culture is considered to be a positive factor for early-marriage people. (More potential for childbearing!) "You can love a person deeply and sincerely whom you do not like. You can like a person passionately whom you do not love," wrote American author Robert Hugh Benson. Act hastily only when you find someone you can like and love. (*Famous examples:* Warren Beatty, Eric Clapton, Michael J. Fox, Steffi Graf, Jack Nicholson, Prince, Kurt Russell.)

Venus in Taurus. Although you tend to be very affectionate and possess deep, enduring emotions, you may encounter delays, obstacles, and disappointments in your marital relationship. Love is an impulse, marriage is a commitment. But it's the strength of your love that helps you to choose again and again over time to weather storms and wait for the sun to shine again. You see, marriage is not a onetime choice that's made when you say, "I do." It's a preference you select

A tenth-century scripture, the *Skanda Purana,* tells of Lord Siva's elopement with his first wife, Sati. The marriage came to a tragic end when her father insulted the lively young god: Sati was so enraged that she committed suicide. Retreating up to the mountains, Siva met and fell in love with the *yogini* Parvati. To start this second marriage properly, Siva asked the astrologer Garga to select the perfect *naksatra* for the nuptials. He chose the *naksatra* Uttaraphalguni. They waited until the exact moment when the Moon passed this fortuitous point. The result: this pair of gods still live in wedded bliss high atop Tibet's Mount Kailash.

every day when you see the person you loved the previous day and you know you still love. (*Famous examples:* Candice Bergen, Johnny Depp, Harrison Ford, Al Gore, Courtney Love, Debbie Reynolds, Brooke Shields, Spencer Tracy, Princess Diana Spencer Windsor, Prince William Windsor.)

Venus in Gemini. You may fall in love more than once and may even carry on two simultaneous liaisons during your life. There's also a possibility you'll walk down the aisle more than once. Your libido emerges before your twenty-fourth birthday, which in Hindu culture is considered to be a positive factor if you want to have children while you're young. It's possible to love two people at the same time, but not with all your heart. Remember, there are few things that devastate someone more than the surprise discovery of an unfaithful mate. We can hurt deepest those who love us most. Is it possible to have an "open marriage" in which you have a spouse but you still date other people? There was a book written about open marriage a few decades ago. The authors divorced shortly after their book of marital advice was published. Open relationships become open competition, producing no winners. With that said, remember: it's better to experiment and make mistakes while you're dating than when you're married. (*Famous examples:* Ben Affleck, Cher, Ray Davies, Tipper Gore, O. J. Simpson.)

Venus in Cancer. There's a good chance you'll have many clandestine love affairs before you settle down with an older or younger spouse. Your marital difficulties could stem from money, parents, or profession. You might consider early loves to be practice for matrimony, as many people do. In reality they provide more of a contrast. The wild storm of courtship prepares you to enjoy the comparative serenity and stability of marriage. Once there, focus on navigating around the rocks and reefs of parental, financial, and professional strife. (*Famous examples:* Lauren Bacall, George W. Bush, John Derek, Madonna, Julia Roberts, Arnold Schwarzenegger, Donald Trump.)

Venus in Leo. Your love life will be as magnanimous as you choose to make it. Romance must be on a grand scale to keep you occupied. Matrimony must satisfy your expectations or you don't bother to stick around. An anguished Indian king built the Taj Mahal as a remembrance to his dead bride. When you fall in love, let your heart build an even grander palace. You have the type of love in your grasp that a heartbroken king would have traded a dozen Taj Mahals to regain. (*Famous examples:* Antonio Banderas, Brigitte Bardot, Catherine Deneuve, Carrie Fisher, Melanie Griffith, Pamela Anderson Lee, Heather Locklear, Richie Sambora, Dwight Yoakam.)

Venus in Virgo. You may experience romantic disappointments or delays, partly because you rarely express your deepest emotions. You may marry a coworker, an employee, a doctor, or someone who needs you as both spouse and primary caregiver. To give of yourself is the most precious gift there is. You have the capacity to provide so steadily that the recipient may feel there is life with you and life without you, just as there are days with sunshine or with clouds. The trouble is, your beloved might not notice or recognize the depth of your passion. You mean it without saying it. Did you ever wonder why people seem attracted to individuals who are full of smooth talk about love but lack sincerity? It's because it means so much for people to hear the words. Verbalize your feelings. Soon you'll be the best of both worlds in someone's eyes. (*Famous examples:* Woody Allen, Bill Clinton, Hillary Rodham Clinton, Prince Charles Windsor.)

Venus in Libra. When you finally decide to settle down, you'll potentially marry well. You're predisposed to prosper financially and socially through your marriage. Don't worry too much about feeling indecisive; you won't vacillate when the right person appears. Age provides you with that wisdom. In the meantime, think of this: married people often reminisce about the wonderful carefree days they had before marriage. So why do they rush to get married? The answer is simple. Some people just don't realize how far the world extends beyond the horizons we saw at birth. (*Famous examples:* Bo Derek, Michael Douglas, Bill Gates, Goldie Hawn, Steven Spielberg, Ted Turner.)

Venus in Scorpio. You may experience many disappointments in both courtship and wedlock. Oh for a love who could be there to witness all of your greatest moments and who would always look the other way when you stumble. Of course, more often life works in reverse. As William Shakespeare wrote in *A Midsummer Night's Dream,* "The course of true love never did run smooth." But take heart, you are not alone and you won't be alone. Financial losses might also occur through romance or marriage. You might want to give your lover everything he or she ever wanted. The trouble is, it not only gets expensive, it also leaves you wondering whether this person adores you or your presents. Be generous with your love, not your wallet. Your libido potentially emerges before your twenty-fourth birthday, which in Hindu culture is considered to be a positive factor if you wish to start a family earlier rather than later. (*Famous examples:* Kim Basinger, Humphrey Bogart, David Bowie, Jane Fonda, Maria Shriver.)

Venus in Sagittarius. You tend to be a romantic at heart. You might even have a long-distance relationship during your life. Chances are you'll also wed more than once. Romance comes in as many forms as there are lovers in this world. As a person who is truly entranced by passion, you may find yourself drawn to very different people at different times, reinventing yourself within your transformed surroundings. It may surprise you to discover that when you read between the lines of a long-distance affair, you simply peruse the love stories you've written for yourself. Before your twenty-fourth birthday, your libido potentially develops, which in Hindu culture is considered to be a positive factor for early-marriage people. (*Famous examples:* Richard Burton, Diane Keaton, John F. Kennedy Jr.)

Venus in Capricorn. You tend to marry for professional, financial, or social reasons rather than love. But without that key ingredient, your mate may become cold, indifferent, or disappointed when the honeymoon's over. To marry for passion alone is to deny that you and your spouse will ever spend a moment out of bed. However, a lack of intimacy can erode the foundation of the most solid and profitable relationship. Flirtation between the two of you is a mutual assurance that you continue to find each other attractive. To find your happiness, marry well but never cease to be a loving mate. (*Famous examples:* Mikhail Gorbachev, Carolyn Bessette Kennedy, Brad Pitt, Elvis Presley, Britney Spears, Jason Timberlake, Oprah Winfrey.)

Venus in Aquarius. You might experience some unconventional or unusual liaisons before you settle down. Matrimony occurs later in your life. Chances are you'll wed someone who's younger or older and quite eccentric. Remember the words of actress Katharine Hepburn: "If you obey all the rules, you miss all the fun." She knew what she was talking about. Her lifelong love affair with actor Spencer Tracy (who refused to divorce his wife because of his deep Catholic beliefs) was one of the twentieth century's greatest romances. (*Famous examples:* Sir Michael Caine, Bridget Fonda, the Reverend Dr. Martin Luther King Jr., Barbra Streisand, John Travolta.)

Venus in Pisces. You tend to be romantically fickle. Naturally attracted to the underdog, you flit through love affairs and marriages with little concern for stability or longevity. The first sip of champagne is filled with effervescence, but if you drink it very slowly, by the time you reach the bottom of the bottle it seems to lose some of its sparkle. A relationship doesn't have to go flat if you stick around to enjoy it. Endless dates with new people may seem like boundless first sips, but it eventually leaves you without something others have: a mate with whom you share a past. One prince or princess is worth a hundred toads. As for those thoughts of regret, regardless of which road you take in life, you'll always wonder what might have been, whether you take every turn or never once stray off the path. (*Famous examples:* Drew Barrymore, Julie Christie, Kurt Cobain, Mia Farrow, George Harrison, Katharine Hepburn, John Lennon, Michelle Pfeiffer, Elizabeth Taylor.)

Using Brad Pitt as an example, the astrologer might conclude that Pitt's Venus in Capricorn makes him inclined to marry for professional, financial, or social reasons rather than love. This information can then be coupled with the planet's location in his chart, as outlined in the following pages, to derive a complete reading of Venus's sway over his love life.

♥ ♥ ♥

The placement of the planet Venus in your birth chart enhances the description of your love life, indicating how romantic and loving you are toward your mate. **You'll need your *bhavacakra* to use this particular section.** Enter your (and/or your mate's) birth date onto Worksheet 7. Look for the Venus symbol (VE) on your *bhavacakra*. Note the number of the house it occupies. (On page 104, fig. 2 highlights Venus's placement in the third house of Brad Pitt's *bhavacakra*). Enter that house number in the space provided on the worksheet. Do the same with your mate's Venus placement. Then locate the house number in the text following to learn how this planet's placement further affects your ability to give and receive affection.

WORKSHEET 7. VENUS'S *BHAVACAKRA* HOUSE LOCATION

	Example:	Name A:	Name B:
	Brad Pitt		
Birth date	18 Dec 1963		
Venus's bhavacakra house location	III (third house)		

Venus in your chart's first house. Venus's placement tends to make you passionate. "A man in passion," wrote seventeenth-century British clergyman Thomas Fuller, "rides a horse that runs away with him." You have a heart that can be swept away. That should be less surprising to you than the fact that not everyone else does. Learn to be a little tolerant of jealous friends who can't feel as deeply. Also, beware of people who might talk of love just to exploit you. (*Famous examples:* Ben Affleck, Lauren Bacall, George W. Bush, Cher, Michael Douglas, Tipper Gore, Carolyn Bessette Kennedy, Julia Roberts, Donald Trump, Dwight Yoakam.)

Venus in your chart's second house. The planet's location potentially affords you a happy domestic life. You may be advised by people that you need your own space and need to "find yourself" by spending a few years not dating anyone in particular before you can enter a relationship as a "whole person." Be gentle with these advice-laden folk. You're blessed with the ability to have a happier home life today than they might have after decades of solitary soul-searching. But they'll never know this because they can't see the world through any eyes but their own. (*Famous examples:* Woody Allen, Bill Clinton, Arnold Schwarzenegger.)

Venus in your chart's third house. Venus's placement quite possibly grants you joie de vivre and strong desires. Don't insist that your love interest must match your outward exhilaration. Let your energy draw them along and you'll both enjoy the ride. When you desire it, you can also draw on the quiet within your lover to slow your pace for a little while. (*Famous examples:* David Bowie, Diane Keaton, Brad Pitt, Elvis Presley, Maria Shriver, Prince Charles Windsor.)

Venus in your chart's fourth house. You're inclined to be lucky in love with Venus in this position. You might receive a lot of advice from people who've been less romantically fortunate. Mostly, they'll extol the virtues of not being in a happy relationship. As pop musician Joe Jackson sang, "Until the time that I can do my dancing with a partner, those happy couples ain't no friends of mine." Be tolerant of them. They'd love to have this Venus placement in their own charts. The world would be a happier place if everyone did. (*Famous examples:* Kim Basinger, Ray Davies, Bridget Fonda, Pamela Anderson Lee, Richie Sambora, Steven Spielberg, Justin Timberlake.)

Venus in your chart's fifth house. Venus's placement tends to afford you romantic happiness. Is Prince Charming or Miss Perfect out there? Who cares when you've got real happiness right here. Believe it or not, some people throw away the real thing to endlessly chase fairy tales. You're smarter than that. (*Famous examples:* Antonio Banderas, Hillary Rodham Clinton, Jane Fonda, Michael J. Fox, Melanie Griffith, John F. Kennedy Jr.)

Venus in your chart's sixth house. In this location, the planet's influence might instigate romantic difficulties. There's an old pop tune the Ink Spots sang that goes, "Into each life some rain must fall, but too much is fallin' in mine." There are no sweeter or more heartfelt frustrations than those that arise from love. And when that passion is strong enough, nothing is insurmountable. (*Famous example:* George Harrison, Katharine Hepburn, John Lennon, Britney Spears, Elizabeth Taylor, Spencer Tracy, Prince William Windsor, Oprah Winfrey.)

Venus in your chart's seventh house. Venus's position may grant you a romantic marriage to an artistic mate. From the *Venus de Milo* to Jimi Hendrix's "Foxy Lady," the history of art is the history of artists who've expressed passion through their work. Who knows what poetry your love might inspire? (*Famous examples:* Candice Bergen, Humphrey Bogart, Heather Locklear, Prince, Princess Diana Spencer Windsor.)

Venus in your chart's eighth house. The planet's placement in this house might instigate romantic difficulties. The smoothest road through life is paved with boredom. To avoid emotional injury, you could try to avoid falling in love. But the truth is, the joy is worth the pain. Keep a journal. Write down only the good times. Read it when you feel blue. (*Famous examples:* Warren Beatty, Eric Clapton, Kurt Cobain, Bo Derek, Carrie Fisher, Courtney Love.)

Venus in your chart's ninth house. Venus's location may send you a spiritually minded spouse from a foreign land. Believe it or not, there's no planetary position or aspect in any form of astrology that would indicate you have a tall, dark, and handsome stranger in your future. However, there is one that almost predicts this, and this is it! (*Famous example:* Sir Michael Caine, Catherine Deneuve, John Derek, Harrison Ford, Debbie Reynolds.)

Venus in your chart's tenth house. The planet's placement potentially grants you professional or social status as well as fame through romance. Behind the scenes, our world is bound together by friendships. In life, promotion and advancement can depend as much on who you know (or who they know) as what you know. There are also some people who just bring out the best in us. You have a good chance of meeting someone who'll have that effect on you. (*Famous examples:* Brigitte Bardot, Julie Christie, Brooke Shields, John Travolta.)

Venus in your chart's eleventh house. With Venus in this location, you potentially experience fortunate opportunities and encounter artistic suitors. This star smiles on you. Enjoy it with one caution. Morality is the difference between artistry and artifice. Look for ethical and forthright behavior in your potential mate. (*Famous examples:* Drew Barrymore, Richard Burton, Steffi Graf, Jack Nicholson, O. J. Simpson, Barbra Streisand.)

Venus in your chart's twelfth house. The planet's placement might instigate a strong sexual appetite, but it also increases your potential for
problems with women and romance. If you're female, you may find
that you just get along better with men.
There's a fundamental double standard
in courtship: men get labeled as studs,
women are branded as sluts (usually by
other women). Whether it's out of jealousy or for some other reason, the label
hurts. Avoid women who apply it in
anger, lest they use it on you. This factor
has the same effect on men: troubles
with women and romance. If you're
male, you might have trouble understanding how your friends can spend
time around women when all they seem
to do for you is cause trouble. (*Famous
examples:* Johnny Depp, Mia Farrow,
Bill Gates, Al Gore, Mikhail Gorbachev,
Goldie Hawn, the Reverend Dr. Martin
Luther King Jr., Madonna, Michelle
Pfeiffer, Kurt Russell, Ted Turner.)

Lord Krishna's passion for his
lover Radha is celebrated
annually in a festival held at the
Dauji Temple in Uttar Pradesh.
One legend narrates that *gopi*
(cowgirls) showered the loving
couple with brightly colored flower
petals when they saw them
together. To commemorate this
event, brilliant vegetable dyes are
mixed with water and showered
upon mobs of young women who
gather at the temple each year,
hoping to be blessed with a tender
husband by Lord Krishna.

With this additional information, Brad Pitt's astrologer would now know
that Venus's placement in the actor's third house quite possibly
grants him a love of life as well as strong desires. Combined with the
planet's association with Capricorn that we discovered in the previous
section, the practitioner might infer that Pitt has a lively and amorous
nature, which he keeps separate from his desire to marry the right
woman, who'll enhance his professional, financial, or social status.

You can't change where Venus was situated when you were born
to diminish its influences. However, Hindu astrologers often pair people who share the same planetary placements as a way to negate the
planet's less desirable effects. It's in this manner that the astrologer
helps a couple avoid the frustrations that can potentially occur when
one person is more romantic or passionate than the other.

Carnal Knowledge:
Mars's Sidereal Placement in Your Chart

Hindu astrologers consider the planet Mars to be the sex-drive planet, influencing love's physical side. This may sound good on paper, but this aggressive celestial body can spell trouble for a mismatched couple. Excessive ambition, competitiveness, and financial dilemmas that might spark matrimonial strife also come under Mars's aggressive sway. The planet's house placement in your chart and its association with a zodiac sign are combined by the astrologer into a synthesized interpretation, determining your carnal nature as well as your general ambitions and drives.

You don't need a *bhavacakra* to use this section. Simply enter your (and/or your mate's) birth date onto Worksheet 8. Using Table 6, look in the first column for the period in which your birth date falls, and in the second column find the zodiac sign associated with that period. (The dates listed are the starting dates for each period: your birth date should fall on or after the appropriate date, and before the date in the row below.) Enter that zodiac sign in the space provided on the worksheet. Do the same with your mate's Mars placement. Then locate the zodiac sign in the text following and read how your physical nature might affect your mate. Naturally, if you have a *bhavacakra,* look for Mars's symbol (MA) and note the zodiac sign associated with that planet on the worksheet. (Fig. 3 illustrates Mars's placement in Brad Pitt's *bhavacakra,* showing it to be in the second house and associated with the zodiac sign Sagittarius, number 9. A list of zodiac signs and their numbers appears on page 96.)

WORKSHEET 8. MARS'S *BHAVACAKRA* PLACEMENT

	Example:	Name A:	Name B:
	Brad Pitt		
Birth date	18 Dec 1963		
Mars's *bhavacakra* placement	9 (Sagittarius)		

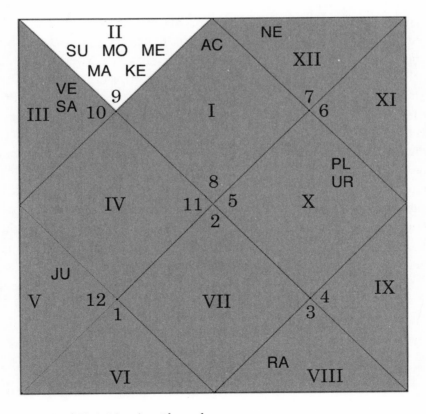

Figure 3. Brad Pitt's Mars in a *Bhavacakra*.

TABLE 6. SIDEREAL PLACEMENTS FOR MARS, 1927–1987

Starting Date	Zodiac Sign	Starting Date	Zodiac Sign
01 Jan 1927	Aries (♈)*	07 Oct 1930	Cancer (♋)
08 Feb 1927	Taurus (♉)	28 May 1931	Leo (♌)
05 Apr 1927	Gemini (♊)	21 Jul 1931	Virgo (♍)
26 May 1927	Cancer (♋)	07 Sep 1931	Libra (♎)
14 Jul 1927	Leo (♌)	21 Oct 1931	Scorpio (♏)
31 Aug 1927	Virgo (♍)	01 Dec 1931	Sagittarius (♐)
16 Oct 1927	Libra (♎)	09 Jan 1932	Capricorn (♑)
28 Nov 1927	Scorpio (♏)	16 Feb 1932	Aquarius (♒)
09 Jan 1928	Sagittarius (♐)	25 Mar 1932	Pisces (♓)
19 Feb 1928	Capricorn (♑)	03 May 1932	Aries (♈)
29 Mar 1928	Aquarius (♒)	13 Jun 1932	Taurus (♉)
08 May 1928	Pisces (♓)	25 Jul 1932	Gemini (♊)
17 Jun 1928	Aries (♈)	09 Sep 1932	Cancer (♋)
29 Jul 1928	Taurus (♉)	31 Oct 1932	Leo (♌)
18 Sep 1928	Gemini (♊)	23 Jun 1933	Virgo (♍)
10 Jan 1929	Taurus (♉)	15 Aug 1933	Libra (♎)
14 Feb 1929	Gemini (♊)	30 Sep 1933	Scorpio (♏)
30 Apr 1929	Cancer (♋)	10 Nov 1933	Sagittarius (♐)
23 Jun 1929	Leo (♌)	19 Dec 1933	Capricorn (♑)
11 Aug 1929	Virgo (♍)	26 Jan 1934	Aquarius (♒)
26 Sep 1929	Libra (♎)	05 Mar 1934	Pisces (♓)
09 Nov 1929	Scorpio (♏)	13 Apr 1934	Aries (♈)
20 Dec 1929	Sagittarius (♐)	24 May 1934	Taurus (♉)
29 Jan 1930	Capricorn (♑)	06 Jul 1934	Gemini (♊)
08 Mar 1930	Aquarius (♒)	20 Aug 1934	Cancer (♋)
16 Apr 1930	Pisces (♓)	07 Oct 1934	Leo (♌)
25 May 1930	Aries (♈)	28 Nov 1934	Virgo (♍)
05 Jul 1930	Taurus (♉)	11 Feb 1935	Libra (♎)
18 Aug 1930	Gemini (♊)	06 Sep 1935	Scorpio (♏)

* (starts at 15° Aries 22')

Starting Date	Zodiac Sign	Starting Date	Zodiac Sign
19 Oct 1935	Sagittarius (♐)	22 Mar 1940	Taurus (♉)
28 Nov 1935	Capricorn (♑)	07 May 1940	Gemini (♊)
06 Jan 1936	Aquarius (♒)	22 Jun 1940	Cancer (♋)
13 Feb 1936	Pisces (♓)	09 Aug 1940	Leo (♌)
23 Mar 1936	Aries (♈)	25 Sep 1940	Virgo (♍)
04 May 1936	Taurus (♉)	10 Nov 1940	Libra (♎)
16 Jun 1936	Gemini (♊)	25 Dec 1940	Scorpio (♏)
31 Jul 1936	Cancer (♋)	08 Feb 1941	Sagittarius (♐)
15 Sep 1936	Leo (♌)	23 Mar 1941	Capricorn (♑)
03 Nov 1936	Virgo (♍)	06 May 1941	Aquarius (♒)
24 Dec 1936	Libra (♎)	21 Jun 1941	Pisces (♓)
22 Feb 1937	Scorpio (♏)	28 Aug 1941	Aries (♈)
05 Jun 1937	Libra (♎)	23 Feb 1942	Taurus (♉)
21 Jul 1937	Scorpio (♏)	15 Apr 1942	Gemini (♊)
20 Sep 1937	Sagittarius (♐)	03 Jun 1942	Cancer (♋)
02 Nov 1937	Capricorn (♑)	21 Jul 1942	Leo (♌)
12 Dec 1937	Aquarius (♒)	07 Sep 1942	Virgo (♍)
21 Jan 1938	Pisces (♓)	22 Oct 1942	Libra (♎)
03 Mar 1938	Aries (♈)	06 Dec 1942	Scorpio (♏)
14 Apr 1938	Taurus (♉)	11 Jan 1943	Sagittarius (♐)
28 May 1938	Gemini (♊)	27 Feb 1943	Capricorn (♑)
12 Jul 1938	Cancer (♋)	08 Apr 1943	Aquarius (♒)
28 Aug 1938	Leo (♌)	18 May 1943	Pisces (♓)
14 Oct 1938	Virgo (♍)	28 Jun 1943	Aries (♈)
01 Dec 1938	Libra (♎)	12 Aug 1943	Taurus (♉)
18 Jan 1939	Scorpio (♏)	14 Mar 1944	Gemini (♊)
09 Mar 1939	Sagittarius (♐)	10 May 1944	Cancer (♋)
06 May 1939	Capricorn (♑)	01 Jul 1944	Leo (♌)
08 Nov 1939	Aquarius (♒)	18 Aug 1944	Virgo (♍)
25 Dec 1939	Pisces (♓)	03 Oct 1944	Libra (♎)
07 Feb 1940	Aries (♈)	16 Nov 1944	Scorpio (♏)

Starting Date	Zodiac Sign	Starting Date	Zodiac Sign
27 Dec 1944	Sagittarius (♐)	13 Mar 1949	Pisces (♓)
05 Feb 1945	Capricorn (♑)	21 Apr 1949	Aries (♈)
16 Mar 1945	Aquarius (♒)	31 May 1949	Taurus (♉)
24 Apr 1945	Pisces (♓)	13 Jul 1949	Gemini (♊)
02 Jun 1945	Aries (♈)	27 Aug 1949	Cancer (♋)
13 Jul 1945	Taurus (♉)	15 Oct 1949	Leo (♌)
27 Aug 1945	Gemini (♊)	10 Dec 1949	Virgo (♍)
23 Oct 1945	Cancer (♋)	30 Jul 1950	Libra (♎)
15 Jan 1946	Gemini (♊)	16 Sep 1950	Scorpio (♏)
05 Apr 1946	Cancer (♋)	28 Oct 1950	Sagittarius (♐)
08 Jun 1946	Leo (♌)	06 Dec 1950	Capricorn (♑)
29 Jul 1946	Virgo (♍)	14 Jan 1951	Aquarius (♒)
14 Sep 1946	Libra (♎)	21 Feb 1951	Pisces (♓)
28 Oct 1946	Scorpio (♏)	01 Apr 1951	Aries (♈)
08 Dec 1946	Sagittarius (♐)	12 May 1951	Taurus (♉)
16 Jan 1947	Capricorn (♑)	24 Jun 1951	Gemini (♊)
24 Feb 1947	Aquarius (♒)	08 Aug 1951	Cancer (♋)
03 Apr 1947	Pisces (♓)	24 Sep 1951	Leo (♌)
12 May 1947	Aries (♈)	12 Nov 1951	Virgo (♍)
21 Jun 1947	Taurus (♉)	06 Jan 1952	Libra (♎)
03 Aug 1947	Gemini (♊)	16 Aug 1952	Scorpio (♏)
19 Sep 1947	Cancer (♋)	02 Oct 1952	Sagittarius (♐)
14 Nov 1947	Leo (♌)	13 Nov 1952	Capricorn (♑)
29 Feb 1948	Cancer (♋)	22 Dec 1952	Aquarius (♒)
29 Apr 1948	Leo (♌)	30 Jan 1953	Pisces (♓)
05 Jul 1948	Virgo (♍)	11 Mar 1953	Aries (♈)
24 Aug 1948	Libra (♎)	21 Apr 1953	Taurus (♉)
07 Oct 1948	Scorpio (♏)	04 Jun 1953	Gemini (♊)
18 Nov 1948	Sagittarius (♐)	19 Jul 1953	Cancer (♋)
27 Dec 1948	Capricorn (♑)	05 Sep 1953	Leo (♌)
03 Feb 1949	Aquarius (♒)	21 Oct 1953	Virgo (♍)

Starting Date	Zodiac Sign	Starting Date	Zodiac Sign
09 Dec 1953	Libra (♎)	02 Sep 1958	Taurus (♉)
29 Jan 1954	Scorpio (♏)	18 Nov 1958	Aries (♈)
27 Mar 1954	Sagittarius (♐)	24 Jan 1958	Taurus (♉)
11 Oct 1954	Capricorn (♑)	29 Mar 1959	Gemini (♊)
25 Nov 1954	Aquarius (♒)	21 May 1959	Cancer (♋)
06 Jan 1955	Pisces (♓)	09 Jul 1959	Leo (♌)
17 Feb 1955	Aries (♈)	26 Aug 1959	Virgo (♍)
01 Apr 1955	Taurus (♉)	11 Oct 1959	Libra (♎)
16 May 1955	Gemini (♊)	24 Nov 1959	Scorpio (♏)
01 Jul 1955	Cancer (♋)	05 Jan 1960	Sagittarius (♐)
17 Aug 1955	Leo (♌)	14 Feb 1960	Capricorn (♑)
03 Oct 1955	Virgo (♍)	24 Mar 1960	Aquarius (♒)
18 Nov 1955	Libra (♎)	02 May 1960	Pisces (♓)
04 Jan 1956	Scorpio (♏)	11 Jun 1960	Aries (♈)
18 Feb 1956	Sagittarius (♐)	23 Jul 1960	Taurus (♉)
04 Apr 1956	Capricorn (♑)	09 Sep 1960	Gemini (♊)
22 May 1956	Aquarius (♒)	23 Apr 1961	Cancer (♋)
03 Aug 1956	Pisces (♓)	17 Jun 1961	Leo (♌)
17 Jan 1957	Aries (♈)	06 Aug 1961	Virgo (♍)
07 Mar 1957	Taurus (♉)	22 Sep 1961	Libra (♎)
24 Apr 1957	Gemini (♊)	04 Nov 1961	Scorpio (♏)
11 Jun 1957	Cancer (♋)	16 Dec 1961	Sagittarius (♐)
28 Jul 1957	Leo (♌)	24 Jan 1962	Capricorn (♑)
13 Sep 1957	Virgo (♍)	03 Mar 1962	Aquarius (♒)
30 Oct 1957	Libra (♎)	11 Apr 1962	Pisces (♓)
13 Dec 1957	Scorpio (♏)	20 May 1962	Aries (♈)
25 Jan 1958	Sagittarius (♐)	29 Jun 1962	Taurus (♉)
08 Mar 1958	Capricorn (♑)	12 Aug 1962	Gemini (♊)
18 Apr 1958	Aquarius (♒)	29 Sep 1962	Cancer (♋)
29 May 1958	Pisces (♓)	09 Dec 1962	Leo (♌)
11 Jul 1958	Aries (♈)	11 Jan 1963	Cancer (♋)

Starting Date	Zodiac Sign	Starting Date	Zodiac Sign
20 May 1963	Leo (♌)	30 Aug 1967	Scorpio (♏)
15 Jul 1963	Virgo (♍)	14 Oct 1967	Sagittarius (♐)
02 Sep 1963	Libra (♎)	23 Nov 1967	Capricorn (♑)
16 Oct 1963	Scorpio (♏)	01 Jan 1968	Aquarius (♒)
26 Nov 1963	Sagittarius (♐)	08 Feb 1968	Pisces (♓)
05 Jan 1964	Capricorn (♑)	19 Mar 1968	Aries (♈)
12 Feb 1964	Aquarius (♒)	29 Apr 1968	Taurus (♉)
21 Mar 1964	Pisces (♓)	11 Jun 1968	Gemini (♊)
28 Apr 1964	Aries (♈)	26 Jul 1968	Cancer (♋)
08 Jun 1964	Taurus (♉)	11 Sep 1968	Leo (♌)
21 Jul 1964	Gemini (♊)	29 Oct 1968	Virgo (♍)
04 Sep 1964	Cancer (♋)	18 Dec 1968	Libra (♎)
25 Oct 1964	Leo (♌)	11 Feb 1969	Scorpio (♏)
30 Dec 1964	Virgo (♍)	10 Sep 1969	Sagittarius (♐)
26 Feb 1965	Leo (♌)	26 Oct 1969	Capricorn (♑)
15 Jun 1965	Virgo (♍)	07 Dec 1969	Aquarius (♒)
10 Aug 1965	Libra (♎)	16 Jan 1970	Pisces (♓)
25 Sep 1965	Scorpio (♏)	26 Feb 1970	Aries (♈)
05 Nov 1965	Sagittarius (♐)	09 Apr 1970	Taurus (♉)
15 Dec 1965	Capricorn (♑)	23 May 1970	Gemini (♊)
22 Jan 1966	Aquarius (♒)	08 Jul 1970	Cancer (♋)
01 Mar 1966	Pisces (♓)	24 Aug 1970	Leo (♌)
09 Apr 1966	Aries (♈)	10 Oct 1970	Virgo (♍)
19 May 1966	Taurus (♉)	26 Nov 1970	Libra (♎)
01 Jul 1966	Gemini (♊)	13 Jan 1971	Scorpio (♏)
15 Aug 1966	Cancer (♋)	01 Mar 1971	Sagittarius (♐)
02 Oct 1966	Leo (♌)	21 Apr 1971	Capricorn (♑)
22 Nov 1966	Virgo (♍)	24 Oct 1971	Aquarius (♒)
23 Jan 1967	Libra (♎)	16 Dec 1971	Pisces (♓)
20 Apr 1967	Virgo (♍)	31 Jan 1972	Aries (♈)
04 Jul 1967	Libra (♎)	17 Mar 1972	Taurus (♉)

Starting Date	Zodiac Sign	Starting Date	Zodiac Sign
02 May 1972	Gemini (♊)	12 Nov 1976	Scorpio (♏)
18 Jun 1972	Cancer (♋)	23 Dec 1976	Sagittarius (♐)
05 Aug 1972	Leo (♌)	01 Feb 1977	Capricorn (♑)
21 Sep 1972	Virgo (♍)	12 Mar 1977	Aquarius (♒)
06 Nov 1972	Libra (♎)	19 Apr 1977	Pisces (♓)
21 Dec 1972	Scorpio (♏)	28 May 1977	Aries (♈)
03 Feb 1973	Sagittarius (♐)	08 Jul 1977	Taurus (♉)
17 Mar 1973	Capricorn (♑)	22 Aug 1977	Gemini (♊)
29 Apr 1973	Aquarius (♒)	13 Oct 1977	Cancer (♋)
11 Jun 1973	Pisces (♓)	20 Feb 1978	Gemini (♊)
30 Jul 1973	Aries (♈)	17 Mar 1978	Cancer (♋)
15 Feb 1974	Taurus (♉)	02 Jun 1978	Leo (♌)
09 Apr 1974	Gemini (♊)	25 Jul 1978	Virgo (♍)
29 May 1974	Cancer (♋)	10 Sep 1978	Libra (♎)
17 Jul 1974	Leo (♌)	24 Oct 1978	Scorpio (♏)
03 Sep 1974	Virgo (♍)	04 Dec 1978	Sagittarius (♐)
18 Oct 1974	Libra (♎)	12 Jan 1979	Capricorn (♑)
01 Dec 1974	Scorpio (♏)	19 Feb 1979	Aquarius (♒)
13 Jan 1975	Sagittarius (♐)	29 Mar 1979	Pisces (♓)
22 Feb 1975	Capricorn (♑)	07 May 1979	Aries (♈)
03 Apr 1975	Aquarius (♒)	17 Jun 1979	Taurus (♉)
13 May 1975	Pisces (♓)	30 Jul 1979	Gemini (♊)
22 Jun 1975	Aries (♈)	14 Sep 1979	Cancer (♋)
04 Aug 1975	Taurus (♉)	06 Nov 1979	Leo (♌)
28 Sep 1975	Gemini (♊)	29 Jun 1980	Virgo (♍)
16 Dec 1975	Taurus (♉)	19 Aug 1980	Libra (♎)
02 Mar 1976	Gemini (♊)	03 Oct 1980	Scorpio (♏)
05 May 1976	Cancer (♋)	13 Nov 1980	Sagittarius (♐)
26 Jun 1976	Leo (♌)	23 Dec 1980	Capricorn (♑)
14 Aug 1976	Virgo (♍)	30 Jan 1981	Aquarius (♒)
29 Sep 1976	Libra (♎)	09 Mar 1981	Pisces (♓)

Starting Date	Zodiac Sign	Starting Date	Zodiac Sign
17 Apr 1981	Aries (♈)	17 Dec 1984	Aquarius (♒)
27 May 1981	Taurus (♉)	25 Jan 1985	Pisces (♓)
09 Jul 1981	Gemini (♊)	06 Mar 1985	Aries (♈)
23 Aug 1981	Cancer (♋)	17 Apr 1985	Taurus (♉)
10 Oct 1981	Leo (♌)	31 May 1985	Gemini (♊)
03 Dec 1981	Virgo (♍)	15 Jul 1985	Cancer (♋)
23 Jul 1982	Libra (♎)	31 Aug 1985	Leo (♌)
10 Sep 1982	Scorpio (♏)	17 Oct 1985	Virgo (♍)
23 Oct 1982	Sagittarius (♐)	04 Dec 1985	Libra (♎)
02 Dec 1982	Capricorn (♑)	22 Jan 1986	Scorpio (♏)
09 Jan 1983	Aquarius (♒)	16 Mar 1986	Sagittarius (♐)
17 Feb 1983	Pisces (♓)	26 Sep 1986	Capricorn (♑)
28 Mar 1983	Aries (♈)	16 Nov 1986	Aquarius (♒)
08 May 1983	Taurus (♉)	30 Dec 1986	Pisces (♓)
20 Jun 1983	Gemini (♊)	11 Feb 1987	Aries (♈)
04 Aug 1983	Cancer (♋)	27 Mar 1987	Taurus (♉)
20 Sep 1983	Leo (♌)	11 May 1987	Gemini (♊)
07 Nov 1983	Virgo (♍)	27 Jun 1987	Cancer (♋)
30 Dec 1983	Libra (♎)	13 Aug 1987	Leo (♌)
07 Mar 1984	Scorpio (♏)	29 Sep 1987	Virgo (♍)
26 Sep 1984	Sagittarius (♐)	14 Nov 1987	Libra (♎)
07 Nov 1984	Capricorn (♑)	30 Dec 1987	Scorpio (♏)

These dates are derived from calculations using *The American Ephemeris for the Twentieth Century* (San Diego: ACS Publications, 1980–1996) and the latitude and longitude for New York City at noon, and applying the Lahiri *ayanamsa* for each year to its placement.

Mars in Aries. You're naturally inclined to be a quarrelsome person, and are incapable of keeping secrets or concealing your emotions. But this placement generally indicates Mars has little negative affect on your physically intimate relationships. What do ulcers, high blood pressure, and heart attacks have in common? Each is aggravated by the internalization of stress. It's healthy to let off steam. However, these illnesses can also be worsened in loved ones who become the brunt of too much released stress. Find constructive ways to let go. As far as secrets are concerned, sometimes the most respected person in a group says, "Don't even tell me!" Also, a person who keeps no secrets has to be honest. (*Famous examples:* John Derek, Madonna.)

Mars in Taurus. Danger from adultery tends to loom in the shadows of your sex life. You're also inclined to cause harm to women or be harmed by women. Your marriage could be potentially jeopardized by either of these indications if you don't monitor their potential existence. Commitment in a relationship means that your partner comes before your friends. Always. This doesn't mean forsaking friendship, but what sort of a friend puts themselves between you and your mate, instigating unnecessary gossip or luring you away for an illicit tryst? (*Famous examples:* Antonio Banderas, Catherine Deneuve, the Reverend Dr. Martin Luther King Jr., Courtney Love, Arnold Schwarzenegger, O. J. Simpson.)

Mars in Gemini. Sudden or unexpected financial losses could cause matrimonial distress. But this placement also indicates Mars has little negative affect on your physically intimate relationships. Furthermore, you develop sexual urges early in life. Some things are more valuable than money. Friendships might not top the list, but they're pretty close. However, even friendships can be compromised by poor choices in sexual relationships. Choose wisely and with restraint. Don't worry too much about short-term finances as long as your long-term savings are on track. (*Famous examples:* John F. Kennedy Jr., Barbra Streisand.)

Mars in Cancer. You tend to nurse negative emotions such as anger and anguish for long periods of time. Within an enduring relationship such as wedlock, this can create resentment and pain where compassion and forgiveness are mandated. Happiness doesn't come from a life without troubles. Everyone has them. It stems from your ability to release painful feelings. It isn't necessary to forget to forgive. Just remember, once you have forgiven an injury it should never be spoken of again, especially in anger. (*Famous examples:* Brigitte Bardot, Candice Bergen, Humphrey Bogart, Cher, Hillary Rodham Clinton, Ray

Davies, Harrison Ford, Michael J. Fox, Mikhail Gorbachev, Al Gore, Goldie Hawn, Diane Keaton.)

Mars in Leo. Your ability to be an aggressive opponent serves you well in business, but it's your inclination to forgive your mate that makes your relationship work. Your libido emerges early in life, so be careful. A victorious conquest, gained in haste, can cost more than it's worth in the long run. Beware of what you pursue. Make sure it's what you want. (*Famous examples:* Ben Affleck, George W. Bush, Sir Michael Caine, Johnny Depp, Melanie Griffith, Richie Sambora, Brooke Shields, Donald Trump, Princess Diana Spencer Windsor.)

In Barar, a man who had been married twice and wished to wed again married a mudar tree, which was considered to be his third wife, before taking the hand of his next wife. No reputable father would ever permit his daughter to become a man's third wife: it was believed to be an unlucky position for both the bride and her family. In the simple ceremony, the man sat next to the tree, and turmeric-dyed rice was tossed over him and at the tree by a priest. The man was then free to marry a fourth wife, who was human.

Mars in Virgo. You may crave fame or power, but you might encounter downfalls, obstacles, reversals, and struggles of a bizarre nature throughout your life. You may wed someone from a lower class than yourself, which may work for your sex life. Your spouse might, however, impede your professional or social ambitions. Who's the winner in this game of life? Is it the one with all the chips at his or her end of the table? Hardly. The precious few who find happiness, hold on to it, and roll with the punches come out ahead in the long run. (*Famous examples:* Kim Basinger, Bill Clinton, Michael Douglas, Bill Gates, Tipper Gore, Pamela Anderson Lee, John Lennon, Elvis Presley, Maria Shriver, Britney Spears, Ted Turner, Prince William Windsor.)

Mars in Libra. You're romantically impulsive and tend to delay thoughts about matrimony. But there may be a good reason why. An early marriage might bust up in a monumental argument. Or a previous heartbreak might cause you to doubt the possibility of total commitment. This placement, however, also indicates Mars has little negative affect on your physically intimate relationships, developing your libido before your twenty-first birthday. "When you really want love," said playwright Oscar Wilde, "you will find it waiting for you." Just be certain you're ready for it. (*Famous examples:* Richard Burton, Kurt Cobain, Heather Locklear.)

Mars in Scorpio. Although you're known by some people for your cold disregard of others' feelings, this perception certainly doesn't influence your sex life. You may have satisfactory liaisons and a beneficial marriage, although you may have to occasionally remind some people that you have a heart, emotions, and strong passions. Others will see it instantly, but only rarely will it be someone you find attractive. Fortunately, when it's mutual, you won't need anyone to point it out. It'll be obvious. Work hard to be open and tender to your mate. (*Famous examples:* Warren Beatty, Steffi Graf, Jack Nicholson, John Travolta, Oprah Winfrey, Prince Charles Windsor.)

Mars in Sagittarius. You may speak and act impulsively with your new lover. But you may not disclose the fact that you've been married more than once (speaking of impulsive acts). It better to have loved and *learned* than never to have loved at all, as long as you know when it's time to move on. "One makes mistakes: that is life," wrote French novelist Romain Rolland. "But it is never quite a mistake to have loved." Also, during the time you're married, you may have some concerns over your mate's health. However, this placement indicates Mars has little negative affect on your physically intimate relationships. (*Famous examples:* David Bowie, George Harrison, Katharine Hepburn, Brad Pitt, Julia Roberts, Steven Spielberg.)

Mars in Capricorn. Serious ambitions for public life and for wealth may influence your lifestyle. You may marry someone who's older or, surprisingly, from a lower social class while you're still young. A hockey team takes to the ice with six players, a marriage takes on the world with two teammates. Choose wisely if your goal is to win. Your ambitions will be better met by someone with more maturity than by someone who might drop the ball in social situations. Love impulsively, but commit carefully. (*Famous examples:* Woody Allen, Drew Barrymore, Julie Christie, Mia Farrow, Bridget Fonda, Carolyn Bessette Kennedy.)

Mars in Aquarius. You may have very abrupt patterns of speech or mannerisms that could offend your lover. An ambitious and highly independent nature may also deter you from focusing your attentions on romance. Mars has little negative effect on your sex life overall, stimulating your libido early in life. There's a secret that romance novelists and mystery writers know: it's not what actually happens, but what could happen, what might happen, what's going to happen, that excites readers. That's why it takes a few hundred pages to build up to the story's climax. Getting there is more than half the fun. And yes, it's the same in life. It's the smiles, first tentative kisses, time spent strolling hand in hand that really ignite the sparks in a relationship, not going to bed together. (*Famous examples:* Lauren Bacall, Eric Clapton, Bo Derek, Jane Fonda, Steffi Graf, Michelle Pfeiffer, Elizabeth Taylor, Justin Timberlake, Dwight Yoakam.)

Mars in Pisces. Indecisiveness is quite possibly the reason you endure numerous romantic disappointments and potentially more than one marriage. To know someone is to see his or her faults. To love someone is to accept those faults. Everyone has them. That fascinating new face may appear to be unblemished by imperfections, but that's just because you haven't stared at it long enough. Don't mistake new love for perfect love. (*Famous examples:* Prince, Debbie Reynolds, Kurt Russell, Spencer Tracy.)

Using Brad Pitt as an example, the astrologer might determine from his planet Mars's association with Sagittarius that he may admit to speaking and acting impulsively but may not disclose to his new lover whether he'd previously been married once or had an earlier serious relationship. This information will then be coupled with Mars's location in his chart to derive a complete reading of Mars's sway over his drives and ambitions.

♥ ♥ ♥

The placement of Mars in your birth chart enhances the description of your sex life, indicating what sort of everyday domestic, financial, or business stresses could cause strife in the bedroom. **You'll need your** *bhavacakra* **to use this particular section.** Enter your (and/or your mate's) birth date onto Worksheet 9. If you already have a *bhavacakra*, look for the Mars symbol (MA), then note the number of the house it occupies. (On page 128, fig. 3 highlights Mars's placement in the second house of Brad Pitt's *bhavacakra*.) Enter that house number in the space provided on the worksheet. Do the same with your mate's Mars placement. Then locate the house number in the text following and read about this planet's additional influence.

WORKSHEET 9. MARS'S *BHAVACAKRA* HOUSE LOCATION

	Example:	Name A:	Name B:
	Brad Pitt		
Birth date	18 Dec 1963		
Mars's **bhavacakra** **house location**	11 (second house)		

Mars in your chart's first house. The planet's placement can potentially incite matrimonial strife. Your union could be harmed by fate. It's been said that the strongest bond is a shared adversary. It is strange that shared adversity can put such an enormous strain on a relationship. Maintain emotional and physical distance. Self-sufficiency is paramount for survival, even in a good marriage. (*Famous examples:* Carolyn Bessette Kennedy, Brooke Shields, Maria Shriver.)

Mars in your chart's second house. Your mutual finances might be shaken up by Mars's influence. This planet may also instigate marital and family difficulties, stemming from financial worries. It's a sad truth that finances can disrupt happiness. It might help if you don't pool your money. Separate accounts don't mean separate lives. In fact, this simple solution can help preserve sanity. The big trick is to not dwell on monetary issues. If you enjoy what you're doing together, it will soften the woes. (*Famous examples:* Antonio Banderas, Kim Basinger, George W. Bush, Bill Clinton, Hillary Rodham Clinton, Johnny Depp, Carrie Fisher, Al Gore, Brad Pitt, Donald Trump.)

Mars in your chart's third house. Mars's placement creates intense desires but has little negative impact on your marital relationship. *I want. I need. I crave:* you've thought these words, you've said them, and you've meant them. Surprisingly, others might not have these feelings as often or as intensely as you do. Take care to weigh your priorities and to treat others' desires as you would have them treat yours. (*Famous examples:* Ben Affleck, Warren Beatty, Humphrey Bogart, Sir Michael Caine, Kurt Cobain, George Harrison, Katharine Hepburn, the Reverend Dr. Martin Luther King Jr.)

Mars in your chart's fourth house. The planet's position can cause strife at home and potential conflicts with either your mother or your mate's mother. You choose your friends, you tolerate your relatives. Your marriage could also potentially be harmed by fate. It's better to maintain distance from a parental adversary than to face him or her, as people tend to judge you on how well you get along with your parents. Rebellion is expected when you're a teenager, and it ends when you get tired of being treated like one. Some people never seem to understand that parents are at least as human as they are. Once you forgive their imperfections, there's nothing left to rebel against. In the case of an in-law, remember one important rule: Blood is thicker than marriage. (*Famous examples:* David Bowie, Tipper Gore, Richie Sambora, Oprah Winfrey.)

Mars in your chart's fifth house. You may fail in the performance of good deeds because of Mars's placement, which can ultimately reflect on your marriage. At times when you try hard but don't succeed, you hope to at least receive an A for effort as a consolation prize. The trouble is, others might see only the failure. As hard as it seems, there are times when only success counts. Fix that which can be fixed and move on. (*Famous examples:* Melanie Griffith, Pamela Anderson Lee, Elizabeth Taylor, Justin Timberlake.)

Mars in your chart's sixth house. Your strong libido (instigated by Mars's position) can be good or bad for your marriage, depending on your mate's planetary placement. Passion is healthy for a union only when it's between the two who said, "I do." If one person has a higher sex drive than the other, it takes a bit of comprehension and compassion on both sides to make the relationship work. (*Famous examples:* Woody Allen, Eric Clapton, Catherine Deneuve, John Derek, Mikhail Gorbachev, Steffi Graf, Jack Nicholson, Julia Roberts, Steven Spielberg.)

Edward Thurston reported in 1906 that Brahmans in southern India traditionally performed an unusual rite prior to a wedding. The bride was dressed up as the groom and another girl was dressed up as the bride. Then they were paraded through the streets. When they finished, the bride, still dressed as the groom, confronted her future husband. During this meeting, she tossed insults at the real groom, accusing him of theft and indulging in a mock fight. It's presumed that this was her opportunity to say all the things she shouldn't say once they were married, and also to let him know what sort of wrath he might encounter if he ever wronged his wife.

Mars in your chart's seventh house. Matrimonial conflicts and confrontations may be ignited by Mars's influence. It's all too easy to fall into a pattern of antagonism with your mate. Look at how many marriages end in divorce. Arguments are inevitable, but they shouldn't be frequent. Take walks together. Be good to each other. There are times in marriage when the only way to win in the long run is to lose the argument. Don't be the first to give in and fight. Don't be the last to give up a fight. (*Famous examples:* Debbie Reynolds, John Travolta, Dwight Yoakam.)

Mars in your chart's eighth house. Your joint finances may be disrupted by difficulties with property and legacies caused by Mars's position. Your marriage could also be potentially harmed by trouble with your spouse's finances. Inheritance is the money we wait for throughout our lives, at the peril of our own success. Spoken words are worth the paper on which they're printed. Even between loved ones, financial and property matters need to be spelled out, signed, and understood. (*Famous examples:* Lauren Bacall, Julie Christie, Jane Fonda, Michael J. Fox, Goldie Hawn, Courtney Love.)

Mars in your chart's ninth house. Mars's placement could bring agony instigated by your father or your mate's father, which can ultimately affect your marriage. It's better to maintain distance from a paternal adversary than to face him, as people tend to judge you by your relationship with your father. Rebellion is part of growing up. It ends when you get tired of being treated like a child. Your father is at least as human as you are. Once you forgive his imperfections, there's no reason to rebel. Remember that blood is thicker than marriage when it comes to a relationship with an in-law. (*Famous examples:* Brigitte Bardot, Candice Bergen, Richard Burton, Heather Locklear, Madonna.)

Mars in your chart's tenth house. The planet's position creates potential conflicts with either your parents or your mate's parents, trickling down to your marriage. It's better to maintain distance from parental adversaries than to face them. People tend to judge you by how you relate to your parents and, to a lesser degree, your in-laws. You may not always believe that your parents are at least as human as you are. Once you forgive their imperfections, there's little cause for rebellion. Have patience with them as they're not likely to change. In the case of an in-law, also remember that blood is thicker than marriage. (*Famous examples:* Diane Keaton, Michelle Pfeiffer, Kurt Russell, O. J. Simpson, Ted Turner, Princess Diana Spencer Windsor, Prince William Windsor.)

Mars in your chart's eleventh house. Your siblings or your mate's siblings could potentially cause a rift in your marital bliss because of the planet's placement. We worry about acceptance by our mate's family. We should also worry about being so accepted that we're dragged into sibling rivalry and other squabbles. The blood that binds siblings

doesn't extend to siblings-in-law, and fights can be permanently detrimental, especially because there's no guarantee your partner will
take your side. Siblings often hold equal footing to a spouse. A little
respectful distance can preserve a relationship. If things get ugly, re-
sort to good manners and minimal contact. (*Famous examples:* Harrison Ford, Bill Gates, John F. Kennedy Jr., Elvis Presley.)

Mars in your chart's twelfth house. Mars's influence might stimulate a
strong libido, which can potentially disrupt your romantic life and marriage, depending on your mate's planetary placement. Sexual compatibility is vital to the success of an enduring relationship. The
nature of physical intimacy can and often does change between two
people over time. There are few surprises and there might be times of
boredom. However, like a couple learning to dance compared to a
couple who have danced together for years, there's much that improves over time. (*Famous examples:* Bo Derek, Michael Douglas, Arnold
Schwarzenegger, Spencer Tracy.)

From Mars's placement in Brad Pitt's second house, an astrologer
might surmise that mutual finances could be a shaky prospect between the actor and his spouse unless they maintain separate bank
accounts. A practitioner might add that, coupled with the planet's
association with Sagittarius, his impulsiveness could be the crux of
the problem. A previous experience or two could also instigate the
need for a clean discussion about expenses and investments.

♥ ♥ ♥

As is the case with Venus, you can't change where Mars was situated
when you were born to diminish its confrontational or aggressive
influences. Hindu astrologers, however, often pair people who share
the same planetary placements to negate the planet's less desirable
effects. Two people who are driven toward the same desires and goals
at the same rate of speed and strength make perfect allies. A couple
whose energy is lopsided or directed onto opposite paths only dimin-

ish their mutual potential for achievement within this lifetime. Some practitioners further believe Mars's initial sway diminishes after your thirtieth birthday. Maturity before marriage does have its advantages after all!

The Marriage Killer: Ketu's Sidereal Placement in Your Chart

Ketu represents the midpoint between the Sun and Moon's orbital paths in the Hindu tradition. (In Western astrology, this imaginary point is called the Moon's South Node, or Dragon's Tail.) According to practitioners, this aggressive celestial point spells marital troubles for a couple if it occupies certain houses in either the bride's or the groom's *bhavacakra*. In fact, Ketu's interpretations do point to facets of your personality or lifestyle that might be a cause of concern for your mate, creating a need for compromise, increased self-control, or clear communication.

You'll need your *bhavacakra* to use this particular section. Enter your (and/or your mate's) birth date onto Worksheet 10. If you already have a *bhavacakra*, look for Ketu's symbol (KE), note the number of the house it occupies, and enter that house number in the space provided on the worksheet. Do the same with your mate's Ketu placement. Locate the house number in the following text and read what quirks in your own personality or lifestyle might grate on your mate's nerves.

Fig. 4 highlights Ketu's location in the second house of Brad Pitt's *bhavacakra*.

WORKSHEET 10. KETU'S *BHAVACAKRA* HOUSE LOCATION

	Example:	Name A:	Name B:
	Brad Pitt		
Birth date	18 Dec 1963		
Ketu's ***bhavacakra*** **house location**	11 (second house)		

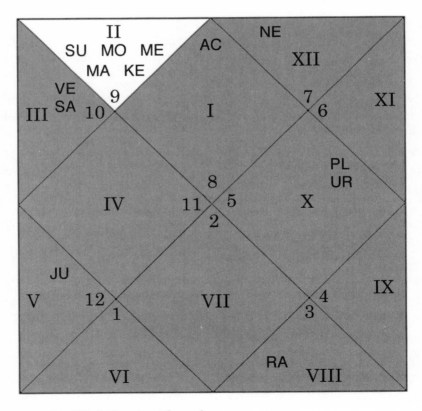

Figure 4. Brad Pitt's Ketu in a *Bhavacakra*.

Ketu in your chart's first house. Your introspective and somewhat spiritual nature may create marital difficulties. For anyone who has discovered their personal path, finding peace is a simple matter of introspection. Once found, inner peace is seductive. There's a temptation to spend a lot of time within yourself. However, this can cause matrimonial strife as it hampers communication and other delicate bonds. A relationship is what happens *between* two people, not just *to* two people who are together. (*Famous examples:* Candice Bergen, Melanie Griffith, Goldie Hawn, Heather Locklear, Debbie Reynolds, Prince William Windsor.)

Ketu in your chart's second house. You tend to own few possessions because your finances might be limited. Although it may not seem like it in this materialistic world, this gives you a great advantage over other people. Human beings are truly possessed by their possessions. Every item you own requires a tiny portion of your attention. These add up to a huge chunk of your life spent as a servant to your car, your house, and your entertainment devices. A mind uncluttered is a mind unfettered. You might also encounter confrontations with your spouse because you don't always present the facts that surround a situation. It's always better to be forthright than to have your mate discover the facts elsewhere. Your spouse is an extension of yourself and will uncover the truth sooner or later. (*Famous examples:* Ben Affleck, Humphrey Bogart, Catherine Deneuve, John Derek, Brad Pitt.)

Ketu in your chart's third house. You may find that your desires are fulfilled easily. Strange as it might seem, this could ignite serious bouts of sibling rivalry, which can ricochet in your mate's direction. It'd be easy for others to celebrate your success if your success didn't highlight their lack of it by comparison. A jealous sibling might find an outlet for his or her frustration by attacking or belittling your spouse. When family attacks family, never side with the attacker. That's like pouring gasoline on a fire. If the attacker is right, find a middle ground (except in extreme cases such as physical abuse). (*Famous examples:* David Bowie, Sir Michael Caine, Kurt Cobain, Bo

Derek, Michael J. Fox, Diane Keaton, Courtney Love, Kurt Russell, O. J. Simpson, John Travolta.)

Ketu in your chart's fourth house. You may encounter some problems with your home or your mother, which might grate on your mate's nerves. Respect is the key to the prevention of strife. If your partner complains about an issue, take that complaint seriously. Be genuine. Be heartfelt in your efforts to remedy the situation. Your mate will be grateful and careful in the future not to complain unless it's serious. The quickest way to gain respect is to give respect. In this instance, respect means the willingness to change and compromise for the sake of your relationship. (*Famous examples:* Eric Clapton, Bill Clinton, Michael Douglas, Steffi Graf, Katharine Hepburn, Julia Roberts, Brooke Shields, Justin Timberlake, Princess Diana Spencer Windsor.)

Ketu in your chart's fifth house. Ketu appears to limit the number of children you might have. This was once considered a curse. In centuries past, there was a reason a large family was vital. More children meant more hands to work the land, and insurance against high infant mortality rates. These days a child needs far more parental attention and supervision. Children born into smaller families have a major asset: attentive, doting parents. There's also the possibility that your offspring may be introspective rather than extroverted in their approach to life. (*Famous examples:* George W. Bush, Carrie Fisher, Al Gore, Tipper Gore, George Harrison, Steven Spielberg, Donald Trump, Ted Turner.)

Ketu in your chart's sixth house. You're inclined to experience difficulties with coworkers or employees. (If you're a student, this aspect applies to classmates.) Coworkers become a second family after a while. This, unfortunately, leads to a general breakdown of professionalism and can give rise to sibling-style rivalries and squabbles. It can be even worse if there are promotions, commissions, or other prizes at stake. The real trouble, however, begins when you bring your job-related frustrations home with you. If you can't leave the stress at work, expect repercussions at home. It might not seem fair, but your spouse is just as human, just as sensitive to stress, and just as tired at the end of the day. Your mate really wants to be able to share good times with you. (*Famous examples:* Hillary Rodham Clinton, Harrison Ford, Johnny Depp, Pamela Anderson Lee, Arnold Schwarzenegger, Spencer Tracy.)

Ketu in your chart's seventh house. Your marriage tends to fluctuate through high and low periods. The union may also be unusual in some way. But then, whose match doesn't seem eccentric? If you'd like to add more highs, keep a relationship diary, but write down only the good occasions. Even little things, like a nice kiss or hug, count. When you're feeling down, read your diary. You may also have a very eccentric or individualist spouse, but this isn't necessarily a negative element in your life or your relationship. If you're going to spend the rest of your life with someone, that person might as well be lively. (*Famous examples:* Lauren Bacall, Bill Gates, John F. Kennedy Jr.)

Ketu in your chart's eighth house. Unhappiness at home experienced during childhood or adolescence, or a chronic illness, might exert some stress on your marriage. Marry a person and you are wedded to his or her past. You bring a bit of baggage with you into a relationship. Some of it you lose as you mature, but sometimes it takes counseling or therapy to help you work through outside issues that stand in the way of your happiness. As for chronic illness, the vow "in sickness and in health" is one that you hope you can live up to if the time comes, while you quietly pray that it never does. It might also be tempting for an ailing spouse to try to break away to free the other from the burden of caring for them. Don't let a relationship be shattered by health or by love. (*Famous example:* Mikhail Gorbachev.)

During Vedic times (circa 1500 B.C.), it was a sin for a younger brother to marry before his elder brother. If he did, he could absolve his sin in a simple ceremony. Reed grass was placed on his stomach as he lay on his back on the ground. The shafts were then washed on his stomach, sprinkled with water, and thrown into a fast-moving stream. It was believed that the foam from the rushing current transported his sin away.

Ketu in your chart's ninth house. Business and travel-related problems are experienced by everyone at some point or another. Okay, so you might have more than your fair share of obstacles and delays, but it isn't necessary to carry that baggage home as a souvenir. Fortunately, there's a lot more to life than travel. Make your home a favorite destination for yourself, your spouse, friends, and relatives. When you have to travel have patience, and be very good to your mate. (*Famous examples:* Brigitte Bardot, Warren Beatty, the Reverend Dr. Martin Luther King Jr., Madonna, Elvis Presley, Maria Shriver.)

Ketu in your chart's tenth house. You might encounter professional or social success, fulfilling your deep-seated ambitions. While you ascend this steep ladder, remember to bring your mate along for the ride as an amenable copilot or front-seat passenger. A great politician keeps a few trusted advisers, surrounding himself or herself with profound thinkers and a spouse. It should put you at ease (not that it'll ever come to it) that a spouse can't testify against you in court. A mate gives a more honest reflection than a mirror. (*Famous examples:* Julie Christie, Dwight Yoakam.)

Ketu in your chart's eleventh house. You may derive a certain portion of your wealth from freelance work or hobbies. One person's labor is another's love. There's a little entrepreneur in you, which you should set free. Recreation doesn't have to be unprofitable. You also tend to attract unusual friends. Think of your mate as a social barometer. Is the new friend you've brought home fascinating, or creepy? Watch and respect your spouse's opinion. At times like these a mate can be the set of objective eyes we always wish we'd had in the back of our heads. (*Famous examples:* Woody Allen, Antonio Banderas, Jane Fonda, Carolyn Bessette Kennedy, Richie Sambora.)

Ketu in your chart's twelfth house. You're inclined to experience romantic and sexual problems. This is such a broad area that it's difficult to give you advice except to say that you should be on the lookout for trouble. And you should try to fix it rather than live with it. You also find it difficult to save money, which can place stress on your and your mate's plans for the future. There are a whole lot of people out there who have devoted their lives to the failure of your savings plan. It's not the extra pair of shoes (actually it is, but there's more to it) so much as the service charges for unused extras on the phone bill, the credit card interest, and all of life's little luxuries that advertisers convince us are necessities. Write down every expense for a month or two. You might be horrified by what you see. (*Famous examples:* Kim Basinger, Richard Burton, Jack Nicholson, Michelle Pfeiffer, Elizabeth Taylor, Oprah Winfrey.)

Actor Brad Pitt's Ketu in his chart's second house suggests to the astrologer that he tends to own few possessions because his finances might be limited from time to time. This factor often creates major marital strife. If he should be wedded to a person who derives pleasure from luxurious and expensive items, his relationship might be strained because he lacks interest in shopping sprees and the exhilaration of acquisition.

You can't change where Ketu was situated when you were born to diminish its influences. This doesn't mean a person born with Ketu in an inopportune position could never have a happy marriage. Hindu astrologers would match you to someone with a similar placement, using the double negative to cancel out its undesirable effects. The astrologer may also recommend an amulet made of cat's-eye stone to ward off Ketu's weakened influence.

The Matchmaker:
The Moon's Sidereal Placement in Your Chart

Using short stories and narratives, the *Nilamata Purana* is one of over a dozen works that explain the complicated religious concepts found in the vedas and dharmasutras, which are the Hindu equivalents of sacred Judaic, Islamic, and Christian texts. This epic volume tells us that "women get beautiful form and great prosperity, so the Full Moon nights should be specially observed by women." Despite this gender-specific instruction, in Hindu culture, the Moon is valued by both sexes.

Whether you're male or female, your personal *naksatra* (lunar mansion) is very important to your marital compatibility, revealing a great deal about your emotional makeup. In the same way that the Moon's orbit around the earth is seen as a path that passes twenty-eight fixed stars in Chinese astrology, this orbital pattern follows a course of twenty-seven fixed stars in the Hindu discipline. When the Moon passes by one of these fixed stars, it's said to enter a particular *naksatra*. When you're born, the Moon's placement is determined by the *naksatra* it entered at that moment. Astrologers use this information for three purposes. First, it serves as the basis for calculating your *vimsottari dasa* (timeline), which we'll discuss later. Second, like the Chinese *sieu* (lunar mansions), the *naksatra* for a chosen day indicates whether it's a lucky day to perform a wedding ceremony (this will be discussed later in this chapter). Third, it provides general information about your character, suggesting how you potentially shape up as a matrimonial prospect in your future mate's eyes.

You'll need your *bhavacakra* to use this particular section. Simply enter your (and/or your mate's) birth date onto Worksheet 11. Look for the Moon's symbol (MO) in the *naksatra* list that accompanies your *bhavacakra* (Fig. 5 illustrates the Moon's *naksatra* in Brad Pitt's *bhavacakra)*, entering that information in the worksheet space. Locate the *naksatra* in the text that follows and read how you fare as a potential spouse through someone else's eyes.

WORKSHEET 11. BIRTH *NAKSATRA*

	Example:	Name A:	Name B:
	Brad Pitt		
Birth date	18 Dec 1963		
Birth *naksatra*	Uttarasadha 29°SAG14'42"		

The Moon in *naksatra* Asvini. You're inclined to be very moral yet passionate, speaking and acting with a positive outlook. Heroes are frequently born under this *naksatra,* and so are good speakers. These

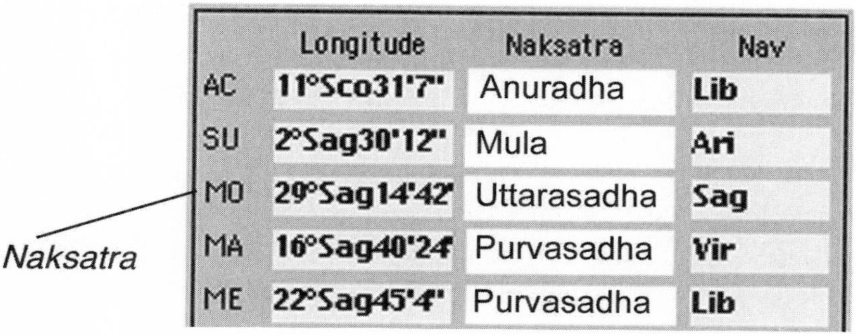

	Longitude	Naksatra	Nav
AC	11°Sco31'7"	Anuradha	Lib
SU	2°Sag30'12"	Mula	Ari
MO	29°Sag14'42"	Uttarasadha	Sag
MA	16°Sag40'24"	Purvasadha	Vir
ME	22°Sag45'4"	Purvasadha	Lib

Naksatra

Figure 5. Brad Pitt's *Naksatra* in a *Bhavacakra*.

public figures are just as scared as anyone else would be in their shoes. Maybe even more so. Fear boosts their adrenaline, which gives them a jolt of energy. They learn to channel that energy. The result might appear to be a superhuman performance, but we're all human. You can prevail in any trial if you just harness the force that surges up within you and tells you to run away. (*Famous examples:* Lauren Bacall, Michael J. Fox, Pamela Anderson Lee, Heather Locklear.)

The Moon in *naksatra* Bharani. You tend to be very sexual, often unforgiving, and preoccupied with material gain. You may also have a small family. Forgiveness is a virtue. Self-preservation is a necessity. Knowing which to lean toward is an art. Do you fight to the death when you're wronged, or do you let water pass under the bridge and move on with life? Be good to your family and your mate. A heartfelt hug costs nothing yet it has a worth beyond any price. Be good to friends and people you meet in a business context and you'll prosper.

The Moon in *naksatra* Krttika. You're inclined to be a materially successful person with high personal aims and a strong libido. There is no achievement without goals. You can clear the highest hurdle if you go through every step, every motion in your mind before you take your first step toward it. There's a river of money that flows through this world. The trick is to find someone who knows where it is and to convince them to show you the way. (*Famous examples:* Bill Clinton, Katharine Hepburn.)

The Moon in *naksatra* Rohini. You tend to be a romantic, affectionate person. But you're also predisposed to be very critical of others and you may have trouble with your parents. The ability to see others' faults is a curse. People rarely like to hear about their shortcomings, and often they'll hold the messenger responsible for the bad news. Allow the good in people to overshadow their imperfections. If you do, your romantic side will flourish. (*Famous examples:* Brigitte Bardot, Carrie Fisher, Steffi Graf, Dwight Yoakam.)

The Moon in *naksatra* Mrgasiras. You're inclined to indecision and self-doubt. You might have a close attachment to your mother. You may also have trouble making a commitment, which creates obstacles to your personal growth. Comedian Jerry Seinfeld joked that when we were kids we didn't think of superheroes as fantasies, we thought of them as options! When you were little, you thought you could do anything. Somewhere along the way you acquired the delusion that you couldn't. Believe in yourself. The longest journey begins with a single step, followed by another, and another, and another. Stick with goals and they will become achievements. (*Famous examples:* Goldie Hawn, Brooke Shields, Spencer Tracy.)

Hindus believe that each planet and lunar node is ruled by a specific deity. Each is worshiped in a prenuptial ceremony called the *navgraha puja*, which literally means "worship of the nine planets." The god of fire, Agni, rules the Sun. The water goddesses, the Apas, govern the Moon. The Earth goddess, Bhumi, oversees Mars. Mercury is ruled by Vishnu the Maintainer, the king of the gods. Indra governs Jupiter. Saturn is overseen by the god of death, Yama. The queen of the gods, Indrani, rules over Venus. The goddess of power, Durga, oversees the Moon's North Node, which the Hindus call Rahu. The god of karma, Citra Gupta, governs the Moon's South Node, which the Hindus call Ketu.

The Moon in *naksatra* Ardra. You tend to be an intense and enthusiastic person. But as the path to enlightenment teaches more than it rewards, you might find yourself in a very static position, becoming critical of others if lessons are not learned and embraced. Nothing actually comes to the person who just waits. The sun will shine on your life if you work to rise above the clouds. (*Famous examples:* Humphrey Bogart, Kurt Cobain, Bo Derek, Prince William Windsor.)

The Moon in *naksatra* Punarvasu. You're a generous person. Like a river, your nurturing support flows to those around you. But also like a river that never ceases to shift its banks and reshape its course, you might change residences often and have difficulty making a pledge to a relationship. Don't fear commitment; no matter which way you turn you will always wonder what might have happened if you'd gone the other way. As for moving around, it is said that nearly 90 percent of the population lives and dies within twenty-five miles of their birthplace. You'll see far more of the world than most. (*Famous examples:* Harrison Ford, Carolyn Bessette Kennedy, Courtney Love, Kurt Russell.)

The Moon in *naksatra* Pusya. You're inclined to be a stable, easygoing person who has a successful career and a good family life. Every house is built on a foundation. With its faithful strength and support a house is a warm and secure place. You are the foundation in the lives of the people closest to you, thus happiness surrounds you. (*Famous example:* Maria Shriver.)

The Moon in *naksatra* Aslesa. You tend to be a self-reliant, sexual person. You're uncomfortable in the company of strangers and you are unkind to people who are not family members or trusted friends. The person who's wary of strangers shelters himself or herself from good times and bad. Neither entirely positive or negative, this life choice is simply an alternative. Kindness, however, should be extended to all until they prove themselves unworthy. (*Famous examples:* David Bowie, Catherine Deneuve, Mikhail Gorbachev.)

The Moon in *naksatra* Magha. You're predisposed to be a sensual, highly successful person with a voracious sex drive, who doesn't like many people and prefers to be served rather than to serve. "All the world's a stage," William Shakespeare wrote in his play *As You Like It*, "and all the men and women merely players: they have their exits and their entrances; and one man in his time plays many parts." Know your parts, play them well, and people will gladly serve you. Never take kindness for granted. You need to be gracious and appreciative. Write your scripts and direct your performance. Be careful who you let peek backstage behind the curtain. Public and private personas rarely match in successful people (even though your ethics and principles must). (*Famous examples:* Candice Bergen, Jane Fonda, Julia Roberts.)

The Moon in *naksatra* Purvaphalguni. More than anyone else, you are blessed by Bhaga the Aditya, who's the protector of marital happiness. You're a generous person who's inclined to succeed in positions of high authority and to prevail without the use of intimidation. A good relationship in a chaotic world is a buffer just like a sheltered cove in a storm. This security allows you to view your environment rationally and objectively: two highly prized traits. Give earnestly of your time and talents and the rewards will come. (*Famous examples:* Richard Burton, Madonna, Michelle Pfeiffer, John Travolta.)

The Moon in *naksatra* Uttaraphalguni. You tend to be very intelligent and you have a high self-opinion. However, your romantic episodes are apt to cause you trouble. It's important to love yourself, but don't show it. And when you select others to love, choose responsibly. Use your head in romantic matters. It can save your heart. (*Famous examples:* Jack Nicholson, Richie Sambora.)

The Moon in *naksatra* Hasta. You tend to be a resourceful person, but somewhat impatient and conservative. The will to find a way can sometimes push you right past patience, which is often the best way to get what you're after. Also, don't dismiss lofty or seemingly outrageous goals. There are times in life when the only insurmountable obstacle we face is our own certainty that we can't succeed. You also have a tendency to manipulate other people for personal ends. For friendship's sake play your cards with an open hand, and reward those who do things for you. (*Famous example:* John Derek.)

The Moon in *naksatra* Citra. You're inclined to be a sexually magnetic person and somewhat self-indulgent. Sensory sensuality is a lust for pleasurable stimulation (even holding hands). While it's an asset to feel and enjoy pleasure (believe it or not, some people can't), its pursuit may be fraught with pitfalls. Take care. You're also likely to move far from home, and tend to condescend toward others. Different cultures, even different parents, teach divergent manners and customs. Don't be too critical of others as your behavior may seem just as strange to them. (*Famous examples:* George W. Bush, Sir Michael Caine, Ted Turner.)

The Moon in *naksatra* Svati. You're inclined to be a quiet person who's likely to live far from your birthplace. You take a long time to execute any task or review new information. Life is measured not so much by what we have done right or wrong but by what we have accomplished, mistakes and all. "Life," John Lennon said, "is what happens to you while you're busy making other plans." Try to include an occasional snap decision or impulsive act in your routine. (*Famous examples:* Ben Affleck, Eric Clapton, Steven Spielberg, Oprah Winfrey.)

The Moon in *naksatra* Visakha. You tend to be a purposeful person. However, you have little patience; you revel in turmoil and enjoy arguments. Debate—verbal dueling that pits point against counterpoint—is a time-honored art. So is yodeling. Each has its fans and its detractors. You have a remarkable ability, but you must rein it in and exercise restraint to avoid alienating people who are important to you. Don't be afraid, however, to unleash it once in a while on their behalf and in their defense. If you do, you will win arguments and forge strong bonds with people you care about. (*Famous examples:* Julie Christie, George Harrison, Elizabeth Taylor.)

The Moon in *naksatra* Anuradha. You're inclined to be a family-loving person. But you are shy in public and suffer from bouts of depression even though many opportunities naturally come your way. The art of polite conversation is still taught in finishing schools around the world. There are even chapters about it in most etiquette books. People study it to avoid embarrassment. The fear of putting your foot in your mouth is the cause of all shyness. Depression in the midst of good fortune is less easily explained, but the remedies are simple.

When your mind paints the world a sullen gray, laugh at the well of moribund humor concealed within you. Reach out to a loved one for a hug, or settle down in front of a good comedy until the darkness lifts. (*Famous example:* Warren Beatty.)

The Moon in *naksatra* Jyestha. You're predisposed to cheerfulness but can be equally irascible. Other people admire you either way. Character makes a mark that lasts long after physical features are forgotten. Positive petulance is an inspiring force. It makes you memorable. In a relationship, it sets the tone. You'll argue. You'll squabble. You'll compete. Do it lovingly, with respect, and you'll be doing it happily together for a very long time. However, if you lose admiration and adoration, the relationship will be torn apart in a shower of sparks like an old satellite crashing back into the atmosphere. (*Famous examples:* Justin Timberlake, Donald Trump.)

The Moon in *naksatra* Mula. A pleasure-loving person who's inclined to be suspicious of other people's motives, you might find marriage causes you problems. Sky divers traditionally pack their own parachutes so that they have no one to blame on the way down if anything's tangled. But when they step out of an airplane they still place their lives in the hands of the person who made the parachute. There comes a point when we must simply have faith in others. It's a choice we make to get what we want. Other people are no different. Remember to enter into commitment with the thought that it will not always be easy. Your entire life is a very long time, whether you share it with someone or not. (*Famous examples:* Michael Douglas, Arnold Schwarzenegger, Al Gore.)

The Moon in *naksatra* Purvasadha. You tend to be an extroverted, independent person who's lucky in love. Few attributes are as attractive as self-assuredness. Your independence is a gift that can easily be shared with someone special. A healthy relationship is based on desire, not need. (*Famous examples:* Kim Basinger, Johnny Depp.)

The Moon in *naksatra* Uttarasadha. You're predisposed to generosity and potentially destined for fame, but you must be aware of enemies. "Keep your friends close, but your enemies closer," said Al Pacino in *The Godfather Part II*. Awareness of an adversary's actions will reduce the possibility of an unpleasant surprise. However, this doesn't mean you should welcome enemies into your life. One of the surest ways to end strife is to cease communication. Words fuel the flames of discord. (*Famous example:* Brad Pitt.)

The Moon in *naksatra* Sravana. You tend to be an intelligent person. If you move far away from your origins, you might find that you're blessed with a happy marriage and even a measure of fame. A person with qualities considered common in one place may be highly valued elsewhere for those same characteristics. You may discover that your greatest asset is your ability to communicate cross-culturally. (*Famous examples:* Melanie Griffith, Diane Keaton.)

The Moon in *naksatra* Dhanista. You tend to be a courageous person, but your aggressive nature sparks frequent marital confrontations. Your ability to champion your cause as part of a couple is an asset when it's focused at the outside world. However, when it comes to communication with your mate, it could cost you your relationship. There's a route to victory that doesn't involve winning or losing. It's called compromise. Negotiation is compromise in action. Sometimes it does mean complete concession, at which time you can simply smile to yourself and chalk one up to relationship preservation. (*Famous examples:* Woody Allen, Tipper Gore, John F. Kennedy Jr., Debbie Reynolds, Princess Diana Spencer Windsor.)

The Moon in *naksatra* Satabhisaj. You're predisposed to privacy, concealing your real thoughts and intentions. You have an unobtrusive nature like the deepest water. Sometimes when you think you've broadcast your desires loud and clear, those closest to you hear only a whisper or silence. They act surprised when you finally explode, as if you'd given them no indication of your undetected needs. Don't hold them entirely responsible. You may be surprised how much your relationship improves if you make a point of not waiting for your mate to realize the obvious. Speak up and say what you want, then you'll get what you want. (*Famous example:* Elvis Presley.)

The Moon in *naksatra* Purvabhadrapada. You tend to be a sensual person who frequently changes residences. You are also uniquely talented, achieving your goals through ingenuity and hard work. Moving from place to place can often work to your advantage. Life's professional, social, and economic ladders can all be climbed by moving from one ladder to another, leveraging each move to include a step up to a rung above the last. New flirtations and excitements make new situations especially enticing. (*Famous examples:* the Reverend Dr. Martin Luther King Jr., O. J. Simpson.)

The Moon in *naksatra* Uttarabhadrapada. You tend to be an eccentric, ethical person. You're also inclined to be shy and fickle. You're self-sacrificing, willing to support and protect others. Someone you're interested in may not take you seriously at first, and may humor you simply because he or she is attracted to you and is enchanted with your unique approach to life. Don't worry about it. Anyone who spends enough time around you will grow to appreciate your underlying integrity and forthrightness, as these are truly your best qualities. (*Famous examples:* Antonio Banderas, Hillary Rodham Clinton, Bill Gates.)

The Moon in *naksatra* Revati. You're inclined to be a sensual person who loves people and is loved in return. Wealth and joy are often spontaneously bestowed upon you. You also find fulfillment through marriage. There's a pleasant (though time-consuming) job in wedlock to which you are ideally suited. You need to play social secretary. It may mean that you send out a hundred Christmas cards every year or spend an hour or two every week on the phone and writing e-mails, but it's important. In this world the lines between good friends and good business often cross. Success is there for you to reach out and grasp, and you'll have a fabulous time in the process.

Brad Pitt's astrologer might determine from the Moon's placement in *naksatra* Uttarasadha that the actor's disposed to generosity and potentially destined for fame, but he must be aware of enemies. His prospects as a potential mate make him an ideal candidate for someone who's equally generous and fated for fame because neither person will become jealous or fail to return shows of affection, compliments, or gifts. The pair can also keep a mutually watchful eye for people who might try to do them harm.

♥ ♥ ♥

In a consultation, the Hindu astrologer would also study your and your mate's *navamsacakra* (ninth-sign charts), which provide key insights into your marriage prospects, and your respective *saptamsacakra* (seventh-sign charts), which present a glimpse of your potential for offspring and your compatibility. The calculations and interpretative material the astrologer filters through to do this are daunting. It can be tough work, even for seasoned professionals who've spent dozens of years learning their craft.

Timing Is Everything: *Dasa* Periods

For the same reason mentioned above, we won't present the construction of the *vimsottari dasa* (timeline) in this chapter. **However, if you already have a *bhavacakra*, you probably also received a list of your *dasa* (time periods) that will allow you to follow along with this section.**

Many Hindu astrologers cast the *vimsottari dasa* to determine when you and your mate will enter your Venus *dasa*. During that period of twenty-two years, it's believed, you experience successful relationships with your true love, an atmosphere of social harmony, and the birth of children, if the planet Venus isn't adversely affected by its placement in your chart. There's also a Jupiter *dasa* of sixteen years, in which marriage, children, and professional success can occur amid fortunate and prosperous times.

These two *dasa* occur at radically different times in each person's life, so it's essential for both of you to be in a complementary (not necessarily the same) *dasa* when you decide to wed. The *dasa* is then further subdivided by the astrologer, using additional calculations to fine-tune the optimal days, months, and years in which a marriage could take place.

In the late 1800s, a Bengali hill tribe known as the Mandas reputedly married each young couple to a pair of trees before the couple's own nuptials could take place. The bride was tied to a mahua tree in an elaborate ceremony, while the groom was tied to a mango tree. Some ethnologists speculate that the Mandas believed the trees' reproductive powers were transferred to the couple during this unusual practice.

There are a few other *dasa* that were considered good periods for marriage in the past but are rarely applied in modern times. According to the classic Hindu astrological text *Philadeepika*, marriage should take place during the *dasa* of a planet that occupies your chart's seventh house; a planet situated three, four, five, eight, nine, or ten houses from your chart's seventh house; or during the *dasa* of a planet that governs the zodiac sign associated with your chart's seventh house.

In actor Brad Pitt's *bhavacakra* (fig. 6), you'll notice that he's due to enter his Jupiter *dasa* on 18 October 2003 and his Venus *dasa* on 18 October 2062. Under normal circumstances, the astrologer would suggest Pitt seek a spouse during the sixteen-year period of his Jupiter *dasa* because his Venus *dasa* doesn't occur until he's ninety-

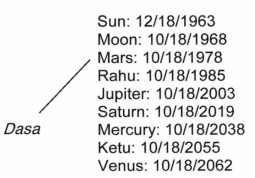

Dasa

Sun: 12/18/1963
Moon: 10/18/1968
Mars: 10/18/1978
Rahu: 10/18/1985
Jupiter: 10/18/2003
Saturn: 10/18/2019
Mercury: 10/18/2038
Ketu: 10/18/2055
Venus: 10/18/2062

Figure 6. Brad Pitt's *Dasa* in a *Bhavacakra*.

nine years old! Many modern astrologers, Ronnie Gale Dreyer included, prefer not to apply the *dasa* in all cases, finding that the planets' placements and house rulerships are far more critical to the outcome of love and marriage.

Walking the Steps: From Betrothal to Marriage

Armed with all of this valuable information, Hindu parents begin the arduous task of finding their child a mate. Rather than by hiring a matchmaker, potential matches are often found through word of mouth, newspaper and Internet advertisements, business connections, by allowing the family astrologer to take on the matchmaker's job, or by letting nature takes its course in matters of love and attraction. Unlike the Chinese, the Hindu bride's family also initiates inquiries.

Once a potential match is found, the action really heats up. The groom's relatives and friends tell the bride's parents about all the past and present faults they might know about the bride's other suitors and exaggerate any of the groom's fine points to the bride's mother. Sir Richard Burton's 1883 translation of the *Kama Sutra* notes that a little cheating also might take place: "One of the friends should also disguise himself as an astrologer, and declare the future good fortune and wealth of his friend by showing the existence of all the lucky omens and signs, the good influence of planets, the auspicious entrance of the Sun into a sign of the zodiac, propitious stars, and fortunate marks on his body." Tales of lucky blue jays flying on a person's left side and the simultaneous throbbing of the groom's right eye and the bride's left eye abound during these consultations. Finally, a troop of the groom's friends rouse the jealousy of the bride's mother by warning that their friend has a chance of getting an even a better catch than her daughter. If that doesn't spark the *vagdanam* (betrothal ceremonies), nothing will.

Choosing the Perfect Day
Before the colorful *vagdanam* can take place, the families must determine the most auspicious date for the actual wedding ceremony.

According to pundit Ramesh Upadhyay, when Venus or the Moon, during its orbit, enters the zodiac sign associated with Saturn in your chart, the chances for finding a mate and actually getting married are extremely favorable. The Hindu almanac known as the *panchang* (five limbs) suggests that the wedding date should fall either five, seven, nine, or eleven months from the groom's lunar birth month. (If you're curious about this, take a look at the lunar month table on pages 58–63.)

The most popular way to choose a wedding date, however, is through the daily *naksatra* (lunar mansion). Just as Chinese astrologers consult the daily *sieu* (lunar mansion) to determine the best date for the wedding, Hindu practitioners consult the *naksatra* for the same purpose. The astrologer refers to a *panchang* for the year, seeking the Moon's location on a day that the family has suggested in order to determine if this day is favorable for matrimony. As with the Chinese almanac, the *panchang* isn't generally available in English. However, we've included some translation here to allow you to see if your proposed wedding date is listed among the favorable *naksatra*. First, enter your potential wedding date onto Worksheet 12. Then, using the data in Table 7, see if your date falls on one of the good *naksatra* dates listed. If it doesn't, it's not a favorable wedding date, so you should consider the closest day in the table to your selection as an option. Next, look at the text following and see if that *naksatra* is favorable for marriage in a manner that pleases you. If it's not, you may want to adjust the date so that it corresponds to another auspicious *naksatra*.

WORKSHEET 12. WEDDING DATE

	Example A:	Example B:	Date Choice	Date Choice
	Brad Pitt's wedding	Brad Pitt's suggested date	A:	B:
Wedding date	29 Jul 2000	27 Jul 2000		
Naksatra	Punarvasu	Mrgasiras		

TABLE 7. OPTIMAL WEDDING DAY *Naksatra* for the Years 2002–2005

Date	*Naksatra*	Date	*Naksatra*
04 Jan 2002	Uttaraphalguni	16 Apr 2002	Rohini
05 Jan 2002	Hasta	17 Apr 2002	Mrgasiras
09 Jan 2002	Anuradha	24 Apr 2002	Uttaraphalguni
18 Jan 2002	Uttarabhadrapada	25 Apr 2002	Hasta
19 Jan 2002	Revati	28 Apr 2002	Anuradha
20 Jan 2002	Revati	08 May 2002	Uttarabhadrapada
24 Jan 2002	Rohini	09 May 2002	Revati
25 Jan 2002	Mrgasiras	13 May 2002	Rohini
31 Jan 2002	Uttaraphalguni	14 May 2002	Mrgasiras
01 Feb 2002	Hasta	21 May 2002	Uttaraphalguni
05 Feb 2002	Anuradha	22 May 2002	Hasta
15 Feb 2002	Uttarabhadrapada	26 May 2002	Anuradha
16 Feb 2002	Revati	04 Jun 2002	Uttarabhadrapada
21 Feb 2002	Mrgasiras	05 Jun 2002	Revati
22 Feb 2002	Mrgasiras	10 Jun 2002	Rohini
28 Feb 2002	Uttaraphalguni	11 Jun 2002	Mrgasiras
01 Mar 2002	Hasta	17 Jun 2002	Uttaraphalguni
03 Mar 2002	Svati	18 Jun 2002	Hasta
05 Mar 2002	Anuradha	22 Jun 2002	Anuradha
14 Mar 2002	Uttarabhadrapada	01 Jul 2002	Uttarabhadrapada
15 Mar 2002	Revati	02 Jul 2002	Uttarabhadrapada
20 Mar 2002	Rohini	03 Jul 2002	Revati
21 Mar 2002	Mrgasiras	07 Jul 2002	Rohini
27 Mar 2002	Uttaraphalguni	08 Jul 2002	Mrgasiras
28 Mar 2002	Hasta	15 Jul 2002	Uttaraphalguni
01 Apr 2002	Anuradha	19 Jul 2002	Anuradha
10 Apr 2002	Uttarabhadrapada	29 Jul 2002	Uttarabhadrapada
11 Apr 2002	Uttarabhadrapada	30 Jul 2002	Revati
12 Apr 2002	Revati	03 Aug 2002	Rohini

Date	Naksatra	Date	Naksatra
04 Aug 2002	Mrgasiras	12 Dec 2002	Uttarabhadrapada
11 Aug 2002	Uttaraphalguni	13 Dec 2002	Revati
12 Aug 2002	Hasta	18 Dec 2002	Rohini
16 Aug 2002	Anuradha	19 Dec 2002	Mrgasiras
25 Aug 2002	Uttarabhadrapada	26 Dec 2002	Uttaraphalguni
26 Aug 2002	Revati	27 Dec 2002	Hasta
31 Aug 2002	Rohini	30 Dec 2002	Anuradha
01 Sep 2002	Mrgasiras	08 Jan 2003	Uttarabhadrapada
07 Sep 2002	Uttaraphalguni	09 Jan 2003	Uttarabhadrapada
08 Sep 2002	Hasta	10 Jan 2003	Revati
12 Sep 2002	Anuradha	14 Jan 2003	Rohini
21 Sep 2002	Uttarabhadrapada	15 Jan 2003	Mrgasiras
22 Sep 2002	Revati	22 Jan 2003	Uttaraphalguni
27 Sep 2002	Rohini	23 Jan 2003	Hasta
28 Sep 2002	Mrgasiras	27 Jan 2003	Anuradha
05 Oct 2002	Uttaraphalguni	05 Feb 2003	Uttarabhadrapada
06 Oct 2002	Hasta	06 Feb 2003	Revati
09 Oct 2002	Anuradha	10 Feb 2003	Rohini
19 Oct 2002	Uttarabhadrapada	11 Feb 2003	Mrgasiras
20 Oct 2002	Revati	12 Feb 2003	Mrgasiras
24 Oct 2002	Rohini	18 Feb 2003	Uttaraphalguni
25 Oct 2002	Mrgasiras	23 Feb 2003	Anuradha
01 Nov 2002	Uttaraphalguni	04 Mar 2003	Uttarabhadrapada
02 Nov 2002	Hasta	05 Mar 2003	Revati
06 Nov 2002	Anuradha	10 Mar 2003	Rohini
15 Nov 2002	Uttarabhadrapada	11 Mar 2003	Mrgasiras
16 Nov 2002	Revati	18 Mar 2003	Uttaraphalguni
20 Nov 2002	Rohini	19 Mar 2003	Hasta
21 Nov 2002	Mrgasiras	22 Mar 2003	Anuradha
29 Nov 2002	Hasta	31 Mar 2003	Uttarabhadrapada
03 Dec 2002	Anuradha	01 Apr 2003	Uttarabhadrapada

Date	Naksatra	Date	Naksatra
02 Apr 2003	Revati	02 Aug 2003	Hasta
06 Apr 2003	Rohini	06 Aug 2003	Anuradha
07 Apr 2003	Mrgasiras	15 Aug 2003	Uttarabhadrapada
14 Apr 2003	Uttaraphalguni	16 Aug 2003	Revati
15 Apr 2003	Hasta	20 Aug 2003	Rohini
19 Apr 2003	Anuradha	21 Aug 2003	Rohini
28 Apr 2003	Uttarabhadrapada	22 Aug 2003	Mrgasiras
29 Apr 2003	Revati	29 Aug 2003	Uttaraphalguni
03 May 2003	Rohini	30 Aug 2003	Hasta
04 May 2003	Mrgasiras	02 Sep 2003	Anuradha
05 May 2003	Mrgasiras	11 Sep 2003	Uttarabhadrapada
12 May 2003	Uttaraphalguni	12 Sep 2003	Revati
16 May 2003	Anuradha	17 Sep 2003	Rohini
25 May 2003	Uttarabhadrapada	18 Sep 2003	Mrgasiras
26 May 2003	Revati	25 Sep 2003	Uttaraphalguni
31 May 2003	Rohini	26 Sep 2003	Hasta
01 Jun 2003	Mrgasiras	30 Sep 2003	Anuradha
08 Jun 2003	Uttaraphalguni	09 Oct 2003	Uttarabhadrapada
09 Jun 2003	Hasta	10 Oct 2003	Revati
21 Jun 2003	Uttarabhadrapada	14 Oct 2003	Rohini
22 Jun 2003	Revati	15 Oct 2003	Mrgasiras
27 Jun 2003	Rohini	23 Oct 2003	Hasta
28 Jun 2003	Mrgasiras	27 Oct 2003	Anuradha
05 Jul 2003	Uttaraphalguni	05 Nov 2003	Uttarabhadrapada
06 Jul 2003	Hasta	06 Nov 2003	Revati
10 Jul 2003	Anuradha	10 Nov 2003	Rohini
19 Jul 2003	Uttarabhadrapada	11 Nov 2003	Rohini
20 Jul 2003	Revati	12 Nov 2003	Mrgasiras
24 Jul 2003	Rohini	19 Nov 2003	Uttaraphalguni
25 Jul 2003	Mrgasiras	20 Nov 2003	Hasta
01 Aug 2003	Uttaraphalguni	02 Dec 2003	Uttarabhadrapada

Date	Naksatra	Date	Naksatra
03 Dec 2003	Revati	27 Mar 2004	Mrgasiras
08 Dec 2003	Rohini	03 Apr 2004	Uttaraphalguni
09 Dec 2003	Mrgasiras	04 Apr 2004	Hasta
16 Dec 2003	Uttaraphalguni	08 Apr 2004	Anuradha
17 Dec 2003	Hasta	17 Apr 2004	Uttarbhadrapada
21 Dec 2003	Anuradha	18 Apr 2004	Revati
29 Dec 2003	Uttarabhadrapada	22 Apr 2004	Rohini
30 Dec 2003	Revati	23 Apr 2004	Mrgasiras
31 Dec 2003	Revati	01 May 2004	Uttaraphalguni
04 Jan 2004	Rohini	02 May 2004	Hasta
05 Jan 2004	Mrgasiras	14 May 2004	Uttarabhadrapada
13 Jan 2004	Uttaraphalguni	15 May 2004	Revati
14 Jan 2004	Hasta	19 May 2004	Rohini
17 Jan 2004	Anuradha	20 May 2004	Rohini
26 Jan 2004	Uttarabhadrapada	21 May 2004	Mrgasiras
27 Jan 2004	Revati	28 May 2004	Uttaraphalguni
31 Jan 2004	Rohini	29 May 2004	Hasta
01 Feb 2004	Mrgasiras	02 Jun 2004	Anuradha
09 Feb 2004	Uttaraphalguni	10 Jun 2004	Uttarabhadrapada
10 Feb 2004	Hasta	11 Jun 2004	Revati
14 Feb 2004	Anuradha	16 Jun 2004	Rohini
22 Feb 2004	Uttarabhadrapada	17 Jun 2004	Mrgasiras
23 Feb 2004	Revati	25 Jun 2004	Uttaraphalguni
28 Feb 2004	Rohini	26 Jun 2004	Hasta
29 Feb 2004	Mrgasiras	29 Jun 2004	Anuradha
07 Mar 2004	Uttaraphalguni	08 Jul 2004	Uttarabhadrapada
08 Mar 2004	Hasta	09 Jul 2004	Revati
12 Mar 2004	Anuradha	13 Jul 2004	Rohini
21 Mar 2004	Uttarabhadrapada	14 Jul 2004	Mrgasiras
22 Mar 2004	Revati	22 Jul 2004	Uttaraphalguni
26 Mar 2004	Rohini	23 Jul 2004	Hasta

Date	Naksatra	Date	Naksatra
27 Jul 2004	Anuradha	27 Nov 2004	Rohini
04 Aug 2004	Uttarabhadrapada	28 Nov 2004	Mrgasiras
05 Aug 2004	Revati	05 Dec 2004	Uttaraphalguni
09 Aug 2004	Rohini	06 Dec 2004	Hasta
11 Aug 2004	Mrgasiras	10 Dec 2004	Anuradha
18 Aug 2004	Uttaraphalguni	18 Dec 2004	Uttarabhadrapada
19 Aug 2004	Hasta	19 Dec 2004	Uttarabhadrapada
23 Aug 2004	Anuradha	20 Dec 2004	Revati
31 Aug 2004	Uttarabhadrapada	24 Dec 2004	Rohini
01 Sep 2004	Revati	25 Dec 2004	Mrgasiras
06 Sep 2004	Rohini	02 Jan 2005	Uttaraphalguni
07 Sep 2004	Mrgasiras	03 Jan 2005	Hasta
14 Sep 2004	Uttaraphalguni	07 Jan 2005	Anuradha
15 Sep 2004	Hasta	15 Jan 2005	Uttarabhadrapada
19 Sep 2004	Anuradha	16 Jan 2005	Revati
28 Sep 2004	Uttarabhadrapada	20 Jan 2005	Rohini
29 Sep 2004	Revati	21 Jan 2005	Mrgasiras
03 Oct 2004	Rohini	29 Jan 2005	Uttaraphalguni
04 Oct 2004	Mrgasiras	30 Jan 2005	Hasta
12 Oct 2004	Uttaraphalguni	03 Feb 2005	Anuradha
13 Oct 2004	Hasta	11 Feb 2005	Uttarabhadrapada
25 Oct 2004	Uttarabhadrapada	12 Feb 2005	Revat
26 Oct 2004	Revati	16 Feb 2005	Rohini
30 Oct 2004	Rohini	17 Feb 2005	Mrgasiras
31 Oct 2004	Mrgasiras	18 Feb 2005	Mrgasiras
01 Nov 2004	Mrgasiras	25 Feb 2005	Uttaraphalguni
08 Nov 2004	Uttaraphalguni	26 Feb 2005	Hasta
09 Nov 2004	Hasta	02 Mar 2005	Anuradha
13 Nov 2004	Anuradha	11 Mar 2005	Uttarabhadrapada
21 Nov 2004	Uttarabhadrapada	12 Mar 2005	Revati
22 Nov 2004	Revati	16 Mar 2005	Rohini

Date	Naksatra	Date	Naksatra
17 Mar 2005	Mrgasiras	13 Jul 2005	Hasta
25 Mar 2005	Uttaraphalguni	17 Jul 2005	Anuradha
26 Mar 2005	Hasta	25 Jul 2005	Uttarabhadrapda
30 Mar 2005	Anuradha	26 Jul 2005	Revati
07 Apr 2005	Uttarabhadrapada	30 Jul 2005	Rohini
08 Apr 2005	Revati	31 Jul 2005	Mrgasiras
12 Apr 2005	Rohini	08 Aug 2005	Uttaraphalguni
13 Apr 2005	Mrgasiras	09 Aug 2005	Hasta
21 Apr 2005	Uttaraphalguni	13 Aug 2005	Anuradha
22 Apr 2005	Hasta	22 Aug 2005	Uttarabhadrapada
26 Apr 2005	Anuradha	27 Aug 2005	Rohini
04 May 2005	Uttarbhadrapada	28 Aug 2005	Mrgasiras
05 May 2005	Revati	04 Sep 2005	Uttaraphalguni
09 May 2005	Rohini	05 Sep 2005	Hasta
10 May 2005	Rohini	06 Sep 2005	Hasta
11 May 2005	Mrgasiras	10 Sep 2005	Anuradha
18 May 2005	Uttaraphalguni	18 Sep 2005	Uttarabhadrapada
19 May 2005	Hasta	19 Sep 2005	Revati
23 May 2005	Anuradha	23 Sep 2005	Rohini
01 Jun 2005	Uttarabhadrapada	24 Sep 2005	Mrgasiras
02 Jun 2005	Revati	02 Oct 2005	Uttaraphalguni
06 Jun 2005	Rohini	03 Oct 2005	Hasta
07 Jun 2005	Mrgasiras	07 Oct 2005	Anuradha
15 Jun 2005	Uttaraphalguni	15 Oct 2005	Uttarabhadrapada
16 Jun 2005	Hasta	16 Oct 2005	Revati
20 Jun 2005	Anuradha	20 Oct 2005	Rohini
28 Jun 2005	Uttarabhadrapada	21 Oct 2005	Mrgasiras
29 Jun 2005	Revati	29 Oct 2005	Uttaraphalguni
03 Jul 2005	Rohini	30 Oct 2005	Hasta
04 Jul 2005	Mrgasiras	03 Nov 2005	Anuradhas
12 Jul 2005	Uttaraphalguni	12 Nov 2005	Uttarabhadrapada

Date	Naksatra	Date	Naksatra
13 Nov 2005	Revati	10 Dec 2005	Revati
17 Nov 2005	Rohini	14 Dec 2005	Rohini
18 Nov 2005	Mrgasiras	15 Dec 2005	Mrgasiras
25 Nov 2005	Uttaraphalguni	23 Dec 2005	Uttaraphalguni
26 Nov 2005	Hasta	24 Dec 2005	Hasta
09 Dec 2005	Uttarabhadrapada	28 Dec 2005	Anuradha

These dates are derived from calculations made with RishiCalc v.01 software created by Michael Taft, using the latitude and longitude for New York City at noon.

Traditionally, the following *naksatra* are considered to be the best times for marriages:

The Moon in *naksatra* Rohini. This is a fortunate day for healing, matrimony, spiritual endeavors, and putting on new jewelry for the first time.

The Moon in *naksatra* Mrgasiras. It's a good day to begin constructing a new building, to travel, and for a wedding ceremony.

The Moon in *naksatra* Uttaraphalguni. The Lord Siva and his second wife, the mountain *yogini* Parvati, were married under this *naksatra,* which is best known for bestowing marital happiness. It's an auspicious day for nuptials and other important ceremonies as well as for making resolutions and entering a new home for the first time.

The Moon in *naksatra* Hasta. Besides being good for a wedding, this is a good day for starting a new course of study, traveling, and taking new purchases home.

The Moon in *naksatra* Anuradha. This day is auspicious for travel, matrimony, and for entering a new vehicle for the first time.

The Moon in *naksatra* Uttarabhadrapada. Aside from being a good day for a wedding, it's also a fortunate time to bless others and make promises.

The Bharias of central India decided that the best way to keep the evil eye and demons from cursing the groom on the day before his wedding was to dress him up in women's jewelry. He'd wear yellow robes over red trousers and red shoes, donning a marriage crown made of date leaves on his head. Then he'd add bangles, necklaces, and earrings to his costume, along with a dagger in his belt and a smudge of ash on his forehead.

The Moon in *naksatra* Revati. This is a good day for marriage, making resolutions, doing construction work (or building things in general), and wearing jewelry.

If you want to check a wedding date that occurred between 1950 and 2000, go to http://www.world-astrology.com, where we've listed those *naksatra*.

As you can see, Brad Pitt's actual date—29 July 2000—wasn't a favorable date for a wedding ceremony in the eyes of a Hindu astrologer. Since it fell under the *naksatra* Punarvasu the astrologer would have suggested that the actor move the date up to 27 July 2000 in order to benefit from an auspicious placement of the Moon in *naksatra* Mrgasiras.

A Traditional Hindu Wedding

Golden Sweets: The *Misri* Ceremony

Filled with color and symbolism, the *vagdanam* (betrothal) celebrations build the festive spirit until it crescendos with the *vivaha* (wedding). The various parts of this elaborate ritual are outlined below. You may want to incorporate some of these beautiful traditions into your own nuptials. At least one part of the Hindu marriage, *mehndi* (the henna ceremony), has become quite popular with women in contemporary Western culture. And, of course, it has never gone out of fashion in India.

The first custom is the *misri* (crystallized sugar) ceremony. In the presence of the couple and their families, seven married women, who represent the spiritual rulers of the days of the week, apply Lord Ganesha's symbol—a clockwise swastika—in red powder on a bowl of *misri,* asking him to bless the nuptial events and the betrothed pair.

A *puja* (worship) dedicated to Lord Ganesha, Varuna Devta,

Laksmi, Narayana, the gods who rule the nine planets, Lord Brahma, Lord Vishnu, and Lord Siva is celebrated by the couple and their parents. A *varmala* (exchange of garlands) is performed by the bride and groom to welcome each other into their respective lives.

Gold represents longevity and fortune in many cultures: beneficial virtues for any union. The exchange of gold rings dates back to the ancient Egyptians, and Hindus have embraced this custom during the past century. The ring finger reputedly has a vein—the *vena amoris*—that leads directly to the heart. To form a symbolically complete heart, the bride wears her ring on her left hand while the groom wears his ring on his right hand.

The groom's parents then give their benediction by placing a basket of fresh fruit, clothes, cosmetics, and ornaments in the bride's lap, wishing her prosperity, happiness, and healthy children. It's a lucky omen to eat sweets at special occasions such as this, so the groom's family offers lumps of *misri* to the bride's family. At this time the groom's parents also give their final verbal consent for the marriage.

Mehndi, Sangeet, and Sagri

Although it's Muslim in origin, Hindus in Rajasthan and Gujarat also perform the *mehndi* (henna) ceremony. (This rite has increasingly become a popular tradition among modern-day urban brides throughout India and in some Western cultures.) The henna's yellowish red hue complements the traditional red wedding sari and elaborate jewelry worn by Hindu brides. Although it's mainly a ladies' tea party, male relatives sometimes attend this four-to-six-hour event, in which the bride's hands and feet are intricately painted with a henna paste made from dried henna powder, warm tea, oil, and lemon juice. The designs are usually inspired by the floral and paisley motifs seen on fabric. While the bride waits for the henna paste to dry, party members usually join in the fun, decoratively painting one another's hands and feet. According to this superstition, the darker the *mehndi* tints the bride's skin, the stronger her marriage will be. The families throw a *sangeet* (prewedding party) that same evening, during which professional singers and musicians perform popular tunes (many from current Hindi films) while family and friends eat, drink, and dance the night away.

The next day, the *sagri* (a ritualized gathering that gives the bride a chance to meet her new sisters-in-law) brings together the groom's sisters, who dress the bride and adorn her with flowers that are strung together, forming bangles, garlands, hairpieces, and earrings. The women apply perfume and cosmetics while engaging the bride in lighthearted conversation as a way to make her feel welcome in her new family. The bride then places a drop of perfume in her mouth, adding "fragrance and sweetness" to her voice.

The Final *Pujas*

Indians believe that Agni, the Apas, Bhumi, Vishnu, Indra, Indrani, Yama, and Durga are the gods who rule the planets and the lunar nodes. Since it's believed that these celestial entities exert tremendous influence over personal destiny, the planetary gods' benediction is considered of supreme importance to the couple's marital bliss. Performed the day before the wedding, the *navgraha puja* (nine-planet worship) unites the families as they implore the gods to bless the couple's union.

The *ghari puja* (worship devoted to the gods Varuna Devta and Lord Ganesha) draws the prenuptial festivities to a close and is performed on the same day as the *navgraha puja*. The priest prays over a spread of fresh foods (rice, coconut, wheat berries, oil, betel nuts, turmeric, and other spices), offering the bounty to the Lord Ganesha. Married women grind wheat, symbolizing that the house will always prosper no matter how the fates may change. The groom offers the priest a handful of the finished flour, indicating his willingness to help others and to perform good deeds. (In some regions, the couple's mothers then mix a little oil with ground yellow turmeric. They rub the mixture on the bride's and groom's hands, legs, feet, and backbones, making their beloved children appear golden.)

Dressed in her finery, the bride's mother steps outdoors accompanied by her elder daughters' husbands, who act as protectors, carrying a pot of water on her head as she walks to the threshold of her house. At the door, the groom cuts through the water with a knife to dispel the evil eye or any spells that someone may have invoked upon the house or its inhabitants. Family members bang pots, yell, and whistle to ward off malicious spirits as well. Friends and relatives adorn the parents with garlands before the party proceeds to the groom's house, where the ceremony is repeated by his mother.

From that moment until the actual wedding day, both the bride and the groom wear torn, old clothes donated by their families. This visually puts an end to their old lives, making them grungy so they will look especially glorious when they enter their new life together.

The *Vivaha*

On the wedding day, the bride's female relatives escort the groom to the bride, who's now dressed in her red wedding sari and adorned with family jewels. The *svagatam* (welcome) begins, which kicks off the elaborate *vivaha* (wedding). Standing at the threshold, the groom places his foot gently on top of his bride's, signifying that he's the dominant figure in their future household. He then enters her house, where her parents wash his feet with milk and water. His future mother-in-law then sprinkles rice and ground red turmeric powder on him and places a dot of red turmeric on his forehead.

The bride and groom are ceremoniously seated, sharing a cup of *madhuparka*, which is a blend of honey, curd (similar to cottage cheese), and clarified butter. The bride's family then officially gives their daughter to her husband and his family in the *kanya danam* (entrustment rite). A sacred fire is then lit in the *viva homa* (sacred fire ceremony), inviting the gods to circle the flame and witness the proceedings. The *hiathialo* (joining of hands) follows. Just as in the handfast ceremonies celebrated in the British isles, the bride and groom's hands are ritually joined together. In this case, the couple's right hands are joined together with a thread that's been blessed by the priest, tying the eternal knot between them.

Assisted by her mother, the bride steps onto a stone in the *shila arohanam* (stone stepping) while the *pujari* (priest) recites passages from the *Atharva Veda* II.13.4: "Tread on this stone. Like a stone be firm." The act signifies her entry into a new life that may have its ups and downs. Fried rice is tossed into the sacred fire by family members before the couple walks around the flame. In the *parikrama* (circling), the groom leads the bride three times around the flame, exchanging vows of duty, love, fidelity, and respect. Then the bride leads the groom around the flame one more time.

Then the most romantic portion of this long matrimonial event takes place: the *saptapadi* (seven steps ritual). First, an edge of the bride's sari is tied to the groom's scarf. Handfuls of uncooked rice are placed in a line on the floor at equal distances in seven places. Positioned toward the north at the start of the line, the groom places his hand on the bride's right shoulder and together they take a step with their right feet in a northeasterly direction onto the first rice pile. With that step they say: "May the first step lead to food that is nourishing and pure." On the second pile, they proclaim: "May the second step lead to strength." At the third, they recite: "May the third step lead to prosperity." At the subsequent steps they declare: "May the fourth step lead to happiness. May the fifth step lead to noble and virtuous children. May the sixth step lead to long life." And at the final step, they say: "May the seventh step lead to friendship." The groom then faces his bride, saying: "Having walked the seven steps, be my lifelong companion, be my associate and helper in my duties as a householder. May we be blessed with many children who will live a full life."

According to Sir James George Frazer's *The Golden Bough*, a Brahman boy's initiation into manhood required him to place his right foot on a large stone while reciting the words "Tread on this stone, like a stone be firm." A bride performs this same ritual, known as the *shila arohanam* (stone stepping), at her wedding ceremony.

The *pujari* further explains the couple's duties to each other and blesses the union in the *asirvada* (blessing). Tradition dictates that a *brahma* marriage must always be sanctified by water. Accordingly, the *pujari* sprinkles water over the couple as an *abhishek* (ablution).

While the Sun sets on the wedding ceremony, the final rites are performed by the bride and groom. Together, they recite verses from the *Rig Veda* VII.66.16: "O God, the illuminator of the Sun! May we live for a hundred years, hear for a hundred years, and speak for a hundred years through your grace. And may we never be dependent upon anyone. May we likewise live even beyond a hundred years!"

The polestar (the star Polaris in the Ursa Minor constellation) and the Arundhati star (the least visible star among the Taurus constellation's Pleiades star cluster) represent fixed points in the nighttime skies, just as the bride and groom are meant to be to each other. Thus, the newlyweds stand together, reciting verses from the *Rig Veda* X.173.4 under these stars. The bride says: "Just as the star Arundhati is attached to the star Vasishtha, so may I be always firmly attached to my husband!" The groom says: "As the heavens are always stable, as the Earth is always stable, as the mountains are always stable, and as the entire universe is always stable, so may my wife be always part of my family. You are the polestar. I see stability and constancy in you. May you always be steadfast in your affection toward me. The great god has united you with me. May you live with me, blessed with children for a hundred years!"

In 1869, Edward J. Wood documented that in some regions of India, a bridal couple performs an additional ritual before asking the stars Polaris and Arundhati to bless their union with steadfastness. The bride and groom sit outdoors under the nighttime skies on a red-tinted cowhide. Pouring a small amount of clarified butter onto the bride's head, the groom prays that they'll be united in *bhur* (the earthly world). He pours a little more butter on her head, praying that they'll be united in *bhuah* (the heavenly world). Then he pours one last splash of butter on her head, praying that they'll be united in *svar* (the spirit world).

After the ceremony, the wedding party adjourns to the groom's house, where the bride's feet are washed by the groom's parents. A veil is placed over her head before she sprinkles milk in all the corners of her in-laws' abode. The *datar* (salt ceremony) commences when the bride picks up a handful of salt and places it in her husband's hands. He passes it back to her, then they repeat this back-and-forth gesture two more times. This symbolic demonstration of the couple's ability to work and share life together concludes the elaborate *vivaha*.

♥ ♥ ♥

The expression "Timing is everything" has been impressed upon the Hindu psyche for centuries. With the amount of planning and preparation that goes into the nuptial process in India, it's not surprising that the astrologer is an integral part of this epic event. The next chapter takes us to a world where the concept of marriage is less publicly linked to the stars, but no less spiritual in its conceptualization.

אני לדודי ודודי לי

צדקה · בית

אהבה · משפחה

ב בשברת לחדש
שנת חמשת אלפים ושבע
לבריאת עולם למנין
טאנר מונין כאן במדינת

מאות

אך החתן
אמר לה כדהדא
הוי לי לאנתו כדת

משה וישראל ואנא אפלח ואוקיר ואיזון ואפרנס יתיכי ליכי
כהלכות גוברין יהודאין דפלחין ומוקרין וזנין ומפרנסין לנשיהון
בקושטא ויהיבנא ליכי כסף זוזי דחזי ליכי
ומזוניכי וכסותיכי וסיפוקיכי ומיעל לותיכי כאורח
כל ארעא וצביאת מרת דא והות
ליה לאנתו ודין נדוניא דהנעלת ליה מבי בין בכסף
בין בדהב בין בתכשיטין במאני דלבושא בשימושי דירה
ובשימושי דערסא הכל קבל עליו חתן דנן
זקוקים כסף צרוף וצבי זקים דן והוסף
לה מן דיליה עוד זקוקים כסף צרוף אחרים כנגדן
סך הכל זקוקים כסף צרוף וכך אמר
חתן דנן אחריות שטר כתובתא דא נדוניא דין
ותוספתא דא קבלית עלי ועל ירתי בתראי להתפרע מכל
שפר ארג נכסין וקנינין דאירת לי תחות כל שמיא דקנאי
ודיעתיד אנא למקנא נכסי דאית להון אחריות ודלית להון
אחריות כלהון יהון אחראין וערבאין לפרוע מנהון שטר
כתובתא דא נדוניא דין ורזו תוספתא דא מנאי ואפילו מן
גלימא דעל כתפאי בחיי ובתר חיי מן יומא דנן ולעלם
ואחריות וחומר שטר כתובתא דא נדוניא דין ותוספתא דא
קבל עליו חתן דנן כחומר כל שטרי
כתובות ותוספתות דנהגין בבנות ישראל העשויין כתקון זקון
חכמינו זכרונם לברכה דלא כאסמכתא ודלא כטופסי
דשטרי וקנינא מן חתן דנן למרת
דא על כל מה דכתוב ומפורש לעיל במנא דכשר למקניא
ביה והכל שריר וקים.

נאם _____ עד
נאם _____ עד

CHAPTER FOUR

Using Judaic Astrology to Find Love and Marriage

THE SONG OF SONGS

He who has found woman has found good.

—Proverbs 18:22

ow will you find your all-important other half? The Talmud's *Sotah* 2a offers a clue from the Jewish perspective: "Rabbi Judah said in the name of Rav: Forty days before the embryo is formed, a heavenly voice calls out and says, 'The daughter of so-and-so shall marry so-and-so.' " Like the Chinese and Hindus, many Jews have always believed that perfect matches are preordained in heaven. They also honor a tradition that ensures that promises made by parents will be kept by their children.

Yiddish playwright S. Ansky presented his view of this eternal bond in his haunting 1914 tale, *The Dybbuk*. Channon was a poverty-stricken yeshiva student who'd been drawn to the study of kabbalah (Jewish mysticism). He'd been in love with Leah since childhood, and the young couple were obviously destined to wed. When Leah's father, Sender, made a marriage contract with a wealthier suitor, Channon fasted, meditated, and cast spells to thwart the arrangement, and he succeeded. Sender found another rich prospect, and another, but Channon managed to stop these attempts as well. Finally, on the fourth attempt, Channon's worst nightmare came true. After extensive negotiation, Sender and a rich family agreed on the terms of a marriage arrangement and Leah was soon to be wed. Upon hearing the news, Channon dropped dead in the middle of the synagogue. Because of his tragic and untimely death he was transformed into a dybbuk, a wandering spirit doomed to take possession of a living body to purify his soul. Channon the dybbuk naturally possessed Leah's body the night before her marriage.

On her wedding day, a day when every precaution is taken to drive away the evil eye, Leah sat in the synagogue's bridal room in a trancelike state. Then, just as she was to leave the room to join to the nuptial ceremony, she tore off her veil and refused to marry her fiancé, Menashe.

The Talmud's *Gittin* 57a documents a charming matrimonial custom that was practiced in ancient Judea. If a boy was born, the family planted a cedar tree in their garden. If a girl was born, they planted a pine tree. When the children married, the *chuppah* (wedding canopy) was woven from the mature branches of each of their trees.

Exorcists were summoned to free Leah from her spiritual captor. Before they began the rites of exorcism, the chief rabbi revealed a dream to the gathered holy men in which he had learned that Sender had broken a promise to Channon's father, Nissen. The two men had pledged during High Holy Days that if their wives became pregnant, one with a boy and the other with a girl, the two children would then be married. But Nissen died before he could see the promise carried out.

A rabbinical court was called and Sender confessed his broken promise. The court sentenced him to give away half of his fortune and to pray over Nissen's unsettled soul.

Leah's exorcism took place anyway and Menashe was summoned so the wedding could proceed. Just as she was called to join in the nuptial service, Leah saw Channon's spirit in the room and walked toward it, saying tenderly: "I am enveloped in a blaze of light. My bridegroom, my destined one, I am united with you for all eternity. Together we will soar higher and higher, ever higher." She died at that moment, joining the man she'd always loved.

In Jewish culture, marriage is viewed as a necessary stage in one's growth and development that will enrich the spirit through the fulfillment of destiny. The Talmud's *Yevamot* 62b reminds us that "a man who has not a wife is doomed to an existence without joy, without blessing, without experiencing life's true goodness, without Torah, without protection, and without peace."

Matchmaker, Matchmaker

From the day a daughter is born, her parents begin accumulating her dowry, money that helps young couples start their new lives together. In many Orthodox Jewish households, parents do most of the spouse hunting with the help of a *shadchen* (matchmaker), who knows the backgrounds of numerous families and keeps track of available sons. If a *shadchen*'s fee is unaffordable to them, a family will either enlist their rabbi's help or just search on their own.

A prime candidate for a son-in-law is someone with *yihus*— distinction through inherited social status, education, a charitable nature, and a reputation for *mitzvot* (good deeds). It doesn't hurt if good health, good looks, and money also enter into the picture.

But what about those of us who don't have overeager parents and paid matchmakers to help us search for our perfect mate? Don't worry. Thorough self-examination and some astrological birth charts can be equally effective in this sometimes daunting endeavor.

Consulting the stars regarding matters of the heart is far less complicated in Judaic astrology than in its Hindu counterpart, where numerous charts are cast for each person. However, it's still more involved than the Chinese system. Judaic astrology is identical to Western astrology in this respect, employing a birth chart that is cast according to the tropical zodiac. One of the first things the Judaic astrologer analyzes on this chart is the seventh house, which is known as the house of marriage. He or she will look at this house along with any planets that occupy it to determine whether or not a person is the marrying kind. Then the planets Venus, Jupiter, the Moon, Mars, and the Moon's South Node are consulted in the same manner as they are in Hindu astrology. The planet Saturn and the Sun are assessed by the same methods used in Western astrology. If two charts are being looked at together to determine the compatibility of a couple, the planets in each chart will be paired up (in a process called synastry) to look for points of unison between the Sun in each chart, the Moon in each chart, the Sun in one and the Moon in the other, Venus in one and Mars in the other, and so forth. Armed with this valuable data, you will have at your fingertips a myriad of insights about you and your mate and the relationship that is possible between you.

In this chapter we'll show you how to read portions of your Judaic birth chart, starting with the zodiac sign that rules the seventh house. We'll also teach you how to interpret the placement of the planets Venus and Jupiter. And then we'll explain how to construct and read a simple synastry between your and your mate's charts.

Are You Marriage Material?: Your Chart's Seventh House

In exactly the same way that Hindu astrologers determine if you're destined to wed, Judaic astrologers assess the zodiac sign that governs your chart's seventh house to find out if you'll marry, the type of spouse you'll have, and the influence marriage might have on your life. The Judaic interpretation, however, will more than likely differ from a Hindu astrologer's assessment. It's simple to explain. Your Judaic house location is usually different from your Hindu house position because one chart is cast according to the tropical zodiac while the other is cast employing the sidereal zodiac. Frequently, the difference between these two zodiacs is equal to a shift of one zodiac sign or house between the two types of charts. In other words, you may have Aquarius as your seventh house's zodiac sign in your *bhavacakra,* but in your Judaic birth chart, your seventh house's zodiac sign might be Pisces instead. You might think that the shift of one whole sign makes the Hindu and Judaic methods contradictory or makes one method better than the other. In truth, the two different interpretations often only complement or enhance each other. If a shift doesn't occur in your particular situation, it just confirms the interpretation from two different perspectives.

You'll need your birth chart to use this particular section. (If you don't already have one, visit our Web site at http://www.world-astrology.

com and click on to the linked site that lets you cast and print out your Western tropical birth chart, which is used for both Judaic and Western readings, free of charge.) Enter your (and/or your mate's) birth date onto Worksheet 13. Look for the zodiac sign associated with your seventh house in your tropical Western birth chart. You'll find that zodiac sign in the outer circle, situated directly across the segment marked with a 7 at the center of the circle. (This appears as the unshaded section in fig. 7.) Figure 7 illustrates that the zodiac sign governing Antonio Banderas's seventh house is Virgo (♍). For reference, here's a list of the symbols used in this type of chart:

Aries	♈
Taurus	♉
Gemini	♊
Cancer	♋
Leo	♌
Virgo	♍
Libra	♎
Scorpio	♏
Sagittarius	♐
Capricorn	♑
Aquarius	♒
Pisces	♓

Enter that zodiac sign in the space provided on the worksheet. Do the same with your mate's birth date. Then find the interpretation of that sign in the text following to determine your marital prospects.

WORKSHEET 13. SEVENTH HOUSE TROPICAL ZODIAC SIGN

	Example:	Name A:	Name B:
	Antonio Banderas		
Birth date	10 Aug 1960		
Seventh house tropical zodiac sign	♍ (Virgo)		

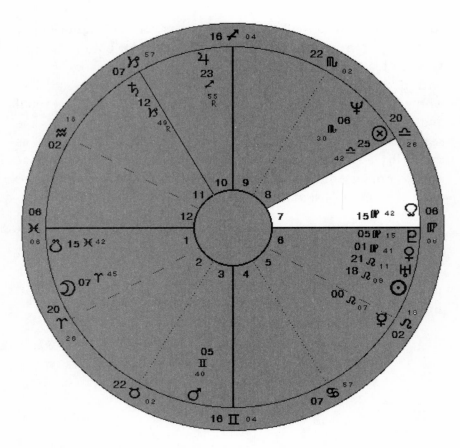

Figure 7. Antonio Banderas's Seventh House in the Birth Chart.

Aries in your chart's seventh house. "My chief want in life," said American essayist Ralph Waldo Emerson, "is someone who shall make me do what I can." You tend to need a spicy mate who likes to argue. You have the potential to marry an assertive person. We tend to seek out what we need in life, whether we realize it or not. An assertive spouse is inclined to be a motivational source, giving you a push when you need it. Arguments can also have a positive effect, if the underlying goal is mutual betterment. Just remember, while quarrels can be positive, fights are always negative. When you debate you attack the problem; when you fight you attack the person. (*Famous examples:* David Bowie, Eric Clapton, Harrison Ford, George Harrison, Katharine Hepburn, Courtney Love, Debbie Reynolds.)

Taurus in your chart's seventh house. You might have a stable and happy marriage that lasts for a long time. With divorce rates soaring toward 60 percent, many married people maintain separate lives and accounts, keeping escape routes ready. All this preparation actually contributes to breakups because when times are tough, people find themselves snared by the traps they've laid for themselves by creating easy ways out. It's a shame for them. You, on the other hand, should plan for a happy lifetime relationship (once you've found a compatible mate), and skip the parachute. (*Famous examples:* Michael Douglas, Diane Keaton, Prince, Justin Timberlake.)

Gemini in your chart's seventh house. You may marry more than once or you may not marry at all. If you do take the leap of faith, your mate might be an educator or a writer, or work in the communications, publishing, or advertising industry. Whether you wed or not, you are likely to have more than one serious relationship during your lifetime. This doesn't indicate traumatic breakups or bad relationships. Life is a lot longer than you realize. Your desires grow and change as you mature. Your potential mate is a communicator, someone with an ability to shape messages for the public. If you learn more about the professions mentioned above, it will facilitate your relationship. It might even help you to find your mate! (*Famous examples:* Brigitte Bardot, Candice Bergen, John Derek, Bridget Fonda, Brad Pitt, Elvis Presley, Elizabeth Taylor, Ted Turner, Princess Diana Spencer Windsor, Prince William Windsor.)

Cancer in your chart's seventh house. There's a good chance you and your mate will have a very close, caring relationship. If you're a man, you might marry someone who strongly resembles your mother or is much younger than yourself. If you're a woman, your potential mate is a dominant person with whom you maintain a strong emotional connection. Like it or not, for the vast majority of us, our parents shaped our understanding of relationships (both how they should and shouldn't be). During childhood there's seldom anyone you communicate with more than your parents. You've been blessed with a clear vision of the ground rules of a relationship that will be healthy for you. With a large age difference or a dominant mate there are clear roles of lead and support. Both parts are essential. (*Famous examples:* Catherine Deneuve, Carrie Fisher, Goldie Hawn, Spencer Tracy.)

Leo in your chart's seventh house. Your ego is liable to be satisfied on a positive level when you're married. A mate is a person and a partner, not an acquisition or a trophy. However, that doesn't mean you can't take pride in your good fortune at being loved by (and seen in public with) such a wonderful attractive person. Don't be surprised if your mate enjoys your attention. (*Famous examples:* Kim Basinger, Michael J. Fox, Mikhail Gorbachev, Carolyn Bessette Kennedy.)

Virgo in your chart's seventh house. You may marry more than once. When you take the plunge, you're inclined to be constructively critical of your mate. One of the roles you take on as a spouse is that of mentor and counselor. It works both ways, as two people invariably arrive in a relationship with different life experience and knowledge to share. However, you might find yourself the teacher far more often than the student. You may also find that at some point graduation comes and your spouse moves on, most likely with your benediction. After you've invested so much of yourself, you can't help being pleased at that person's continued success. This doesn't mean you'll break up. There may be a progressive distance in an area such as profession, but the independence will be healthy. (*Famous examples:* Antonio Banderas, Richard Burton.)

Libra in your chart's seventh house. You'll probably enjoy marriage, but you may equate romantic gestures and charm with emotional commitment. In the end, you might find it difficult to settle down or form a permanent union. Although romance and commitment are often associated, they aren't the same. Infatuation is hormonal, betrothal is (or should be) rational. Beware of someone who bombards you with passionate advances. This isn't love or commitment, it's seduction. If you're in a relationship and a new person showers you with compliments, he or she might naturally be more desirable than the person you're with day after day. If you think about falling for the new person, just remember, the sweet talk you hear has probably been used elsewhere, and will be used on other people, possibly during a relationship with you. (*Famous examples:* Ray Davies, Bo Derek, the Reverend Dr. Martin Luther King Jr., John Lennon, Heather Locklear, Barbra Streisand.)

Scorpio in your chart's seventh house. You tend to attract an intellectual or powerful mate. You're also inclined to wield control in your marriage. Plus, you harbor a secret or mystery that's attached to your relationship. There's always potential for friction when you attempt to control a dominant person. Boundaries and limits set early in a union will provide a foundation for later happiness. As for secrets, there are skeletons in every family's closet. Listen to your heart, as long as your heart tells you to play by the rules. In the end, you can make it work. (*Famous examples:* Mia Farrow, Melanie Griffith, Maria Shriver.)

Sagittarius in your chart's seventh house. You're probably attracted to a mate who thinks and acts on a grand scale. You must have personal freedom within your marriage. To maintain moderate independence, you need an independent spouse. Someone who strives

The *mizpah* coin has been exchanged as a sentimental love token since at least the Victorian era. Its name, roughly translated, means watchtower. The face of the coin is inscribed with a verse from Genesis 31:49: "The Lord watch between me and thee, when we are absent from one another." The token is designed so that it can be split into two halves that fit back together along a jagged edge. Like the lovers it represents, the *mizpah* coin can be whole only when the two halves are joined together. Commonly worn as rings or pendants, *mizpah* coins became popular during the Second World War, when many American soldiers gave them as parting gifts to the brides they left at home. During the 1970s, gold *mizpah* coins reemerged when gold jewelry became the height of fashion.

to realize big dreams is perfect for that. Just remember, the person with whom you truly share your life with isn't necessarily the person you married: it's the person with whom you spend the most time. Is that individual your mate, or a close friend? It's your choice. You make it every day by being with your mate or being with your friends.

(*Famous examples:* Drew Barrymore, Humphrey Bogart, Sir Michael Caine, Julie Christie, Hillary Rodham Clinton, Steffi Graf, Michelle Pfeiffer, Richie Sambora, John Travolta.)

Capricorn in your chart's seventh house. You tend to happily take on marital responsibilities. If you wait until your twenty-seventh birthday has come and gone, you've got a chance to attain a stable and enduring union. Romance is fun. Infatuation is wonderful. Enjoy them early and you won't have regrets later about what might have been. Marriage is work—delightful work, but work nonetheless. As with any enterprise, if you bring more skills to the job, you increase your chances of success. Interaction, compassion, empathy, respect, patience, and self-awareness improve with age. Don't worry about relationship-based mistakes during courtship. Think of it as practice. Learning to love is like studying the violin. You must first master the rules to make music. Only then can you close your eyes and let your heart guide the melody. (*Famous examples:* Ben Affleck, Lauren Bacall, Cher, Bill Gates, Tipper Gore, Jack Nicholson, Kurt Russell, Arnold Schwarzenegger, Steven Spielberg.)

Aquarius in your chart's seventh house. You're inclined to marry more than once or you may not wed at all. If you do take that major step, you'll unite with an unconventional mate and have an equally nonconformist marriage. According to modern science, all the cells in our bodies are replaced by new ones within a five-year period. This means that you're quite literally not the person you were five years ago, and in another five years you'll be someone else entirely. Is it any wonder that we can fall in and out of love, and cherish different people at different times? Also, there's no such thing as a normal relationship, and there's no reason for you to want one. At times when life seems especially off-kilter, consider this: it isn't the conformists who change the world. (*Famous examples:* George W. Bush, Bill Clinton, Johnny Depp, Jane Fonda, Al Gore, Julia Roberts, O. J. Simpson, Donald Trump, Prince Charles Windsor.)

Pisces rules your chart's seventh house. You're inclined to establish some fairly unrealistic expectations about marriage. In fact, you might marry someone who's very artistic, from a minority group, or addicted to drugs or alcohol. An intense personality is an attractive one. For you, this is potentially very positive or very negative. Obsessions and addictions can be constructive or destructive. Before you commit, make sure your love has positive interests. You may not be dragged down by a mate's self-destructive behavior, but you certainly won't move forward as quickly. The word "tolerance" has two meanings. Both are important. You'll need to be tolerant of your mate's eccentricities. You'll also need to build a tolerance to your environment so that your mate's negative aspects don't affect you. (*Famous examples:* Woody Allen, Warren Beatty, Kurt Cobain, John F. Kennedy Jr., Madonna, Brooke Shields, Britney Spears, Oprah Winfrey, Dwight Yoakam.)

We'll use actor Antonio Banderas's seventh house position as an example. The astrologer might deduce that Virgo in his chart's seventh house implies he might marry or have a serious relationship more than once during his lifetime.

Will You Feel the Earth Move?: Venus's Tropical Placement in Your Chart

There are people who believe that lust ignites passion but it takes matrimony to build love. Whether a marriage comes about through parental intervention or through independent reconnaissance, the question of love always enters the picture sooner or later. Hindu astrologers look for love by directing their attention toward Venus's placement in your chart. So do Judaic astrologers.

Normally, the interpretations of Venus's house placement and associated zodiac sign are combined by the Judaic astrologer into a personal description, just as a Hindu astrologer would do in the same circumstances. However, there is one radical difference. Venus might not be placed in the same house or zodiac sign in your Judaic birth chart as it was in your *bhavacakra*. Because Judaic and Hindu charts are calculated with different zodiacs, there is a potential shift from one zodiac sign to the next or one house to the next. This makes for varying interpretations.

You don't need a birth chart to use this section. Simply enter your (and/or your mate's) birth date onto Worksheet 14. Using Table 8, look for the time period in which your birth date falls and find the zodiac sign associated with that period. (The dates listed are the starting dates for each period: your birth date should fall on or after the appropriate date, and before the date in the row below.) Enter that zodiac sign in the space provided on the worksheet. Do the same for your mate. Then locate the zodiac sign in the text following and read how your tendency toward romance might influence your love life.

Naturally, if you have a Western birth chart cast according to the tropical zodiac, look for Venus's symbol (♀) (fig. 8 illustrates Venus's zodiac sign and house placement in Antonio Banderas's birth chart) and enter the zodiac sign that appears on the same line with Venus's symbol in the worksheet space provided. For example, fig. 8 shows that the zodiac sign associated with Venus in Banderas's chart is Virgo (♍). This appears as the unshaded section in fig. 8. (A list of zodiac signs and their symbols can be found on page 183.)

For a reading that combines Venus's house placement and zodiac sign, look for Venus's symbol (♀) on your Judaic (tropical Western) birth chart. Then note the number of the house it occupies, toward the center of the circle. (This appears in the unshaded section in fig. 8.) Locate that house number on pages 123–26 in Chapter 3. Then synthesize what you learned in this section with your house interpretation in Chapter 3.

WORKSHEET 14. VENUS'S TROPICAL ZODIAC SIGN AND HOUSE LOCATION

	Example:	Name A:	Name B:
	Antonio Banderas		
Birth date	10 Aug 1960		
Venus's tropical zodiac sign	♍ (Virgo)		
Venus's house location	6 (sixth house)		

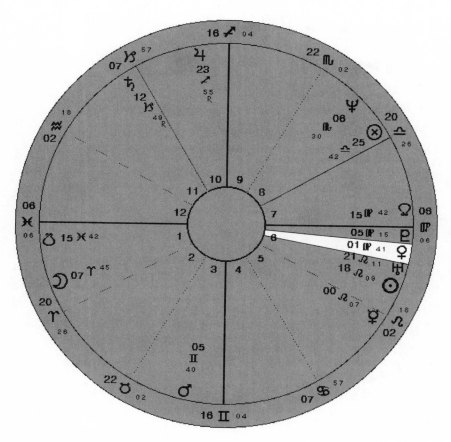

Figure 8. Antonio Banderas's Venus in the Birth Chart.

TABLE 8. TROPICAL PLACEMENT FOR VENUS, 1927–1987

Starting Date	Zodiac Sign	Starting Date	Zodiac Sign
01 Jan 1927	Capricorn (♑)	03 Jun 1929	Taurus (♉)
09 Jan 1927	Aquarius (♒)	08 Jul 1929	Gemini (♊)
02 Feb 1927	Pisces (♓)	05 Aug 1929	Cancer (♋)
27 Feb 1927	Aries (♈)	31 Aug 1929	Leo (♌)
23 Mar 1927	Taurus (♉)	26 Sep 1929	Virgo (♍)
17 Apr 1927	Gemini (♊)	20 Oct 1929	Libra (♎)
12 May 1927	Cancer (♋)	13 Nov 1929	Scorpio (♏)
08 Jun 1927	Leo (♌)	07 Dec 1929	Sagittarius (♐)
08 Jul 1927	Virgo (♍)	31 Dec 1929	Capricorn (♑)
10 Nov 1927	Libra (♎)	24 Jan 1930	Aquarius (♒)
09 Dec 1927	Scorpio (♏)	17 Feb 1930	Pisces (♓)
04 Jan 1928	Sagittarius (♐)	13 Mar 1930	Aries (♈)
29 Jan 1928	Capricorn (♑)	06 Apr 1930	Taurus (♉)
23 Feb 1928	Aquarius (♒)	01 May 1930	Gemini (♊)
18 Mar 1928	Pisces (♓)	25 May 1930	Cancer (♋)
12 Apr 1928	Aries (♈)	19 Jun 1930	Leo (♌)
06 May 1928	Taurus (♉)	15 Jul 1930	Virgo (♍)
30 May 1928	Gemini (♊)	10 Aug 1930	Libra (♎)
24 Jun 1928	Cancer (♋)	07 Sep 1930	Scorpio (♏)
18 Jul 1928	Leo (♌)	12 Oct 1930	Sagittarius (♐)
12 Aug 1928	Virgo (♍)	22 Nov 1930	Scorpio (♏)
05 Sep 1928	Libra (♎)	04 Jan 1931	Sagittarius (♐)
29 Sep 1928	Scorpio (♏)	07 Feb 1931	Capricorn (♑)
25 Oct 1928	Sagittarius (♐)	06 Mar 1931	Aquarius (♒)
17 Nov 1928	Capricorn (♑)	01 Apr 1931	Pisces (♓)
12 Dec 1928	Aquarius (♒)	26 Apr 1931	Aries (♈)
07 Jan 1929	Pisces (♓)	21 May 1931	Taurus (♉)
03 Feb 1929	Aries (♈)	15 Jun 1931	Gemini (♊)
08 Mar 1929	Taurus (♉)	10 Jul 1931	Cancer (♋)
20 Apr 1929	Aries (♈)	03 Aug 1931	Leo (♌)

Starting Date	Zodiac Sign	Starting Date	Zodiac Sign
27 Aug 1931	Virgo (♍)	06 Apr 1934	Pisces (♓)
21 Sep 1931	Libra (♎)	06 May 1934	Aries (♈)
15 Oct 1931	Scorpio (♏)	02 Jun 1934	Taurus (♉)
08 Nov 1931	Sagittarius (♐)	28 Jun 1934	Gemini (♊)
02 Dec 1931	Capricorn (♑)	24 Jul 1934	Cancer (♋)
26 Dec 1931	Aquarius (♒)	18 Aug 1934	Leo (♌)
19 Jan 1932	Pisces (♓)	11 Sep 1934	Virgo (♍)
13 Feb 1932	Aries (♈)	05 Oct 1934	Libra (♎)
09 Mar 1932	Taurus (♉)	29 Oct 1934	Scorpio (♏)
05 Apr 1932	Gemini (♊)	22 Nov 1934	Sagittarius (♐)
06 May 1932	Cancer (♋)	16 Dec 1934	Capricorn (♑)
13 Jul 1932	Gemini (♊)	09 Jan 1935	Aquarius (♒)
28 Jul 1932	Cancer (♋)	02 Feb 1935	Pisces (♓)
09 Sep 1932	Leo (♌)	26 Feb 1935	Aries (♈)
07 Oct 1932	Virgo (♍)	22 Mar 1935	Taurus (♉)
02 Nov 1932	Libra (♎)	16 Apr 1935	Gemini (♊)
27 Nov 1932	Scorpio (♏)	12 May 1935	Cancer (♋)
21 Dec 1932	Sagittarius (♐)	08 Jun 1935	Leo (♌)
14 Jan 1933	Capricorn (♑)	08 Jul 1935	Virgo (♍)
07 Feb 1933	Aquarius (♒)	10 Nov 1935	Libra (♎)
03 Mar 1933	Pisces (♓)	09 Dec 1935	Scorpio (♏)
28 Mar 1933	Aries (♈)	04 Jan 1936	Sagittarius (♐)
21 Apr 1933	Taurus (♉)	29 Jan 1936	Capricorn (♑)
15 May 1933	Gemini (♊)	22 Feb 1936	Aquarius (♒)
09 Jun 1933	Cancer (♋)	18 Mar 1936	Pisces (♓)
03 Jul 1933	Leo (♌)	11 Apr 1936	Aries (♈)
28 Jul 1933	Virgo (♍)	05 May 1936	Taurus (♉)
22 Aug 1933	Libra (♎)	30 May 1936	Gemini (♊)
16 Sep 1933	Scorpio (♏)	23 Jun 1936	Cancer (♋)
11 Oct 1933	Sagittarius (♐)	18 Jul 1936	Leo (♌)
07 Nov 1933	Capricorn (♑)	11 Aug 1936	Virgo (♍)
06 Dec 1933	Aquarius (♒)	04 Sep 1936	Libra (♎)

Starting Date	Zodiac Sign	Starting Date	Zodiac Sign
29 Sep 1936	Scorpio (♏)	31 Mar 1939	Pisces (♓)
23 Oct 1936	Sagittarius (♐)	26 Apr 1939	Aries (♈)
17 Nov 1936	Capricorn (♑)	21 May 1939	Taurus (♉)
12 Dec 1936	Aquarius (♒)	14 Jun 1939	Gemini (♊)
06 Jan 1937	Pisces (♓)	09 Jul 1939	Cancer (♋)
02 Feb 1937	Aries (♈)	03 Aug 1939	Leo (♌)
10 Mar 1937	Taurus (♉)	27 Aug 1939	Virgo (♍)
14 Apr 1937	Aries (♈)	20 Sep 1939	Libra (♎)
04 Jun 1937	Taurus (♉)	14 Oct 1939	Scorpio (♏)
08 Jul 1937	Gemini (♊)	07 Nov 1939	Sagittarius (♐)
05 Aug 1937	Cancer (♋)	01 Dec 1939	Capricorn (♑)
31 Aug 1937	Leo (♌)	25 Dec 1939	Aquarius (♒)
25 Sep 1937	Virgo (♍)	19 Jan 1940	Pisces (♓)
20 Oct 1937	Libra (♎)	12 Feb 1940	Aries (♈)
13 Nov 1937	Scorpio (♏)	09 Mar 1940	Taurus (♉)
07 Dec 1937	Sagittarius (♐)	05 Apr 1940	Gemini (♊)
31 Dec 1937	Capricorn (♑)	07 May 1940	Cancer (♋)
23 Jan 1938	Aquarius (♒)	06 Jul 1940	Gemini (♊)
16 Feb 1938	Pisces (♓)	01 Aug 1940	Cancer (♋)
12 Mar 1938	Aries (♈)	09 Sep 1940	Leo (♌)
06 Apr 1938	Taurus (♉)	07 Oct 1940	Virgo (♍)
30 Apr 1938	Gemini (♊)	02 Nov 1940	Libra (♎)
25 May 1938	Cancer (♋)	27 Nov 1940	Scorpio (♏)
19 Jun 1938	Leo (♌)	21 Dec 1940	Sagittarius (♐)
14 Jul 1938	Virgo (♍)	14 Jan 1941	Capricorn (♑)
10 Aug 1938	Libra (♎)	07 Feb 1941	Aquarius (♒)
07 Sep 1938	Scorpio (♏)	03 Mar 1941	Pisces (♓)
14 Oct 1938	Sagittarius (♐)	27 Mar 1941	Aries (♈)
16 Nov 1938	Capricorn (♑)	20 Apr 1941	Taurus (♉)
05 Jan 1939	Sagittarius (♐)	15 May 1941	Gemini (♊)
06 Feb 1939	Capricorn (♑)	08 Jun 1941	Cancer (♋)
06 Mar 1939	Aquarius (♒)	03 Jul 1941	Leo (♌)

Starting Date	Zodiac Sign	Starting Date	Zodiac Sign
27 Jul 1941	Virgo (♍)	05 May 1944	Taurus (♉)
21 Aug 1941	Libra (♎)	29 May 1944	Gemini (♊)
15 Sep 1941	Scorpio (♏)	23 Jun 1944	Cancer (♋)
11 Oct 1941	Sagittarius (♐)	17 Jul 1944	Leo (♌)
06 Nov 1941	Capricorn (♑)	11 Aug 1944	Virgo (♍)
06 Dec 1941	Aquarius (♒)	04 Sep 1944	Libra (♎)
07 Apr 1942	Pisces (♓)	28 Sep 1944	Scorpio (♏)
06 May 1942	Aries (♈)	23 Oct 1944	Sagittarius (♐)
02 Jun 1942	Taurus (♉)	16 Nov 1944	Capricorn (♑)
28 Jun 1942	Gemini (♊)	11 Dec 1944	Aquarius (♒)
23 Jul 1942	Cancer (♋)	06 Jan 1945	Pisces (♓)
17 Aug 1942	Leo (♌)	02 Feb 1945	Aries (♈)
11 Sep 1942	Virgo (♍)	11 Mar 1945	Taurus (♉)
05 Oct 1942	Libra (♎)	08 Apr 1945	Aries (♈)
29 Oct 1942	Scorpio (♏)	05 Jun 1945	Taurus (♉)
22 Nov 1942	Sagittarius (♐)	08 Jul 1945	Gemini (♊)
16 Dec 1942	Capricorn (♑)	04 Aug 1945	Cancer (♋)
08 Jan 1943	Aquarius (♒)	31 Aug 1945	Leo (♌)
01 Feb 1943	Pisces (♓)	25 Sep 1945	Virgo (♍)
26 Feb 1943	Aries (♈)	19 Oct 1945	Libra (♎)
22 Mar 1943	Taurus (♉)	12 Nov 1945	Scorpio (♏)
16 Apr 1943	Gemini (♊)	06 Dec 1945	Sagittarius (♐)
11 May 1943	Cancer (♋)	30 Dec 1945	Capricorn (♑)
08 Jun 1943	Leo (♌)	23 Jan 1946	Aquarius (♒)
08 Jul 1943	Virgo (♍)	16 Feb 1946	Pisces (♓)
10 Nov 1943	Libra (♎)	12 Mar 1946	Aries (♈)
08 Dec 1943	Scorpio (♏)	05 Apr 1946	Taurus (♉)
03 Jan 1944	Sagittarius (♐)	29 Apr 1946	Gemini (♊)
28 Jan 1944	Capricorn (♑)	24 May 1946	Cancer (♋)
22 Feb 1944	Aquarius (♒)	18 Jun 1946	Leo (♌)
17 Mar 1944	Pisces (♓)	14 Jul 1946	Virgo (♍)
11 Apr 1944	Aries (♈)	09 Aug 1946	Libra (♎)

Starting Date	Zodiac Sign	Starting Date	Zodiac Sign
07 Sep 1946	Scorpio (♏)	02 Mar 1949	Pisces (♓)
16 Oct 1946	Sagittarius (♐)	26 Mar 1949	Aries (♈)
08 Nov 1946	Scorpio (♏)	20 Apr 1949	Taurus (♉)
06 Jan 1947	Sagittarius (♐)	14 May 1949	Gemini (♊)
06 Feb 1947	Capricorn (♑)	07 Jun 1949	Cancer (♋)
05 Mar 1947	Aquarius (♒)	02 Jul 1949	Leo (♌)
31 Mar 1947	Pisces (♓)	27 Jul 1949	Virgo (I)
25 Apr 1947	Aries (♈)	21 Aug 1949	Libra (♎)
20 May 1947	Taurus (♉)	15 Sep 1949	Scorpio (♏)
14 Jun 1947	Gemini (♊)	10 Oct 1949	Sagittarius (♐)
09 Jul 1947	Cancer (♋)	06 Nov 1949	Capricorn (♑)
02 Aug 1947	Leo (♌)	06 Dec 1949	Aquarius (♒)
26 Aug 1947	Virgo (♍)	07 Apr 1950	Pisces (♓)
20 Sep 1947	Libra (♎)	06 May 1950	Aries (♈)
14 Oct 1947	Scorpio (♏)	02 Jun 1950	Taurus (♉)
07 Nov 1947	Sagittarius (♐)	27 Jun 1950	Gemini (♊)
01 Dec 1947	Capricorn (♑)	23 Jul 1950	Cancer (♋)
25 Dec 1947	Aquarius (♒)	17 Aug 1950	Leo (♌)
18 Jan 1948	Pisces (♓)	10 Sep 1950	Virgo (♍)
12 Feb 1948	Aries (♈)	04 Oct 1950	Libra (♎)
08 Mar 1948	Taurus (♉)	28 Oct 1950	Scorpio (♏)
05 Apr 1948	Gemini (♊)	21 Nov 1950	Sagittarius (♐)
07 May 1948	Cancer (♋)	15 Dec 1950	Capricorn (♑)
29 Jun 1948	Gemini (♊)	08 Jan 1951	Aquarius (♒)
03 Aug 1948	Cancer (♋)	01 Feb 1951	Pisces (♓)
09 Sep 1948	Leo (♌)	25 Feb 1951	Aries (♈)
07 Oct 1948	Virgo (♍)	21 Mar 1951	Taurus (♉)
01 Nov 1948	Libra (♎)	15 Apr 1951	Gemini (♊)
26 Nov 1948	Scorpio (♏)	11 May 1951	Cancer (♋)
20 Dec 1948	Sagittarius (♐)	07 Jun 1951	Leo (♌)
13 Jan 1949	Capricorn (♑)	08 Jul 1951	Virgo (♍)
06 Feb 1949	Aquarius (♒)	10 Nov 1951	Libra (♎)

Starting Date	Zodiac Sign	Starting Date	Zodiac Sign
08 Dec 1951	Scorpio (♏)	04 Apr 1954	Taurus (♉)
03 Jan 1952	Sagittarius (♐)	29 Apr 1954	Gemini (♊)
28 Jan 1952	Capricorn (♑)	24 May 1954	Cancer (♋)
21 Feb 1952	Aquarius (♒)	18 Jun 1954	Leo (♌)
17 Mar 1952	Pisces (♓)	13 Jul 1954	Virgo (♍)
10 Apr 1952	Aries (♈)	09 Aug 1954	Libra (♎)
04 May 1952	Taurus (♉)	07 Sep 1954	Scorpio (♏)
29 May 1952	Gemini (♊)	24 Oct 1954	Sagittarius (♐)
22 Jun 1952	Cancer (♋)	27 Oct 1954	Capricorn (♑)
17 Jul 1952	Leo (♌)	06 Jan 1955	Sagittarius (♐)
10 Aug 1952	Virgo (♍)	06 Feb 1955	Capricorn (♑)
03 Sep 1952	Libra (♎)	05 Mar 1955	Aquarius (♒)
28 Sep 1952	Scorpio (♏)	30 Mar 1955	Pisces (♓)
22 Oct 1952	Sagittarius (♐)	25 Apr 1955	Aries (♈)
16 Nov 1952	Capricorn (♑)	20 May 1955	Taurus (♉)
11 Dec 1952	Aquarius (♒)	13 Jun 1955	Gemini (♊)
05 Jan 1953	Pisces (♓)	08 Jul 1955	Cancer (♋)
02 Feb 1953	Aries (♈)	01 Aug 1955	Leo (♌)
15 Mar 1953	Taurus (♉)	26 Aug 1955	Virgo (♍)
31 Mar 1953	Aries (♈)	19 Sep 1955	Libra (♎)
05 Jun 1953	Taurus (♉)	13 Oct 1955	Scorpio (♏)
07 Jul 1953	Gemini (♊)	06 Nov 1955	Sagittarius (♐)
04 Aug 1953	Cancer (♋)	30 Nov 1955	Capricorn (♑)
30 Aug 1953	Leo (♌)	24 Dec 1955	Aquarius (♒)
24 Sep 1953	Virgo (♍)	18 Jan 1956	Pisces (♓)
19 Oct 1953	Libra (♎)	11 Feb 1956	Aries (♈)
12 Nov 1953	Scorpio (♏)	08 Mar 1956	Taurus (♉)
06 Dec 1953	Sagittarius (♐)	04 Apr 1956	Gemini (♊)
30 Dec 1953	Capricorn (♑)	08 May 1956	Cancer (♋)
22 Jan 1954	Aquarius (♒)	24 Jun 1956	Gemini (♊)
15 Feb 1954	Pisces (♓)	04 Aug 1956	Cancer (♋)
11 Mar 1954	Aries (♈)	08 Sep 1956	Leo (♌)

Starting Date	Zodiac Sign	Starting Date	Zodiac Sign
06 Oct 1956	Virgo (♍)	21 Mar 1959	Taurus (♉)
01 Nov 1956	Libra (♎)	15 Apr 1959	Gemini (♊)
26 Nov 1956	Scorpio (♏)	11 May 1959	Cancer (♋)
20 Dec 1956	Sagittarius (♐)	07 Jun 1959	Leo (♌)
13 Jan 1957	Capricorn (♑)	09 Jul 1959	Virgo (♍)
06 Feb 1957	Aquarius (♒)	20 Sep 1959	Leo (♌)
04 Mar 1957	Pisces (♓)	25 Sep 1959	Virgo (♍)
26 Mar 1957	Aries (♈)	10 Nov 1959	Libra (♎)
19 Apr 1957	Taurus (♉)	08 Dec 1959	Scorpio (♏)
13 May 1957	Gemini (♊)	02 Jan 1960	Sagittarius (♐)
07 Jun 1957	Cancer (♋)	27 Jan 1960	Capricorn (♑)
13 Jul 1957	Leo (♌)	21 Feb 1960	Aquarius (♒)
30 Jul 1957	Virgo (♍)	16 Mar 1960	Pisces (♓)
20 Aug 1957	Libra (♎)	09 Apr 1960	Aries (♈)
14 Sep 1957	Scorpio (♏)	04 May 1960	Taurus (♉)
10 Oct 1957	Sagittarius (♐)	28 May 1960	Gemini (♊)
06 Nov 1957	Capricorn (♑)	22 Jun 1960	Cancer (♋)
07 Dec 1957	Aquarius (♒)	16 Jul 1960	Leo (♌)
07 Apr 1958	Pisces (♓)	09 Aug 1960	Virgo (♍)
05 May 1958	Aries (♈)	03 Sep 1960	Libra (♎)
01 Jun 1958	Taurus (♉)	27 Sep 1960	Scorpio (♏)
27 Jun 1958	Gemini (♊)	22 Oct 1960	Sagittarius (♐)
22 Jul 1958	Cancer (♋)	15 Nov 1960	Capricorn (♑)
16 Aug 1958	Leo (♌)	10 Dec 1960	Aquarius (♒)
10 Sep 1958	Virgo (♍)	05 Jan 1961	Pisces (♓)
04 Oct 1958	Libra (♎)	02 Feb 1961	Aries (♈)
28 Oct 1958	Scorpio (♏)	06 Jun 1961	Taurus (♉)
21 Nov 1958	Sagittarius (♐)	07 Jul 1961	Gemini (♊)
14 Dec 1958	Capricorn (♑)	04 Aug 1961	Cancer (♋)
07 Jan 1959	Aquarius (♒)	30 Aug 1961	Leo (♌)
31 Jan 1959	Pisces (♓)	24 Sep 1961	Virgo (♍)
24 Feb 1959	Aries (♈)	18 Oct 1961	Libra (♎)

Starting Date	Zodiac Sign	Starting Date	Zodiac Sign
11 Nov 1961	Scorpio (♏)	09 May 1964	Cancer (♋)
01 Dec 1961	Sagittarius (♐)	18 Jun 1964	Gemini (♊)
20 Dec 1961	Capricorn (♑)	05 Aug 1964	Cancer (♋)
22 Jan 1962	Aquarius (♒)	08 Sep 1964	Leo (♌)
15 Feb 1962	Pisces (♓)	06 Oct 1964	Virgo (♍)
11 Mar 1962	Aries (♈)	31 Oct 1964	Libra (♎)
04 Apr 1962	Taurus (♉)	25 Nov 1964	Scorpio (♏)
28 Apr 1962	Gemini (♊)	19 Dec 1964	Sagittarius (♐)
23 May 1962	Cancer (♋)	12 Jan 1965	Capricorn (♑)
17 Jun 1962	Leo (♌)	05 Feb 1965	Aquarius (♒)
13 Jul 1962	Virgo (♍)	01 Mar 1965	Pisces (♓)
09 Aug 1962	Libra (♎)	25 Mar 1965	Aries (♈)
07 Sep 1962	Scorpio (♏)	19 Apr 1965	Taurus (♉)
07 Jan 1963	Sagittarius (♐)	13 May 1965	Gemini (♊)
06 Feb 1963	Capricorn (♑)	06 Jun 1965	Cancer (♋)
04 Mar 1963	Aquarius (♒)	01 Jul 1965	Leo (♌)
30 Mar 1963	Pisces (♓)	26 Jul 1965	Virgo (♍)
24 Apr 1963	Aries (♈)	20 Aug 1965	Libra (♎)
19 May 1963	Taurus (♉)	14 Sep 1965	Scorpio (♏)
13 Jun 1963	Gemini (♊)	10 Oct 1965	Sagittarius (♐)
07 Jul 1963	Cancer (♋)	06 Nov 1965	Capricorn (♑)
01 Aug 1963	Leo (♌)	07 Dec 1965	Aquarius (♒)
25 Aug 1963	Virgo (♍)	07 Feb 1966	Capricorn (♑)
18 Sep 1963	Libra (♎)	25 Feb 1966	Aquarius (♒)
12 Oct 1963	Scorpio (♏)	07 Apr 1966	Pisces (♓)
06 Nov 1963	Sagittarius (♐)	05 May 1966	Aries (♈)
30 Nov 1963	Capricorn (♑)	01 Jun 1966	Taurus (♉)
24 Dec 1963	Aquarius (♒)	26 Jun 1966	Gemini (♊)
17 Jan 1964	Pisces (♓)	22 Jul 1966	Cancer (♋)
11 Feb 1964	Aries (♈)	16 Aug 1966	Leo (♌)
08 Mar 1964	Taurus (♉)	09 Sep 1966	Virgo (♍)
04 Apr 1964	Gemini (♊)	03 Oct 1966	Libra (♎)

Starting Date	Zodiac Sign	Starting Date	Zodiac Sign
27 Oct 1966	Scorpio (♏)	06 Jun 1969	Taurus (♉)
20 Nov 1966	Sagittarius (♐)	07 Jul 1969	Gemini (♊)
14 Dec 1966	Capricorn (♑)	03 Aug 1969	Cancer (♋)
07 Jan 1967	Aquarius (♒)	29 Aug 1969	Leo (♌)
31 Jan 1967	Pisces (♓)	23 Sep 1969	Virgo (♍)
24 Feb 1967	Aries (♈)	18 Oct 1969	Libra (♎)
20 Mar 1967	Taurus (♉)	11 Nov 1969	Scorpio (♏)
14 Apr 1967	Gemini (♊)	05 Dec 1969	Sagittarius (♐)
10 May 1967	Cancer (♋)	28 Dec 1969	Capricorn (♑)
07 Jun 1967	Leo (♌)	21 Jan 1970	Aquarius (♒)
09 Jul 1967	Virgo (♍)	14 Feb 1970	Pisces (♓)
09 Sep 1967	Leo (♌)	10 Mar 1970	Aries (♈)
02 Oct 1967	Virgo (♍)	03 Apr 1970	Taurus (♉)
10 Nov 1967	Libra (♎)	28 Apr 1970	Gemini (♊)
07 Dec 1967	Scorpio (♏)	23 May 1970	Cancer (♋)
02 Jan 1968	Sagittarius (♐)	17 Jun 1970	Leo (♌)
27 Jan 1968	Capricorn (♑)	13 Jul 1970	Virgo (♍)
20 Feb 1968	Aquarius (♒)	08 Aug 1970	Libra (♎)
16 Mar 1968	Pisces (♓)	07 Sep 1970	Scorpio (♏)
09 Apr 1968	Aries (♈)	07 Jan 1971	Sagittarius (♐)
03 May 1968	Taurus (♉)	06 Feb 1971	Capricorn (♑)
28 May 1968	Gemini (♊)	04 Mar 1971	Aquarius (♒)
21 Jun 1968	Cancer (♋)	30 Mar 1971	Pisces (♓)
16 Jul 1968	Leo (♌)	24 Apr 1971	Aries (♈)
09 Aug 1968	Virgo (♍)	19 May 1971	Taurus (♉)
02 Sep 1968	Libra (♎)	07 Jun 1971	Gemini (♊)
27 Sep 1968	Scorpio (♏)	07 Jul 1971	Cancer (♋)
21 Oct 1968	Sagittarius (♐)	01 Aug 1971	Leo (♌)
15 Nov 1968	Capricorn (♑)	25 Aug 1971	Virgo (♍)
10 Dec 1968	Aquarius (♒)	18 Sep 1971	Libra (♎)
05 Jan 1969	Pisces (♓)	12 Oct 1971	Scorpio (♏)
02 Feb 1969	Aries (♈)	05 Nov 1971	Sagittarius (♐)

Starting Date	Zodiac Sign	Starting Date	Zodiac Sign
29 Nov 1971	Capricorn (♑)	31 May 1974	Taurus (♉)
23 Dec 1971	Aquarius (♒)	26 Jun 1974	Gemini (♊)
17 Jan 1972	Pisces (♓)	21 Jul 1974	Cancer (♋)
10 Feb 1972	Aries (♈)	15 Aug 1974	Leo (♌)
07 Mar 1972	Taurus (♉)	08 Sep 1974	Virgo (♍)
04 Apr 1972	Gemini (♊)	03 Oct 1974	Libra (♎)
11 May 1972	Cancer (♋)	27 Oct 1974	Scorpio (♏)
12 Jun 1972	Gemini (♊)	19 Nov 1974	Sagittarius (♐)
06 Aug 1972	Cancer (♋)	13 Dec 1974	Capricorn (♑)
08 Sep 1972	Leo (♌)	06 Jan 1975	Aquarius (♒)
05 Oct 1972	Virgo (♍)	30 Jan 1975	Pisces (♓)
31 Oct 1972	Libra (♎)	23 Feb 1975	Aries (♈)
25 Nov 1972	Scorpio (♏)	20 Mar 1975	Taurus (♉)
19 Dec 1972	Sagittarius (♐)	14 Apr 1975	Gemini (♊)
12 Jan 1973	Capricorn (♑)	10 May 1975	Cancer (♋)
05 Feb 1973	Aquarius (♒)	06 Jun 1975	Leo (♌)
01 Mar 1973	Pisces (♓)	09 Jul 1975	Virgo (♍)
25 Mar 1973	Aries (♈)	03 Sep 1975	Leo (♌)
18 Apr 1973	Taurus (♉)	04 Oct 1975	Virgo (♍)
12 May 1973	Gemini (♊)	10 Nov 1975	Libra (♎)
06 Jun 1973	Cancer (♋)	07 Dec 1975	Scorpio (♏)
30 Jun 1973	Leo (♌)	02 Jan 1976	Sagittarius (♐)
25 Jul 1973	Virgo (♍)	26 Jan 1976	Capricorn (♑)
19 Aug 1973	Libra (♎)	20 Feb 1976	Aquarius (♒)
13 Sep 1973	Scorpio (♏)	15 Mar 1976	Pisces (♓)
09 Oct 1973	Sagittarius (♐)	08 Apr 1976	Aries (♈)
06 Nov 1973	Capricorn (♑)	03 May 1976	Taurus (♉)
08 Dec 1973	Aquarius (♒)	27 May 1976	Gemini (♊)
30 Jan 1974	Capricorn (♑)	21 Jun 1976	Cancer (♋)
01 Mar 1974	Aquarius (♒)	15 Jul 1976	Leo (♌)
07 Apr 1974	Pisces (♓)	08 Aug 1976	Virgo (♍)
05 May 1974	Aries (♈)	02 Sep 1976	Libra (♎)

Starting Date	Zodiac Sign	Starting Date	Zodiac Sign
26 Sep 1976	Scorpio (♏)	06 Jul 1979	Cancer (♋)
21 Oct 1976	Sagittarius (♐)	31 Jul 1979	Leo (♌)
14 Nov 1976	Capricorn (♑)	24 Aug 1979	Virgo (♍)
10 Dec 1976	Aquarius (♒)	17 Sep 1979	Libra (♎)
05 Jan 1977	Pisces (♓)	11 Oct 1979	Scorpio (♏)
02 Feb 1977	Aries (♈)	04 Nov 1979	Sagittarius (♐)
06 Jun 1977	Taurus (♉)	29 Nov 1979	Capricorn (♑)
07 Jul 1977	Gemini (♊)	23 Dec 1979	Aquarius (♒)
03 Aug 1977	Cancer (♋)	16 Jan 1980	Pisces (♓)
29 Aug 1977	Leo (♌)	10 Feb 1980	Aries (♈)
23 Sep 1977	Virgo (♍)	07 Mar 1980	Taurus (♉)
17 Oct 1977	Libra (♎)	04 Apr 1980	Gemini (♊)
10 Nov 1977	Scorpio (♏)	13 May 1980	Cancer (♋)
04 Dec 1977	Sagittarius (♐)	05 Jun 1980	Gemini (♊)
28 Dec 1977	Capricorn (♑)	07 Aug 1980	Cancer (♋)
21 Jan 1978	Aquarius (♒)	08 Sep 1980	Leo (♌)
14 Feb 1978	Pisces (♓)	05 Oct 1980	Virgo (♍)
10 Mar 1978	Aries (♈)	30 Oct 1980	Libra (♎)
03 Apr 1978	Taurus (♉)	24 Nov 1980	Scorpio (♏)
27 Apr 1978	Gemini (♊)	18 Dec 1980	Sagittarius (♐)
22 May 1978	Cancer (♋)	11 Jan 1981	Capricorn (♑)
16 Jun 1978	Leo (♌)	04 Feb 1981	Aquarius (♒)
12 Jul 1978	Virgo (♍)	28 Feb 1981	Pisces (♓)
08 Aug 1978	Libra (♎)	24 Mar 1981	Aries (♈)
07 Sep 1978	Scorpio (♏)	18 Apr 1981	Taurus (♉)
07 Jan 1979	Sagittarius (♐)	12 May 1981	Gemini (♊)
05 Feb 1979	Capricorn (♑)	05 Jun 1981	Cancer (♋)
04 Mar 1979	Aquarius (♒)	30 Jun 1981	Leo (♌)
29 Mar 1979	Pisces (♓)	25 Jul 1981	Virgo (♍)
18 Apr 1979	Aries (♈)	19 Aug 1981	Libra (♎)
18 May 1979	Taurus (♉)	13 Sep 1981	Scorpio (♏)
12 Jun 1979	Gemini (♊)	09 Oct 1981	Sagittarius (♐)

Starting Date	Zodiac Sign	Starting Date	Zodiac Sign
06 Nov 1981	Capricorn (♑)	02 May 1984	Taurus (♉)
09 Dec 1981	Aquarius (♒)	27 May 1984	Gemini (♊)
23 Jan 1982	Capricorn (♑)	20 Jun 1984	Cancer (♋)
02 Mar 1982	Aquarius (♒)	14 Jul 1984	Leo (♌)
07 Apr 1982	Pisces (♓)	08 Aug 1984	Virgo (♍)
05 May 1982	Aries (♈)	01 Sep 1984	Libra (♎)
31 May 1982	Taurus (♉)	26 Sep 1984	Scorpio (♏)
26 Jun 1982	Gemini (♊)	20 Oct 1984	Sagittarius (♐)
21 Jul 1982	Cancer (♋)	14 Nov 1984	Capricorn (♑)
14 Aug 1982	Leo (♌)	09 Dec 1984	Aquarius (♒)
08 Sep 1982	Virgo (♍)	04 Jan 1985	Pisces (♓)
02 Oct 1982	Libra (♎)	02 Feb 1985	Aries (♈)
26 Oct 1982	Scorpio (♏)	06 Jun 1985	Taurus (♉)
19 Nov 1982	Sagittarius (♐)	06 Jul 1985	Gemini (♊)
13 Dec 1982	Capricorn (♑)	02 Aug 1985	Cancer (♋)
06 Jan 1983	Aquarius (♒)	28 Aug 1985	Leo (♌)
23 Jan 1983	Pisces (♓)	22 Sep 1985	Virgo (♍)
23 Feb 1983	Aries (♈)	17 Oct 1985	Libra (♎)
19 Mar 1983	Taurus (♉)	10 Nov 1985	Scorpio (♏)
13 Apr 1983	Gemini (♊)	04 Dec 1985	Sagittarius (♐)
09 May 1983	Cancer (♋)	27 Dec 1985	Capricorn (♑)
06 Jun 1983	Leo (♌)	20 Jan 1986	Aquarius (♒)
10 Jul 1983	Virgo (♍)	11 Feb 1986	Pisces (♓)
27 Aug 1983	Leo (♌)	09 Mar 1986	Aries (♈)
06 Oct 1983	Virgo (♍)	02 Apr 1986	Taurus (♉)
09 Nov 1983	Libra (♎)	27 Apr 1986	Gemini (♊)
07 Dec 1983	Scorpio (♏)	22 May 1986	Cancer (♋)
01 Jan 1984	Sagittarius (♐)	16 Jun 1986	Leo (♌)
26 Jan 1984	Capricorn (♑)	12 Jul 1986	Virgo (♍)
19 Feb 1984	Aquarius (♒)	08 Aug 1986	Libra (♎)
15 Mar 1984	Pisces (♓)	07 Sep 1986	Scorpio (♏)
08 Apr 1984	Aries (♈)	07 Jan 1987	Sagittarius (♐)

Starting Date	Zodiac Sign	Starting Date	Zodiac Sign
05 Feb 1987	Capricorn (♑)	30 Jul 1987	Leo (♌)
03 Mar 1987	Aquarius (♒)	24 Aug 1987	Virgo (♍)
29 Mar 1987	Pisces (♓)	17 Sep 1987	Libra (♎)
23 Apr 1987	Aries (♈)	11 Oct 1987	Scorpio (♏)
17 May 1987	Taurus (♉)	04 Nov 1987	Sagittarius (♐)
11 Jun 1987	Gemini (♊)	28 Nov 1987	Capricorn (♑)
06 Jul 1987	Cancer (♋)	22 Dec 1987	Aquarius (♒)

These dates are derived from calculations using *The American Ephemeris for the Twentieth Century* (San Diego: ACS Publications, 1980–1996).

Venus in Aries. You're inclined to appreciate the opposite sex. Consequently, you may marry very early or hastily. You may also encounter an inharmonious union because of your own impulsiveness. One of the most valuable pieces of wisdom we gain in our lifetime comes the moment we realize how little we actually know. Never lull yourself into believing you've made a completely informed decision. Life has an odd way of humbling anyone who dares to be rash and overconfident. Give yourself plenty of time, even if you're sure. Picture yourself looking back after forty years of blissful wedlock. Those few extra months (or years!) of courtship may have a very special place among your most treasured memories; don't rush through them. (*Famous examples:* Matthew Broderick, Julie Christie, Mia Farrow, Lukas Haas, George Harrison, Katharine Hepburn, Taylor Hanson, Jack Nicholson, Sarah Jessica Parker, Kurt Russell, Elizabeth Taylor, Liv Tyler.)

Venus in Taurus. Although you're inclined to be very affectionate and you possess deep, enduring emotions, you may encounter some delays during your marriage. You set goals for yourself because you know you can achieve them. However, getting there can be tougher than you might imagine. You might expect rock-solid support from your mate, only to discover that he or she is just as human as you and trying just as hard to get through life. In the words of the modern-day balladeer and poet Rod McKuen, "In loving, you lean on someone to hold them up." (*Famous examples:* Warren Beatty, Eric Clapton, Johnny

Depp, Michael J. Fox, Al Gore, Steffi Graf, Prince, Debbie Reynolds, Spencer Tracy, Steven Tyler, Princess Diana Spencer Windsor, Prince William Windsor.)

Venus in Gemini. You potentially fall in love more than once and may even carry on two simultaneous love affairs at some point during your life. There's also a possibility you may marry more than once. There are loads of reasons to love someone, and we cherish different people for different reasons. Life would be simple if we met our soulmate and then never met another attractive person again. The truth is, some people spend a lot of time alone, while others meet more than one wonderful person. Is infidelity acceptable? Look into your heart for the answer to the question that's on your mind. Don't look for forgiveness after doing wrong to others or to yourself. (*Famous examples:* Candice Bergen, Bebe Buell, Cher, Amy Chow, Harrison Ford, Courtney Love, Brooke Shields.)

Venus in Cancer. There's a good chance you'll have many clandestine liaisons before you settle down with an older or younger spouse. Age is not the number on your driver's license, it's something you feel. Are you more mature, or more youthful, than others your age? You'll find more fulfillment in a relationship with someone who's as old as you feel. Also, beware of reality's imposition upon your happiness. Your marital difficulties stem from money, parents, or profession. If you could live on love alone, you might never feel another tense moment. External pressures are actually the leading cause of marital strife. Work, bills, and responsibilities to parents or children can leave you tense and argumentative. These emotions can be hard on the strongest relationship, so try to release them when you're alone. (*Famous examples:* Ben Affleck, Ray Davies, John Derek, Tipper Gore, Ashley Olsen, Mary-Kate Olsen, Natalie Portman, Todd Rundgren, Arnold Schwarzenegger, O. J. Simpson, Donald Trump.)

Venus in Leo. Your love life will probably be as magnificent as you can make it. Romances must be on a grand scale to keep you occupied. Marriage must satisfy your expectations or you don't bother to stick around. The world is filled with stories of great never-ending romances. Deep inside, you know what life can offer and you won't allow yourself to settle for less. At least not for long. "Love," wrote Lebanese poet Kahlil Gibran, "is the only freedom in the world because it so elevates the spirit that the laws of humanity and the phenomena of nature do not alter its course." For lasting happiness, choose carefully. (*Famous examples:* Lauren Bacall, George H. Bush, Madonna.)

> Each soul is sent down from heaven with both male and female traits, according to the *Zohar (Book of Mysticism)*. Once it arrives on Earth, it splits into two beings. A boy receives the soul's male half, while a girl is the recipient of the female half. Thus, marriage reunites that which God created as a single spirit, rejoining the two halves into a whole entity.

Venus in Virgo. You're inclined to experience disappointments or delays in romance, partly because you rarely express your deepest emotions. Unexpressed love is unrequited love. Sometimes it's the walls around our hearts that cause the very pain we hope to avoid. You might marry a coworker, an employee, a doctor, or someone who needs you as both spouse and primary caregiver. You can't truly cherish someone until you know them well. At work or in school you not only meet people, you witness their approach to life. You see them practice their personal beliefs and apply their values every day. Behavior is the real mirror to the soul. Someone who shares your sense of humor, likes and dislikes, and your personal code of ethics (we all have one whether we acknowledge it or not) will be an ideal life partner. They'll also be fortunate to have you. In the words of the French writer Simone De Beauvoir, "Marriage is a career which brings about more benefits than many others." (*Famous examples:* Antonio Banderas, Brigitte Bardot, Catherine Deneuve, Carrie Fisher, Melanie Griffith, John Lennon, Heather Locklear, Julia Roberts, Richie Sambora, Evan Rachel Wood, Dwight Yoakam.)

Venus in Libra. When you finally decide to settle down, you marry well. You're also predisposed to financial and social prosperity throughout your marriage. The ideal spouse is someone who completes you. Don't look for someone who competes only on common ground. It's all right for your strengths to be your mate's weaknesses, and vice versa. Don't try to be alike, simply try to be together. This way you can become an indomitable team when you're united. You'll weather the storms and share the victories. Be sure to adhere to positive goals and care genuinely for those who are less fortunate. (*Famous examples:* Woody Allen, Bill Clinton, Bo Derek, Michael Douglas, Zac Hanson, Prince Charles Windsor.)

Venus in Scorpio. You're inclined to experience many disappointments in both courtship and marriage. Financial losses might also occur through love or matrimony. "Love," said American essayist Ralph Waldo Emerson, "and you shall be loved." If only it were that simple. All too often the object of one's affections is interested in someone else. There's an old proverb that says you can't force anyone to love you or lend you money. Asking a person you're interested in a simple question can spare you a lot of heartache: "Could you see yourself falling in love with someone like me?" Any answer that's not a straight no is a yes or a maybe. Don't bother trying to impress a date with lavish gifts or expensive dinners. In the end you'll find someone who's interested in you, not just the luxuries you can provide. Even a fairy-tale prince and princess live a lot more like Cinderella when they're at home. (*Famous examples:* Hillary Rodham Clinton, Leonardo DiCaprio, Bill Gates, Goldie Hawn, Steven Spielberg, Ted Turner.)

Venus in Sagittarius. A romantic at heart, you're inclined to conduct a long-distance relationship at some point during your life. Chances are you'll also marry more than once. French philosopher Blaise Pascal wrote, "When we are in love we seem to ourselves quite different from what we were before." And we *are* different. We're changed by those we love. There's no greater teacher than passion. We listen, we observe, we imitate. Our lover's thoughts become our own. Cherish the insight and wisdom you gain. Also, remember that love comes in many forms. You may cherish someone intellectually, emotionally, physically, or in any combination of these. A successful relationship is built between people who love each other in the same ways. (*Famous examples:* Christina Aguilera, Kim Basinger, Humphrey Bogart, David Bowie, Laura Bush, Jane Fonda, Maria Shriver, Michael Stipe.)

Venus in Capricorn. You tend to marry for professional, financial, or social reasons rather than love. Without that key ingredient, your mate might become cold, indifferent, or disappointed when the honeymoon's over. "I've been rich and I've been poor," actress Mae West once said; "Believe me, rich is better." But in truth, even she would've traded money for happiness in a heartbeat. Success might motivate you. Money might make you happy outside of marriage, but only real love will satisfy your desire to love and be loved. To have wealth and attachment, you must look for both and refuse to settle for less. (*Famous examples:* Richard Burton, Mayte Garcia, Mikhail Gorbachev, Diane Keaton, John F. Kennedy Jr., Brad Pitt, Elvis Presley, Britney Spears, Justin Timberlake.)

Venus in Aquarius. You're inclined to have some unconventional or unusual love affairs before you settle down. Marriage happens later in life for you. Chances are you'll wed someone who is younger or older and quite eccentric. "Love is a canvas pattern furnished by Nature, and embroidered by imagination," wrote the French writer Voltaire. Life is a great experiment. There are so many options, it's amazing that anyone would make a lifetime commitment while he or she is still young. Isn't it? For you, there's a great desire to explore. To deny that is to live a long life with regrets. Eccentricities are the visible manifestations of genius. Don't think of them as negative. (*Famous examples:* Garth Brooks, Carolyn Bessette Kennedy, Bob Moffatt, Clint Moffatt, Dave Moffatt, Kate Moss, Oprah Winfrey.)

Venus in Pisces. You tend to be romantically fickle. Naturally attracted to the underdog, you flit through love affairs and marriages with little concern for stability or longevity. The Spanish writer Miguel de Unamuno said, "Love is the child of illusion and the parent of disillusion." Just as there are fashion fads, there are fashion staples like jeans. Likewise, there are witty fun acquaintances and there are people you could be around day in and day out for life. The trouble is that it's the fun ones, not the stable ones, who stand out in the crowd. You can't bottle a romance and put it on a back shelf while you try out someone new. As life moves on for you, it progresses for those you love. If you remain in someone's life, you grow together. If not, you grow apart. Remember, you can't get what you want until you know what you want. Once you do, don't look back. Stability is valued only by those who truly desire it. (*Famous examples:* Drew Barrymore, Helen Gurley Brown, Sir Michael Caine, Kurt Cobain, Claire Danes, Bridget Fonda, the Reverend Dr. Martin Luther King Jr., Michelle Pfeiffer, Jamie Renée Smith, Barbra Streisand, John Travolta.)

The astrologer might surmise from Antonio Banderas's Venus in Virgo that he's inclined to experience disappointment or delay in romance, partly because he rarely expresses his deepest emotions. A combined reading of the zodiac sign associated with Venus and its location in his chart might suggest that he will experience some disappointment or delay in the romance department. Most of his problems emerge because he rarely expresses his deepest emotions.

Are You Lucky in Love?: Jupiter's Tropical Placement in Your Chart

Ancient Hebrews believed the planet Mazal, or Jupiter, was a very favorable star. Said to bestow a portion of prosperity and good fortune to each person, Jupiter's influence extends to matrimony as well. It's no coincidence that wedding guests toast the happy couple with a rousing *"Mazal tov!"* which, loosely translated, means, "May you live under Jupiter's influence." In fact, the location of Jupiter in your birth chart, as well as its associated zodiac sign, can tell you a great deal about the measure of good fortune you've been allotted in the relationship area.

You don't need a birth chart to use this section. Simply enter your (and/or your mate's) birth date onto Worksheet 15. Using Table 9, look for the time period in which your birth date falls, and find the zodiac sign associated with that period. (The dates listed are the starting dates for each period: your birth date should fall on or after the appropriate date, and before the date in the row below.) Enter that zodiac sign in the space provided on the worksheet. Do the same with your mate's Jupiter placement. Then locate the zodiac sign in the text

following and read how Jupiter bestows its abundance upon your relationship.

Naturally, if you have a tropical Western birth chart, look for
Jupiter's symbol (♃) and enter the zodiac sign that appears on the
same line as Jupiter in the worksheet space provided. Fig. 9 illustrates
that Sagittarius (♐) is Jupiter's zodiac sign in Antonio Banderas's
chart; this appears as the unshaded section in this figure. (A list of
zodiac signs and their symbols can be found on page 183.)

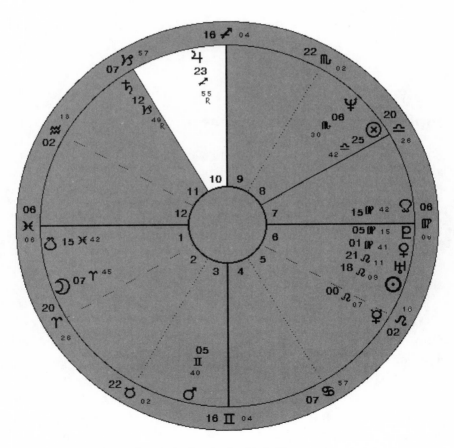

Figure 9. Antonio Banderas's Jupiter in the Birth Chart.

WORKSHEET 15. TROPICAL PLACEMENT FOR JUPITER

	Example:	Name A:	Name B:
	Antonio Banderas		
Birth date	10 Aug 1960		
Jupiter's tropical placement	♐ (Sagittarius)		

TABLE 9. TROPICAL PLACEMENT FOR JUPITER, 1927–1987

Starting Date	Zodiac Sign	Starting Date	Zodiac Sign
01 Jan 1927	Aquarius (♒)	27 May 1941	Gemini (♊)
18 Jan 1927	Pisces (♓)	10 Jun 1942	Cancer (♋)
06 Jun 1927	Aries (♈)	01 Jul 1943	Leo (♌)
11 Sep 1927	Pisces (♓)	26 Jul 1944	Virgo (♍)
23 Jan 1928	Aries (♈)	25 Aug 1945	Libra (♎)
04 Jun 1928	Taurus (♉)	25 Sep 1946	Scorpio (♏)
13 Jun 1929	Gemini (♊)	24 Oct 1947	Sagittarius (♐)
27 Jun 1930	Cancer (♋)	15 Nov 1948	Capricorn (♑)
17 Jul 1931	Leo (♌)	13 Apr 1949	Aquarius (♒)
11 Aug 1932	Virgo (♍)	28 Jun 1949	Capricorn (♑)
10 Sep 1933	Libra (♎)	01 Dec 1949	Aquarius (♒)
11 Oct 1934	Scorpio (♏)	15 Apr 1950	Pisces (♓)
09 Nov 1935	Sagittarius (♐)	15 Sep 1950	Aquarius (♒)
02 Dec 1936	Capricorn (♑)	02 Dec 1950	Pisces (♓)
20 Dec 1937	Aquarius (♒)	22 Apr 1951	Aries (♈)
14 May 1938	Pisces (♓)	29 Apr 1952	Taurus (♉)
30 Jul 1938	Aquarius (♒)	10 May 1953	Gemini (♊)
30 Dec 1938	Pisces (♓)	24 May 1954	Cancer (♋)
12 May 1939	Aries (♈)	13 Jun 1955	Leo (♌)
30 Oct 1939	Pisces (♓)	17 Nov 1955	Virgo (♍)
21 Dec 1939	Aries (♈)	18 Jan 1956	Leo (♌)
16 May 1940	Taurus (♉)	08 Jul 1956	Virgo (♍)

Starting Date	Zodiac Sign	Starting Date	Zodiac Sign
13 Dec 1956	Libra (♎)	17 Dec 1969	Scorpio (♏)
20 Feb 1957	Virgo (♍)	30 Apr 1970	Libra (♎)
07 Aug 1957	Libra (♎)	16 Aug 1970	Scorpio (♏)
14 Jan 1958	Scorpio (♏)	14 Jan 1971	Sagittarius (♐)
21 Mar 1958	Libra (♎)	05 Jun 1971	Scorpio (♏)
07 Sep 1958	Scorpio (♏)	12 Sep 1971	Sagittarius (♐)
11 Feb 1959	Sagittarius (♐)	07 Feb 1972	Capricorn (♑)
25 Apr 1959	Scorpio (♏)	25 Jul 1972	Sagittarius (♐)
06 Oct 1959	Sagittarius (♐)	26 Sep 1972	Capricorn (♑)
02 Mar 1960	Capricorn (♑)	23 Feb 1973	Aquarius (♒)
10 Jun 1960	Sagittarius (♐)	08 Mar 1974	Pisces (♓)
26 Oct 1960	Capricorn (♑)	19 Mar 1975	Aries (♈)
15 Mar 1961	Aquarius (♒)	26 Mar 1976	Taurus (♉)
12 Aug 1961	Capricorn (♑)	23 Aug 1976	Gemini (♊)
04 Nov 1961	Aquarius (♒)	17 Oct 1976	Cancer (♋)
26 Mar 1962	Pisces (♓)	04 Apr 1977	Gemini (♊)
04 Apr 1963	Aries (♈)	21 Aug 1977	Cancer (♋)
12 Apr 1964	Taurus (♉)	31 Dec 1977	Gemini (♊)
23 Apr 1965	Gemini (♊)	12 Apr 1978	Cancer (♋)
21 Sep 1965	Cancer (♋)	05 Sep 1978	Leo (♌)
17 Nov 1965	Gemini (♊)	01 Mar 1979	Cancer (♋)
06 May 1966	Cancer (♋)	20 Apr 1979	Leo (♌)
28 Sep 1966	Leo (♌)	29 Sep 1979	Virgo (♍)
17 Jan 1967	Cancer (♋)	27 Oct 1980	Libra (♎)
23 May 1967	Leo (♌)	27 Nov 1981	Scorpio (♏)
19 Oct 1967	Virgo (♍)	26 Dec 1982	Sagittarius (♐)
27 Feb 1968	Leo (♌)	20 Jan 1984	Capricorn (♑)
16 Jun 1968	Virgo (♍)	07 Feb 1985	Aquarius (♒)
16 Nov 1968	Libra (♎)	21 Feb 1986	Pisces (♓)
31 Mar 1969	Virgo (♍)	03 Mar 1987	Aries (♈)
16 Jul 1969	Libra (♎)		

These dates are derived from calculations using *The American Ephemeris for the Twentieth Century* (San Diego: ACS Publications, 1980–1996).

Jupiter in Aries. While you're married, you might experience good fortune and business success. A recent study of corporate executives revealed that the right spouse was as crucial to success as a college degree. Not only can a spouse motivate you and become your greatest ally and teammate; people scrutinize your choice of a mate in order to learn more about you. "Tell me whom you love," wrote the French poet Arsène Houssaye, "and I will tell you who you are." What does your choice say about you? Infatuation is hormonal, love is emotional. If commitment were rational there would be a lot more successful marriages in this world. (*Famous examples:* Johnny Depp, Bridget Fonda, Brad Pitt.)

Jupiter in Taurus. Although you tend to encounter marital happiness, you may experience ingratitude from friends. Associations with friends might become strained for a variety of reasons. Single friends may feel abandoned, out of place, or even jealous. A spouse requires (and deserves) most of your social attention. You may not intend to jilt friends, but in all likelihood you will. It's a consequence of commitment. Married friends will be far more amenable. However, they may prove equally unreliable at times for the same reasons pointed out about you by your unmarried friends. After all, they have spouses who come first in their lives, too. Just remember, when you select your mate, you also choose the person with whom you want to share your life. (*Famous examples:* Julie Christie, the Reverend Dr. Martin Luther King Jr., John Lennon, Sarah Jessica Parker.)

Jupiter in Gemini. Good fortune tends to follow you in marriage, but you might encounter sudden reversals toward your forty-fifth birthday. There are so many clichés that sum up the wisdom you need to live by: save for a rainy day, forewarned is forearmed, a penny saved, an ounce of prevention, and so on. You need what's known in the business world as a "go to hell fund." Save a little money every week or every month. By the time you're in your forties you'll need enough savings to live on for six months (in case the world goes to hell or you need to tell your boss to go there). It may seem like an annoyance, skipping the purchase of a nice pair of shoes or a new CD now and then. But your future self will be eternally grateful for those sacrifices.

Can you think of a better charity? (*Famous examples:* Kim Basinger, Bebe Buell, Carolyn Bessette Kennedy, Courtney Love, Brooke Shields, Barbra Streisand, John Travolta, Liv Tyler, Oprah Winfrey.)

Elaborate wedding bands are considered tasteless in a Jewish marriage. Designed without engravings on the inside or outside, the ring signifies the simple beauty and value of the couple's union. Ornate trappings such as diamonds would only cheapen the sublime nature of the event. For the same reason, some traditions dictate that the *chattan* (groom) shouldn't carry money, silver or gold articles, precious jewels, or any other valuables in his pockets or hands during the ceremony.

Jupiter in Cancer. While you're married, your prominence may be as fleeting and flimsy as a Hollywood backdrop. Your wealth might come from your popularity rather than your hard work. A false sense of self-confidence can potentially lead you to make an ill-advised decision, such as leaving a good job to pursue an entrepreneurial or freelance position. The riches that arise from popularity rather than performance are tenuous at best. When the budget axe swings, only the hard workers survive. For your entire married life you need to subscribe to a strong work ethic combined with conservative career movements. We shape our future with our present actions, just as we shaped our present with our actions in the past. (*Famous examples:* Kurt Cobain, Claire Danes, Harrison Ford, Mikhail Gorbachev, George Harrison, Katharine Hepburn.)

Jupiter in Leo. Your married life might possibly afford you a rich and complete personal existence. It's no secret that happy couples tend to live longer, more fulfilled lives than an unhappy pair or a perennially single person. However, this is especially true for you. Family life should provide the focal point of your personal existence. You might find yourself not only in love with your mate but genuinely proud of that person. "There is nothing nobler or more admirable," according to Homer, "than when two people who see eye to eye keep house as man and wife, confounding their enemies and delighting their friends."

(*Famous examples:* Ray Davies, Catherine Deneuve, Bill Gates, Debbie Reynolds, Maria Shriver, Elizabeth Taylor.)

Jupiter in Virgo. You potentially have a prosperous marriage. Landing a rich spouse, however, is no assurance that you'll have wealth later in life. There's an old Yiddish proverb: "Parents can give a dowry, but not good luck." Found cash disappears quickly. Money means the most to people who earn it. Now, any relationship involves three personalities: me, you, and us. In your case, it's the "us" personality that brings together the necessary ingredients for success. Your mate may be effective at making money but not at saving it. You might be better at budget and investment issues than the steady acquisition of paychecks. Separately, neither of you might do as well as you will together. Remember this when you analyze what your mate contributes to your relationship. It might actually be more than you realize. (*Famous examples:* Sir Michael Caine, Eric Clapton, Bo Derek, Michael Douglas, Mia Farrow, Carrie Fisher, Steffi Graf, Julia Roberts, Dwight Yoakam.)

Jupiter in Libra. You're inclined to experience much happiness while you're married. The best years of your life aren't something you give to someone. They're something you experience with that person. They become the best years in part because you're with your mate. When you commit to someone, don't attempt to live part of your life separately or secretly. The rules for success are honesty, respect, and admiration. Also, remember how your mate made you feel when you first met, and how you acted toward your mate. Those feelings are the model of respect and admiration. Above all, when you are blessed with happiness guard it jealously. (*Famous examples:* Christina Aguilera, Brigitte Bardot, Candice Bergen, Helen Gurley Brown, George W. Bush, Cher, Bill Clinton, Melanie Griffith, Goldie Hawn, Diane Keaton, Madonna, Michelle Pfeiffer, Natalie Portman, Prince, Donald Trump, Justin Timberlake.)

Jupiter in Scorpio. For you, marriage may not bestow personal fulfillment. Beware of your own unrealistic expectations of the changes matrimony might make to your life. A spouse isn't there to fix all of life's problems, just to share them with you. To love someone is to cherish their strengths and accept their weaknesses. This also applies to loving yourself. Don't claim to adulate yourself while you're inwardly uncertain. Get to know yourself, forgive your failures, and stop hiding behind your successes. In the words of Canadian author Merle Shain: "Loving can cost a lot but not loving always costs more, and those who fear to love often find that want of love is an emptiness that robs the joy from life." (*Famous examples:* Humphrey Bogart, David Bowie, Laura Bush, Elvis Presley, Richie Sambora, Arnold Schwarzenegger, O. J. Simpson, Britney Spears, Steven Spielberg, Prince William Windsor.)

Jupiter in Sagittarius. You might achieve both success and good fortune during your marriage. An auspicious destiny is a lucky break delivered on a silver platter. Success depends on what you make of that opportunity. It takes keen awareness and self-discipline to avoid relaxing and enjoying the ride when a little effort can carry you farther faster. The confidence and determination you derive from your marriage are the raw materials required to deliver that success. (*Famous examples:* Ben Affleck, Woody Allen, Lauren Bacall, Antonio Banderas, Hillary Rodham Clinton, Al Gore, Tipper Gore, Todd Rundgren, Michael Stipe, Spencer Tracy, Steven Tyler, Prince Charles Windsor.)

Jupiter in Capricorn: Your small ambitions may lead to an unsatisfactory marital existence. Low sights reap scant rewards. Set your aims high and be prepared to weather adversity to attain what you desire. The balance you must strive to achieve is embodied in a pair of questions from the Talmud's *Hillel:* "If I am not for myself, who is for me? And if I am only for myself, what am I?" Be at once for yourself and for the common good, and actively seek the best for both. (*Famous examples:* Warren Beatty, Richard Burton, John F. Kennedy Jr., Heather Locklear, Jack Nicholson.)

Jupiter in Aquarius: Marriage to an older person or marriage later in life may bring you good fortune. Any twenty-year-old will tell you that you won't really know who you are until you're eighteen. A forty-year-old might say you can't possibly know yourself until you've hit thirty-five. A sixty-five-year-old knows the magic number is sixty. An eighty-year-old can tell you that the truth is you never really know yourself, but as time passes you get more comfortable with the lack of knowledge. Maturity enters to a relationship in three ways: You bring it. Your mate brings it. You nurture it together. Believe it or not, relationships have a better chance to thrive if at least one person provides maturity. (*Famous examples:* Garth Brooks, Matthew Broderick, John Derek, Jane Fonda, Michael J. Fox, Ted Turner, Princess Diana Spencer Windsor.)

Jupiter in Pisces. Increased fortunes may accompany your marriage, but so do scandals. With success comes scrutiny. If you do your best to do no wrong, then you can never be rightfully accused. It's far easier to defend your integrity when you're virtuous, and your innocence when you're blameless. When fortunes fly in your favor you must be prepared to defend both. It's better to end a commitment than to treat it with disregard. A breakup and a new start are preferable to adultery because your integrity will remain intact. However, it's better still to stay together and work through the dull times. Be careful not to trade the prince or princess for the toad. (*Famous examples:* Drew Barrymore, Leonardo DiCaprio, Ashley Olsen, Mary-Kate Olsen, Kurt Russell.)

Using this information, one might say that Antonio Banderas's Jupiter in Sagittarius suggests that success and good fortune will occur during his marriage. During a personal consultation, a Judaic astrologer might also check Jupiter's house placement in a birth chart for more enhanced information.

When Like Minds Fall in Love: Synastry

Judaic astrologers use a few different methods to determine a couple's compatibility by looking at their charts together. In one of the most popular, practitioners take the degrees of a planet's position in one chart and subtract them from the degrees of a planet's position in the other chart to find degrees of separation between those two planets. Known as angles, there are five commonly interpreted degrees of separation that astrologers look for: conjunctions (00°–08° difference), sextiles (52°–68° difference), squares (82°–98° difference), trines (112°–128° difference), and oppositions (172°–188° difference). There is, however, a much simpler way to explore how the stars will affect your relationship that does not involve math. This method was developed by astrologer Marc Robertson and is based on concepts formulated by the second-century astrologer Claudius Ptolemy. In this system, the location of conjunctions between the planets is employed to provide substantial insight into the true nature of a couple's compatibility.

Riddle:

What grows without rain? What burns without a fire? What cries without tears?

Can you answer the riddles on pages 88, 99, and 308? Then visit www.world-astrology.com.

You don't need a birth chart to use most of this section. You will, however, need your birth chart to locate the Moon's zodiac sign for one particular part. Enter both your and your mate's birth dates onto Worksheet 16. Using Table 10, which provides the Sun's zodiac sign for the entire year, look for the time period in which your birth date falls, and find the zodiac sign associated with that period. Enter that zodiac sign in the space provided on the worksheet. Repeat these steps using Table 11, which shows Mercury's zodiac sign; Table 12, which shows Mars's zodiac sign; Table 13, which shows Venus's zodiac sign; Table 14, which shows Jupiter's zodiac sign; and Table 15, which shows Saturn's zodiac sign. Then enter your and your mate's information in the spaces provided on the worksheet.

To find the Moon's zodiac sign, look for the Moon's symbol (☽) in your birth chart—fig. 10 illustrates the Moon's zodiac sign (Aries) and house placement (first house) in Antonio Banderas's birth chart, appearing as the unshaded section in the figure—and enter the zodiac sign that appears on the same line with the Moon's symbol in the worksheet space provided. (A list of zodiac signs and their symbols can be found on page 183.) Do the same with your mate's information.

Once you've filled in the entire worksheet, take a look at the zodiac sign associated with Name A's Sun placement. Look down name B's column to see if there's an identical sign associated with any of the planets in that column. If you find a match, write the words "Sun to Sun" in the blank column marked "Conjunctions." Repeat the process with Name A's Mercury, Mars, Venus, Jupiter, Saturn, and the Moon's placements.

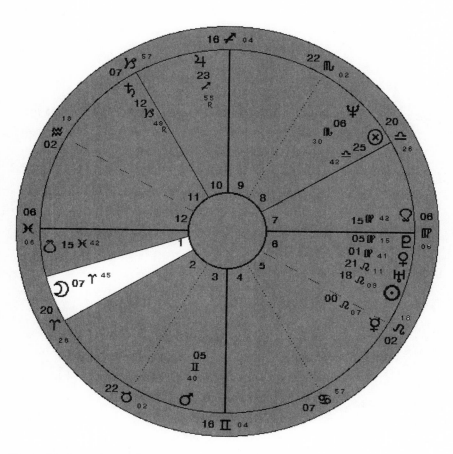

Figure 10. Antonio Banderas's Moon in the Birth Chart.

If you have conjunctions in your worksheet, find the planetary pair (Sun and Sun, Sun and Moon, Mars and Jupiter, and so forth) in the text that follows and read how your and your mate's planetary placements influence each other. If you don't find any conjunctions, don't worry. As we mentioned before, a professional astrologer can help you discover other combinations in your charts such as trines, sextiles, squares, and oppositions, which would yield far more insight into the nature of your union. You must always take into consideration that it requires years of education and experience before an astrologer can truly help you reveal the fragile fabric of which a relationship is made. However, the material provided in these pages can help open your eyes to an infinite ocean of possibilities, and even answer questions you might not yet have thought to ask.

WORKSHEET 16. TROPICAL PLACEMENTS FOR THE SUN, MERCURY, MARS, VENUS, JUPITER, SATURN, AND THE MOON

	Example A:	Example B:	Conjunctions:	Name A:	Name B:	Conjunctions:
	Melanie Griffith	Antonio Banderas				
Birth date	09 Aug 1957	10 Aug 1960	none			
The Sun's tropical placement	Leo (♌)	Leo (♌)	Sun to Sun; Sun to Mercury			
Mercury's tropical placement	Virgo (♍)	Leo (♌)	Mercury to Venus			

	Example A:	Example B:	Conjunctions:	Name A:	Name B:	Conjunctions:
	Melanie Griffith	Antonio Banderas				
Mars's tropical placement	Virgo (♍)	Gemini (♊) Venus	Mars to Venus			
Venus's tropical placement	Virgo (♍)	Virgo (♍) Venus	Venus to Venus			
Jupiter's tropical placement	Libra (♎)	Sagittarius (♐)	none			
Saturn's tropical placement	Sagittarius (♐)	Capricorn (♑)				
The Moon's tropical placement	Aquarius (♒)	Aries (♈)	none			

TABLE 10. TROPICAL PLACEMENT FOR THE SUN, 1927–1987

Starting Date	Zodiac Sign
1 Jan	Capricorn (♑)
21 Jan (There are exceptions. The Sun moved into this zodiac sign on 20 Jan in the following years: 1933, 1937, 1941, 1945, 1949, 1953, 1957, 1961, 1965, 1969, 1970, 1973, 1974, 1977, 1978, 1981, 1982, 1985, and 1986.)	Aquarius (♒)
19 Feb (There are exceptions. The Sun moved into this zodiac sign on 20 Feb in the following years: 1927, 1928, 1931, 1932, 1935, 1936, 1939, 1940, 1943, 1944, 1948, 1952, 1956, 1960, 1964, 1968, 1972, 1976, and 1980.)	Pisces (♓)
21 Mar (There are exceptions. The Sun moved into this zodiac sign on 22 Mar in the following years: 1931, 1932, 1935, 1939, and 1943. Changed on 20 Mar: 1976, 1980, and 1984.)	Aries (♈)
21 Apr (There are exceptions. The Sun moved into this zodiac sign on 20 Apr in the following years: 1928, 1932, 1936, 1940, 1941, 1944, 1945, 1948, 1949, 1952, 1953, 1956, 1957, 1960, 1961, 1964, 1965, 1968, 1969, 1972, 1973, 1974, 1976, 1977, 1978, 1980, 1981, 1982, 1984, 1985, and 1986.)	Taurus (♉)
22 May (There are exceptions. The Sun moved into this zodiac sign on 21 May in the following years: 1928, 1932, 1936, 1937, 1940, 1941, 1944, 1945, 1948, 1949, 1952, 1953, 1956, 1957, 1960, 1961, 1964, 1965, 1968, 1969, 1970, 1972, 1973, 1974, 1976, 1977, 1978, 1980, 1981, 1982, 1984, 1985, and 1986.)	Gemini (♊)
22 Jun (There are exceptions. The Sun moved into this zodiac sign on 21 June in the following years: 1952, 1956, 1960, 1964, 1968, 1972, 1976,1980, 1981, 1984, and 1985.)	Cancer (♋)

Starting Date	Zodiac Sign
23 Jul	Leo (♌)
(There are exceptions. The Sun moved into this zodiac sign on 24 Jul in the following years: 1930, 1931, 1934, 1935, 1938, 1939, 1942, 1943, 1947, 1951, 1955, 1959, 1963, 1967, and 1971.)	
24 Aug	Virgo (♍)
(There are exceptions. The Sun moved into this zodiac sign on 23 Aug in the following years: 1928, 1932, 1936, 1940, 1944, 1948, 1949, 1952, 1953, 1956, 1957, 1960, 1961, 1964, 1965, 1968, 1969, 1972, 1973, 1976, 1977, 1978, 1980, 1981, 1982, 1984, 1985, and 1986.)	
24 Sep	Libra (♎)
(There are exceptions. The Sun moved into this zodiac sign on 23 Sep in the following years: 1928, 1932, 1933, 1936, 1937, 1940, 1941, 1944, 1945, 1948, 1949, 1952, 1953, 1956, 1957, 1960, 1961, 1964, 1965, 1966, 1968, 1969, 1970, 1972, 1973, 1974, 1976, 1977, 1978, 1980, 1981, 1982, 1984, 1985, and 1986.)	
24 Oct	Scorpio (♏)
(There are exceptions. The Sun moved into this zodiac sign on 23 Oct in the following years: 1952, 1956, 1960, 1964, 1968, 1972, 1976, 1980, 1984, and 1985.)	
23 Nov	Sagittarius (♐)
(There are exceptions. The Sun moved into this zodiac sign on 22 Nov in the following years: 1940, 1944, 1948, 1952, 1956, 1960, 1964, 1968, 1969, 1972, 1973, 1976, 1977, 1980, 1981, 1984, and 1985.)	
23 Dec	Capricorn (♑)
(There are exceptions. The Sun moved into this zodiac sign on 22 Dec in the following years: 1930, 1931, 1934, 1935, 1938, 1939, 1943, 1947, 1951, 1955, 1959, 1963, 1967, and 1971.)	

These dates are derived from calculations using *The American Ephemeris for the Twentieth Century* (San Diego: ACS Publications, 1980–1996).

TABLE 11. TROPICAL PLACEMENT FOR MERCURY, 1927–1987

Starting Date	Zodiac Sign	Starting Date	Zodiac Sign
01 Jan 1927	Sagittarius (♐)	02 Dec 1928	Sagittarius (♐)
05 Jan 1927	Capricorn (♑)	21 Dec 1928	Capricorn (♑)
24 Jan 1927	Aquarius (♒)	08 Jan 1929	Aquarius (♒)
10 Feb 1927	Pisces (♓)	16 Mar 1929	Pisces (♓)
18 Apr 1927	Aries (♈)	04 Apr 1929	Aries (♈)
06 May 1927	Taurus (♉)	19 Apr 1929	Taurus (♉)
21 May 1927	Gemini (♊)	04 May 1929	Gemini (♊)
05 Jun 1927	Cancer (♋)	12 Jul 1929	Cancer (♋)
29 Jun 1927	Leo (♌)	28 Jul 1929	Leo (♌)
14 Jul 1927	Cancer (♋)	12 Aug 1929	Virgo (♍)
12 Aug 1927	Leo (♌)	20 Aug 1929	Libra (♎)
29 Aug 1927	Virgo (♍)	06 Nov 1929	Scorpio (♏)
14 Sep 1927	Libra (♎)	25 Nov 1929	Sagittarius (♐)
03 Oct 1927	Scorpio (♏)	14 Dec 1929	Capricorn (♑)
09 Dec 1927	Sagittarius (♐)	02 Jan 1930	Aquarius (♒)
29 Dec 1927	Capricorn (♑)	23 Jan 1930	Capricorn (♑)
17 Jan 1928	Aquarius (♒)	16 Feb 1930	Aquarius (♒)
03 Feb 1928	Pisces (♓)	10 Mar 1930	Pisces (♓)
29 Feb 1928	Aquarius (♒)	27 Mar 1930	Aries (♈)
18 Mar 1928	Pisces (♓)	11 Apr 1930	Taurus (♉)
11 Apr 1928	Aries (♈)	01 May 1930	Gemini (♊)
27 Apr 1928	Taurus (♉)	17 May 1930	Taurus (♉)
12 May 1928	Gemini (♊)	15 Jun 1930	Gemini (♊)
29 May 1928	Cancer (♋)	05 Jul 1930	Cancer (♋)
05 Aug 1928	Leo (♌)	19 Jul 1930	Leo (♌)
20 Aug 1928	Virgo (♍)	04 Aug 1930	Virgo (♍)
06 Sep 1928	Libra (♎)	27 Aug 1930	Libra (♎)
28 Sep 1928	Scorpio (♏)	07 Sep 1930	Virgo (♍)
25 Oct 1928	Libra (♎)	11 Oct 1930	Libra (♎)
11 Nov 1928	Scorpio (♏)	30 Oct 1930	Scorpio (♏)

Starting Date	Zodiac Sign	Starting Date	Zodiac Sign
17 Nov 1930	Sagittarius (♐)	18 Apr 1933	Aries (♈)
07 Dec 1930	Capricorn (♑)	10 May 1933	Taurus (♉)
12 Feb 1931	Aquarius (♒)	26 May 1933	Gemini (♊)
03 Mar 1931	Pisces (♓)	09 Jun 1933	Cancer (♋)
19 Mar 1931	Aries (♈)	27 Jun 1933	Leo (♌)
04 Apr 1931	Taurus (♉)	02 Sep 1933	Virgo (♍)
11 Jun 1931	Gemini (♊)	18 Sep 1933	Libra (♎)
27 Jun 1931	Cancer (♋)	07 Oct 1933	Scorpio (♏)
11 Jul 1931	Leo (♌)	30 Oct 1933	Sagittarius (♐)
29 Jul 1931	Virgo (♍)	16 Nov 1933	Capricorn (♑)
05 Oct 1931	Libra (♎)	12 Dec 1933	Sagittarius (♐)
22 Oct 1931	Scorpio (♏)	02 Jan 1934	Capricorn (♑)
10 Nov 1931	Sagittarius (♐)	20 Jan 1934	Aquarius (♒)
15 Jan 1932	Capricorn (♑)	07 Feb 1934	Pisces (♓)
05 Feb 1932	Aquarius (♒)	15 Apr 1934	Aries (♈)
23 Feb 1932	Pisces (♓)	03 May 1934	Taurus (♉)
10 Mar 1932	Aries (♈)	17 May 1934	Gemini (♊)
16 May 1932	Taurus (♉)	01 Jun 1934	Cancer (♋)
03 Jun 1932	Gemini (♊)	10 Aug 1934	Leo (♌)
17 Jun 1932	Cancer (♋)	15 Aug 1934	Virgo (♍)
02 Jul 1932	Leo (♌)	10 Sep 1934	Libra (♎)
28 Jul 1932	Virgo (♍)	01 Oct 1934	Scorpio (♏)
10 Aug 1932	Leo (♌)	06 Dec 1934	Sagittarius (♐)
09 Sep 1932	Virgo (♍)	26 Dec 1934	Capricorn (♑)
26 Sep 1932	Libra (♎)	13 Jan 1935	Aquarius (♒)
14 Oct 1932	Scorpio (♏)	01 Feb 1935	Pisces (♓)
03 Nov 1932	Sagittarius (♐)	15 Feb 1935	Aquarius (♒)
08 Jan 1933	Capricorn (♑)	19 Mar 1935	Pisces (♓)
28 Jan 1933	Aquarius (♒)	09 Apr 1935	Aries (♈)
14 Feb 1933	Pisces (♓)	25 Apr 1935	Taurus (♉)
03 Mar 1933	Aries (♈)	09 May 1935	Gemini (♊)
26 Mar 1933	Taurus (♉)	30 May 1935	Cancer (♋)

Starting Date	Zodiac Sign	Starting Date	Zodiac Sign
21 Jun 1935	Gemini (♊)	08 Oct 1937	Libra (♎)
14 Jul 1935	Cancer (♋)	26 Oct 1937	Scorpio (♏)
02 Aug 1935	Leo (♌)	14 Nov 1937	Sagittarius (♐)
17 Aug 1935	Virgo (♍)	04 Dec 1937	Capricorn (♑)(♑)
03 Sep 1935	Libra (♎)	07 Jan 1938	Sagittarius (♐)
29 Sep 1935	Scorpio (♏)	13 Jan 1938	Capricorn (♑)
13 Oct 1935	Sagittarius (♐)	09 Feb 1938	Aquarius (♒)
10 Nov 1935	Scorpio (♏)	27 Feb 1938	Pisces (♓)
29 Nov 1935	Sagittarius (♐)	15 Mar 1938	Aries (♈)
18 Dec 1935	Capricorn (♑)	02 Apr 1938	Taurus (♉)
06 Jan 1936	Aquarius (♒)	24 Apr 1938	Gemini (♊)
13 Mar 1936	Pisces (♓)	17 May 1938	Taurus (♉)
31 Mar 1936	Aries (♈)	08 Jun 1938	Gemini (♊)
15 Apr 1936	Taurus (♉)	23 Jun 1938	Cancer (♋)
01 May 1936	Gemini (♊)	07 Jul 1938	Leo (♌)
09 Jul 1936	Cancer (♋)	27 Jul 1938	Virgo (♍)
24 Jul 1936	Leo (♌)	03 Sep 1938	Libra (♎)
08 Aug 1936	Virgo (♍)	11 Sep 1938	Scorpio (♏)
28 Aug 1936	Libra (♎)	01 Oct 1938	Libra (♎)
02 Nov 1936	Scorpio (♏)	19 Oct 1938	Scorpio (♏)
21 Nov 1936	Sagittarius (♐)	07 Nov 1938	Sagittarius (♐)
10 Dec 1936	Capricorn (♑)	12 Jan 1939	Capricorn (♑)
02 Jan 1937	Aquarius (♒)	02 Feb 1939	Aquarius (♒)
10 Jan 1937	Capricorn (♑)	19 Feb 1939	Pisces (♓)
14 Feb 1937	Aquarius (♒)	07 Mar 1939	Aries (♈)
07 Mar 1937	Pisces (♓)	15 May 1939	Taurus (♉)
23 Mar 1937	Aries (♈)	31 May 1939	Gemini (♊)
07 Apr 1937	Taurus (♉)	14 Jun 1939	Cancer (♋)
14 Jun 1937	Gemini (♊)	30 Jun 1939	Leo (♌)
01 Jul 1937	Cancer (♋)	07 Sep 1939	Virgo (♍)
15 Jul 1937	Leo (♌)	23 Sep 1939	Libra (♎)
01 Aug 1937	Virgo (♍)	11 Oct 1939	Scorpio (♏)

Starting Date	Zodiac Sign	Starting Date	Zodiac Sign
01 Nov 1939	Sagittarius (♐)	30 Oct 1941	Libra (♎)
03 Dec 1939	Scorpio (♏)	12 Nov 1941	Scorpio (♏)
14 Dec 1939	Sagittarius (♐)	03 Dec 1941	Sagittarius (♐)
06 Jan 1940	Capricorn (♑)	22 Dec 1941	Capricorn (♑)
25 Jan 1940	Aquarius (♒)	10 Jan 1942	Aquarius (♒)
12 Feb 1940	Pisces (♓)	17 Mar 1942	Pisces (♓)
04 Mar 1940	Aries (♈)	05 Apr 1942	Aries (♈)
08 Mar 1940	Taurus (♉)	21 Apr 1942	Taurus (♉)
17 Apr 1940	Aries (♈)	05 May 1942	Gemini (♊)
07 May 1940	Taurus (♉)	13 Jul 1942	Cancer (♋)
22 May 1940	Gemini (♊)	29 Jul 1942	Leo (♌)
05 Jun 1940	Cancer (♋)	13 Aug 1942	Virgo (♍)
27 Jun 1940	Leo (♌)	31 Aug 1942	Libra (♎)
21 Jul 1940	Cancer (♋)	07 Nov 1942	Scorpio (♏)
12 Aug 1940	Leo (♌)	26 Nov 1942	Sagittarius (♐)
29 Aug 1940	Virgo (♍)	15 Dec 1942	Capricorn (♑)
14 Sep 1940	Libra (♎)	03 Jan 1943	Aquarius (♒)
04 Oct 1940	Scorpio (♏)	28 Jan 1943	Pisces (♓)
10 Dec 1940	Sagittarius (♐)	16 Feb 1943	Aquarius (♒)
29 Dec 1940	Capricorn (♑)	11 Mar 1943	Pisces (♓)
17 Jan 1941	Aquarius (♒)	28 Mar 1943	Aries (♈)
04 Feb 1941	Pisces (♓)	12 Apr 1943	Taurus (♉)
07 Mar 1941	Aquarius (♒)	01 May 1943	Gemini (♊)
17 Mar 1941	Pisces (♓)	26 May 1943	Cancer (♋)
12 Apr 1941	Aries (♈)	14 Jun 1943	Gemini (♊)
29 Apr 1941	Taurus (♉)	06 Jul 1943	Cancer (♋)
13 May 1941	Gemini (♊)	21 Jul 1943	Leo (♌)
30 May 1941	Cancer (♋)	05 Aug 1943	Virgo (♍)
06 Aug 1941	Leo (♌)	27 Aug 1943	Libra (♎)
21 Aug 1941	Virgo (♍)	25 Sep 1943	Virgo (♍)
07 Sep 1941	Libra (♎)	12 Oct 1943	Libra (♎)
28 Sep 1941	Scorpio (♏)	31 Oct 1943	Scorpio (♏)

Starting Date	Zodiac Sign	Starting Date	Zodiac Sign
19 Nov 1943	Sagittarius (♐)	04 Mar 1946	Aries (♈)
08 Dec 1943	Capricorn (♑)	02 Apr 1946	Pisces (♓)
13 Feb 1944	Aquarius (♒)	17 Apr 1946	Aries (♈)
03 Mar 1944	Pisces (♓)	12 May 1946	Taurus (♉)
19 Mar 1944	Aries (♈)	27 May 1946	Gemini (♊)
04 Apr 1944	Taurus (♉)	10 Jun 1946	Cancer (♋)
11 Jun 1944	Gemini (♊)	28 Jun 1946	Leo (♌)
27 Jun 1944	Cancer (♋)	04 Sep 1946	Virgo (♍)
11 Jul 1944	Leo (♌)	20 Sep 1946	Libra (♎)
29 Jul 1944	Virgo (♍)	08 Oct 1946	Scorpio (♏)
05 Oct 1944	Libra (♎)	30 Oct 1946	Sagittarius (♐)
22 Oct 1944	Scorpio (♏)	21 Nov 1946	Scorpio (♏)
10 Nov 1944	Sagittarius (♐)	13 Dec 1946	Sagittarius (♐)
02 Dec 1944	Capricorn (♑)	03 Jan 1947	Capricorn (♑)
24 Dec 1944	Sagittarius (♐)	22 Jan 1947	Aquarius (♒)
14 Jan 1945	Capricorn (♑)	08 Feb 1947	Pisces (♓)
05 Feb 1945	Aquarius (♒)	16 Apr 1947	Aries (♈)
23 Feb 1945	Pisces (♓)	04 May 1947	Taurus (♉)
11 Mar 1945	Aries (♈)	19 May 1947	Gemini (♊)
17 May 1945	Taurus (♉)	03 Jun 1947	Cancer (♋)
04 Jun 1945	Gemini (♊)	11 Aug 1947	Leo (♌)
19 Jun 1945	Cancer (♋)	27 Aug 1947	Virgo (♍)
04 Jul 1945	Leo (♌)	12 Sep 1947	Libra (♎)
27 Jul 1945	Virgo (♍)	02 Oct 1947	Scorpio (♏)
17 Aug 1945	Leo (♌)	08 Dec 1947	Sagittarius (♐)
10 Sep 1945	Virgo (♍)	27 Dec 1947	Capricorn (♑)
28 Sep 1945	Libra (♎)	14 Jan 1948	Aquarius (♒)
15 Oct 1945	Scorpio (♏)	02 Feb 1948	Pisces (♓)
04 Nov 1945	Sagittarius (♐)	20 Feb 1948	Aquarius (♒)
10 Jan 1946	Capricorn (♑)	18 Mar 1948	Pisces (♓)
29 Jan 1946	Aquarius (♒)	09 Apr 1948	Aries (♈)
16 Feb 1946	Pisces (♓)	25 Apr 1948	Taurus (♉)

Starting Date	Zodiac Sign	Starting Date	Zodiac Sign
09 May 1948	Gemini (♊)	17 Jul 1950	Leo (♌)
28 May 1948	Cancer (♋)	02 Aug 1950	Virgo (♍)
29 Jun 1948	Gemini (♊)	28 Aug 1950	Libra (♎)
12 Jul 1948	Cancer (♋)	11 Sep 1950	Virgo (♍)
03 Aug 1948	Leo (♌)	10 Oct 1950	Libra (♎)
18 Aug 1948	Virgo (I)	27 Oct 1950	Scorpio (♏)
04 Sep 1948	Libra (♎)	15 Nov 1950	Sagittarius (♐)
27 Sep 1948	Scorpio (♏)	05 Dec 1950	Capricorn (♑)
17 Oct 1948	Libra (♎)	10 Feb 1951	Aquarius (♒)
10 Nov 1948	Scorpio (♏)	01 Mar 1951	Pisces (♓)
30 Nov 1948	Sagittarius (♐)	16 Mar 1951	Aries (♈)
19 Dec 1948	Capricorn (♑)	02 Apr 1951	Taurus (♉)
06 Jan 1949	Aquarius (♒)	02 May 1951	Aries (♈)
14 Mar 1949	Pisces (♓)	15 May 1951	Taurus (♉)
02 Apr 1949	Aries (♈)	09 Jun 1951	Gemini (♊)
17 Apr 1949	Taurus (♉)	24 Jun 1951	Cancer (♋)
02 May 1949	Gemini (♊)	09 Jul 1951	Leo (♌)
10 Jul 1949	Cancer (♋)	28 Jul 1951	Virgo (♍)
25 Jul 1949	Leo (♌)	03 Oct 1951	Libra (♎)
09 Aug 1949	Virgo (♍)	20 Oct 1951	Scorpio (♏)
29 Aug 1949	Libra (♎)	08 Nov 1951	Sagittarius (♐)
04 Nov 1949	Scorpio (♏)	02 Dec 1951	Capricorn (♑)
22 Nov 1949	Sagittarius (♐)	13 Dec 1951	Sagittarius (♐)
12 Dec 1949	Capricorn (♑)	13 Jan 1952	Capricorn (♑)
02 Jan 1950	Aquarius (♒)	03 Feb 1952	Aquarius (♒)
15 Jan 1950	Capricorn (♑)	21 Feb 1952	Pisces (♓)
15 Feb 1950	Aquarius (♒)	08 Mar 1952	Aries (♈)
08 Mar 1950	Pisces (♓)	15 May 1952	Taurus (♉)
25 Mar 1950	Aries (♈)	01 Jun 1952	Gemini (♊)
08 Apr 1950	Taurus (♉)	15 Jun 1952	Cancer (♋)
15 Jun 1950	Gemini (♊)	30 Jun 1952	Leo (♌)
03 Jul 1950	Cancer (♋)	08 Jul 1952	Virgo (♍)

Starting Date	Zodiac Sign	Starting Date	Zodiac Sign
24 Sep 1952	Libra (♎)	05 Nov 1954	Libra (♎)
12 Oct 1952	Scorpio (♏)	11 Nov 1954	Scorpio (♏)
01 Nov 1952	Sagittarius (♐)	04 Dec 1954	Sagittarius (♐)
07 Jan 1953	Capricorn (♑)	24 Dec 1954	Capricorn (♑)
26 Jan 1953	Aquarius (♒)	11 Jan 1955	Aquarius (♒)
12 Feb 1953	Pisces (♓)	18 Mar 1955	Pisces (♓)
03 Mar 1953	Aries (♈)	07 Apr 1955	Aries (♈)
16 Mar 1953	Pisces (♓)	22 Apr 1955	Taurus (♉)
18 Apr 1953	Aries (♈)	07 May 1955	Gemini (♊)
08 May 1953	Taurus (♉)	14 Jul 1955	Cancer (♋)
23 May 1953	Gemini (♊)	31 Jul 1955	Leo (♌)
06 Jun 1953	Cancer (♋)	15 Aug 1955	Virgo (♍)
26 Jun 1953	Leo (♌)	02 Sep 1955	Libra (♎)
29 Jul 1953	Cancer (♋)	08 Nov 1955	Scorpio (♏)
12 Aug 1953	Leo (♌)	27 Nov 1955	Sagittarius (♐)
31 Aug 1953	Virgo (♍)	16 Dec 1955	Capricorn (♑)
16 Sep 1953	Libra (♎)	04 Jan 1956	Aquarius (♒)
05 Oct 1953	Scorpio (♏)	03 Feb 1956	Capricorn (♑)
01 Nov 1953	Sagittarius (♐)	15 Feb 1956	Aquarius (♒)
07 Nov 1953	Scorpio (♏)	11 Mar 1956	Pisces (♓)
11 Dec 1953	Sagittarius (♐)	29 Mar 1956	Aries (♈)
31 Dec 1953	Capricorn (♑)	13 Apr 1956	Taurus (♉)
18 Jan 1954	Aquarius (♒)	30 Apr 1956	Gemini (♊)
05 Feb 1954	Pisces (♓)	07 Jul 1956	Cancer (♋)
13 Apr 1954	Aries (♈)	21 Jul 1956	Leo (♌)
30 Apr 1954	Taurus (♉)	06 Aug 1956	Virgo (♍)
15 May 1954	Gemini (♊)	27 Aug 1956	Libra (♎)
13 May 1954	Cancer (♋)	30 Sep 1956	Virgo (♍)
08 Aug 1954	Leo (♌)	11 Oct 1956	Libra (♎)
23 Aug 1954	Virgo (♍)	21 Oct 1956	Scorpio (♏)
08 Sep 1954	Libra (♎)	19 Nov 1956	Sagittarius (♐)
29 Sep 1954	Scorpio (♏)	08 Dec 1956	Capricorn (♑)

Starting Date	Zodiac Sign	Starting Date	Zodiac Sign
13 Feb 1957	Aquarius (♒)	29 May 1959	Gemini (♊)
04 Mar 1957	Pisces (♓)	12 Jun 1959	Cancer (♋)
21 Mar 1957	Aries (♈)	29 Jun 1959	Leo (♌)
05 Apr 1957	Taurus (♉)	05 Sep 1959	Virgo (♍)
13 Jun 1957	Gemini (♊)	21 Sep 1959	Libra (♎)
29 Jun 1957	Cancer (♋)	09 Oct 1959	Scorpio (♏)
13 Jul 1957	Leo (♌)	31 Oct 1959	Sagittarius (♐)
30 Jul 1957	Virgo (♍)	25 Nov 1959	Scorpio (♏)
06 Oct 1957	Libra (♎)	14 Dec 1959	Sagittarius (♐)
24 Oct 1957	Scorpio (♏)	04 Jan 1960	Capricorn (♑)
12 Nov 1957	Sagittarius (♐)	23 Jan 1960	Aquarius (♒)
02 Dec 1957	Capricorn (♑)	09 Feb 1960	Pisces (♓)
29 Dec 1957	Sagittarius (♐)	16 Apr 1960	Aries (♈)
14 Jan 1958	Capricorn (♑)	05 May 1960	Taurus (♉)
07 Feb 1958	Aquarius (♒)	19 May 1960	Gemini (♊)
25 Feb 1958	Pisces (♓)	03 Jun 1960	Cancer (♋)
13 Mar 1958	Aries (♈)	01 Jul 1960	Leo (♌)
17 May 1958	Taurus (♉)	06 Jul 1960	Cancer (♋)
08 Jun 1958	Gemini (♊)	10 Aug 1960	Leo (♌)
20 Jun 1958	Cancer (♋)	27 Aug 1960	Virgo (♍)
05 Jul 1958	Leo (♌)	12 Sep 1960	Libra (♎)
26 Jul 1958	Virgo (♍)	02 Oct 1960	Scorpio (♏)
24 Aug 1958	Leo (♌)	08 Dec 1960	Sagittarius (♐)
11 Sep 1958	Virgo (♍)	27 Dec 1960	Capricorn (♑)
29 Sep 1958	Libra (♎)	15 Jan 1961	Aquarius (♒)
16 Oct 1958	Scorpio (♏)	02 Feb 1961	Pisces (♓)
05 Nov 1958	Sagittarius (♐)	25 Feb 1961	Aquarius (♒)
11 Jan 1959	Capricorn (♑)	18 Mar 1961	Pisces (♓)
31 Jan 1959	Aquarius (♒)	10 Apr 1961	Aries (♈)
17 Feb 1959	Pisces (♓)	27 Apr 1961	Taurus (♉)
05 Mar 1959	Aries (♈)	11 May 1961	Gemini (♊)
13 May 1959	Taurus (♉)	29 May 1961	Cancer (♋)

Starting Date	Zodiac Sign	Starting Date	Zodiac Sign
04 Aug 1961	Leo (♌)	27 Aug 1963	Libra (♎)
19 Aug 1961	Virgo (♍)	17 Sep 1963	Virgo (♍)
05 Sep 1961	Libra (♎)	11 Oct 1963	Libra (♎)
28 Sep 1961	Scorpio (♏)	29 Oct 1963	Scorpio (♏)
22 Oct 1961	Libra (♎)	16 Nov 1963	Sagittarius (♐)
11 Nov 1961	Scorpio (♏)	06 Dec 1963	Capricorn (♑)
01 Dec 1961	Sagittarius (♐)	11 Feb 1964	Aquarius (♒)
20 Dec 1961	Capricorn (♑)	01 Mar 1964	Pisces (♓)
08 Jan 1962	Aquarius (♒)	17 Mar 1964	Aries (♈)
15 Mar 1962	Pisces (♓)	02 Apr 1964	Taurus (♉)
02 Apr 1962	Aries (♈)	10 Jun 1964	Gemini (♊)
18 Apr 1962	Taurus (♉)	25 Jun 1964	Cancer (♋)
03 May 1962	Gemini (♊)	09 Jul 1964	Leo (♌)
11 Jul 1962	Cancer (♋)	27 Jul 1964	Virgo (♍)
26 Jul 1962	Leo (♌)	03 Oct 1964	Libra (♎)
11 Aug 1962	Virgo (♍)	20 Oct 1964	Scorpio (♏)
20 Aug 1962	Libra (♎)	08 Nov 1964	Sagittarius (♐)
05 Nov 1962	Scorpio (♏)	01 Dec 1964	Capricorn (♑)
24 Nov 1962	Sagittarius (♐)	17 Dec 1964	Sagittarius (♐)
13 Dec 1962	Capricorn (♑)	13 Jan 1965	Capricorn (♑)
02 Jan 1963	Aquarius (♒)	03 Feb 1965	Aquarius (♒)
20 Jan 1963	Capricorn (♑)	21 Feb 1965	Pisces (♓)
15 Feb 1963	Aquarius (♒)	09 Mar 1965	Aries (♈)
09 Mar 1963	Pisces (♓)	16 May 1965	Taurus (♉)
26 Mar 1963	Aries (♈)	02 Jun 1965	Gemini (♊)
10 Apr 1963	Taurus (♉)	16 Jun 1965	Cancer (♋)
03 May 1963	Gemini (♊)	02 Jul 1965	Leo (♌)
11 May 1963	Taurus (♉)	31 Jul 1965	Virgo (♍)
15 Jun 1963	Gemini (♊)	03 Aug 1965	Leo (♌)
04 Jul 1963	Cancer (♋)	09 Sep 1965	Virgo (♍)
18 Jul 1963	Leo (♌)	25 Sep 1965	Libra (♎)
03 Aug 1963	Virgo (♍)	13 Oct 1965	Scorpio (♏)

Starting Date	Zodiac Sign	Starting Date	Zodiac Sign
02 Nov 1965	Sagittarius (♐)	12 Feb 1968	Aquarius (♒)
08 Jan 1966	Capricorn (♑)	18 Mar 1968	Pisces (♓)
27 Jan 1966	Aquarius (♒)	07 Apr 1968	Aries (♈)
13 Feb 1966	Pisces (♓)	23 Apr 1968	Taurus (♉)
03 Mar 1966	Aries (♈)	07 May 1968	Gemini (♊)
22 Mar 1966	Pisces (♓)	30 May 1968	Cancer (♋)
18 Apr 1966	Aries (♈)	14 Jun 1968	Gemini (♊)
10 May 1966	Taurus (♉)	13 Jul 1968	Cancer (♋)
25 May 1966	Gemini (♊)	31 Jul 1968	Leo (♌)
09 Jun 1966	Cancer (♋)	15 Aug 1968	Virgo (♍)
27 Jun 1966	Leo (♌)	02 Sep 1968	Libra (♎)
01 Sep 1966	Virgo (♍)	29 Sep 1968	Scorpio (♏)
17 Sep 1966	Libra (♎)	08 Oct 1968	Libra (♎)
06 Oct 1966	Scorpio (♏)	08 Nov 1968	Scorpio (♏)
20 Oct 1966	Sagittarius (♐)	28 Nov 1968	Sagittarius (♐)
13 Nov 1966	Scorpio (♏)	17 Dec 1968	Capricorn (♑)
12 Dec 1966	Sagittarius (♐)	05 Jan 1969	Aquarius (♒)
01 Jan 1967	Capricorn (♑)	13 Mar 1969	Pisces (♓)
20 Jan 1967	Aquarius (♒)	30 Mar 1969	Aries (♈)
06 Feb 1967	Pisces (♓)	14 Apr 1969	Taurus (♉)
15 Apr 1967	Aries (♈)	01 May 1969	Gemini (♊)
02 May 1967	Taurus (♉)	08 Jul 1969	Cancer (♋)
16 May 1967	Gemini (♊)	23 Jul 1969	Leo (♌)
01 Jun 1967	Cancer (♋)	07 Aug 1969	Virgo (♍)
09 Aug 1967	Leo (♌)	27 Aug 1969	Libra (♎)
24 Aug 1967	Virgo (♍)	07 Oct 1969	Virgo (♍)
10 Sep 1967	Libra (♎)	10 Oct 1969	Libra (♎)
30 Sep 1967	Scorpio (♏)	02 Nov 1969	Scorpio (♏)
06 Dec 1967	Sagittarius (♐)	20 Nov 1969	Sagittarius (♐)
25 Dec 1967	Capricorn (♑)	10 Dec 1969	Capricorn (♑)
12 Jan 1968	Aquarius (♒)	14 Feb 1970	Aquarius (♒)
02 Feb 1968	Pisces (♓)	06 Mar 1970	Pisces (♓)

Starting Date	Zodiac Sign	Starting Date	Zodiac Sign
22 Mar 1970	Aries (♈)	29 May 1972	Gemini (♊)
06 Apr 1970	Taurus (♉)	12 Jun 1972	Cancer (♋)
14 Jun 1970	Gemini (♊)	29 Jun 1972	Leo (♌)
30 Jun 1970	Cancer (♋)	05 Sep 1972	Virgo (♍)
14 Jul 1970	Leo (♌)	22 Sep 1972	Libra (♎)
31 Jul 1970	Virgo (♍)	09 Oct 1972	Scorpio (♏)
08 Oct 1970	Libra (♎)	31 Oct 1972	Sagittarius (♐)
25 Oct 1970	Scorpio (♏)	29 Nov 1972	Scorpio (♏)
13 Nov 1970	Sagittarius (♐)	13 Dec 1972	Sagittarius (♐)
03 Dec 1970	Capricorn (♑)	05 Jan 1973	Capricorn (♑)
03 Jan 1971	Sagittarius (♐)	24 Jan 1973	Aquarius (♒)
14 Jan 1971	Capricorn (♑)	10 Feb 1973	Pisces (♓)
08 Feb 1971	Aquarius (♒)	17 Apr 1973	Aries (♈)
26 Feb 1971	Pisces (♓)	06 May 1973	Taurus (♉)
14 Mar 1971	Aries (♈)	21 May 1973	Gemini (♊)
02 Apr 1971	Taurus (♉)	04 Jun 1973	Cancer (♋)
19 Apr 1971	Aries (♈)	27 Jun 1973	Leo (♌)
17 May 1971	Taurus (♉)	16 Jul 1973	Cancer (♋)
07 Jun 1971	Gemini (♊)	12 Aug 1973	Leo (♌)
22 Jun 1971	Cancer (♋)	29 Aug 1973	Virgo (♍)
06 Jul 1971	Leo (♌)	14 Sep 1973	Libra (♎)
27 Jul 1971	Virgo (♍)	03 Oct 1973	Scorpio (♏)
30 Aug 1971	Leo (♌)	09 Dec 1973	Sagittarius (♐)
11 Sep 1971	Virgo (♍)	29 Dec 1973	Capricorn (♑)
30 Sep 1971	Libra (♎)	16 Jan 1974	Aquarius (♒)
18 Oct 1971	Scorpio (♏)	03 Feb 1974	Pisces (♓)
06 Nov 1971	Sagittarius (♐)	03 Mar 1974	Aquarius (♒)
12 Jan 1972	Capricorn (♑)	18 Mar 1974	Pisces (♓)
01 Feb 1972	Aquarius (♒)	12 Apr 1974	Aries (♈)
19 Feb 1972	Pisces (♓)	28 Apr 1974	Taurus (♉)
06 Mar 1972	Aries (♈)	12 May 1974	Gemini (♊)
13 May 1972	Taurus (♉)	28 May 1974	Cancer (♋)

Starting Date	Zodiac Sign	Starting Date	Zodiac Sign
05 Aug 1974	Leo (♌)	26 Aug 1976	Libra (♎)
20 Aug 1974	Virgo (♍)	21 Sep 1976	Virgo (♍)
06 Sep 1974	Libra (♎)	11 Oct 1976	Libra (♎)
28 Sep 1974	Scorpio (♏)	29 Oct 1976	Scorpio (♏)
27 Oct 1974	Libra (♎)	17 Nov 1976	Sagittarius (♐)
12 Nov 1974	Scorpio (♏)	06 Dec 1976	Capricorn (♑)
02 Dec 1974	Sagittarius (♐)	11 Feb 1977	Aquarius (♒)
21 Dec 1974	Capricorn (♑)	02 Mar 1977	Pisces (♓)
09 Jan 1975	Aquarius (♒)	18 Mar 1977	Aries (♈)
17 Mar 1975	Pisces (♓)	03 Apr 1977	Taurus (♉)
05 Apr 1975	Aries (♈)	11 Jun 1977	Gemini (♊)
20 Apr 1975	Taurus (♉)	26 Jun 1977	Cancer (♋)
04 May 1975	Gemini (♊)	10 Jul 1977	Leo (♌)
12 Jul 1975	Cancer (♋)	28 Jul 1977	Virgo (♍)
28 Jul 1975	Leo (♌)	04 Oct 1977	Libra (♎)
12 Aug 1975	Virgo (♍)	22 Oct 1977	Scorpio (♏)
31 Aug 1975	Libra (♎)	10 Nov 1977	Sagittarius (♐)
06 Nov 1975	Scorpio (♏)	01 Dec 1977	Capricorn (♑)
25 Nov 1975	Sagittarius (♐)	21 Dec 1977	Sagittarius (♐)
13 Dec 1975	Capricorn (♑)	12 Jan 1978	Capricorn (♑)
03 Jan 1976	Aquarius (♒)	05 Feb 1978	Aquarius (♒)
25 Jan 1976	Capricorn (♑)	23 Feb 1978	Pisces (♓)
16 Feb 1976	Aquarius (♒)	11 Mar 1978	Aries (♈)
10 Mar 1976	Pisces (♓)	16 May 1978	Taurus (♉)
27 Mar 1976	Aries (♈)	04 Jun 1978	Gemini (♊)
10 Apr 1976	Taurus (♉)	18 Jun 1978	Cancer (♋)
30 Apr 1976	Gemini (♊)	03 Jul 1978	Leo (♌)
20 May 1976	Taurus (♉)	27 Jul 1978	Virgo (♍)
14 Jun 1976	Gemini (♊)	13 Aug 1978	Leo (♌)
05 Jul 1976	Cancer (♋)	10 Sep 1978	Virgo (♍)
19 Jul 1976	Leo (♌)	27 Sep 1978	Libra (♎)
04 Aug 1976	Virgo (♍)	14 Oct 1978	Scorpio (♏)

Starting Date	Zodiac Sign	Starting Date	Zodiac Sign
03 Nov 1978	Sagittarius (♐)	16 Feb 1981	Aquarius (♒)
09 Jan 1979	Capricorn (♑)	18 Mar 1981	Pisces (♓)
29 Jan 1979	Aquarius (♒)	08 Apr 1981	Aries (♈)
15 Feb 1979	Pisces (♓)	24 Apr 1981	Taurus (♉)
04 Mar 1979	Aries (♈)	08 May 1981	Gemini (♊)
28 Mar 1979	Pisces (♓)	29 May 1981	Cancer (♋)
18 Apr 1979	Aries (♈)	23 Jun 1981	Gemini (♊)
11 May 1979	Taurus (♉)	13 Jul 1981	Cancer (♋)
26 May 1979	Gemini (♊)	02 Aug 1981	Leo (♌)
09 Jun 1979	Cancer (♋)	17 Aug 1981	Virgo (♍)
27 Jun 1979	Leo (♌)	03 Sep 1981	Libra (♎)
03 Sep 1979	Virgo (♍)	27 Sep 1981	Scorpio (♏)
19 Sep 1979	Libra (♎)	14 Oct 1981	Libra (♎)
07 Oct 1979	Scorpio (♏)	10 Nov 1981	Scorpio (♏)
30 Oct 1979	Sagittarius (♐)	29 Nov 1981	Sagittarius (♐)
18 Nov 1979	Scorpio (♏)	18 Dec 1981	Capricorn (♑)
13 Dec 1979	Sagittarius (♐)	06 Jan 1982	Aquarius (♒)
02 Jan 1980	Capricorn (♑)	14 Mar 1982	Pisces (♓)
21 Jan 1980	Aquarius (♒)	01 Apr 1982	Aries (♈)
07 Feb 1980	Pisces (♓)	16 Apr 1982	Taurus (♉)
15 Apr 1980	Aries (♈)	02 May 1982	Gemini (♊)
02 May 1980	Taurus (♉)	09 Jul 1982	Cancer (♋)
17 May 1980	Gemini (♊)	24 Jul 1982	Leo (♌)
01 Jun 1980	Cancer (♋)	09 Aug 1982	Virgo (♍)
09 Aug 1980	Leo (♌)	28 Aug 1982	Libra (♎)
25 Aug 1980	Virgo (♍)	03 Nov 1982	Scorpio (♏)
08 Sep 1980	Libra (♎)	22 Nov 1982	Sagittarius (♐)
30 Sep 1980	Scorpio (♏)	11 Dec 1982	Capricorn (♑)
06 Dec 1980	Sagittarius (♐)	02 Jan 1983	Aquarius (♒)
25 Dec 1980	Capricorn (♑)	12 Jan 1983	Capricorn (♑)
13 Jan 1981	Aquarius (♒)	14 Feb 1983	Aquarius (♒)
01 Feb 1981	Pisces (♓)	07 Mar 1983	Pisces (♓)

Starting Date	Zodiac Sign	Starting Date	Zodiac Sign
24 Mar 1983	Aries (♈)	31 May 1985	Gemini (♊)
08 Apr 1983	Taurus (♉)	14 Jun 1985	Cancer (♋)
14 Jun 1983	Gemini (♊)	30 Jun 1985	Leo (♌)
02 Jul 1983	Cancer (♋)	07 Sep 1985	Virgo (♍)
16 Jul 1983	Leo (♌)	23 Sep 1985	Libra (♎)
01 Aug 1983	Virgo (♍)	11 Oct 1985	Scorpio (♏)
29 Aug 1983	Libra (♎)	01 Nov 1985	Sagittarius (♐)
06 Sep 1983	Virgo (♍)	05 Dec 1985	Scorpio (♏)
09 Oct 1983	Libra (♎)	12 Dec 1985	Sagittarius (♐)
27 Oct 1983	Scorpio (♏)	06 Jan 1986	Capricorn (♑)
14 Nov 1983	Sagittarius (♐)	25 Jan 1986	Aquarius (♒)
04 Dec 1983	Capricorn (♑)	11 Feb 1986	Pisces (♓)
09 Feb 1984	Aquarius (♒)	03 Mar 1986	Aries (♈)
28 Feb 1984	Pisces (♓)	12 Mar 1986	Pisces (♓)
15 Mar 1984	Aries (♈)	18 Apr 1986	Aries (♈)
01 Apr 1984	Taurus (♉)	08 May 1986	Taurus (♉)
25 Apr 1984	Aries (♈)	22 May 1986	Gemini (♊)
16 May 1984	Taurus (♉)	06 Jun 1986	Cancer (♋)
08 Jun 1984	Gemini (♊)	27 Jun 1986	Leo (♌)
22 Jun 1984	Cancer (♋)	24 Jul 1986	Cancer (♋)
07 Jul 1984	Leo (♌)	12 Aug 1986	Leo (♌)
26 Jul 1984	Virgo (♍)	30 Aug 1986	Virgo (♍)
01 Oct 1984	Libra (♎)	15 Sep 1986	Libra (♎)
18 Oct 1984	Scorpio (♏)	04 Oct 1986	Scorpio (♏)
07 Nov 1984	Sagittarius (♐)	10 Dec 1986	Sagittarius (♐)
02 Dec 1984	Capricorn (♑)	30 Dec 1986	Capricorn (♑)
08 Dec 1984	Sagittarius (♐)	18 Jan 1987	Aquarius (♒)
12 Jan 1985	Capricorn (♑)	04 Feb 1987	Pisces (♓)
01 Feb 1985	Aquarius (♒)	12 Mar 1987	Aquarius (♒)
19 Feb 1985	Pisces (♓)	14 Mar 1987	Pisces (♓)
07 Mar 1985	Aries (♈)	13 Apr 1987	Aries (♈)
14 May 1985	Taurus (♉)	30 Apr 1987	Taurus (♉)

Starting Date	Zodiac Sign	Starting Date	Zodiac Sign
14 May 1987	Gemini (♊)	29 Sep 1987	Scorpio (♏)
30 May 1987	Cancer (♋)	01 Nov 1987	Libra (♎)
07 Aug 1987	Leo (♌)	12 Nov 1987	Scorpio (♏)
22 Aug 1987	Virgo (♍)	04 Dec 1987	Sagittarius (♐)
08 Sep 1987	Libra (♎)	23 Dec 1987	Capricorn (♑)

These dates are derived from calculations using *The American Ephemeris for the Twentieth Century* (San Diego: ACS Publications, 1980–1996).

TABLE 12. TROPICAL PLACEMENT FOR MARS, 1927–1987

Starting Date	Zodiac Sign	Starting Date	Zodiac Sign
01 Jan 1927	Taurus (♉)	07 Oct 1929	Scorpio (♏)
22 Feb 1927	Gemini (♊)	19 Nov 1929	Sagittarius (♐)
17 Apr 1927	Cancer (♋)	29 Dec 1929	Capricorn (♑)
06 Jun 1927	Leo (♌)	07 Feb 1930	Aquarius (♒)
25 Jul 1927	Virgo (♍)	17 Mar 1930	Pisces (♓)
11 Sep 1927	Libra (♎)	25 Apr 1930	Aries (♈)
26 Oct 1927	Scorpio (♏)	03 Jun 1930	Taurus (♉)
08 Dec 1927	Sagittarius (♐)	15 Jul 1930	Gemini (♊)
19 Jan 1928	Capricorn (♑)	28 Aug 1930	Cancer (♋)
28 Feb 1928	Aquarius (♒)	21 Oct 1930	Leo (♌)
08 Apr 1928	Pisces (♓)	13 Feb 1931	Cancer (♋)
17 May 1928	Aries (♈)	30 Mar 1931	Leo (♌)
26 Jun 1928	Taurus (♉)	11 Jun 1931	Virgo (♍)
09 Aug 1928	Gemini (♊)	02 Aug 1931	Libra (♎)
03 Oct 1928	Cancer (♋)	17 Sep 1931	Scorpio (♏)
20 Dec 1928	Gemini (♊)	31 Oct 1931	Sagittarius (♐)
11 Mar 1929	Cancer (♋)	10 Dec 1931	Capricorn (♑)
13 May 1929	Leo (♌)	18 Jan 1932	Aquarius (♒)
04 Jul 1929	Virgo (♍)	25 Feb 1932	Pisces (♓)
22 Aug 1929	Libra (♎)	03 Apr 1932	Aries (♈)

Starting Date	Zodiac Sign	Starting Date	Zodiac Sign
12 May 1932	Taurus (♉)	15 May 1937	Scorpio (♏)
22 Jun 1932	Gemini (♊)	09 Aug 1937	Sagittarius (♐)
05 Aug 1932	Cancer (♋)	30 Sep 1937	Capricorn (♑)
21 Sep 1932	Leo (♌)	12 Nov 1937	Aquarius (♒)
14 Nov 1932	Virgo (♍)	22 Dec 1937	Pisces (♓)
07 Jul 1933	Libra (♎)	31 Jan 1938	Aries (♈)
26 Aug 1933	Scorpio (♏)	12 Mar 1938	Taurus (♉)
09 Oct 1933	Sagittarius (♐)	24 Apr 1938	Gemini (♊)
19 Nov 1933	Capricorn (♑)	07 Jun 1938	Cancer (♋)
28 Dec 1933	Aquarius (♒)	23 Jul 1938	Leo (♌)
04 Feb 1934	Pisces (♓)	08 Sep 1938	Virgo (♍)
14 Mar 1934	Aries (♈)	25 Oct 1938	Libra (♎)
23 Apr 1934	Taurus (♉)	12 Dec 1938	Scorpio (♏)
03 Jun 1934	Gemini (♊)	29 Jan 1939	Sagittarius (♐)
16 Jul 1934	Cancer (♋)	21 Mar 1939	Capricorn (♑)
31 Aug 1934	Leo (♌)	25 Mar 1939	Aquarius (♒)
18 Oct 1934	Virgo (♍)	22 Jul 1939	Capricorn (♑)
11 Dec 1934	Libra (♎)	24 Sep 1939	Aquarius (♒)
30 Jul 1935	Scorpio (♏)	20 Nov 1939	Pisces (♓)
17 Sep 1935	Sagittarius (♐)	04 Jan 1940	Aries (♈)
29 Oct 1935	Capricorn (♑)	17 Feb 1940	Taurus (♉)
07 Dec 1935	Aquarius (♒)	02 Apr 1940	Gemini (♊)
15 Jan 1936	Pisces (♓)	18 May 1940	Cancer (♋)
22 Feb 1936	Aries (♈)	03 Jul 1940	Leo (♌)
02 Apr 1936	Taurus (♉)	20 Aug 1940	Virgo (♍)
13 May 1936	Gemini (♊)	06 Oct 1940	Libra (♎)
26 Jun 1936	Cancer (♋)	21 Nov 1940	Scorpio (♏)
10 Aug 1936	Leo (♌)	15 Jan 1941	Sagittarius (♐)
27 Sep 1936	Virgo (♍)	18 Feb 1941	Capricorn (♑)
15 Nov 1936	Libra (♎)	02 Apr 1941	Aquarius (♒)
06 Jan 1937	Scorpio (♏)	16 May 1941	Pisces (♓)
13 Mar 1937	Sagittarius (♐)	02 Jul 1941	Aries (♈)

Starting Date	Zodiac Sign	Starting Date	Zodiac Sign
12 Jan 1942	Taurus (♉)	25 Sep 1946	Scorpio (♏)
07 Mar 1942	Gemini (♊)	07 Nov 1946	Sagittarius (♐)
26 Apr 1942	Cancer (♋)	17 Dec 1946	Capricorn (♑)
14 Jun 1942	Leo (♌)	25 Jan 1947	Aquarius (♒)
01 Aug 1942	Virgo (♍)	05 Mar 1947	Pisces (♓)
17 Sep 1942	Libra (♎)	12 Apr 1947	Aries (♈)
02 Nov 1942	Scorpio (♏)	21 May 1947	Taurus (♉)
16 Dec 1942	Sagittarius (♐)	14 Jun 1947	Gemini (♊)
27 Jan 1943	Capricorn (♑)	14 Aug 1947	Cancer (♋)
09 Mar 1943	Aquarius (♒)	01 Oct 1947	Leo (♌)
17 Apr 1943	Pisces (♓)	01 Dec 1947	Virgo (♍)
27 May 1943	Aries (♈)	12 Feb 1948	Leo (♌)
08 Jul 1943	Taurus (♉)	19 May 1948	Virgo (♍)
24 Aug 1943	Gemini (♊)	17 Jul 1948	Libra (♎)
28 Mar 1944	Cancer (♋)	04 Sep 1948	Scorpio (♏)
23 May 1944	Leo (♌)	17 Oct 1948	Sagittarius (♐)
12 Jul 1944	Virgo (♍)	27 Nov 1948	Capricorn (♑)
29 Aug 1944	Libra (♎)	05 Jan 1949	Aquarius (♒)
14 Oct 1944	Scorpio (♏)	12 Feb 1949	Pisces (♓)
26 Nov 1944	Sagittarius (♐)	22 Mar 1949	Aries (♈)
06 Jan 1945	Capricorn (♑)	30 Apr 1949	Taurus (♉)
14 Feb 1945	Aquarius (♒)	10 Jun 1949	Gemini (♊)
25 Mar 1945	Pisces (♓)	23 Jul 1949	Cancer (♋)
03 May 1945	Aries (♈)	07 Sep 1949	Leo (♌)
11 Jun 1945	Taurus (♉)	27 Oct 1949	Virgo (♍)
23 Jul 1945	Gemini (♊)	26 Dec 1949	Libra (♎)
08 Sep 1945	Cancer (♋)	28 Mar 1950	Virgo (♍)
12 Nov 1945	Leo (♌)	12 Jun 1950	Libra (♎)
27 Dec 1945	Cancer (♋)	11 Aug 1950	Scorpio (♏)
23 Apr 1946	Leo (♌)	26 Sep 1950	Sagittarius (♐)
20 Jun 1946	Virgo (♍)	06 Nov 1950	Capricorn (♑)
10 Aug 1946	Libra (♎)	15 Dec 1950	Aquarius (♒)

Starting Date	Zodiac Sign	Starting Date	Zodiac Sign
23 Jan 1951	Pisces (♓)	27 Aug 1955	Virgo (♍)
02 Mar 1951	Aries (♈)	13 Oct 1955	Libra (♎)
10 Apr 1951	Taurus (♉)	29 Nov 1955	Scorpio (♏)
22 May 1951	Gemini (♊)	14 Jan 1956	Sagittarius (♐)
04 Jul 1951	Cancer (♋)	29 Feb 1956	Capricorn (♑)
18 Aug 1951	Leo (♌)	15 Apr 1956	Aquarius (♒)
05 Oct 1951	Virgo (♍)	03 Jun 1956	Pisces (♓)
24 Nov 1951	Libra (♎)	06 Dec 1956	Aries (♈)
20 Jan 1952	Scorpio (♏)	28 Jan 1957	Taurus (♉)
28 Aug 1952	Sagittarius (♐)	18 Mar 1957	Gemini (♊)
12 Oct 1952	Capricorn (♑)	05 May 1957	Cancer (♋)
22 Nov 1952	Aquarius (♒)	22 Jun 1957	Leo (♌)
31 Dec 1952	Pisces (♓)	08 Aug 1957	Virgo (♍)
08 Feb 1953	Aries (♈)	24 Sep 1957	Libra (♎)
20 Mar 1953	Taurus (♉)	09 Nov 1957	Scorpio (♏)
01 May 1953	Gemini (♊)	23 Dec 1957	Sagittarius (♐)
14 Jun 1953	Cancer (♋)	04 Feb 1958	Capricorn (♑)
30 Jul 1953	Leo (♌)	17 Mar 1958	Aquarius (♒)
15 Sep 1953	Virgo (♍)	27 Apr 1958	Pisces (♓)
02 Nov 1953	Libra (♎)	07 Jun 1958	Aries (♈)
20 Dec 1953	Scorpio (♏)	21 Jul 1958	Taurus (♉)
10 Feb 1954	Sagittarius (♐)	21 Sep 1958	Gemini (♊)
13 Apr 1954	Capricorn (♑)	28 Oct 1958	Cancer (♋)
03 Jul 1954	Sagittarius (♐)	11 Feb 1959	Gemini (♊)
25 Aug 1954	Capricorn (♑)	10 Apr 1959	Cancer (♋)
22 Oct 1954	Aquarius (♒)	01 Jun 1959	Leo (♌)
04 Dec 1954	Pisces (♓)	20 Jul 1959	Virgo (♍)
15 Jan 1955	Aries (♈)	06 Sep 1959	Libra (♎)
26 Feb 1955	Taurus (♉)	21 Oct 1959	Scorpio (♏)
11 Apr 1955	Gemini (♊)	04 Dec 1959	Sagittarius (♐)
26 May 1955	Cancer (♋)	14 Jan 1960	Capricorn (♑)
11 Jul 1955	Leo (♌)	23 Feb 1960	Aquarius (♒)

Starting Date	Zodiac Sign	Starting Date	Zodiac Sign
02 Apr 1960	Pisces (♓)	06 Nov 1964	Virgo (♍)
11 May 1960	Aries (♈)	29 Jun 1965	Libra (♎)
20 Jun 1960	Taurus (♉)	21 Aug 1965	Scorpio (♏)
02 Aug 1960	Gemini (♊)	04 Oct 1965	Sagittarius (♐)
21 Sep 1960	Cancer (♋)	14 Nov 1965	Capricorn (♑)
05 Feb 1961	Gemini (♊)	23 Dec 1965	Aquarius (♒)
07 Feb 1961	Cancer (♋)	01 Feb 1966	Pisces (♓)
06 May 1961	Leo (♌)	01 Apr 1966	Aries (♈)
29 Jun 1961	Virgo (♍)	18 Apr 1966	Taurus (♉)
17 Aug 1961	Libra (♎)	29 May 1966	Gemini (♊)
02 Oct 1961	Scorpio (♏)	11 Jul 1966	Cancer (♋)
14 Nov 1961	Sagittarius (♐)	26 Aug 1966	Leo (♌)
25 Dec 1961	Capricorn (♑)	13 Oct 1966	Virgo (♍)
02 Feb 1962	Aquarius (♒)	04 Dec 1966	Libra (♎)
12 Mar 1962	Pisces (♓)	13 Feb 1967	Scorpio (♏)
20 Apr 1962	Aries (♈)	31 Mar 1967	Libra (♎)
29 May 1962	Taurus (♉)	20 Jul 1967	Scorpio (♏)
09 Jul 1962	Gemini (♊)	10 Sep 1967	Sagittarius (♐)
22 Aug 1962	Cancer (♋)	23 Oct 1967	Capricorn (♑)
12 Oct 1962	Leo (♌)	02 Dec 1967	Aquarius (♒)
03 Jun 1963	Virgo (♍)	09 Jan 1968	Pisces (♓)
27 Jul 1963	Libra (♎)	17 Feb 1968	Aries (♈)
12 Sep 1963	Scorpio (♏)	28 Mar 1968	Taurus (♉)
26 Oct 1963	Sagittarius (♐)	09 May 1968	Gemini (♊)
05 Dec 1963	Capricorn (♑)	21 Jun 1968	Cancer (♋)
13 Jan 1964	Aquarius (♒)	06 Aug 1968	Leo (♌)
20 Feb 1964	Pisces (♓)	22 Sep 1968	Virgo (♍)
29 Mar 1964	Aries (♈)	09 Nov 1968	Libra (♎)
08 May 1964	Taurus (♉)	30 Dec 1968	Scorpio (♏)
17 Jun 1964	Gemini (♊)	25 Feb 1969	Sagittarius (♐)
01 Aug 1964	Cancer (♋)	21 Sep 1969	Capricorn (♑)
15 Sep 1964	Leo (♌)	05 Nov 1969	Aquarius (♒)

Starting Date	Zodiac Sign	Starting Date	Zodiac Sign
16 Dec 1969	Pisces (♓)	28 Jul 1974	Virgo (♍)
25 Jan 1970	Aries (♈)	13 Sep 1974	Libra (♎)
07 Mar 1970	Taurus (♉)	28 Oct 1974	Scorpio (♏)
19 Apr 1970	Gemini (♊)	11 Dec 1974	Sagittarius (♐)
02 Jun 1970	Cancer (♋)	22 Jan 1975	Capricorn (♑)
18 Jul 1970	Leo (♌)	03 Mar 1975	Aquarius (♒)
03 Sep 1970	Virgo (♍)	12 Apr 1975	Pisces (♓)
20 Oct 1970	Libra (♎)	21 May 1975	Aries (♈)
07 Dec 1970	Scorpio (♏)	01 Jul 1975	Taurus (♉)
14 Jan 1971	Sagittarius (♐)	15 Aug 1975	Gemini (♊)
12 Mar 1971	Capricorn (♑)	17 Oct 1975	Cancer (♋)
04 May 1971	Aquarius (♒)	26 Nov 1975	Gemini (♊)
07 Nov 1971	Pisces (♓)	19 Mar 1976	Cancer (♋)
24 Dec 1971	Aries (♈)	16 May 1976	Leo (♌)
11 Feb 1972	Taurus (♉)	07 Jul 1976	Virgo (♍)
27 Mar 1972	Gemini (♊)	24 Aug 1976	Libra (♎)
13 May 1972	Cancer (♋)	09 Oct 1976	Scorpio (♏)
29 Jun 1972	Leo (♌)	21 Nov 1976	Sagittarius (♐)
15 Aug 1972	Virgo (♍)	01 Jan 1977	Capricorn (♑)
01 Oct 1972	Libra (♎)	09 Feb 1977	Aquarius (♒)
16 Nov 1972	Scorpio (♏)	20 Mar 1977	Pisces (♓)
31 Dec 1972	Sagittarius (♐)	28 Apr 1977	Aries (♈)
12 Feb 1973	Capricorn (♑)	06 Jun 1977	Taurus (♉)
27 Mar 1973	Aquarius (♒)	18 Jul 1977	Gemini (♊)
08 May 1973	Pisces (♓)	01 Sep 1977	Cancer (♋)
21 Jun 1973	Aries (♈)	27 Oct 1977	Leo (♌)
13 Aug 1973	Taurus (♉)	26 Jan 1978	Cancer (♋)
30 Oct 1973	Aries (♈)	11 Apr 1978	Leo (♌)
24 Dec 1973	Taurus (♉)	14 Jun 1978	Virgo (♍)
27 Feb 1974	Gemini (♊)	04 Aug 1978	Libra (♎)
20 Apr 1974	Cancer (♋)	20 Sep 1978	Scorpio (♏)
09 Jun 1974	Leo (♌)	02 Nov 1978	Sagittarius (♐)

Starting Date	Zodiac Sign	Starting Date	Zodiac Sign
13 Dec 1978	Capricorn (♑)	17 May 1983	Gemini (♊)
21 Jan 1979	Aquarius (♒)	29 Jun 1983	Cancer (♋)
28 Feb 1979	Pisces (♓)	14 Aug 1983	Leo (♌)
07 Apr 1979	Aries (♈)	30 Sep 1983	Virgo (♍)
16 May 1979	Taurus (♉)	18 Nov 1983	Libra (♎)
26 Jun 1979	Gemini (♊)	11 Jan 1984	Scorpio (♏)
09 Aug 1979	Cancer (♋)	18 Aug 1984	Sagittarius (♐)
25 Sep 1979	Leo (♌)	05 Oct 1984	Capricorn (♑)
20 Nov 1979	Virgo (♍)	16 Nov 1984	Aquarius (♒)
12 Mar 1980	Leo (♌)	25 Dec 1984	Pisces (♓)
04 May 1980	Virgo (♍)	03 Feb 1985	Aries (♈)
11 Jul 1980	Libra (♎)	15 Mar 1985	Taurus (♉)
29 Aug 1980	Scorpio (♏)	26 Apr 1985	Gemini (♊)
12 Oct 1980	Sagittarius (♐)	09 Jun 1985	Cancer (♋)
22 Nov 1980	Capricorn (♑)	25 Jul 1985	Leo (♌)
31 Dec 1980	Aquarius (♒)	10 Sep 1985	Virgo (♍)
07 Feb 1981	Pisces (♓)	28 Oct 1985	Libra (♎)
17 Mar 1981	Aries (♈)	15 Dec 1985	Scorpio (♏)
25 Apr 1981	Taurus (♉)	02 Feb 1986	Sagittarius (♐)
05 Jun 1981	Gemini (♊)	28 Mar 1986	Capricorn (♑)
18 Jul 1981	Cancer (♋)	09 Oct 1986	Aquarius (♒)
02 Sep 1981	Leo (♌)	26 Nov 1986	Pisces (♓)
21 Oct 1981	Virgo (♍)	09 Jan 1987	Aries (♈)
16 Dec 1981	Libra (♎)	21 Feb 1987	Taurus (♉)
03 Aug 1982	Scorpio (♏)	06 Apr 1987	Gemini (♊)
20 Sep 1982	Sagittarius (♐)	21 May 1987	Cancer (♋)
01 Nov 1982	Capricorn (♑)	07 Jul 1987	Leo (♌)
10 Dec 1982	Aquarius (♒)	23 Aug 1987	Virgo (♍)
18 Jan 1983	Pisces (♓)	09 Oct 1987	Libra (♎)
25 Feb 1983	Aries (♈)	24 Nov 1987	Scorpio (♏)
06 Apr 1983	Taurus (♉)		

These dates are derived from calculations using *The American Ephemeris for the Twentieth Century* (San Diego: ACS Publications, 1980–1996).

TABLE 13. TROPICAL PLACEMENT FOR VENUS, 1927–1987

Starting Date	Zodiac Sign	Starting Date	Zodiac Sign
01 Jan 1927	Capricorn (♑)	20 Apr 1929	Aries (♈)
09 Jan 1927	Aquarius (♒)	03 Jun 1929	Taurus (♉)
02 Feb 1927	Pisces (♓)	08 Jul 1929	Gemini (♊)
27 Feb 1927	Aries (♈)	05 Aug 1929	Cancer (♋)
23 Mar 1927	Taurus (♉)	31 Aug 1929	Leo (♌)
17 Apr 1927	Gemini (♊)	26 Sep 1929	Virgo (♍)
12 May 1927	Cancer (♋)	20 Oct 1929	Libra (♎)
08 Jun 1927	Leo (♌)	13 Nov 1929	Scorpio (♏)
08 Jul 1927	Virgo (♍)	07 Dec 1929	Sagittarius (♐)
10 Nov 1927	Libra (♎)	31 Dec 1929	Capricorn (♑)
09 Dec 1927	Scorpio (♏)	24 Jan 1930	Aquarius (♒)
04 Jan 1928	Sagittarius (♐)	17 Feb 1930	Pisces (♓)
29 Jan 1928	Capricorn (♑)	13 Mar 1930	Aries (♈)
23 Feb 1928	Aquarius (♒)	06 Apr 1930	Taurus (♉)
18 Mar 1928	Pisces (♓)	01 May 1930	Gemini (♊)
12 Apr 1928	Aries (♈)	25 May 1930	Cancer (♋)
06 May 1928	Taurus (♉)	19 Jun 1930	Leo (♌)
30 May 1928	Gemini (♊)	15 Jul 1930	Virgo (♍)
24 Jun 1928	Cancer (♋)	10 Aug 1930	Libra (♎)
18 Jul 1928	Leo (♌)	07 Sep 1930	Scorpio (♏)
12 Aug 1928	Virgo (♍)	12 Oct 1930	Sagittarius (♐)
05 Sep 1928	Libra (♎)	22 Nov 1930	Scorpio (♏)
29 Sep 1928	Scorpio (♏)	04 Jan 1931	Sagittarius (♐)
25 Oct 1928	Sagittarius (♐)	07 Feb 1931	Capricorn (♑)
17 Nov 1928	Capricorn (♑)	06 Mar 1931	Aquarius (♒)
12 Dec 1928	Aquarius (♒)	01 Apr 1931	Pisces (♓)
07 Jan 1929	Pisces (♓)	26 Apr 1931	Aries (♈)
03 Feb 1929	Aries (♈)	21 May 1931	Taurus (♉)
08 Mar 1929	Taurus (♉)	15 Jun 1931	Gemini (♊)

Starting Date	Zodiac Sign	Starting Date	Zodiac Sign
10 Jul 1931	Cancer (♋)	07 Nov 1933	Capricorn (♑)
03 Aug 1931	Leo (♌)	06 Dec 1933	Aquarius (♒)
27 Aug 1931	Virgo (♍)	06 Apr 1934	Pisces (♓)
21 Sep 1931	Libra (♎)	06 May 1934	Aries (♈)
15 Oct 1931	Scorpio (♏)	02 Jun 1934	Taurus (♉)
08 Nov 1931	Sagittarius (♐)	28 Jun 1934	Gemini (♊)
02 Dec 1931	Capricorn (♑)	24 Jul 1934	Cancer (♋)
26 Dec 1931	Aquarius (♒)	18 Aug 1934	Leo (♌)
19 Jan 1932	Pisces (♓)	11 Sep 1934	Virgo (♍)
13 Feb 1932	Aries (♈)	05 Oct 1934	Libra (♎)
09 Mar 1932	Taurus (♉)	29 Oct 1934	Scorpio (♏)
05 Apr 1932	Gemini (♊)	22 Nov 1934	Sagittarius (♐)
06 May 1932	Cancer (♋)	16 Dec 1934	Capricorn (♑)
13 Jul 1932	Gemini (♊)	09 Jan 1935	Aquarius (♒)
28 Jul 1932	Cancer (♋)	02 Feb 1935	Pisces (♓)
09 Sep 1932	Leo (♌)	26 Feb 1935	Aries (♈)
07 Oct 1932	Virgo (♍)	22 Mar 1935	Taurus (♉)
02 Nov 1932	Libra (♎)	16 Apr 1935	Gemini (♊)
27 Nov 1932	Scorpio (♏)	12 May 1935	Cancer (♋)
21 Dec 1932	Sagittarius (♐)	08 Jun 1935	Leo (♌)
14 Jan 1933	Capricorn (♑)	08 Jul 1935	Virgo (♍)
07 Feb 1933	Aquarius (♒)	10 Nov 1935	Libra (♎)
03 Mar 1933	Pisces (♓)	09 Dec 1935	Scorpio (♏)
28 Mar 1933	Aries (♈)	04 Jan 1936	Sagittarius (♐)
21 Apr 1933	Taurus (♉)	29 Jan 1936	Capricorn (♑)
15 May 1933	Gemini (♊)	22 Feb 1936	Aquarius (♒)
09 Jun 1933	Cancer (♋)	18 Mar 1936	Pisces (♓)
03 Jul 1933	Leo (♌)	11 Apr 1936	Aries (♈)
28 Jul 1933	Virgo (♍)	05 May 1936	Taurus (♉)
22 Aug 1933	Libra (♎)	30 May 1936	Gemini (♊)
16 Sep 1933	Scorpio (♏)	23 Jun 1936	Cancer (♋)
11 Oct 1933	Sagittarius (♐)	18 Jul 1936	Leo (♌)

Starting Date	Zodiac Sign	Starting Date	Zodiac Sign
11 Aug 1936	Virgo (♍)	06 Feb 1939	Capricorn (♑)
04 Sep 1936	Libra (♎)	06 Mar 1939	Aquarius (♒)
29 Sep 1936	Scorpio (♏)	31 Mar 1939	Pisces (♓)
23 Oct 1936	Sagittarius (♐)	26 Apr 1939	Aries (♈)
17 Nov 1936	Capricorn (♑)	21 May 1939	Taurus (♉)
12 Dec 1936	Aquarius (♒)	14 Jun 1939	Gemini (♊)
06 Jan 1937	Pisces (♓)	09 Jul 1939	Cancer (♋)
02 Feb 1937	Aries (♈)	03 Aug 1939	Leo (♌)
10 Mar 1937	Taurus (♉)	27 Aug 1939	Virgo (♍)
14 Apr 1937	Aries (♈)	20 Sep 1939	Libra (♎)
04 Jun 1937	Taurus (♉)	14 Oct 1939	Scorpio (♏)
08 Jul 1937	Gemini (♊)	07 Nov 1939	Sagittarius (♐)
05 Aug 1937	Cancer (♋)	01 Dec 1939	Capricorn (♑)
31 Aug 1937	Leo (♌)	25 Dec 1939	Aquarius (♒)
25 Sep 1937	Virgo (♍)	19 Jan 1940	Pisces (♓)
20 Oct 1937	Libra (♎)	12 Feb 1940	Aries (♈)
13 Nov 1937	Scorpio (♏)	09 Mar 1940	Taurus (♉)
07 Dec 1937	Sagittarius (♐)	05 Apr 1940	Gemini (♊)
31 Dec 1937	Capricorn (♑)	07 May 1940	Cancer (♋)
23 Jan 1938	Aquarius (♒)	06 Jul 1940	Gemini (♊)
16 Feb 1938	Pisces (♓)	01 Aug 1940	Cancer (♋)
12 Mar 1938	Aries (♈)	09 Sep 1940	Leo (♌)
06 Apr 1938	Taurus (♉)	07 Oct 1940	Virgo (♍)
30 Apr 1938	Gemini (♊)	02 Nov 1940	Libra (♎)
25 May 1938	Cancer (♋)	27 Nov 1940	Scorpio (♏)
19 Jun 1938	Leo (♌)	21 Dec 1940	Sagittarius (♐)
14 Jul 1938	Virgo (♍)	14 Jan 1941	Capricorn (♑)
10 Aug 1938	Libra (♎)	07 Feb 1941	Aquarius (♒)
07 Sep 1938	Scorpio (♏)	03 Mar 1941	Pisces (♓)
14 Oct 1938	Sagittarius (♐)	27 Mar 1941	Aries (♈)
16 Nov 1938	Capricorn (♑)	20 Apr 1941	Taurus (♉)
05 Jan 1939	Sagittarius (♐)	15 May 1941	Gemini (♊)

Starting Date	Zodiac Sign	Starting Date	Zodiac Sign
08 Jun 1941	Cancer (♋)	17 Mar 1944	Pisces (♓)
03 Jul 1941	Leo (♌)	11 Apr 1944	Aries (♈)
27 Jul 1941	Virgo (♍)	05 May 1944	Taurus (♉)
21 Aug 1941	Libra (♎)	29 May 1944	Gemini (♊)
15 Sep 1941	Scorpio (♏)	23 Jun 1944	Cancer (♋)
11 Oct 1941	Sagittarius (♐)	17 Jul 1944	Leo (♌)
06 Nov 1941	Capricorn (♑)	11 Aug 1944	Virgo (♍)
06 Dec 1941	Aquarius (♒)	04 Sep 1944	Libra (♎)
07 Apr 1942	Pisces (♓)	28 Sep 1944	Scorpio (♏)
06 May 1942	Aries (♈)	23 Oct 1944	Sagittarius (♐)
02 Jun 1942	Taurus (♉)	16 Nov 1944	Capricorn (♑)
28 Jun 1942	Gemini (♊)	11 Dec 1944	Aquarius (♒)
23 Jul 1942	Cancer (♋)	06 Jan 1945	Pisces (♓)
17 Aug 1942	Leo (♌)	02 Feb 1945	Aries (♈)
11 Sep 1942	Virgo (♍)	11 Mar 1945	Taurus (♉)
05 Oct 1942	Libra (♎)	08 Apr 1945	Aries (♈)
29 Oct 1942	Scorpio (♏)	05 Jun 1945	Taurus (♉)
22 Nov 1942	Sagittarius (♐)	08 Jul 1945	Gemini (♊)
16 Dec 1942	Capricorn (♑)	04 Aug 1945	Cancer (♋)
08 Jan 1943	Aquarius (♒)	31 Aug 1945	Leo (♌)
01 Feb 1943	Pisces (♓)	25 Sep 1945	Virgo (♍)
26 Feb 1943	Aries (♈)	19 Oct 1945	Libra (♎)
22 Mar 1943	Taurus (♉)	12 Nov 1945	Scorpio (♏)
16 Apr 1943	Gemini (♊)	06 Dec 1945	Sagittarius (♐)
11 May 1943	Cancer (♋)	30 Dec 1945	Capricorn (♑)
08 Jun 1943	Leo (♌)	23 Jan 1946	Aquarius (♒)
08 Jul 1943	Virgo (♍)	16 Feb 1946	Pisces (♓)
10 Nov 1943	Libra (♎)	12 Mar 1946	Aries (♈)
08 Dec 1943	Scorpio (♏)	05 Apr 1946	Taurus (♉)
03 Jan 1944	Sagittarius (♐)	29 Apr 1946	Gemini (♊)
28 Jan 1944	Capricorn (♑)	24 May 1946	Cancer (♋)
22 Feb 1944	Aquarius (♒)	18 Jun 1946	Leo (♌)

Starting Date	Zodiac Sign	Starting Date	Zodiac Sign
14 Jul 1946	Virgo (♍)	13 Jan 1949	Capricorn (♑)
09 Aug 1946	Libra (♎)	06 Feb 1949	Aquarius (♒)
07 Sep 1946	Scorpio (♏)	02 Mar 1949	Pisces (♓)
16 Oct 1946	Sagittarius (♐)	26 Mar 1949	Aries (♈)
08 Nov 1946	Scorpio (♏)	20 Apr 1949	Taurus (♉)
06 Jan 1947	Sagittarius (♐)	14 May 1949	Gemini (♊)
06 Feb 1947	Capricorn (♑)	07 Jun 1949	Cancer (♋)
05 Mar 1947	Aquarius (♒)	02 Jul 1949	Leo (♌)
31 Mar 1947	Pisces (♓)	27 Jul 1949	Virgo (♍)
25 Apr 1947	Aries (♈)	21 Aug 1949	Libra (♎)
20 May 1947	Taurus (♉)	15 Sep 1949	Scorpio (♏)
14 Jun 1947	Gemini (♊)	10 Oct 1949	Sagittarius (♐)
09 Jul 1947	Cancer (♋)	06 Nov 1949	Capricorn (♑)
02 Aug 1947	Leo (♌)	06 Dec 1949	Aquarius (♒)
26 Aug 1947	Virgo (♍)	07 Apr 1950	Pisces (♓)
20 Sep 1947	Libra (♎)	06 May 1950	Aries (♈)
14 Oct 1947	Scorpio (♏)	02 Jun 1950	Taurus (♉)
07 Nov 1947	Sagittarius (♐)	27 Jun 1950	Gemini (♊)
01 Dec 1947	Capricorn (♑)	23 Jul 1950	Cancer (♋)
25 Dec 1947	Aquarius (♒)	17 Aug 1950	Leo (♌)
18 Jan 1948	Pisces (♓)	10 Sep 1950	Virgo (♍)
12 Feb 1948	Aries (♈)	04 Oct 1950	Libra (♎)
08 Mar 1948	Taurus (♉)	28 Oct 1950	Scorpio (♏)
05 Apr 1948	Gemini (♊)	21 Nov 1950	Sagittarius (♐)
07 May 1948	Cancer (♋)	15 Dec 1950	Capricorn (♑)
29 Jun 1948	Gemini (♊)	08 Jan 1951	Aquarius (♒)
03 Aug 1948	Cancer (♋)	01 Feb 1951	Pisces (♓)
09 Sep 1948	Leo (♌)	25 Feb 1951	Aries (♈)
07 Oct 1948	Virgo (♍)	21 Mar 1951	Taurus (♉)
01 Nov 1948	Libra (♎)	15 Apr 1951	Gemini (♊)
26 Nov 1948	Scorpio (♏)	11 May 1951	Cancer (♋)
20 Dec 1948	Sagittarius (♐)	07 Jun 1951	Leo (♌)

Starting Date	Zodiac Sign	Starting Date	Zodiac Sign
08 Jul 1951	Virgo (♍)	15 Feb 1954	Pisces (♓)
10 Nov 1951	Libra (♎)	11 Mar 1954	Aries (♈)
08 Dec 1951	Scorpio (♏)	04 Apr 1954	Taurus (♉)
03 Jan 1952	Sagittarius (♐)	29 Apr 1954	Gemini (♊)
28 Jan 1952	Capricorn (♑)	24 May 1954	Cancer (♋)
21 Feb 1952	Aquarius (♒)	18 Jun 1954	Leo (♌)
17 Mar 1952	Pisces (♓)	13 Jul 1954	Virgo (♍)
10 Apr 1952	Aries (♈)	09 Aug 1954	Libra (♎)
04 May 1952	Taurus (♉)	07 Sep 1954	Scorpio (♏)
29 May 1952	Gemini (♊)	24 Oct 1954	Sagittarius (♐)
22 Jun 1952	Cancer (♋)	27 Oct 1954	Capricorn (♑)
17 Jul 1952	Leo (♌)	06 Jan 1955	Sagittarius (♐)
10 Aug 1952	Virgo (♍)	06 Feb 1955	Capricorn (♑)
03 Sep 1952	Libra (♎)	05 Mar 1955	Aquarius (♒)
28 Sep 1952	Scorpio (♏)	30 Mar 1955	Pisces (♓)
22 Oct 1952	Sagittarius (♐)	25 Apr 1955	Aries (♈)
16 Nov 1952	Capricorn (♑)	20 May 1955	Taurus (♉)
11 Dec 1952	Aquarius (♒)	13 Jun 1955	Gemini (♊)
05 Jan 1953	Pisces (♓)	08 Jul 1955	Cancer (♋)
02 Feb 1953	Aries (♈)	01 Aug 1955	Leo (♌)
15 Mar 1953	Taurus (♉)	26 Aug 1955	Virgo (♍)
31 Mar 1953	Aries (♈)	19 Sep 1955	Libra (♎)
05 Jun 1953	Taurus (♉)	13 Oct 1955	Scorpio (♏)
07 Jul 1953	Gemini (♊)	06 Nov 1955	Sagittarius (♐)
04 Aug 1953	Cancer (♋)	30 Nov 1955	Capricorn (♑)
30 Aug 1953	Leo (♌)	24 Dec 1955	Aquarius (♒)
24 Sep 1953	Virgo (♍)	18 Jan 1956	Pisces (♓)
19 Oct 1953	Libra (♎)	11 Feb 1956	Aries (♈)
12 Nov 1953	Scorpio (♏)	08 Mar 1956	Taurus (♉)
06 Dec 1953	Sagittarius (♐)	04 Apr 1956	Gemini (♊)
30 Dec 1953	Capricorn (♑)	08 May 1956	Cancer (♋)
22 Jan 1954	Aquarius (♒)	24 Jun 1956	Gemini (♊)

Starting Date	Zodiac Sign	Starting Date	Zodiac Sign
04 Aug 1956	Cancer (♋)	31 Jan 1959	Pisces (♓)
08 Sep 1956	Leo (♌)	24 Feb 1959	Aries (♈)
06 Oct 1956	Virgo (♍)	21 Mar 1959	Taurus (♉)
01 Nov 1956	Libra (♎)	15 Apr 1959	Gemini (♊)
26 Nov 1956	Scorpio (♏)	11 May 1959	Cancer (♋)
20 Dec 1956	Sagittarius (♐)	07 Jun 1959	Leo (♌)
13 Jan 1957	Capricorn (♑)	09 Jul 1959	Virgo (♍)
06 Feb 1957	Aquarius (♒)	20 Sep 1959	Leo (♌)
04 Mar 1957	Pisces (♓)	25 Sep 1959	Virgo (♍)
26 Mar 1957	Aries (♈)	10 Nov 1959	Libra (♎)
19 Apr 1957	Taurus (♉)	08 Dec 1959	Scorpio (♏)
13 May 1957	Gemini (♊)	02 Jan 1960	Sagittarius (♐)
07 Jun 1957	Cancer (♋)	27 Jan 1960	Capricorn (♑)
13 Jul 1957	Leo (♌)	21 Feb 1960	Aquarius (♒)
30 Jul 1957	Virgo (♍)	16 Mar 1960	Pisces (♓)
20 Aug 1957	Libra (♎)	09 Apr 1960	Aries (♈)
14 Sep 1957	Scorpio (♏)	04 May 1960	Taurus (♉)
10 Oct 1957	Sagittarius (♐)	28 May 1960	Gemini (♊)
06 Nov 1957	Capricorn (♑)	22 Jun 1960	Taurus (♉)
07 Dec 1957	Aquarius (♒)	16 Jul 1960	Leo (♌)
07 Apr 1958	Pisces (♓)	09 Aug 1960	Virgo (♍)
05 May 1958	Aries (♈)	03 Sep 1960	Libra (♎)
01 Jun 1958	Taurus (♉)	27 Sep 1960	Scorpio (♏)
27 Jun 1958	Gemini (♊)	22 Oct 1960	Sagittarius (♐)
22 Jul 1958	Cancer (♋)	15 Nov 1960	Capricorn (♑)
16 Aug 1958	Leo (♌)	10 Dec 1960	Aquarius (♒)
10 Sep 1958	Virgo (♍)	05 Jan 1961	Pisces (♓)
04 Oct 1958	Libra (♎)	02 Feb 1961	Aries (♈)
28 Oct 1958	Scorpio (♏)	06 Jun 1961	Taurus (♉)
21 Nov 1958	Sagittarius (♐)	07 Jul 1961	Gemini (♊)
14 Dec 1958	Capricorn (♑)	04 Aug 1961	Cancer (♋)
07 Jan 1959	Aquarius (♒)	30 Aug 1961	Leo (♌)

Starting Date	Zodiac Sign	Starting Date	Zodiac Sign
24 Sep 1961	Virgo (♍)	08 Mar 1964	Taurus (♉)
18 Oct 1961	Libra (♎)	04 Apr 1964	Gemini (♊)
11 Nov 1961	Scorpio (♏)	09 May 1964	Cancer (♋)
01 Dec 1961	Sagittarius (♐)	18 Jun 1964	Gemini (♊)
20 Dec 1961	Capricorn (♑)	05 Aug 1964	Cancer (♋)
22 Jan 1962	Aquarius (♒)	08 Sep 1964	Leo (♌)
15 Feb 1962	Pisces (♓)	06 Oct 1964	Virgo (♍)
11 Mar 1962	Aries (♈)	31 Oct 1964	Libra (♎)
04 Apr 1962	Taurus (♉)	25 Nov 1964	Scorpio (♏)
28 Apr 1962	Gemini (♊)	19 Dec 1964	Sagittarius (♐)
23 May 1962	Cancer (♋)	12 Jan 1965	Capricorn (♑)
17 Jun 1962	Leo (♌)	05 Feb 1965	Aquarius (♒)
13 Jul 1962	Virgo (♍)	01 Mar 1965	Pisces (♓)
09 Aug 1962	Libra (♎)	25 Mar 1965	Aries (♈)
07 Sep 1962	Scorpio (♏)	19 Apr 1965	Taurus (♉)
07 Jan 1963	Sagittarius (♐)	13 May 1965	Gemini (♊)
06 Feb 1963	Capricorn (♑)	06 Jun 1965	Cancer (♋)
04 Mar 1963	Aquarius (♒)	01 Jul 1965	Leo (♌)
30 Mar 1963	Pisces (♓)	26 Jul 1965	Virgo (♍)
24 Apr 1963	Aries (♈)	20 Aug 1965	Libra (♎)
19 May 1963	Taurus (♉)	14 Sep 1965	Scorpio (♏)
13 Jun 1963	Gemini (♊)	10 Oct 1965	Sagittarius (♐)
07 Jul 1963	Cancer (♋)	06 Nov 1965	Capricorn (♑)
01 Aug 1963	Leo (♌)	07 Dec 1965	Aquarius (♒)
25 Aug 1963	Virgo (♍)	07 Feb 1966	Capricorn (♑)
18 Sep 1963	Libra (♎)	25 Feb 1966	Aquarius (♒)
12 Oct 1963	Scorpio (♏)	07 Apr 1966	Pisces (♓)
06 Nov 1963	Sagittarius (♐)	05 May 1966	Aries (♈)
30 Nov 1963	Capricorn (♑)	01 Jun 1966	Taurus (♉)
24 Dec 1963	Aquarius (♒)	26 Jun 1966	Gemini (♊)
17 Jan 1964	Pisces (♓)	22 Jul 1966	Cancer (♋)
11 Feb 1964	Aries (♈)	16 Aug 1966	Leo (♌)

Starting Date	Zodiac Sign	Starting Date	Zodiac Sign
09 Sep 1966	Virgo (♍)	05 Jan 1969	Pisces (♓)
03 Oct 1966	Libra (♎)	02 Feb 1969	Aries (♈)
27 Oct 1966	Scorpio (♏)	06 Jun 1969	Taurus (♉)
20 Nov 1966	Sagittarius (♐)	07 Jul 1969	Gemini (♊)
14 Dec 1966	Capricorn (♑)	03 Aug 1969	Cancer (♋)
07 Jan 1967	Aquarius (♒)	29 Aug 1969	Leo (♌)
31 Jan 1967	Pisces (♓)	23 Sep 1969	Virgo (♍)
24 Feb 1967	Aries (♈)	18 Oct 1969	Libra (♎)
20 Mar 1967	Taurus (♉)	11 Nov 1969	Scorpio (♏)
14 Apr 1967	Gemini (♊)	05 Dec 1969	Sagittarius (♐)
10 May 1967	Cancer (♋)	28 Dec 1969	Capricorn (♑)
07 Jun 1967	Leo (♌)	21 Jan 1970	Aquarius (♒)
09 Jul 1967	Virgo (♍)	14 Feb 1970	Pisces (♓)
09 Sep 1967	Leo (♌)	10 Mar 1970	Aries (♈)
02 Oct 1967	Virgo (♍)	03 Apr 1970	Taurus (♉)
10 Nov 1967	Libra (♎)	28 Apr 1970	Gemini (♊)
07 Dec 1967	Scorpio (♏)	23 May 1970	Cancer (♋)
02 Jan 1968	Sagittarius (♐)	17 Jun 1970	Leo (♌)
27 Jan 1968	Capricorn (♑)	13 Jul 1970	Virgo (♍)
20 Feb 1968	Aquarius (♒)	08 Aug 1970	Libra (♎)
16 Mar 1968	Pisces (♓)	07 Sep 1970	Scorpio (♏)
09 Apr 1968	Aries (♈)	07 Jan 1971	Sagittarius (♐)
03 May 1968	Taurus (♉)	06 Feb 1971	Capricorn (♑)
28 May 1968	Gemini (♊)	04 Mar 1971	Aquarius (♒)
21 Jun 1968	Cancer (♋)	30 Mar 1971	Pisces (♓)
16 Jul 1968	Leo (♌)	24 Apr 1971	Aries (♈)
09 Aug 1968	Virgo (♍)	19 May 1971	Taurus (♉)
02 Sep 1968	Libra (♎)	07 Jun 1971	Gemini (♊)
27 Sep 1968	Scorpio (♏)	07 Jul 1971	Cancer (♋)
21 Oct 1968	Sagittarius (♐)	01 Aug 1971	Leo (♌)
15 Nov 1968	Capricorn (♑)	25 Aug 1971	Virgo (♍)
10 Dec 1968	Aquarius (♒)	18 Sep 1971	Libra (♎)

Starting Date	Zodiac Sign	Starting Date	Zodiac Sign
12 Oct 1971	Scorpio (♏)	07 Apr 1974	Pisces (♓)
05 Nov 1971	Sagittarius (♐)	05 May 1974	Aries (♈)
29 Nov 1971	Capricorn (♑)	31 May 1974	Taurus (♉)
23 Dec 1971	Aquarius (♒)	26 Jun 1974	Gemini (♊)
17 Jan 1972	Pisces (♓)	21 Jul 1974	Cancer (♋)
10 Feb 1972	Aries (♈)	15 Aug 1974	Leo (♌)
07 Mar 1972	Taurus (♉)	08 Sep 1974	Virgo (♍)
04 Apr 1972	Gemini (♊)	03 Oct 1974	Libra (♎)
11 May 1972	Cancer (♋)	27 Oct 1974	Scorpio (♏)
12 Jun 1972	Gemini (♊)	19 Nov 1974	Sagittarius (♐)
06 Aug 1972	Cancer (♋)	13 Dec 1974	Capricorn (♑)
08 Sep 1972	Leo (♌)	06 Jan 1975	Aquarius (♒)
05 Oct 1972	Virgo (♍)	30 Jan 1975	Pisces (♓)
31 Oct 1972	Libra (♎)	23 Feb 1975	Aries (♈)
25 Nov 1972	Scorpio (♏)	20 Mar 1975	Taurus (♉)
19 Dec 1972	Sagittarius (♐)	14 Apr 1975	Gemini (♊)
12 Jan 1973	Capricorn (♑)	10 May 1975	Cancer (♋)
05 Feb 1973	Aquarius (♒)	06 Jun 1975	Leo (♌)
01 Mar 1973	Pisces (♓)	09 Jul 1975	Virgo (♍)
25 Mar 1973	Aries (♈)	03 Sep 1975	Leo (♌)
18 Apr 1973	Taurus (♉)	04 Oct 1975	Virgo (♍)
12 May 1973	Gemini (♊)	10 Nov 1975	Libra (♎)
06 Jun 1973	Cancer (♋)	07 Dec 1975	Scorpio (♏)
30 Jun 1973	Leo (♌)	02 Jan 1976	Sagittarius (♐)
25 Jul 1973	Virgo (♍)	26 Jan 1976	Capricorn (♑)
19 Aug 1973	Libra (♎)	20 Feb 1976	Aquarius (♒)
13 Sep 1973	Scorpio (♏)	15 Mar 1976	Pisces (♓)
09 Oct 1973	Sagittarius (♐)	08 Apr 1976	Aries (♈)
06 Nov 1973	Capricorn (♑)	03 May 1976	Taurus (♉)
08 Dec 1973	Aquarius (♒)	27 May 1976	Gemini (♊)
30 Jan 1974	Capricorn (♑)	21 Jun 1976	Cancer (♋)
01 Mar 1974	Aquarius (♒)	15 Jul 1976	Leo (♌)

Starting Date	Zodiac Sign	Starting Date	Zodiac Sign
08 Aug 1976	Virgo (♍)	18 May 1979	Taurus (♉)
02 Sep 1976	Libra (♎)	12 Jun 1979	Gemini (♊)
26 Sep 1976	Scorpio (♏)	06 Jul 1979	Cancer (♋)
21 Oct 1976	Sagittarius (♐)	31 Jul 1979	Leo (♌)
14 Nov 1976	Capricorn (♑)	24 Aug 1979	Virgo (♍)
10 Dec 1976	Aquarius (♒)	17 Sep 1979	Libra (♎)
05 Jan 1977	Pisces (♓)	11 Oct 1979	Scorpio (♏)
02 Feb 1977	Aries (♈)	04 Nov 1979	Sagittarius (♐)
06 Jun 1977	Taurus (♉)	29 Nov 1979	Capricorn (♑)
07 Jul 1977	Gemini (♊)	23 Dec 1979	Aquarius (♒)
03 Aug 1977	Cancer (♋)	16 Jan 1980	Pisces (♓)
29 Aug 1977	Leo (♌)	10 Feb 1980	Aries (♈)
23 Sep 1977	Virgo (♍)	07 Mar 1980	Taurus (♉)
17 Oct 1977	Libra (♎)	04 Apr 1980	Gemini (♊)
10 Nov 1977	Scorpio (♏)	13 May 1980	Cancer (♋)
04 Dec 1977	Sagittarius (♐)	05 Jun 1980	Gemini (♊)
28 Dec 1977	Capricorn (♑)	07 Aug 1980	Cancer (♋)
21 Jan 1978	Aquarius (♒)	08 Sep 1980	Leo (♌)
14 Feb 1978	Pisces (♓)	05 Oct 1980	Virgo (♍)
10 Mar 1978	Aries (♈)	30 Oct 1980	Libra (♎)
03 Apr 1978	Taurus (♉)	24 Nov 1980	Scorpio (♏)
27 Apr 1978	Gemini (♊)	18 Dec 1980	Sagittarius (♐)
22 May 1978	Cancer (♋)	11 Jan 1981	Capricorn (♑)
16 Jun 1978	Leo (♌)	04 Feb 1981	Aquarius (♒)
12 Jul 1978	Virgo (♍)	28 Feb 1981	Pisces (♓)
08 Aug 1978	Libra (♎)	24 Mar 1981	Aries (♈)
07 Sep 1978	Scorpio (♏)	18 Apr 1981	Taurus (♉)
07 Jan 1979	Sagittarius (♐)	12 May 1981	Gemini (♊)
05 Feb 1979	Capricorn (♑)	05 Jun 1981	Cancer (♋)
04 Mar 1979	Aquarius (♒)	30 Jun 1981	Leo (♌)
29 Mar 1979	Pisces (♓)	25 Jul 1981	Virgo (♍)
18 Apr 1979	Aries (♈)	19 Aug 1981	Libra (♎)

Starting Date	Zodiac Sign	Starting Date	Zodiac Sign
13 Sep 1981	Scorpio (♏)	15 Mar 1984	Pisces (♓)
09 Oct 1981	Sagittarius (♐)	08 Apr 1984	Aries (♈)
06 Nov 1981	Capricorn (♑)	02 May 1984	Taurus (♉)
09 Dec 1981	Aquarius (♒)	27 May 1984	Gemini (♊)
23 Jan 1982	Capricorn (♑)	20 Jun 1984	Cancer (♋)
02 Mar 1982	Aquarius (♒)	14 Jul 1984	Leo (♌)
07 Apr 1982	Pisces (♓)	08 Aug 1984	Virgo (♍)
05 May 1982	Aries (♈)	01 Sep 1984	Libra (♎)
31 May 1982	Taurus (♉)	26 Sep 1984	Scorpio (♏)
26 Jun 1982	Gemini (♊)	20 Oct 1984	Sagittarius (♐)
21 Jul 1982	Cancer (♋)	14 Nov 1984	Capricorn (♑)
14 Aug 1982	Leo (♌)	09 Dec 1984	Aquarius (♒)
08 Sep 1982	Virgo (♍)	04 Jan 1985	Pisces (♓)
02 Oct 1982	Libra (♎)	02 Feb 1985	Aries (♈)
26 Oct 1982	Scorpio (♏)	06 Jun 1985	Taurus (♉)
19 Nov 1982	Sagittarius (♐)	06 Jul 1985	Gemini (♊)
13 Dec 1982	Capricorn (♑)	02 Aug 1985	Cancer (♋)
06 Jan 1983	Aquarius (♒)	28 Aug 1985	Leo (♌)
23 Jan 1983	Pisces (♓)	22 Sep 1985	Virgo (♍)
23 Feb 1983	Aries (♈)	17 Oct 1985	Libra (♎)
19 Mar 1983	Taurus (♉)	10 Nov 1985	Scorpio (♏)
13 Apr 1983	Gemini (♊)	04 Dec 1985	Sagittarius (♐)
09 May 1983	Cancer (♋)	27 Dec 1985	Capricorn (♑)
06 Jun 1983	Leo (♌)	20 Jan 1986	Aquarius (♒)
10 Jul 1983	Virgo (♍)	11 Feb 1986	Pisces (♓)
27 Aug 1983	Leo (♌)	09 Mar 1986	Aries (♈)
06 Oct 1983	Virgo (♍)	02 Apr 1986	Taurus (♉)
09 Nov 1983	Libra (♎)	27 Apr 1986	Gemini (♊)
07 Dec 1983	Scorpio (♏)	22 May 1986	Cancer (♋)
01 Jan 1984	Sagittarius (♐)	16 Jun 1986	Leo (♌)
26 Jan 1984	Capricorn (♑)	12 Jul 1986	Virgo (♍)
19 Feb 1984	Aquarius (♒)	08 Aug 1986	Libra (♎)

Starting Date	Zodiac Sign	Starting Date	Zodiac Sign
07 Sep 1986	Scorpio (♏)	06 Jul 1987	Cancer (♋)
07 Jan 1987	Sagittarius (♐)	30 Jul 1987	Leo (♌)
05 Feb 1987	Capricorn (♑)	24 Aug 1987	Virgo (♍)
03 Mar 1987	Aquarius (♒)	17 Sep 1987	Libra (♎)
29 Mar 1987	Pisces (♓)	11 Oct 1987	Scorpio (♏)
23 Apr 1987	Aries (♈)	04 Nov 1987	Sagittarius (♐)
17 May 1987	Taurus (♉)	28 Nov 1987	Capricorn (♑)
11 Jun 1987	Gemini (♊)	22 Dec 1987	Aquarius (♒)

These dates are derived from calculations using The American Ephemeris for the Twentieth Century (San Diego: ACS Publications, 1980–1996).

TABLE 14. TROPICAL PLACEMENT FOR JUPITER, 1927–1987

Starting Date	Zodiac Sign	Starting Date	Zodiac Sign
01 Jan 1927	Aquarius (♒)	30 Dec 1938	Pisces (♓)
18 Jan 1927	Pisces (♓)	12 May 1939	Aries (♈)
06 Jun 1927	Aries (♈)	30 Oct 1939	Pisces (♓)
11 Sep 1927	Pisces (♓)	21 Dec 1939	Aries (♈)
23 Jan 1928	Aries (♈)	16 May 1940	Taurus (♉)
04 Jun 1928	Taurus (♉)	27 May 1941	Gemini (♊)
13 Jun 1929	Gemini (♊)	10 Jun 1942	Cancer (♋)
27 Jun 1930	Cancer (♋)	01 Jul 1943	Leo (♌)
17 Jul 1931	Leo (♌)	26 Jul 1944	Virgo (♍)
11 Aug 1932	Virgo (♍)	25 Aug 1945	Libra (♎)
10 Sep 1933	Libra (♎)	25 Sep 1946	Scorpio (♏)
11 Oct 1934	Scorpio (♏)	24 Oct 1947	Sagittarius (♐)
09 Nov 1935	Sagittarius (♐)	15 Nov 1948	Capricorn (♑)
02 Dec 1936	Capricorn (♑)	13 Apr 1949	Aquarius (♒)
20 Dec 1937	Aquarius (♒)	28 Jun 1949	Capricorn (♑)
14 May 1938	Pisces (♓)	01 Dec 1949	Aquarius (♒)
30 Jul 1938	Aquarius (♒)	15 Apr 1950	Pisces (♓)

Starting Date	Zodiac Sign	Starting Date	Zodiac Sign
15 Sep 1950	Aquarius (♒)	28 Sep 1966	Leo (♌)
02 Dec 1950	Pisces (♓)	17 Jan 1967	Cancer (♋)
22 Apr 1951	Aries (♈)	23 May 1967	Leo (♌)
29 Apr 1952	Taurus (♉)	19 Oct 1967	Virgo (♍)
10 May 1953	Gemini (♊)	27 Feb 1968	Leo (♌)
24 May 1954	Cancer (♋)	16 Jun 1968	Virgo (♍)
13 Jun 1955	Leo (♌)	16 Nov 1968	Libra (♎)
17 Nov 1955	Virgo (♍)	31 Mar 1969	Virgo (♍)
18 Jan 1956	Leo (♌)	16 Jul 1969	Libra (♎)
08 Jul 1956	Virgo (♍)	17 Dec 1969	Scorpio (♏)
13 Dec 1956	Libra (♎)	30 Apr 1970	Libra (♎)
20 Feb 1957	Virgo (♍)	16 Aug 1970	Scorpio (♏)
07 Aug 1957	Libra (♎)	14 Jan 1971	Sagittarius (♐)
14 Jan 1958	Scorpio (♏)	05 Jun 1971	Scorpio (♏)
21 Mar 1958	Libra (♎)	12 Sep 1971	Sagittarius (♐)
07 Sep 1958	Scorpio (♏)	07 Feb 1972	Capricorn (♑)
11 Feb 1959	Sagittarius (♐)	25 Jul 1972	Sagittarius (♐)
25 Apr 1959	Scorpio (♏)	26 Sep 1972	Capricorn (♑)
06 Oct 1959	Sagittarius (♐)	23 Feb 1973	Aquarius (♒)
02 Mar 1960	Capricorn (♑)	08 Mar 1974	Pisces (♓)
10 Jun 1960	Sagittarius (♐)	19 Mar 1975	Aries (♈)
26 Oct 1960	Capricorn (♑)	26 Mar 1976	Taurus (♉)
15 Mar 1961	Aquarius (♒)	23 Aug 1976	Gemini (♊)
12 Aug 1961	Capricorn (♑)	17 Oct 1976	Cancer (♋)
04 Nov 1961	Aquarius (♒)	04 Apr 1977	Gemini (♊)
26 Mar 1962	Pisces (♓)	21 Aug 1977	Cancer (♋)
04 Apr 1963	Aries (♈)	31 Dec 1977	Gemini (♊)
12 Apr 1964	Taurus (♉)	12 Apr 1978	Cancer (♋)
23 Apr 1965	Gemini (♊)	05 Sep 1978	Leo (♌)
21 Sep 1965	Cancer (♋)	01 Mar 1979	Cancer (♋)
17 Nov 1965	Gemini (♊)	20 Apr 1979	Leo (♌)
06 May 1966	Cancer (♋)	29 Sep 1979	Virgo (♍)

Starting Date	Zodiac Sign	Starting Date	Zodiac Sign
27 Oct 1980	Libra (♎)	07 Feb 1985	Aquarius (♒)
27 Nov 1981	Scorpio (♏)	21 Feb 1986	Pisces (♓)
26 Dec 1982	Sagittarius (♐)	03 Mar 1987	Aries (♈)
20 Jan 1984	Capricorn (♑)		

These dates are derived from calculations using *The American Ephemeris for the Twentieth Century* (San Diego: ACS Publications, 1980–1996).

TABLE 15. TROPICAL PLACEMENT FOR SATURN, 1927–1987

Starting Date	Zodiac Sign	Starting Date	Zodiac Sign
01 Jan 1927	Sagittarius (♐)	08 Mar 1951	Virgo (♍)
06 Mar 1929	Capricorn (♑)	14 Aug 1951	Libra (♎)
05 May 1929	Sagittarius (♐)	23 Oct 1953	Scorpio (♏)
30 Nov 1929	Capricorn (♑)	13 Jan 1956	Sagittarius (♐)
24 Feb 1932	Aquarius (♒)	14 May 1956	Scorpio (♏)
13 Aug 1932	Capricorn (♑)	11 Oct 1956	Sagittarius (♐)
20 Nov 1932	Aquarius (♒)	06 Jan 1959	Capricorn (♑)
15 Feb 1935	Pisces (♓)	04 Jan 1962	Aquarius (♒)
25 Apr 1937	Aries (♈)	24 Mar 1964	Pisces (♓)
18 Oct 1937	Pisces (♓)	17 Sep 1964	Aquarius (♒)
14 Jan 1938	Aries (♈)	16 Dec 1964	Pisces (♓)
06 Jul 1939	Taurus (♉)	04 Mar 1967	Aries (♈)
22 Sep 1939	Aries (♈)	30 Apr 1969	Taurus (♉)
20 Mar 1940	Taurus (♉)	19 Jun 1971	Gemini (♊)
09 May 1942	Gemini (♊)	10 Jan 1972	Taurus (♉)
20 Jun 1944	Cancer (♋)	22 Feb 1972	Gemini (♊)
03 Aug 1946	Leo (♌)	02 Aug 1973	Cancer (♋)
19 Sep 1948	Virgo (♍)	08 Jan 1974	Gemini (♊)
03 Apr 1949	Leo (♌)	19 Apr 1974	Cancer (♋)
30 May 1949	Virgo (♍)	17 Sep 1975	Leo (♌)
21 Nov 1950	Libra (♎)	15 Jan 1976	Cancer (♋)

Starting Date	Zodiac Sign	Starting Date	Zodiac Sign
05 Jun 1976	Leo (♌)	29 Nov 1982	Scorpio (♏)
17 Nov 1977	Virgo (♍)	07 May 1983	Libra (♎)
05 Jan 1978	Leo (♌)	24 Aug 1983	Scorpio (♏)
27 Jul 1978	Virgo (♍)	17 Nov 1985	Sagittarius (♐)
21 Sep 1980	Libra (♎)		

These dates are derived from calculations using *The American Ephemeris for the Twentieth Century* (San Diego: ACS Publications, 1980–1996).

The Sun and the Sun. Potential plus and minus points exist in this type of relationship. There is plenty of comprehension between the two of you, but there's always the chance you'll stimulate an excessive display of your shared signs' strengths and weaknesses. Two of a like mind may seem to be the ideal match, but be aware that you might feed each other's obsessions.

Two **Aries** individuals, for example, may be too driven and quarrelsome to see each other's point of view. A **Taurus** couple might squander too much money on fine dinners and luxurious gifts with little concern over future security. A pair of **Geminis** might live too much in the mind to remember each has a sensitive heart. Endless mood swings can make a pair of **Cancers** a less than grounded match, because in the absence of any stable influences they constantly change their minds. Too much drama and extravagance might hinder two **Leo** individuals' ability to maintain a levelheaded approach to life. A pair of **Virgos** may find themselves with the world's most organized CD collection, missing out on quite a few of life's more spontaneous pleasures in the meantime. A **Libra** couple may have the neatest, most beautifully decorated home on earth but may find agreement on serious issues troublesome. Critical and sometimes overly shrewd, a pair of **Scorpios** might make more unintentional trouble for each other than either expects. Although a **Sagittarius** couple may win a tandem triathlon hands down, their extreme optimism and outspoken natures may not get them through life's more delicate situations. Persistent depression and overt practicality may sink a pair of **Capricorns** deep into the dark clouds of despondency and heavy responsibility, so that they never rise into the random lightness and inexplicable joy that every relationship needs. A mutual fear of rejection may cause a pair of eccentric **Aquarians** to form stronger likes and dislikes than any union or human can bear. A secretive **Pisces** couple may lack the self-confidence, stability, and mutual trust a relationship needs to survive.

Naturally, all of these prognostications are augmented to some degree with the introduction of other planetary combinations into the final synthesis. (*Famous examples:* Antonio Banderas and Melanie Griffith, Michael Douglas and Catherine Zeta-Jones, Todd Rundgren and Bebe Buell, Warren Beatty and Julie Christie, Matthew Broderick and Sarah Jessica Parker.)

The Sun and the Moon. This is considered by many astrologers to be the most frequent and fundamental planetary pairing found among happily married couples. It's also potentially the most romantic and sexual combination. The Moon shines only where it's touched by the Sun. The Sun's brilliance is never so apparent as when it's reflected off the Moon's full face. This is passion, this shared light, soft glow, and warmth that illuminate both day and night. (*Famous examples:* Richard Burton and Elizabeth Taylor, Kurt Cobain and Courtney Love, Michael J. Fox and Tracy Pollan, Woody Allen and Mia Farrow, Justin Timberlake and Britney Spears.)

In May 1995, *The New York Times* reported that nearly twenty Orthodox Jewish fathers living in New York City used an ambiguous passage from the Torah to gain the upper hand in civil divorce cases. According to the passage, a father can arrange his daughter's marriage while she is still under the age of thirteen, making it impossible for her to marry anyone else without her father's permission. In each case, the father who'd been sued for divorce threatened to contract a bad match for his daughter. If his estranged wife didn't comply with his conditions for their divorce settlement, he would make life unbearable for his own daughter. The rabbis interviewed by the newspaper called the practice "disgusting and abhorrent, but valid."

The Sun and Mercury. There's a strong potential for a lucrative exchange of ideas and the combined power to execute them. Compatibility in this case is inclined to be extremely intellectual and communicative.

The Sun and Sun may share their thoughts, but you and your mate have the ability to build on your ideas. This is an expansive and productive union. Explore the world around you. Together you may discover far more than you could apart. (*Famous examples:* John F. Kennedy Jr. and Carolyn Bessette Kennedy, Warren Beatty and Julie Christie, Ted Turner and Jane Fonda, Antonio Banderas and Melanie Griffith, Todd Rundgren and Bebe Buell, Michael J. Fox and Tracy Pollan.)

The Sun and Venus. You tend to follow the same social circuit and share many similar interests. This match is inclined to stimulate a strong romantic attraction. You might have heard the old saying "To love, we must first be able to love ourselves." In the words of the Scottish poet Alexander Smith: "Love is but the discovery of ourselves in others, and the delight in the recognition." What we love about ourselves is often what first attracts us when we see it in someone else. You might have met through friends, or you might have become friends long before you realized you'd fallen in love. (*Famous examples:* Warren Beatty and Julie Christie, John F. Kennedy Jr. and Carolyn Bessette Kennedy, Todd Rundgren and Bebe Buell, Spencer Tracy and Katharine Hepburn.)

The Sun and Mars. This relationship tends to require a lot of negotiation to survive. The potential demands for independence are high. The spirit of competition may soar. Possible conflicts are inclined to be ego-related and filled with fireworks. Compromise and respect for individuality are the keys to stability. (Don't try to change your mate. And let him or her know right up front that you're unlikely to change either.) The lust monster might rage in this union, while love and tenderness linger far off the radar screen. There's a huge difference between physical and emotional attraction. Although both are pleasant, one can't satisfy the need for the other. (*Famous examples:* Woody Allen and Diane Keaton, Humphrey Bogart and Lauren Bacall, Todd Rundgren and Bebe Buell, Bill Clinton and Hillary Rodham Clinton, Al Gore and Tipper Gore.)

The Sun and Jupiter. If you plan to have children, this is the ideal match. You tend to build each other's confidence and integrity. You're both inclined to cooperate, share responsibilities, and give generously to each other. A stable environment is a nurturing environment. This may not sound like a union filled with excitement, but remember the proverb "Love is like butter, it goes well with bread." (*Famous examples:* John F. Kennedy Jr. and Carolyn Bessette Kennedy, Kurt Cobain and Courtney Love, Warren Beatty and Diane Keaton, Arnold Schwarzenegger and Maria Shriver.)

The Sun and Saturn. This planetary match can potentially create the foundation for a long-term relationship. However, this doesn't help nurture romance because it places heavy responsibilities and seriousness on situations. If love were a light, some unions would be fireworks: ablaze with passion and delightful to admire, only to disappear in a grand puff of smoke. Your union, however, would be a lighthouse: a forlorn beacon at times, but built safely above the seas and beaming steadily into the darkness. Which would you choose to guide you through life's storms? Which would you expect to be there for you tomorrow, and all the days after? Hopefully, you have other planetary combinations that supplement and add lightness to the spirit of this solid match. (*Famous examples:* John F. Kennedy and Carolyn Bessette Kennedy, Kurt Cobain and Courtney Love, John Derek and Bo Derek, Bill Clinton and Hillary Rodham Clinton, Al Gore and Tipper Gore.)

The Moon and the Moon. This union is predisposed to emotional excess. "Everyone is a moon," wrote American author Mark Twain, "and has a dark side which he never shows to anybody." Anybody except a Moon-matched mate, that is. You may empathize with each other's ups and downs, feeling them just as if they were your own. Fortunately, one of you may be up and in the mood to do a little spirit lifting while the other is down and morose. When you're both down, however, who's going to help you get up? To make this work, you must learn to laugh off depression, and as surely as the waxing Moon eventually becomes full, light will gradually creep back into your lives. (*Famous examples:* Kurt Cobain and Courtney Love, Warren Beatty and Julie Christie.)

The Moon and Mercury. Communication between you and your mate should be fine if you can both resist the urge to add too many details, which can trigger outbursts in the other person. Also, avoid the urge to burden conversations with too much emotion. Otherwise you'll both get swept up in the tension and be unable to figure out what's really been said. Speech is only half of communication. The rest is what the other person hears. Emotion can be a smoke screen between you, distorting words and causing troubles. You'll always be heard, but you must remain calm and logical to be understood. (*Famous examples:* Woody Allen and Mia Farrow, Justin Timberlake and Britney Spears.)

The Moon and Venus. This match is inclined to be seriously romantic. You tend to harmoniously follow each other's moods, understanding their ebb and flow. There's a rare and ephemeral transition in ballet in which the dancers become the dance. Nights when 1960s' ballet greats Rudolf Nureyev and Dame Margot Fontaine took the stage to perform *Swan Lake* have become legendary. There's a similar transformation in romance when the lovers become the love. Only a precious few will ever know this blissful world. This pair is one. (*Famous examples:* John F. Kennedy Jr. and Carolyn Bessette Kennedy, Richie Sambora and Heather Locklear, John Derek and Bo Derek, Prince Charles Windsor and Princess Diana Spencer Windsor, Spencer Tracy and Katharine Hepburn.)

The Moon and Mars. Domestic bliss might not be in the cards within this type of union. The Moon is moody, while Mars is both pushy and impatient. A person of many moods is best matched with a tolerant mate. Mars is not tolerant. Although the sexual attraction is strong, the love factor is low. Lust won't sustain a bond for long, so a breakup in this match isn't unlikely. However, remember that no single aspect rules the entire chart comparison. There are other influences, for better or worse. (*Famous examples:* John F. Kennedy Jr. and Carolyn Bessette Kennedy, Woody Allen and Mia Farrow.)

The Moon and Jupiter. Trust is a necessary element in any good relationship. In this match, there's strong potential for trust to flourish.

Trust is the root system of a relationship. Positivity, confidence, and happiness are the branches and leaves that spring forth from those solid roots. Trust at home brings peace to all aspects of your life. Guard it carefully, and beware of temptations that could diminish it. Its value can't be overstated. (*Famous example:* Kurt Cobain and Courtney Love.)

During the Middle Ages, Jews living in Egypt performed a symbolic dance with somewhat feminist overtones. The bride led the wedding dance wearing a helmet on her head and wielding a sword in her hand. Her new husband, on the other hand, led the next dance wearing feminine attire and jewelry.

The Moon and Saturn. This match tends to manifest itself as a chilly relationship on the inside and a secure one on the outside. Think of this influence as a cottage in the woods. It's welcoming, provides shelter, and is very charming, but it doesn't include a fire in the fireplace. Moodiness (the Moon) and insensitivity (Saturn) can't comfortably live on the same plane without some assistance. If there are other planetary combinations to create warmth, this one element will provide safety and security. (*Famous examples:* Richard Burton and Elizabeth Taylor, Arnold Schwarzenegger and Maria Shriver, Kurt Russell and Goldie Hawn.)

Mercury and Mercury. "I'm just a soul whose intentions are good," goes the plaintive lyric of the Animals' song "Don't Let Me Be Misunderstood." Isn't it amazing when you finally encounter someone who really comprehends what you're saying? You can finish a thought together. Your arguments are often ones you might have with yourself. You tend to interact extremely well on exactly the same level. But perfect communication is a double-edged sword. It has a negative side as well. At times when you're tired or tense, you have to be twice as careful not to unintentionally spout hurtful words, as they will invariably hit home. (*Famous examples:* Michael J. Fox and Tracy Pollan, Warren Beatty and Julie Christie, Woody Allen and Diane Keaton.)

Mercury and Venus. Art and life potentially become one in this union. You tend to communicate deep emotional thoughts and aesthetic interests to each other. Creativity is the highest level of intelligence. To communicate on this plane is a blessing. Art is not simply beauty, it is interaction itself. Concepts, ideas, or entire worlds are arranged by the artist and perceived by the viewer. This aspect can be fostered through the exploration of creative pursuits with your mate. (*Famous examples:* Antonio Banderas and Melanie Griffith, Ted Turner and Jane Fonda, Warren Beatty and Julie Christie, Spencer Tracy and Katharine Hepburn.)

Mercury and Mars. This relationship is inclined either to stir up positive action or to create phenomenal fireworks if bossiness and criticism are allowed to take precedence. The first phrase in too many arguments is "You're wrong." It never needs to be said, or even implied. It's sometimes worse to win an argument than it is to lose one when you're in love. If your mate is incorrect, start with a description of what you think is right without the use of negative statements. You can win your mate with logic or lose that loved one with quarrels. The stakes are high as you both have much to gain when you think and work together. Diplomacy and deference aren't like your best china; they shouldn't be reserved for company. (*Famous examples:* Warren Beatty and Diane Keaton, Lukas Haas and Natalie Portman, Todd Rundgren and Bebe Buell, Steven Tyler and Bebe Buell, Bill Clinton and Hillary Rodham Clinton.)

Mercury and Jupiter. There's the potential for shared interests on a number of different levels, ranging from educational and religious to cultural and ideological. This relationship also tends to instill tons of optimism into the atmosphere. To share interests is to share lives. To pursue knowledge together is to grow together. We are born surrounded by the accumulated knowledge of numerous generations. This is the base from which we step into the unknown and the unexplored, which is far more vast than the known in this world. It's exciting! You'll go further faster together. (*Famous example:* Woody Allen and Diane Keaton.)

Mercury and Saturn. A strong sense of duty and responsibility is necessary in some relationships. This relationship is inclined to provide that type of depth. The soldier serves in the army not for the pay but for love of country. The lover in this relationship shows adulation with the same sense of purposeful commitment and willingness. Tragically, like the soldier this love is cherished and relied upon in adversity, but may be forsaken in good times. (*Famous examples:* Kurt Cobain and Courtney Love, Lukas Haas and Natalie Portman, Steven Tyler and Bebe Buell, Todd Rundgren and Bebe Buell, Spencer Tracy and Katharine Hepburn, Bill Clinton and Hillary Rodham Clinton.)

> Just before the *chattan* (groom) goes to the *chuppah* to tie the proverbial knot, he loosens any knots in his garments (such as his tie, shoelaces, and sash). This signifies that to him all bonds are eliminated except the most intimate one: marriage.

Venus and Venus. The romance that emerges from this union tends to run emotionally hot. This pair might find that they have as much fascination as infatuation. Perhaps neither of you thought you could ever feel this way. If, as William Shakespeare said, all the world's a stage, then you and your mate have the lead roles in each other's plays. So where do you go from here? "There is no remedy for love," wrote American poet Henry David Thoreau, "but to love more." (*Famous examples:* Antonio Banderas and Melanie Griffith, Matthew Broderick and Sarah Jessica Parker, Richie Sambora and Heather Locklear, Justin Timberlake and Britney Spears.)

Venus and Mars. There's a lot of potential sexual magnetism here. You may begin to wonder how your life will ever be able to go back to normal after it's been disrupted by such intense passion. This love fills your heart and mind the way a million red rose petals fill a bedroom. Possessiveness and jealousy could be a problem in some cases. Flirtation with others might seem fun, and it'll get your mate's focused fascination, but it's not the kind of attention you want. A relationship is never strengthened by severing the delicate strands of trust. Instead, be reassuring and expect love, lots of love, in return. (*Famous examples:* Antonio Banderas and Melanie Griffith, Michael J. Fox and Tracy Pollan, Lukas Haas and Natalie Portman, Woody Allen and Diane Keaton, Dwight Yoakam and Bridget Fonda.)

Venus and Jupiter. If there are clouds in your relationship, this match gives them a silver lining. It even clears them away, highlighting mutual admiration for each other's values and interests. Any couple with active hormones can happily share a bed. But sharing respect is a true quality of love. You'll also tend to accrue financial and social status while you're in this relationship. (*Famous examples:* Warren Beatty and Julie Christie, Woody Allen and Diane Keaton, Humphrey Bogart and Lauren Bacall.)

Venus and Saturn. Affection and security may not always meet eye to eye, but this match does tend to lend itself to a mutual interest in financial status. It also adds stability to the relationship as a whole. A successful long-term union is, in part, a business partnership. There's a lot more to it than that. But the business alliance is an essential ingredient. Even if your jobs and professions are unrelated, you and your mate must still work together to pay the bills, maintain the household, and build your own personal empire. It may not sound romantic, but is. Anything you do with your love, any time spent with your love, is time spent in love. Think of it as living happily and comfortably ever after. (*Famous examples:* Kurt Cobain and Courtney Love, Lukas Haas and Natalie Portman, Warren Beatty and Julie Christie.)

Mars and Mars. An equal match of sexual attraction and physical activity tends to exist in an electric and impulsive atmosphere when this match occurs. You might love to jog or work out together. You'll probably cheer each other on toward anything that improves your individual sense of self. Competitiveness has two faces. The first is "I want to win, and I want you to see me win. So I don't care who beats us as long as I finish ahead of you." The second is "I want us to win, and I'm going to push you carefully because I want to see you do better than you ever dreamed you could." Which type will you have? The choice is yours to make. (*Famous examples:* Prince and Mayte Garcia, Woody Allen and Mia Farrow.)

Mars and Jupiter. You have a greater potential for success with outside ambitions while you're in this relationship, if you're aggressively striving for the top of the business or social heap. Your mutual enthusiasm could become infectious, influencing everyone around you. This facet is a true leadership quality. Your motivation as a couple even tows others along. It's a gravitational pull that draws people to you and carries them on the mutual pursuit of your goals. Remember to take care of them along the way. In the words of American publisher Malcolm Forbes: "You can easily judge the character of others by how they treat those who can do nothing for them or to them." Treat others well (your mate first and foremost), and your success can be a lasting one.

Mars and Saturn. Cross-purposes tend to make this a less than ideal union. While one of you impulsively forges ahead, the other instills concentrated discipline and slows the action down. There are two approaches to any task. You can work hard or you can work smart. The hard worker dives in immediately to get the job done. The smart worker plots an approach to the task, weighs the alternatives, considers the outcome, and then starts the job right about the time the hard worker is half done, but finishes at the same time. Neither approach is always better, though one thing is certain: the two approaches don't mix. The hard worker is driven nuts by the smart worker's apparent laziness, and the smart worker can't concentrate while the hard worker charges forward making a mess of things. Jealousy and resentment have the potential to creep up more times than not. You can improve the situation through mutual understanding. (*Famous examples:* Prince Charles Windsor and Princess Diana Spencer Windsor, Spencer Tracy and Katharine Hepburn, Bill Clinton and Hillary Rodham Clinton, Al Gore and Tipper Gore.)

Naturally, most couples have more than one or two planetary combinations that need to be synthesized into a cohesive profile. For example, Antonio Banderas and Melanie Griffith share five planetary conjunctions between them (Worksheet 16). Their Sun and Sun conjunction suggests that excessive drama and extravagance might hinder these two Leo individuals' ability to maintain a levelheaded approach to life unless other combinations temper their grand designs. A Sun and Mercury conjunction indicates a strong potential for a lucrative exchange of ideas and the combined power to execute them. Compatibility, in this case, is inclined to be extremely intellectual and communicative. The Sun and Sun may allow them to share their thoughts, but this couple has the ability to build on their ideas as well. This is an expansive and productive union. Together they may discover far more than they could individually. A Mercury and Venus conjunction suggests that art and life potentially become one. They communicate deep emotional thoughts and creative interests to each other. A Venus and Venus conjunction suggests the romance that emerges tends to run emotionally hot. A Venus and Mars conjunction suggests there's so much potential sexual magnetism here, they might wonder how normal life will could ever continue when it's disrupted by such intense passion. However, possessiveness and jealousy could be a problem.

As you can see, conjunctions alone can provide extensive insight. However, you can go further. In addition to conjunctions between planets, the astrologer also calculates any squares, trines, oppositions, and sextiles, adding the information into the synthesized mix. Judaic astrologers like Rabbi Joel C. Dobin also suggest a review of your ascendant (or rising sign), which is the zodiac sign associated with your chart's first house. He believes this sign reveals insights into your sexuality and character. The astrologer might also cast a composite chart, calculating the midpoints between each of the houses and the planetary positions in your and your mate's charts. The resulting chart is said to represent the embodiment of your combined traits, which you share during the course of your relationship.

Seizing the Right Day: *Carpe Diem Optimum*

Just like the Chinese calendar, the Jewish months follow the lunar cycle rather than the solar pattern used in the rest of the Western hemisphere. Among Orthodox Jews the first half of a lunar month is the ideal time for nuptials. But the whole months of Kislev (late November to late December), Adar (late February to late March), and Ellul (late August to late September) are also considered to be optimal choices.

There are a few exceptions. Weddings are prohibited by Judaic law on Shabbat, which begins at sundown every Friday and ends at sundown on Saturday. The High Holy Days of Rosh Hashanah and Yom Kippur are also off-limits. Legal business is prohibited during these sacred times, and marriage is considered a business transaction within this culture. For obvious reasons marriage ceremonies also can't occur during specific periods of mourning.

But weddings also aren't permitted on joyous occasions, such as the seven-day celebrations of Pessah (Passover), during March or April, and Sukkot (harvest festival), during September or October, because according to the Talmud, you can't mix joy with joy. There's no other restriction as to the day of the week or time that the ceremony can occur. The only other constraint is that a week should be set aside prior to the wedding day so that proper announcements, fasts, and prayers can take place before the couple enters into their new life together. A week should also be set aside after the wedding so the couple can continue to celebrate for a little longer before settling down to everyday life.

Sealing the Deal

The lively and very social Orthodox Jewish wedding ceremony is still celebrated in many communities, especially among the Hassidim. But even among Conservative and Reform Jewish communities, many young couples have revived traditions that even their parents may not have honored during the 1960s and 1970s. Various parts of this marriage ritual—from the announcement to the breaking of the wineglass—are outlined below. You may want to incorporate some of these beautiful traditions into your own nuptials.

Among Orthodox Jewish families, the Shabbat that occurs a week before the nuptials is when the betrothal is first publicly recognized. This happens during the *auf ruf* (calling up), which honors the groom and bride at a synagogue service. The *chattan* (groom) is called up before the Torah, where the rabbi blesses the couple and announces their upcoming marriage. This observance also serves to remind the couple to look to the Torah for guidance during their married life. The congregation then showers him with raisins and nuts, wishing them a sweet and fruitful marriage blessed with many children. On that same day, the *kallah*'s (bride's) family throws a *forshpiel* (bridal open house).

Among some Orthodox Jewish sects, once the contracts are completed, the *mesader kiddushin* (presiding rabbi) presents the *chattan* with a handkerchief that he holds to symbolize his acceptance of his bridal *kinyan* (acquisition) and the obligations outlined in the *ketubah*. Called the *kinyan sudder*, the ceremony dates back to ancient Israel.

Over the balance of that week, the couple mustn't see each other at all. Additionally, neither person can be seen in public without an escort, because each is traditionally treated as royalty until a week after the nuptials. In very traditional households, the couple fast the day of the ceremony until noon on the wedding day, adding Yom Kippur (Day of Atonement) confessions to their prayers and asking God to forgive their past transgressions. This act of penance is critical because it's believed that God will absolve the couple of their sins before they enter their new life.

The Big Day: A Traditional Jewish Wedding

On the wedding day, the actual festivities start with the *kabblat panim* (greeting). It's considered to be a special *mitzvah* (good deed) to wish the couple well before the ceremony. Because the bridal pair can't see each other even at this late moment, guests visit the *kallah* and *chattan* in separate rooms at the wedding site, wishing them well. In the groom's reception room, a *chattan's tisch* (groom's table) is set up, where two very important documents are drawn up.

The first is the *tena'im* (betrothal conditions), which state the size of the dowry and the penalty the groom has to pay if the betrothal is called off. The finished document is read aloud and signed by two witnesses who aren't members of the immediate families and who must be Jewish. A brightly painted earthenware plate is then broken by the couple's mothers, symbolizing that like a broken plate, a matrimonial pledge is permanent. The second document is the *ketubah* (marriage contract). Written in Aramaic and signed by the witnesses, this document isn't read aloud until the actual nuptial ceremony. This instrument outlines the *chattan*'s promise to provide for, honor, and support his wife. It also spells out his *kallah*'s rights during their marriage and stipulations of financial settlement in the event of a *get* (divorce) or her *chattan*'s death.

Accompanied by his father, future father-in-law, friends, and relatives, the *chattan* meets his *kallah* in her reception room, seeing her for the first time in a week. He brings her veil down over her face to characterize her virtue. The *bedeken* (veiling ceremony) ensures that he's marrying the woman he's negotiated to wed. It also reminds the guests that his *kallah* is officially off-limits to other men. A Hassidic or other Orthodox *chattan* might don the *kittel* (white robe) that he normally wears during Yom Kippur, before he enters the wedding site.

Now, the *unterferers* (married couples) join in the procession to the *chuppah* (canopy). Escorted by his father, father-in-law, and *unterferers*, the *chattan* walks to the *chuppah* in a candlelight procession. The veiled *kallah* is also escorted

Frequently, the *ketubah* is written in calligraphy and illuminated instead of printed. Some families go all out, commissioning a hand-painted document or one that's written on handmade paper. Among some Orthodox Jews, if this valuable contract is lost, the couple can't live together until another one is drawn up and signed. You don't have to be Jewish to have a *ketubah* made to signify your marital bond. Simply contact a *ketubah* artist, such as Marion Zimmer, who created the illuminated document that appears on page 178, at www.ketubah-by-marion.com, or through the Ketubah Gallery at www.ketubahgallery.com

by candlelight to the spot by her mother, mother-in-law, and *unterferers*. Back in biblical times, it was customary to perform the nuptials in the synagogue's courtyard at night so the stars could shine on the couple under the *chuppah* and bless their union with children as numerous and bright as the stars themselves.

Once the couple unite under the *chuppah*, the *kallah*, parents, and *unterferers* circle the *chattan* seven times, representing the Earth's seven rotations on its axis during the seven days of creation. The seven cycles of creation are symbolically reenacted because marriage creates a new world for a couple and their children.

The *kiddushin* (sanctification) begins when the rabbi pours wine into a glass and recites two blessings. He then hands it to the couple to sip. Next the *chattan* places a simple gold band on his *kallah*'s right forefinger, while saying: "Behold, you are consecrated to me with this ring according to the laws of Moses and Israel."

Some authorities believe that the *bedeken* (veiling ceremony) hearkens back to biblical days, when Jacob was promised Rachel's hand in marriage if he served her father, Laban, for seven years. When the wedding ceremony began, however, he discovered that he'd married her older sister, Leah! The *bedeken* assures the *chattan* (groom) that he's marrying the woman he wants.

The *ketubah* is then read aloud, signed by the couple, and handed to the *kallah*. Next, seven different people individually recite seven separate blessings in front of the couple during the *sheva brachot* (seven nuptial blessings). The first person thanks God as the creator and recites the blessing over a second glass of wine, signifying that this is a time to rejoice. The second person thanks God for the world's creation and honors the wedding guests. The third person honors the physical and spiritual creation of human beings. The fourth person acknowledges that with their marriage the couple has begun life as a completed and whole human being. The fifth person expresses the hope for the restoration of Jerusalem and the rebuilding of the holy Temple. The sixth person prays that the newlyweds grow in their exclusive love for each other. And the seventh person prays for peace and tranquillity throughout the world.

The couple drinks from the second glass of wine. Then the *chattan* breaks the glass with his right foot, reminding the newlyweds that relationships are fragile: they must accept joy and sorrow into their lives in equal measure. With the breaking of the glass, the guests usually break out into cries of *"Mazal tov! Mazal tov!"*

♥ ♥ ♥

Symbolism fraught with religious meaning is the centerpiece of Judaic belief and its associated rites. The links between God and human beings, God and his messengers, family and child, as well as husband

and wife, that are commemorated and celebrated in the marriage ceremony have been passed down for centuries. Although divination was condemned by Talmudic scholars, astrology has been accepted in its purest form since the days when Abraham was consulted by "all the kings of the East and of the West" because he was a "Chaldean" (astrologer). The Talmud's *Shabbath* 156a even noted that "the planet under which a person is born determines whether he is wise and rich, and the planets do affect the lives of the Israelites." Next we'll move on to a culture where the mystical world of past lives and predestined unions are not considerations in the world of marriage, but where the positions of the planets and the phases of the Moon are often consulted to determine who will find love and who will marry.

After the *chuppah* ceremony, the newlyweds are escorted to the *yichud* (private room) by their two witnesses. A silver spoon is placed at the threshold, which the *chattan* and then the *kallah* step over as they enter. They spend their first private time together as husband and wife, sharing a bowl of broth to break their fast before joining the wedding feast.

CHAPTER FIVE

Using Western Astrology to Find Love and Marriage

HAVE YOU FOUND YOUR SOULMATE?

Come live with me and be my love,
And we will all the pleasures prove. . . .
The shepherd swains shall dance and sing
For thy delight each May morning;
If these delights thy mind may move,
Then live with me and be my love.

—from Christopher Marlowe,
"The Passionate Shepherd to His Love"

hat happens when love blossoms but isn't destined to be consummated? Sir Thomas Malory recounted the classic legend of the star-crossed lovers Tristan and Isolde in his epic fifteenth-century tale *Le Morte d'Arthur,* which laid bare the agony of love unfulfilled.

Tristan's parents were King Meliodas and Queen Elizabeth of Lyonesse. His mother died shortly after he was born, and Tristan was sent to be raised by his uncle King Mark. However, as Tristan grew, King Mark became more and more jealous of his good looks and charm, which quickly won him the heart of every beautiful woman in the kingdom. Tristan also distinguished himself in combat, defeating and killing Queen Isolde of Ireland's brother Sir Marhaus, and becoming a knight as a result of his bravery. During the battle, however,

Tristan was wounded by Sir Marhaus's poison-coated sword, and he was sent to Ireland under an assumed name to be cured by Queen Isolde. The queen had created the poison and was the only person who knew the antidote. While recovering he fell in love with Isolde's daughter, Isolde the Fair. When Queen Isolde discovered that Tristan (whom she held in special esteem) was her brother's killer, the young knight was sent back home.

A few months after Tristan's return, King Mark declared that he wished to marry Isolde the Fair himself. He sent Tristan to seek her hand for him. More than once Tristan had unintentionally stolen women's hearts away from the monarch. And this was King Mark's revenge for Tristan's past conquests. Thwarting his nephew's obvious love for the maiden seemed like a perfect a way to get his revenge. Out of respect and a strong sense of duty toward his uncle, Tristan complied, and after hearing his heartfelt entreaties, King Anguish and Queen Isolde gave their consent to the marriage of Isolde the Fair and King Mark. Before Isolde began her journey to become King Mark's bride, the queen gave her daughter's maid, Brangwayne, a love potion with instructions to give it to the newlyweds on their wedding night. It was an elixir guaranteed to bond them in eternal love.

Tristan, Isolde the Fair, and Brangwayne sailed to Cornwall. But during the journey, Tristan and Isolde the Fair mistook the potion for a flask of wine and accidentally drank it, spiritually *and* chemically locking themselves into perpetual passion. Nonetheless, when they arrived in Cornwall, Isolde the Fair married King Mark.

After the wedding, Tristan left his uncle's court and joined King Arthur's Round Table. While doing battle for Howel of Brittany, he became enamored with another maiden named Isolde (Isolde of the White Hands) and married her. He was mortally wounded a few months later and on his deathbed gave orders to bring Isolde the Fair to see him one last time. If she returned with the ship, he instructed, a white flag should be flown from the mast. If she wasn't on board, then a black flag was to be flown. From his bed he asked Isolde of the White Hands to report which flag she saw. Out of jealousy, Tristan's wife told him it was the black flag, although the white was hoisted. His grief was so great that he expired in moments. When Isolde the Fair arrived at his room, she too died from the pain of loss.

While it is possible to love someone without reciprocal affection, being *in* love is never a one-sided proposition. It takes two people to ignite and tend the fires of true love. But even then, love isn't necessarily practical or even possible. Just look at poor Tristan, who was sent to ask for the hand of the woman he loved on his uncle's behalf! While it seems to be the breath of life itself, not every love leads to a transcendental bond, a physical or spiritual marriage, or even plain and simple happiness.

Unlike the Chinese, Hindus, and Jews described in previous chapters, most Europeans and Americans have simply allowed their hearts and hormones to take charge when they set out to find a spouse. Of course, without the benefit of sage guidance, emotions impede upon logic more times than not during the tricky business of searching for love. This is often where astrology can play a role.

Although the Egyptians initiated the custom and Hindus adopted it as well, the giving of engagement rings didn't become common in Europe until A.D. 1477. That was the year Austria's archduke Maximilian placed a diamond ring on Mary of Burgundy's finger, thwarting her father's plan to marry her off to a richer suitor. The ring proved the archduke's matrimonial intentions were genuine and her acceptance sealed the deal. It also launched the modern Western custom of giving engagement rings.

Back in Tristan and Isolde's time, it wasn't uncommon for someone to consult an astrologer about their love life and marriageability. Imported from the Spanish Moors, astrology was taught in Europe's finest universities from medieval times up until the end of the Renaissance. When the Roman Catholic Church began trying and executing anyone who practiced astrology for any purpose other than medical diagnosis during the 1400s and 1500s, kings, queens, and the nobility still secretly consulted astrologers on matters of the heart. Even today, many people in the Western hemisphere seek astrological guidance while they're looking for their soulmate or thinking about making the big leap of faith into a serious relationship.

In this chapter we'll show you two different ways to use the Moon's placement to determine your emotional nature and how it influences your love life and marriage. We'll illustrate how the ancient Druids may have interpreted the Moon's position and how modern Western astrologers derive critical information from the Moon's daily travels through the zodiac. Then we'll show you how the zodiac sign associated with Saturn can put a monkey wrench into your relationship happiness. We'll also teach you how to interpret Saturn's house placement in your birth chart, to determine when you're ready for a serious romantic commitment. Finally, we'll show you a unique way to interpret the compatibility of your and your mate's Sun placement to gain a greater understanding of your relationship's outcome.

Under a Celtic Moon: What the Moon Can Tell You About Your Love Life

There's no written record that explains exactly how the Celts' Druidic priests used their observations of the Moon's motions to determine information about one's emotional nature, love life, destiny, and even physical appearance. However, a handful of modern astrologers such as Helena Paterson have taken it upon themselves to decipher what little evidence exists from Celtic oral traditions. According to Paterson, the Druids segmented their calendar into thirteen lunar months. This is not unlike the twelve-month lunar calendars used by the Chinese, Hindus, and Jews, which occasionally contain a thirteenth month (also called an intercalary month) to rectify the lunar calendar with the solar calendar. Paterson also believes that each lunar month was associated with one of thirteen dryads (tree spirits): Birch, Rowan, Ash, Alder, Willow, Hawthorn, Oak, Holly, Hazel, Vine, Ivy, Reed, and Elder. There's also a Mistletoe dryad linked to the nameless day that falls between the lunar months associated with Birch and Elder. According to Paterson, you're endowed with characteristics associated with your lunar birth month's dryad. Your love destiny—whether your love will take root and flourish or fizzle like fireworks—can also be derived from that dryad's influence.

You don't need a birth chart to use this section. Enter your (and/or your mate's) birth date onto Worksheet 17. Using Table 16, look for the period in which your birth date falls and find the Celtic lunar month associated with that period. (The dates listed are the starting dates for each period: your birth date should fall on or after the appropriate date and before the date in the row below). Enter that lunar month in the space provided on the worksheet. Do the same with your mate's data. Locate the lunar month in the text following and read how the dryad that was active during your birth influences your love life.

WORKSHEET 17. CELTIC LUNAR MONTH

	Example: Michael J. Fox	Name A:	Name B:
Birth date	09 Jun 1961		
Celtic lunar month	Hawthorn		

TABLE 16. CELTIC LUNAR MONTHS

Starting Date	Lunar Month	Starting Date	Lunar Month
24 Dec	Birch	08 Jul	Holly
21 Jan	Rowan	05 Aug	Hazel
18 Feb	Ash	02 Sep	Vine
18 Mar	Alder	30 Sep	Ivy
15 Apr	Willow	28 Oct	Reed
13 May	Hawthorn	25 Nov	Elder
10 Jun	Oak	23 Dec	Mistletoe
		("the nameless day")	

These dates are derived from *The Celtic Lunar Zodiac* (Minneapolis: Llewellyn Publications, 1997).

The Moon in the lunar month of the Birch. Your passionate love affairs sometimes burn out like spent fireworks. You tend to succeed at marriage if you wed later in life to someone who can live within your rigid routines. You're inclined to stick it out even if affections go sour. A marriage wears many faces in its time. The first blush of infatuation has only a fraction of an old relationship's intimacy and understanding. When the flames of romance die down, what's left might be closer to cold ashes than glowing coals. You might choose to stay with your mate simply because you have a history with that person. It may be because you've found someone who just suits your lifestyle. What's important is that you realize it's your and your mate's choice to make. (*Famous examples:* David Bowie, Diane Keaton, Carolyn Bessette Kennedy, the Reverend Dr. Martin Luther King Jr., Elvis Presley, Michael Stipe.)

The Moon in the lunar month of the Rowan. Your erratic nature is the cause of Byronic pitfalls. Although you're not very romantic and prefer your independence, you can enter into a successful marriage if your spouse takes this institution as seriously as you do. It's easy to fall in love. It just happens. In fact, some studies say it takes people less than half a minute, on first meeting, to subconsciously decide if they're attracted to each other. If only *being* in love were so easy. It doesn't just happen. You make a choice. You make a commitment that you must work to maintain. Your partner has to do the same. The good news is it becomes much easier over time, as long as you don't throw it all away over minor issues that look like mountains. (*Famous examples:* Humphrey Bogart, Garth Brooks, Mia Farrow, Bridget Fonda, Justin Timberlake, Oprah Winfrey.)

The Moon in the lunar month of the Ash. You tend to take life as it comes even though your feelings are easily wounded. A gentle, tender person, you believe in romance and are sometimes accused of living within your own fantasies. There's a big difference between rolling with the punches and putting yourself in the line of fire. However, it's not always an obvious distinction. Luckily, each of us is blessed with the power of choice. If something hurts you, fix it. If a situation can't be repaired, walk away. Life will never be faultless. Perfection isn't the nature of life. But when you believe in happiness, it's only one small step farther to believe that *you* can be elated. Then, all that's left is to seize the rapture you know you deserve. (*Famous examples:* Drew Barrymore, Helen Gurley Brown, Sir Michael Caine, Kurt Cobain, Mikhail Gorbachev, George Harrison, Kurt Russell, Elizabeth Taylor, John Travolta.)

The Moon in the lunar month of the Alder. You tend to marry hastily because of your passionate nature and your need to be loved. Consequently, you're a better paramour than a spouse. That same ardor and affection also make you a good parent. This ability to love is the gift you bring to the relationship. To make marriage work, you'll need to take care never to let your passions wander. Your mate loves your attention more than you know, and would be hurt deeply by any hint of infidelity. (*Famous examples:* Warren Beatty, Matthew Broderick, Julie Christie, Eric Clapton, Al Gore, Sarah Jessica Parker, Debbie Reynolds, Spencer Tracy, Steven Tyler.)

The Moon in the lunar month of the Willow. You're inclined to marry a younger or older spouse before your twenty-seventh birthday. You need to be in a close, intimate relationship with someone who allows you to release your desires and passions within a secure union. There's a level of expectation you face when you're around someone your own age. Someone who's your peer tends to judge you on the level that only peers can. Someone who is older or younger won't hold you to their standards, but will accept you as the individual that you really are. This gives you the freedom to at least be who you want to be when you're behind closed doors. (*Famous examples:* Candice Bergen, Katharine Hepburn, Jack Nicholson, Michelle Pfeiffer, Barbra Streisand.)

The Moon in the lunar month of the Hawthorn. You might find it difficult to establish a relationship because you never stay in one place long enough. You're easily bored, which contributes to your wanderlust. There is a solution to this. While nine out of ten people live and die within twenty-five miles of their birthplace, there are a few like yourself who will never be truly happy until they've seen more of the world. Find someone who is willing to join you on the perpetual road through life, and don't look back. (*Famous examples:* Barbara Bush, Cher, Johnny Depp, Michael J. Fox, Prince, Brooke Shields.)

The Moon in the lunar month of the Oak. You attract powerful friends. You also tend to place trust in people before you learn enough about them to determine whether they deserve your confidence. Because of this, you're vulnerable when it comes to love. You may also set too high a standard for paramours or a spouse, rejecting anyone who can't live up to your ideals. Powerful people don't necessarily have higher morals than other human beings. Sometimes they aren't even as smart. They just have a remarkable ability to make things happen. When you let a person into your life, you give that individual the opportunity to make things happen to you. Whether these are good or bad things depends on that person. But you'll never know which it might be until you've looked deep inside a potential mate. Try to get to know an individual before you give them your heart. That way you're less likely to hand it to someone who'll trample it. (*Famous examples:* George H. Bush, George W. Bush, Ray Davies, Steffi Graf, Natalie Portman, Donald Trump, Liv Tyler, Princess Diana Spencer Windsor, Prince William Windsor.)

The Associated Press recently reported about a couple living in upstate New York who were celebrating their 75th wedding anniversary. Richard and Margie Stewart were married at age 20, and then took their relationship, in Richard's words "one day at a time." Their anniversary marked day number 27,393.

How did they make their marriage last? They never let the romance slip away. They still have arguments, "but at night, we'll kiss and make up and I'll rub her back."

The Moon in the lunar month of the Holly. Extremely affectionate and protective, you tend to marry your childhood sweetheart without ever exploring the rest of the world. There's nothing wrong with this. But be prepared for a rough midlife crisis, when you might wonder if you made the right decision and if it's time for sweeping changes to make up for it. You can survive this and get back to having a great and permanent relationship. When the crisis hits, you need to look at the time and effort you had to invest to build the level of understanding and intimacy you have with your spouse. It would take years with another person just to see if it was possible to re-create that closeness. Remember to be forgiving of your spouse, too, as you won't be the only one experiencing these feelings. Fortunately, you're tolerant and prudent, and you take the responsibilities of marriage seriously.

Because you are romantically discreet, your friends may find you a bit mysterious. Don't feel obligated to kiss and tell, however. Better that people admire your integrity than your love life. (*Famous examples:* Bebe Buell, Harrison Ford, Courtney Love, Richie Sambora, Arnold Schwarzenegger, O. J. Simpson.)

The Moon in the lunar month of the Hazel. Sometimes you view life through a microscopic lens, seeing every detail of love and existence almost too clearly. A joke is funny because the punch line catches you off guard. Some of the best romantic moments are like that, too. They are wonderful for no discernible reason. They are meant to be enjoyed, not understood. Once you fall in love, you are very tender and honest. Once you marry, you're inclined to bend over backward to indulge your spouse's every wish. Love can be expressed by giving it well and receiving it well. In a relationship, both are equally important. Sometimes a person will make an absurd demand or complaint just because they're cranky and want a fight. If you take someone seriously when they do this, rather than giving in and fighting, they'll be less likely to do it again in the future because a person who's taken seriously will learn to wish prudently. By giving so much, you may make your spouse into a more pleasant cohabitant. (*Famous examples:* Ben Affleck, Antonio Banderas, Bill Clinton, John Derek, Tipper Gore, Melanie Griffith, Madonna.)

The Moon in the lunar month of the Vine. Earthy and aloof, you're a passionate person who's easily hurt by other people's lack of consideration. You may find intimate relationships difficult to sustain. Protection from heartache is nothing less than a shield against love itself. There's only one way to guard yourself against emotional injury in a relationship: maintain emotional distance. This, however, sends a message to your mate that you don't trust and don't love him or her enough to let go. One of the most misused quotes of modern times comes from American poet Robert Frost's poem "Mending Wall": "Good fences make good neighbors." This isn't the message Frost intended. In the poem, he actually questioned why his neighbor insisted on keeping a wall between them. "Before I built a wall I'd ask to know what I was walling in or walling out, and to whom I was like to give offense." (*Famous examples:* Lauren Bacall, Brigitte Bardot, Michael Douglas, Heather Locklear.)

The size of a diamond is measured in carats. The word stems from the ancient practice of weighing a gemstone by the number of carob seeds it took to balance the scale.

The Moon in the lunar month of the Ivy. You tend to be romantically fickle and extremely sensitive. If an infatuation transforms itself into love, you become excessively dependent upon your lover. "On a good day," an old friend once said, "I can fall in love half a dozen times." There's a rapture to the possibility of what sort of life you could have with each beautiful stranger. But that isn't devotion. Love is the commitment that remains after the initial ecstasy is gone. But love holds a danger for you. You must never lose sight of the fact that while you are intimate with your mate, while you rely on your mate for emotional support, you can get by without these things. If you believe you can't live without someone, you become that person's hostage. "To love is to place our happiness in the happiness of another," the German philosopher Gottfried Wilhelm Leibniz wrote. Enjoy love for what it is, but always know that you are your own person. You breath on your own. You eat on your own. You would be happy on your own. Only when you've accepted these truths can you share happiness with someone else, because you must bring your own happiness into a relationship to be able to share happiness with another. (*Famous examples:* Hillary Rodham Clinton, Catherine Deneuve, Carrie Fisher, John Lennon, Dwight Yoakam.)

The Moon in the lunar month of the Reed. Because you are an intensely passionate person, your jealous nature stands at the center of your romantic and marital difficulties. There's a term for fears that cause problems that cause dismay: self-fulfilling prophecies. If you voice your jealousies long and loud enough, your mate is quite likely to seek solace in someone else's arms. "If you would be loved, love and be lovable," wrote Benjamin Franklin in *Poor Richard's Almanac.* A person who has everything they want at home won't look elsewhere. If you crave "variety" then you just aren't ready for commitment. If you are frequently annoyed by your mate, then perhaps you don't love that individual as much as you love the person you think he or she is. (*Famous examples:* Richard Burton, Laura Bush, Bo Derek, Bill Gates, Mayte Garcia, Goldie Hawn, Julia Roberts, Maria Shriver, Ted Turner, Prince Charles Windsor.)

The Moon in the lunar month of the Elder. You tend to stay on the shallow side of love's pool, never falling completely in love with anyone. Although you're honest in your relationships, you never become emotionally involved to the fullest extent. Ask yourself one question: what do you want out of a relationship? Do you want the most passionate romance of all time, or a light fling? Both are possible and both are acceptable. You don't have to sacrifice the rest of your life for passion, unless you want it. If you decide you want an epic love, you must accept that it may lead to monumental heartache. To get this love you have to bare your soul to your mate. You have to be completely open. If you can't do it, then simply let yourself be happy with your decision and accept your relationship as it is. (*Famous examples:* Christina Aguilera, Woody Allen, Kim Basinger, Jane Fonda, John F. Kennedy Jr., Vanessa Paradis, Brad Pitt, Britney Spears, Steven Spielberg.)

The Moon in the nameless lunar day of the Mistletoe. You're reticent to become intimate with anyone, fearing rejection and failure. If you take the plunge, it's because you've given it serious consideration and permanent commitment. Congratulations, you're destined to have a good relationship, if and when you let yourself fall in love. If love were a banquet, you'd be the one who skips the appetizers and side dishes and waits for the main course. There may be temptations along the way, but deep inside you know what you want. How will you know when it's time? You'll know. In the words of the American poet Henry Wadsworth Longfellow, "It is difficult to know at what moment love begins; it is less difficult to know that it has begun."

Using this method to assess actor Michael J. Fox, the astrologer might suggest that he could find it difficult to establish a relationship because he never stays in one place long enough. The Hawthorn dryad also inclines him to be easily bored. He can overcome these obstacles by finding someone who would be willing to accept his wanderlust in order to maintain a happy relationship.

♥ ♥ ♥

Contemporary astrologers in the British isles, Western Europe, and North America rely on methods passed down by the ancient Greeks, Egyptians, and Persians rather than the Celts. Besides being more widely practiced, these astrological calculations and interpretations have been well documented and enhanced over the past two millennia, and this has made them a comprehensive and insightful source for viewing the influence of the Sun, Moon, and planets on an individual's traits and behaviors, particularly in the realm of love.

From the day of her wedding, a Ndebele woman in South Africa has a lifelong obligation to pay *ukuhlonipha* or "respect" to her father-in-law. This means she has to avoid him at all costs, even though they live in the same compound and he has unlimited freedom to move around the family property. If she accidentally runs into him, she must turn her back to him and cover her face. Also, she may never say his first name at any time.

There's an old Irish verse that best exemplifies the Moon's importance to romance: "Moon, Moon, tell unto me, when my true love I shall see. What fine clothes am I to wear? How many children will I bear? For if my love comes not to me, dark and dismal my life will be." To determine how the Moon will influence your love life you'll need to know which zodiac sign was associated with it on the day of your birth.

You'll need your birth chart to use this particular section. Enter your (and/or your mate's) birth date onto Worksheet 18. Look for the Moon's symbol (☽) in your chart (fig. 11 illustrates the Moon's placement in Michael J. Fox's Western birth chart). Then note the zodiac sign that accompanies it, which can be found on the same line as the Moon's symbol. For reference, here's a list of the symbols used in this type of chart:

Aries	♈
Taurus	♉
Gemini	♊
Cancer	♋
Leo	♌
Virgo	♍
Libra	♎
Scorpio	♏
Sagittarius	♐
Capricorn	♑
Aquarius	♒
Pisces	♓

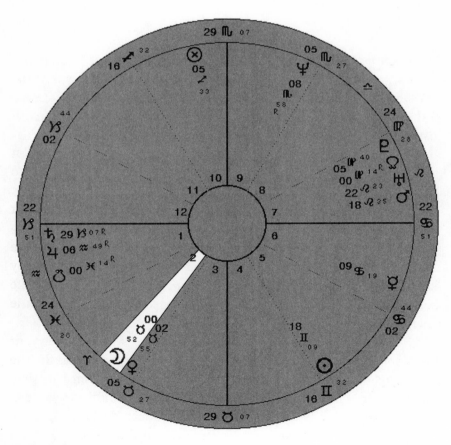

Figure 11. Michael J. Fox's Moon in the Birth Chart.

Enter that information in the space provided on the worksheet. Do the same with your mate's Moon placement. Then locate the zodiac sign in the text following and read how your and your mate's emotional makeup may influence your love life.

WORKSHEET 18. MOON PLACEMENTS

	Example:	Name A:	Name B:
	Michael J. Fox		
Birth date	09 Jun 1961		
Moon's zodiac sign	☉ (Taurus)		

The Moon in Aries. You're a highly imaginative and quick-tempered lover who's very self-reliant. There's nothing as alluring as self-confidence. It makes men handsome and women beautiful. Don't bother to wonder why there are so few people who know this secret, just be glad you've got the gift. (*Famous examples:* Lauren Bacall, Antonio Banderas, Heather Locklear.)

The Moon in Taurus. You're driven by love, marriage, and friendship. Your financial life is even aided by the opposite sex. The fact that the most important thing in your life is a happy relationship might come as less of a surprise than the news that it isn't the most important thing in everyone's existence. By making love a priority, you actually have a better chance of having a good marriage. (*Famous examples:* Bill Clinton, Carrie Fisher, Michael J. Fox, Katharine Hepburn, Prince Charles Windsor.)

The Moon in Gemini. A warmhearted and humane lover, you dislike arguments of any kind. You're sometimes drawn into embarrassing situations on the romantic front. To avoid problems of this sort, just remember that civility and good manners are ideal for diffusing life's awkward moments. (*Famous examples:* Brigitte Bardot, Steffi Graf, Goldie Hawn, Brooke Shields, Spencer Tracy, Dwight Yoakam.)

The Moon in Cancer. You tend to be an agreeable and sympathetic lover who follows the path of least resistance even when it comes to romance. Some people spend their lives in search of love. This doesn't mean love is rare and elusive. More often than not, these people pass up true happiness in order to keep searching for what they believe is perfection. You're blessed with the ability to recognize love when it stares you in the face. (*Famous examples:* Drew Barrymore, Humphrey Bogart, Kurt Cobain, Ray Davies, Bo Derek, Bridget Fonda, Harrison Ford, Carolyn Bessette Kennedy, Courtney Love, Kurt Russell, Prince William Windsor.)

According to the *Washington Post* (20 April 1997), Roman Catholics in the United States have the world's highest church-annulment rate, even though 90 percent of divorced Catholic couples never go through the annulment process. The report stated that in 1994 the Roman Catholic Church in the United States "granted 54,463 annulments of a worldwide total of 72,744 granted by the Church. Before 1910, there were probably only 100 annulments anywhere in the world granted by the Church, and in 1968, before the current liberalization norms, there were 450 worldwide."

The Moon in Leo. You're so popular with the opposite sex, you might have a problem with a jealous mate if you're not careful. Popularity is a double-edged sword. The same attractiveness that got you into a great relationship can cause the relationship problems that end it. Be careful not to flirt with other people unless you're not serious about your lover or spouse. Despite this potential flaw, you're very generous to your mate. (*Famous examples:* David Bowie, Catherine Deneuve, Jane Fonda, Mikhail Gorbachev, Julia Roberts, Maria Shriver, Barbra Streisand.)

The Moon in Virgo. Most of your friends are of the opposite sex, so you might have to deal with your mate's jealousy and possessiveness if you're not careful. It takes a very compassionate person to accept that their mate has friends of the opposite sex. Don't mourn the loss of someone who leaves you for this reason. You can never be yourself in a relationship unless your mate accepts you for who you are. (*Famous examples:* Candice Bergen, Matthew Broderick, Richard Burton,

Madonna, Jack Nicholson, Michelle Pfeiffer, Richie Sambora, John Travolta.)

The Moon in Libra. You are a true romantic who's very affectionate and extremely influenced by your environs. You also need luxury to feel loved or to give affection. To avoid leaving the impression that you're just out for money, try to create some showing of that requisite luxury yourself. Also, learn the fine art of appreciation, and no one will ever regret their generosity toward you. (*Famous examples:* Sir Michael Caine, John Derek, Ted Turner.)

The Moon in Scorpio. You tend to have numerous problems with the opposite sex because of your impulsive nature. However, you willingly make sacrifices for all the right reasons. One of the greatest relinquishments a person can make in a relationship is to lose an argument. There's a perfect reason to do it. An apology will never erase a rash act, but it might change a bad moment into a good one. (*Famous examples:* Ben Affleck, Warren Beatty, Helen Gurley Brown, Julie Christie, Eric Clapton, George Harrison, Steven Spielberg, Elizabeth Taylor.)

The Moon in Sagittarius. Your love life may be erratic because you frequently move from one place to another, rarely setting down roots. There are two solutions: make sure the person you love doesn't mind hitting the road with you, or else plan on having a few relationships in your lifetime. (*Famous examples:* Justin Timberlake, Donald Trump, Oprah Winfrey.)

The Moon in Capricorn. You may have romantic troubles that stem from other people's perception of you. Many potential lovers sense you have little care for others' feelings even though they may find you inspirational in many ways. Compassion comes in all sorts of forms. The difference between sympathy and empathy is the difference between simply recognizing and actually sharing another person's feelings. You need to open up to those around you and show a little more empathetic emotion. Then people will realize you're not cold at all. (*Famous examples:* Kim Basinger, Cher, Johnny Depp, Michael Douglas,

Mia Farrow, Al Gore, Sarah Jessica Parker, Brad Pitt, Arnold Schwarzenegger.)

The Moon in Aquarius. Your desire for independence combined with your unconventional attitude toward love and romance might be the cause of some concern for a potential paramour who's more traditional. It's a tough choice. Do you change to make the relationship work, or find someone who accepts you just as you are? Compromise is a part of every successful union. There's no way to avoid it. Just make sure you don't jeopardize your happiness. (*Famous examples:* Woody Allen, Tipper Gore, Melanie Griffith, John Lennon, Diane Keaton, John F. Kennedy Jr., Debbie Reynolds, Princess Diana Spencer Windsor.)

The Moon in Pisces. An emotional commitment in romance is hard for you to make. You prefer infatuation to serious love. There's a huge difference between feeling in love and being in love. You might not always feel like you are when you are, and you aren't necessarily enamored just because you feel like it. Do you remember what the Oracle told Neo in the 1999 film *The Matrix,* after she explained the sign over her door, which said: "Know thyself"? It means a lot when you're looking for true love. The Oracle said: "Being the One is just like being in love. No one can tell you you're in love. You just know it through and through. Balls to bones." Love's not just a feeling, it's also a commitment. It's a choice. You can choose to have a long relationship or many relationships, but you can't have both. (*Famous examples:* Garth Brooks,

Prenup is a relatively new word in English, but it's been a tradition in some cultures for thousands of years. It's a contract between the bride and groom, signed before the nuptials take place, which spells out financial and other responsibilities, and things each person expects out of the relationship, as well as how assets would be divided in a divorce. The real difference between a prenup and a Jewish *ketubah* (also includes ceremonial language about the marriage), is that a *ketubah* gets framed and prominently displayed in the newlyweds' house. A postnup, on the other hand, is an entirely new concept. It's a contract, drawn up after a couple is married, usually when one or both people are thinking that the marriage won't last.

Hillary Rodham Clinton, Bill Gates, the Reverend Dr. Martin Luther King Jr., Elvis Presley, Prince, O. J. Simpson, Britney Spears, Michael Stipe.)

♥ ♥ ♥

The Moon's influence is also accentuated by its placement in your birth chart. **You'll need your birth chart to use this particular section.** Look for the Moon's symbol (☽) in your chart and note the number of the house it occupies (fig. 11 illustrates Michael J. Fox's Moon in his Western birth chart). Enter that house number in the space provided on the worksheet. Do the same with your mate's Moon placement. Then locate the house number in the text following and read how the Moon enhances or detracts from your relationship with the opposite sex, depending on whether you're a man or a woman. The Moon's influence is very sensitive to its relationship with other planets. In other words, if the Moon in your chart forms an adverse relationship with another planet, it could negate the more positive inclinations in the interpretation. It's always best to consult with a professional astrologer to determine if any of these adverse relationships exist with the Moon in your particular Western birth chart.

WORKSHEET 19. THE MOON'S HOUSE LOCATION

	Example:	Name A:	Name B:
	Michael J. Fox		
Birth date	09 Jun 1961		
The Moon's house location	II or 2 (second house)		

The Moon in your chart's first house. If you're a woman, the Moon triggers strength and self-assertiveness, which can attract or repel a lover. Be true to yourself. Your ideal lover will find your strength attractive.

If you're a man, the Moon tends to place a woman at the helm of every major decision. (*Famous examples:* Antonio Banderas, Humphrey Bogart, Eric Clapton, Jane Fonda, George Harrison, Heather Locklear, Madonna, Julia Roberts, Justin Timberlake.)

The Moon in your chart's second house. If you're a woman, you might have considerable financial success or marry into money. If you're a man, you might experience financial gain through women. The secret to wealth is, of course, that getting rich doesn't depend solely on how much you earn. What counts is how much you save. (*Famous examples:* Drew Barrymore, Warren Beatty, Michael Douglas, Michael J. Fox, Brad Pitt, Princess Diana Spencer Windsor.)

The Moon in your chart's third house. If you're a woman, the Moon may bring intellectual powers that can attract or repel a lover. Never compromise your thoughts. In the words of British author James Allen, "You are today where your thoughts have brought you; you will be tomorrow where your thoughts take you." If you're a man, this lunar position may bestow intellectual powers that are strongly influenced by a woman. (If the Moon is adversely affected by another planet in the chart, a woman might consider other women to be her intellectual rivals, while a man may intellectually reject women.) (*Famous examples:* George W. Bush, Bo Derek, Diane Keaton, Jack Nicholson, Elvis Presley.)

The Moon in your chart's fourth house. With the Moon in this position, your expectations about domestic life and love's nurturing side might be modeled on your mother's strong influence regardless of your gender. (If the Moon is adversely affected by another planet in the chart, there's

A Reuters News Service article (17 October 2000) reported that a global survey determined that the French play the field the most, claiming an average of seventeen lovers per person during their lifetime. Greeks averaged fifteen lovers per person, while Brazilians and Americans averaged twelve. Hindus, however, were the least likely to wander beyond one true mate. Eighty-two percent of Hindus surveyed said they'd had sex with only one person.

the potential rejection of a mother's influence as well as a tendency toward homosexuality.) (*Famous examples:* Carrie Fisher, Michelle Pfeiffer, Prince, Richie Sambora, Maria Shriver, John Travolta, Oprah Winfrey.)

The Moon in your chart's fifth house. The Moon's occupation of this house suggests that you might lack sexual inhibitions regardless of your gender. Though society dictates and judges most of our actions, there is a more fundamental rule that applies when you are behind closed doors: do no harm to yourself or anyone else. Adhere to this, and avoid discussing your intimate interests with others. Also, remember, there is a difference between fantasies and reality. What goes on inside your head is for you alone. Never feel obligated to share your inner thoughts with anyone. (*Famous examples:* Ben Affleck, Sir Michael Caine, Ray Davies, Al Gore, Debbie Reynolds, Steven Spielberg, Barbra Streisand, Donald Trump.)

The Moon in your chart's sixth house. If you're a woman, you may have a strong sense of hierarchy in the workplace. If you're a man, you may maintain a positive dependence upon women in the workplace. Not all marriages are greater than the sum of their participants. Yours is. The key to your success is teamwork built on trust and commitment. (*Famous examples:* Woody Allen, Brigitte Bardot, Richard Burton, Julie Christie, Johnny Depp, Mikhail Gorbachev, Goldie Hawn, Carolyn Bessette Kennedy, John F. Kennedy Jr., Arnold Schwarzenegger, Britney Spears, Spencer Tracy.)

The Moon in your chart's seventh house. The Moon in this position suggests that you tend to encounter success through marriage regardless of your gender. (*Famous examples:* Cher, Bridget Fonda, Catherine Deneuve, Prince William Windsor.)

The Moon in your chart's eighth house. If you're a woman, you may have many children or inherit some great talent or wisdom from your mother. If you're a man, you may encounter financial success through marriage. (*Famous examples:* Candice Bergen, Tipper Gore, Katharine Hepburn, O. J. Simpson.)

The Moon in your chart's ninth house. The Moon tends to bestow on you a talent for languages and trips abroad, where you might potentially encounter a foreign lover or an unattainable person, if you're a woman. You may wed or have a serious love affair with a foreigner or an unattainable person, if you're a man. (*Famous examples:* Mia Farrow, Courtney Love, Brooke Shields.)

The Moon in your chart's tenth house. If you're a woman, you may experience professional success as well as maternal fulfillment. If you're a man, you might encounter elevated professional or social status through a woman. (*Famous examples:* Lauren Bacall, David Bowie, Bill Clinton, Hillary Rodham Clinton, Kurt Cobain, John Derek, Harrison Ford, Bill Gates, Melanie Griffith, Ted Turner, Prince Charles Windsor, Dwight Yoakam.)

The Moon in your chart's eleventh house. The Moon's position suggests that if you're a woman, you may benefit from your friendships. If you're a man, you tend to establish close friendships with women. People might tell you that you have to make your mark as an individual. Ignore them. To acknowledge that your greatest successes will come as part of a team is to recognize your true potential. (*Famous examples:* Kim Basinger, John Lennon, Elizabeth Taylor.)

The Moon in your chart's twelfth house. If you're a woman, you tend to work well in seclusion. If you're a man, you may have secret but positive personal relationships with women. Protect your privacy. (*Famous examples:* Steffi Graf, the Reverend Dr. Martin Luther King Jr.)

An astrologer will combine the influence of the Moon's placement in a particular house and its association with a specific zodiac sign into a synthesized interpretation during a personal consultation. Michael J. Fox's Moon in his chart's second house in Taurus, for example, might be viewed as an indication that he could experience financial gain through women. It also suggests that he's emotionally driven by love, marriage, and friendship.

In another scenario, the astrologer might blend the Celtic and

Western delineations, creating an alternate way to view the Moon's placement on the day of Fox's birth. The Hawthorn dryad from the Celtic view combined with the Taurus position in his Western chart might suggest that although Fox is naturally driven by love, marriage, and friendship, he might find it difficult to establish a relationship because he never stays in one place long enough and is often bored. His financial life, however, is aided by his associations with the opposite sex.

♥ ♥ ♥

As with the other forms of astrology we've discussed in this book, the Moon is only one of the elements used in Western astrology to determine your ability to love and be loved. The zodiac sign associated with the seventh house is assessed, and the planets in each chart are paired up in a process called synastry in the same way they are in Judaic astrology (see page 217). Additionally, the location of the planets Venus, Mars, and Jupiter in your birth chart, as well as their association with a zodiac sign, are reviewed in the same manner as they are in Hindu and Judaic astrology (see pages 91 and 179 for instructions). Plus there's one other planet that all of these practitioners assess to see what sort of difficulties or disappointments you might encounter in a romantic or marital relationship. That planet is Saturn.

What Kinds of Difficulties Lie Ahead?
Saturn's Tropical Placement in Your Chart

In many astrologers' eyes the planet Saturn is a celestial wrench in the works. Face it. Not everyone is consistently pleased with every facet of life (especially love and marriage). But the delays, obstacles, and disappointments that Saturn often imparts also tend to redirect your impulses and emotions, allowing you to view the hard facts of married life and romance in a different light than you may have earlier. This can be very beneficial as you travel the often rough waters of romance.

You don't need a birth chart to use this section. Simply enter your (and/or your mate's) birth date onto Worksheet 20. Using Table 17, look for the period in which your birth date falls, and find the zodiac sign associated with that period. (The dates listed are the starting dates for each period: your birth date should fall on or after the appropriate date and before the date in the row below.) Enter that sign in the space provided on the worksheet. Do the same with your mate's birth date. Then locate the zodiac sign in the text following and read how Saturn might ignite difficulties or delays in your love life.

Naturally, if you have a tropical Western birth chart cast according to the tropical zodiac, look for Saturn's symbol (♄) in your chart (fig. 12 illustrates Saturn's placement in Michael J. Fox's Western birth chart) and note the zodiac sign that's on the same line as Saturn's symbol. Enter that sign in the worksheet space provided. (A list of the symbols appears on page 183.) Then locate the zodiac sign in the following text and read about the potholes Saturn can create in the road to happiness.

WORKSHEET 20. TROPICAL PLACEMENT FOR SATURN

	Example:	Name A:	Name B:
	Michael J. Fox		
Birth date	09 Jun 1961		
Saturn's tropical placement	♄ (Capricorn)		

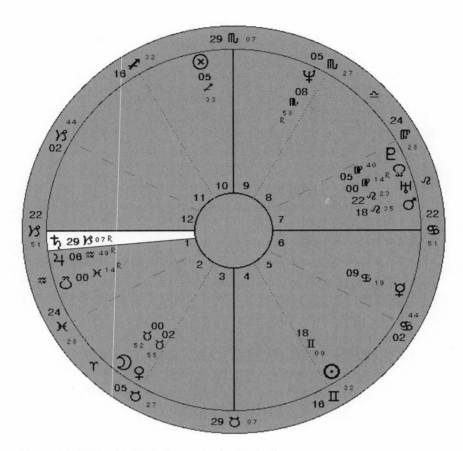

Figure 12. Michael J. Fox's Saturn in the Birth Chart.

TABLE 17. TROPICAL PLACEMENTS FOR SATURN, 1927–1987

Starting Date	Zodiac Sign	Starting Date	Zodiac Sign
01 Jan 1927	Sagittarius (♐)	11 Oct 1956	Sagittarius (♐)
06 Mar 1929	Capricorn (♑)	06 Jan 1959	Capricorn (♑)
05 May 1929	Sagittarius (♐)	04 Jan 1962	Aquarius (♒)
30 Nov 1929	Capricorn (♑)	24 Mar 1964	Pisces (♓)
24 Feb 1932	Aquarius (♒)	17 Sep 1964	Aquarius (♒)
13 Aug 1932	Capricorn (♑)	16 Dec 1964	Pisces (♓)
20 Nov 1932	Aquarius (♒)	04 Mar 1967	Aries (♈)
15 Feb 1935	Pisces (♓)	30 Apr 1969	Taurus (♉)
25 Apr 1937	Aries (♈)	19 Jun 1971	Gemini (♊)
18 Oct 1937	Pisces (♓)	10 Jan 1972	Taurus (♉)
14 Jan 1938	Aries (♈)	22 Feb 1972	Gemini (♊)
06 Jul 1939	Taurus (♉)	02 Aug 1973	Cancer (♋)
22 Sep 1939	Aries (♈)	08 Jan 1974	Gemini (♊)
20 Mar 1940	Taurus (♉)	19 Apr 1974	Cancer (♋)
09 May 1942	Gemini (♊)	17 Sep 1975	Leo (♌)
20 Jun 1944	Cancer (♋)	15 Jan 1976	Cancer (♋)
03 Aug 1946	Leo (♌)	05 Jun 1976	Leo (♌)
19 Sep 1948	Virgo (♍)	17 Nov 1977	Virgo (♍)
03 Apr 1949	Leo (♌)	05 Jan 1978	Leo (♌)
30 May 1949	Virgo (♍)	27 Jul 1978	Virgo (♍)
21 Nov 1950	Libra (♎)	21 Sep 1980	Libra (♎)
08 Mar 1951	Virgo (♍)	29 Nov 1982	Scorpio (♏)
14 Aug 1951	Libra (♎)	07 May 1983	Libra (♎)
23 Oct 1953	Scorpio (♏)	24 Aug 1983	Scorpio (♏)
13 Jan 1956	Sagittarius (♐)	17 Nov 1985	Sagittarius (♐)
14 May 1956	Scorpio (♏)		

These dates are derived from calculations using *The American Ephemeris for the Twentieth Century* (San Diego: ACS Publications, 1980–1996).

Saturn in Aries. An envious spouse may create difficulties in your married life. "Jealousy," said the duc de La Rochefoucauld, "comes from self-love rather than from true love." Although love might also exist, envy has more to do with feelings of insecurity and possessiveness. You might feel like this is something that needs to be fixed in your spouse (and you're right). However, you need to take a little care in the meantime not to set off the fireworks that are stockpiled just below the surface. (*Famous examples:* Julia Roberts, Ted Turner.)

Saturn in Taurus. Your domestic life and relationship with kin may be strained at times. Every marriage is a merger. You bring your family (and family arguments rooted from childhood) with you. No one can open old wounds and dump salt in them like a sibling or a parent. They know your weak points and you know theirs. Pity the innocent bystander like your spouse when the claws come out and the fur starts to fly. If you can't end the fights, then at least get as far away from them as you can, for the sake of your relatioinship. (*Famous examples:* Julie Christie, Steffi Graf, John Lennon, Barbra Streisand.)

Saturn in Gemini. You have so many outside interests that your home life might be troublesome to you at times. So, you've got this great relationship and now you want to get on with your life. Unless your spouse shares your interests, you might hear a lot of complaints that you spend way too much time in your own world. You can try to encourage their interest, set your goals aside, or go back to the single life. If you opt not to decide, your spouse might surprise you, making the decision for you. Otherwise your mate might make your life miserable just to get your attention. (*Famous examples:* Ben Affleck, Catherine Deneuve, Harrison Ford, George Harrison.)

Saturn in Cancer. You may be dissatisfied at home, finding sorrows in your domestic life. The outside world can be a harsh place, but it's more difficult to face external dilemmas if things aren't happy at home. A good relationship is like a soft warm blanket. It wraps you up and soothes you. It gives you the strength to face the day. Arguments and infidelities are fingernails on the chalkboard that's known as your nervous system. You may find that you immerse yourself in work to escape the house until you have a happy love life. (*Famous examples:* Drew Barrymore, Candice Bergen, George W. Bush, Cher, Eric Clapton, Ray Davies, Leonardo DiCaprio, Michael Douglas, Mia Farrow, Goldie Hawn, Diane Keaton, Kurt Russell, Donald Trump.)

Saturn in Leo. Your natural generosity toward your object of desire may be unrequited, creating sorrows in romance. You're free to choose whom you love, but it won't be mutual unless that person also decides to love you. Be prepared to bow out graciously and move on if the spark isn't there. A little heartache now will spare you a truckload of anguish later. Plus, you'll be back on the path toward the person out there who's perfect for you. (*Famous examples:* Christina Aguilera, David Bowie, Laura Bush, Bill Clinton, Hillary Rodham Clinton, Bill Gates, Al Gore, Tipper Gore, Arnold Schwarzenegger, O. J. Simpson, Steven Spielberg, Liv Tyler, Steven Tyler.)

Saturn in Virgo: If you marry during the first half of your life, you may encounter matrimonial troubles or serious obstacles that hinder your marriage. This deterrent does dissipate as you age. It's a lot easier to get what you want when you know what you want. When it comes to matrimony, you may not discover what it is you need until you've experienced a fair share of life. Until then, you'll have to satisfy yourself with what you want without knowing if that's what you need. (*Famous examples:* Claire Danes, Prince Charles Windsor.)

Saturn in Libra. Whether you're male or female, women could become a source of difficulty in your life. Men and women, on the whole, behave differently. You fit in better with men. This doesn't mean you shouldn't have any female friends, just that overall your male friends will prove more reliable. The planet Saturn delays marriage for you and has been known to bestow sorrow at the loss of a deep attachment. This placement can be read two ways. No great heartache can occur where there hasn't first been great love. We all suffer losses. It's part of life. However, we don't all get to enjoy an epic attachment. (*Famous examples:* Bebe Buell, Helen Gurley Brown, Natalie Portman, Britney Spears, Justin Timberlake, Prince William Windsor.)

Saturn in Scorpio. Your passionate and oftentimes jealous nature causes you to face sorrows in liaisons and romantic intrigues as well as domestic difficulties. Passion is a relationship creator, jealousy is a destroyer. If you're attracted to someone, chances are this is an attractive person, and other people will be enticed, too. You can't expect people to look the other way because you've replaced your paramour's "Available" sign for one that reads "Taken." In fact, it's quite the opposite. People take your interest in someone as a sign that someone is fascinating. The trick is to draw the lines about what's worth being angry about and what isn't. You can even discuss this with your love. (Be tactful and do it early in the relationship.) (*Famous examples:* Lauren Bacall, Kim Basinger, Richard Burton, John Derek, Bob Moffatt, Clint Moffatt, Dave Moffatt, Maria Shriver, John Travolta, Oprah Winfrey.)

Some couples can't live without each other. An Associated Press story published in 2000 related the tale of one such pair. Mary and Jerry Siens met at a Jimi Hendrix concert in 1973, when Mary was still a teenager. They got married in 1976. Their marriage lasted twenty-seven years. They even worked together at a Denver post office in the same sorting room for twenty-four of those years. They raised three sons together, and kept homes in the city and in the mountains. Shortly after midnight on Saturday, 25 November, 2000, Mary was driving to her second job when her vehicle was hit by a drunken driver. She was mortally injured. Minutes after the police arrived at the Sienses' home to tell Jerry about the accident, he collapsed in one of his sons' arms and died of a heart attack.

Saturn in Sagittarius. During your marriage, you may discover that opposition creates resentment. It takes careful judgment to figure out which issues are important enough to fight about, and you'll need to if you want your relationship to work. If you didn't agree on most things, you wouldn't (or shouldn't) be together. Try to choose your battles carefully; many of the things you might argue about really aren't worth it. (Who cares which way the toilet paper faces on the roller or who did dishes last?) In the words of American author Dr. William Arthur Ward: "Flatter me, and I may not believe you. Criticize me, and I may not like you. Ignore me, and I may not forgive you.

Encourage me, and I will not forget you. Love me and I may be forced to love you." (*Famous examples:* Humphrey Bogart, Bo Derek, Carrie Fisher, Melanie Griffith, the Reverend Dr. Martin Luther King Jr., Madonna, Michelle Pfeiffer, Prince, Dwight Yoakam.)

Saturn in Capricorn. You're very anxious to succeed, and you ultimately will, but you must be cautious about marriage. An unsatisfactory union could diminish your achievements on many levels. There's an old saying: You can judge a man by the company he keeps. Look at the spouse and you know a lot about the person. For better or worse, your mate represents you in the world's eyes. Beware of thinking that you can shape someone as needed, or that a person will mature into the role you want them to play. Eventually that person will sense that you feel they're not perfect, and there will be resentment and resistance. Choose carefully. Your future depends on it. (*Famous examples:* Antonio Banderas, Michael J. Fox, Mikhail Gorbachev, John F. Kennedy Jr., Heather Locklear, Richie Sambora, Michael Stipe, Spencer Tracy, Princess Diana Spencer Windsor.)

Saturn in Aquarius. The planet Saturn graces you with something rare and precious. It's quite possible you'll find one real romantic attachment that lasts. The trick is knowing that you've got it and accepting it. Relationships suffer when they're overanalyzed. Take a song, one you really like. Put on the headphones, close your eyes, and let the sound sweep you away. Now, track down the sheet music for that song. Read it while the tune is playing in the background. Look for grammatical errors. Try to find at least three spots that need improvement, and while the music plays, try to figure out how the melody or lyrics could be better. Stop it every few seconds and rewind, just to be sure you heard it correctly. Doesn't exactly sweep you away anymore, does it? It's the same with a relationship. Enjoy it for what it is. If it really doesn't sweep you away, maybe it's time for a new one. However, if it does sweep you away, don't question it. (*Famous examples:* Brigitte Bardot, Matthew Broderick, Garth Brooks, Sir Michael Caine, Johnny Depp, Bridget Fonda, Brad Pitt, Elvis Presley, Debbie Reynolds, Elizabeth Taylor.)

Saturn in Pisces. Your emotions are sometimes the source of your own demise when it comes to love. You may even consider yourself unlucky where romance or matrimony is concerned. It isn't just bad luck. When your emotions man the steering wheel, you drive blindly. You might need to take control. Never treat your pets better than you treat your spouse. It's easy to shower affection on small animals, acquaintances, and new friends. It's more difficult to perpetuate that excitement about someone you see day and night. But if you want to keep your mate, you must make that person feel wanted and desired. (*Famous examples:* Woody Allen, Warren Beatty, Kurt Cobain, Jane Fonda, Katharine Hepburn, Carolyn Bessette Kennedy, Courtney Love, Jack Nicholson, Sarah Jessica Parker, Brooke Shields.)

During a personal consultation, an astrologer might consider Michael J. Fox's Saturn in Capricorn a cautionary matrimonial flag. Because he's very anxious to succeed and ultimately does, the selection of a spouse had to be approached shrewdly and carefully. An unsatisfactory union could diminish his achievements on many levels: socially, financially, and professionally.

♥ ♥ ♥

You can also look at the planet Saturn as the parental control in astrology, which creates a state of discipline and responsibility. Not everyone's ready for marriage straight out of high school or even graduate school. For some people, tying the knot is something that best occurs after the outside world has been conquered romantically, professionally, or emotionally. Other people are ready much sooner. Saturn is the matrimonial alarm clock, advising you when you're ready for marriage by its placement in your chart. Astrologer Ted George believes if a marriage takes place before this planet says you're ready to face the responsibilities, problems occur.

　　You'll need your birth chart to use this particular section. Enter your (and/or your mate's) birth date onto Worksheet 21. Look for Saturn's symbol (♄) in your chart and note the house number in which the planet resides. (On page 300, fig. 12 illustrates Saturn's house location in Michael J. Fox's Western birth chart.) Enter the house number from your birth chart in the space provided on the worksheet. Do the same with your mate's birth date. Then locate that house number in the text following to determine when you're potentially ripe for marriage.

WORKSHEET 21. SATURN'S TROPICAL HOUSE LOCATION

	Example: Michael J. Fox	Name A:	Name B:
Birth date	09 Jun 1961		
Saturn's tropical house location	I (first house)		

Saturn in your chart's first house. You're ready for marriage by your fifteenth birthday. Of course, this doesn't mean you should consider matrimony when you're fifteen, simply that you stand a better chance to have a happy marriage than other people who start at a young age. Be sure to check your potential mate's chart, too. If your mate isn't ready, then it doesn't matter if you are. Even if you're both ready, there's no hurry. Life is too long to rush the early parts of it. (*Famous examples:* Cher, Al Gore, Carolyn Bessette Kennedy, John Lennon, Princess Diana Spencer Windsor.)

Saturn in your chart's second house. Marriage is something for you to consider after you turn forty years old. It may sound like a long time to wait for matrimony, and you might not wait. But don't be surprised if you find yourself in a second marriage when you reach that age (or at least, you might finally discover what's truly wonderful about the person whom you married). You can no more know your future self than you can know a complete stranger from their photograph. After all, you are merely a snapshot of your future self. (*Famous examples:* Brigitte Bardot, Drew Barrymore, Bridget Fonda, Prince, Arnold Schwarzenegger, Britney Spears, Steven Spielberg, Barbra Streisand, Elizabeth Taylor, Prince Charles Windsor.)

Saturn in your chart's third house. The marriage time for you begins around the age of thirty-eight. Courtship and romance are the training grounds for matrimony. This is the time to learn how not to destroy a marriage; it's also the time to get tired of endless dates and to discover that it's not as fun to know a little about an endless succession of people. It's better to know one person nearly as well as you know yourself. There's no point to rush into matrimony, especially if you envision escape routes before you begin to plan the nuptials. When the time comes, you'll know it. (*Famous examples:* Hillary Rodham Clinton, Ray Davies, Mia Farrow, Tipper Gore, Brad Pitt, Elvis Presley, Oprah Winfrey, Dwight Yoakam.)

Riddle:

If I am four intertwined for two, who are one, what am I?

Can you answer the riddles on pages 88, 99, and 218? Then visit www.world-astrology.com.

Saturn in your chart's fourth house. The chances of an early marriage followed by divorce are high until you're thirty-six years old. It's so easy to decide what you want if you look at what other people have. Everyone seems to meet the love of his or her life in college or at their first job, then they wed and have a family. This is also why the divorce rate hovers close to 60 percent. Half of these people do it because they really met the one for them; the other half do it just because the first half did. There's a lot of pressure, too. "So," the refrain goes, "when are you going to get married?" Do it when you're ready and you won't wonder whether you should get divorced. (*Famous examples:* Lauren Bacall, Madonna, Kurt Russell, Ted Turner.)

Saturn in your chart's fifth house. You're ready for marital bliss after you're thirty-four years old. Anything worthwhile is worth the wait. However, you don't exactly have to linger. You can date, have wonderful romances, fall in love. You can even tell yourself that you've met the absolutely perfect person for you. Just hold off on the wedding or things might not work out as well as you envisioned. (*Famous examples:* Bill Gates, Katharine Hepburn, John F. Kennedy Jr., Courtney Love, Debbie Reynolds.)

Saturn in your chart's sixth house. Even though you're ready for matrimony after your thirty-second birthday, difficulties may still arise once you're married. Perfect happiness was invented by poets to give us hope. In reality, life is a bumpy road that we travel as best we can. It's better to have someone with whom you share that journey, but you must also maintain your independence and sense of self. (*Famous examples:* Warren Beatty, Humphrey Bogart, Catherine Deneuve, Brooke Shields, Maria Shriver, John Travolta.)

Saturn in your chart's seventh house. Although you're ready for marriage after your thirtieth birthday, difficulties may still arise once you're married. "By all means marry," said Socrates; "if you get a good wife, you'll be happy. If you get a bad one, you'll become a philosopher." Relationships aren't easy. There's a lot of work involved and sometimes it might seem like the rewards are few and far between. You might picture yourself living happily alone, but in truth, the solo life is highly overrated. More often than not, singles excessively wonder when they'll find that special person with whom they can share their life. (*Famous examples:* Woody Allen, Candice Bergen, Kurt Cobain, Johnny Depp, Melanie Griffith, Goldie Hawn, Michelle Pfeiffer, Richie Sambora.)

Saturn in your chart's eighth house. The marriage time for you begins around your twenty-seventh birthday, which is a period some astrologers refer to as your Saturn return. This is a time in which you may question the priorities you set for yourself. This is the point when life's fantasies strip away. Maturity is the knowledge that a single practicality is worth two ideals. The lack of depth in certain people you admired becomes as apparent as the two-by-fours that hold up the Western-town façade on a Hollywood set. You might discover with your newly sharpened vision that what you really want in life is a partner rather than a trophy, someone less exciting and more well rounded. (*Famous examples:* Kim Basinger, Richard Burton, Bo Derek, Michael Douglas, Jane Fonda, George Harrison, Diane Keaton.)

Saturn in your chart's ninth house. You might find a suitable marriage partner after you turn twenty-four years old. It's okay to be certain that a youthful romance is the first, last, and only love of your life. "Love," wrote the British poet Alfred, Lord Tennyson, "is the only gold." It enriches you, and when it's lost you feel poor indeed. But those who have lost it deserve far less pity than those who've never had it. Just know in your heart that whether you commit early or not, your life partner is not likely to become apparent until after your twenty-fourth birthday. (*Famous examples:* Sir Michael Caine, Eric Clapton, Harrison Ford, the Reverend Dr. Martin Luther King Jr., Jack Nicholson, Julie Roberts, Prince William Windsor.)

Saturn in your chart's tenth house. Your suitable partner may appear after you turn twenty-two. Believe it or not, it's rather rare to encounter the right match at such an early age. Your own existence might last one hundred years. Even if you wait a few years, you might still celebrate a sixtieth wedding anniversary. There's no such thing as the right person who got away. Your paths might cross again and again. You might even be involved with other people. But when you're around each other, you'll know. It won't be a hormonal weak-in-the-knees swoon. (Well, actually it might be, but that isn't the feeling that'll let you know this is the right person. That's just the feeling that lets you know this is a really cute individual.) The revelation comes when you're comfortable around someone. You can talk to each other. You're entertained by each other. There's a mutual feeling of admiration. (*Famous examples:* David Bowie, Carrie Fisher, Heather Locklear.)

Saturn in your chart's eleventh house. You have an urgent need for love and are fortunately ready for marriage when you're nineteen years old. Nothing else in this world feels like love. But love is not the passion, the romance, or the desire. It's the discovery that you still want to be with someone at times when those other sensations are gone. Just remember, though you might be ready at an early age, a successful union is a bridge between two solid shores. If one side is built on sand, it'll sink. (*Famous examples:* Antonio Banderas, Julie Christie, Bill Clinton, Mikhail Gorbachev, Steffi Graf, Justin Timberlake.)

Saturn in your chart's twelfth house. You're ready for marriage after your seventeenth birthday. For you, the unnoticed road is the time you give or deny yourself before you take on the responsibility of marriage. The misdirection is an equally young mate who's not as prepared as you to make a lifetime commitment. Check your mate's birth date. If this person doesn't have a similar placement, it's better to wait. The real comfort is not the act of getting married itself but simply knowing that the maturity is there when you finally do decide to do it. (*Famous examples:* Ben Affleck, George W. Bush, John Derek, Michael J. Fox, O. J. Simpson, Spencer Tracy, Donald Trump.)

In Germany's Lausitz region, it was customary for the bride and groom to plant a pair of young oak trees on the morning of their wedding. As they grew, the trees served as a superstitious barometer of the couple's marriage and health.

During a personal consultation, an astrologer might determine that Michael J. Fox's Saturn in the first house placement suggests he was ready for marriage when he celebrated his fifteenth birthday, having reached the maturity to face marital responsibilities early in his life. Combined with Saturn's placement in Capricorn, this would suggest that although he had to be very careful who he picked as his mate in life, he was already able to make that decision at an early age; this allowed him to achieve his financial, social, and professional goals with the right person by his side.

Discovering Your True Essence: The Sun's Tropical Placement in Your Chart

The Sun represents the essence of who you are, shaping your inner self, defining your basic characteristics. It does not, however, necessarily define what people see in you.

The Sun also directs your ability to get along with people who possess different temperaments. Astrologer Linda Goodman would use the element (water, earth, fire, or air) that rules the Sun's particular position in your chart to analyze your potential in this area. This view is similar to a theory established by the father of modern medicine, Hippocrates, who assigned temperaments, or humors, to each element. According to this system, a sanguine temperament is associ-

ated with air, a phlegmatic temperament is coupled with water, a cho-
leric temperament is paired with fire, and the melancholic temperament is associated with earth.

You don't need your birth chart to use this particular section. Simply
enter your (and/or your mate's) birth date onto Worksheet 22. Using
Table 18, look for the period in which your birth date resides. Read
across to find the zodiac sign and the element associated with that
period. (The dates listed are the starting dates for each period: your
birth date should fall on or after the appropriate date and before the
date in the row below.) Enter that zodiac sign and element in the
spaces provided on the worksheet. Then do the same with your
mate's birth date. Finally, locate the pair of elements associated with
you and your mate (for example, *air with air* or *earth with water*) in the
text following and read how your temperaments might influence each
other.

WORKSHEET 22. SUN PERIODS

	Example 1: Michael J. Fox	Example 2: Tracy Pollan	Name A:	Name B:
Birthdate	09 Jun 1961	22 Jun 1960		
Sun's tropical placement	Gemini (♊)	Cancer (♋)		
Element	air	water		

Table 18. Tropical Placements for the Sun, 1927–1987

Starting Date	Zodiac Sign	Element
1 Jan	Capricorn (γ_o)	earth
21 Jan (There are exceptions. The Sun moved into this zodiac sign on 20 Jan in the following years: 1933, 1937, 1941, 1945, 1949, 1953, 1957, 1961, 1965, 1969, 1970, 1973, 1974, 1977, 1978, 1981, 1982, 1985, and 1986.)	Aquarius ($\approx$)	air
19 Feb (There are exceptions. The Sun moved into this zodiac sign on 20 Feb in the following years: 1927, 1928, 1931, 1932, 1935, 1936, 1939, 1940, 1943, 1944, 1948, 1952, 1956, 1960, 1964, 1968, 1972, 1976, and 1980.)	Pisces ($\mathcal{H}$)	water
21 Mar (There are exceptions. The Sun moved into this zodiac sign on 22 Mar in the following years: 1931, 1932, 1935, 1939, and 1943. Changed on 20 Mar: 1976, 1980, and 1984.)	Aries (Υ)	fire
21 Apr (There are exceptions. The Sun moved into this zodiac sign on 20 Apr in the following years: 1928, 1932, 1936, 1940, 1941, 1944, 1945, 1948, 1949, 1952, 1953, 1956, 1957, 1960, 1961, 1964, 1965, 1968, 1969, 1972, 1973, 1974, 1976, 1977, 1978, 1980, 1981, 1982, 1984, 1985, and 1986.)	Taurus ($\emptyset$)	earth
22 May (There are exceptions. The Sun moved into this zodiac sign on 21 May in the following years: 1928, 1932, 1936, 1937, 1940, 1941, 1944, 1945, 1948, 1949,	Gemini ($\mathrm{I\!I}$)	air

Starting Date	Zodiac Sign	Element
1952, 1953, 1956, 1957, 1960, 1961,1964, 1965, 1968, 1969, 1970, 1972, 1973, 1974, 1976, 1977, 1978, 1980, 1981, 1982, 1984, 1985, and 1986.)		
22 Jun (There are exceptions. The Sun moved into this zodiac sign on 21 June in the following years: 1952, 1956, 1960, 1964, 1968, 1972, 1976, 1980, 1981, 1984, and 1985.)	Cancer (♋)	water
23 Jul (There are exceptions. The Sun moved into this zodiac sign on 24 Jul in the following years: 1930, 1931, 1934, 1935, 1938, 1939, 1942, 1943, 1947, 1951, 1955, 1959, 1963, 1967, and 1971.)	Leo (♌)	fire
24 Aug (There are exceptions. The Sun moved into this zodiac sign on 23 Aug in the following years: 1928, 1932, 1936, 1940, 1944, 1948, 1949, 1952, 1953, 1956, 1957, 1960, 1961, 1964, 1965, 1968, 1969, 1972, 1973, 1976, 1977, 1978, 1980, 1981, 1982, 1984, 1985, and 1986.)	Virgo (♍)	earth
24 Sep (There are exceptions. The Sun moved into this zodiac sign on 23 Sep in the following years: 1928, 1932, 1933, 1936, 1937, 1940, 1941, 1944, 1945, 1948, 1949, 1952, 1953, 1956, 1957, 1960, 1961, 1964, 1965, 1966, 1968, 1969, 1970, 1972, 1973, 1974, 1976, 1977, 1978, 1980, 1981, 1982, 1984, 1985, and 1986.)	Libra (♎)	air

Starting Date	Zodiac Sign	Element
24 Oct (There are exceptions. The Sun moved into this zodiac sign on 23 Oct in the following years: 1952, 1956, 1960, 1964, 1968, 1972, 1976, 1980, 1984, and 1985.)	Scorpio (♏)	water
23 Nov (There are exceptions. The Sun moved into this zodiac sign on 22 Nov in the following years: 1940, 1944, 1948, 1952, 1956, 1960, 1964, 1968, 1969, 1972, 1973, 1976, 1977, 1980, 1981, 1984, and 1985.)	Sagittarius (♐)	fire
23 Dec (There are exceptions. The Sun moved into this zodiac sign on 22 Dec in the following years: 1930, 1931, 1934, 1935, 1938, 1939, 1943, 1947, 1951, 1955, 1959, 1963, 1967, and 1971.)	Capricorn (♑)	earth

Air with air. The bywords of this match are freedom and optimism. Since you both tend to intellectualize love and the material world, it's not always easy for you to find emotional fulfillment unless other planetary factors bring you both back to the physical realm. Don Quixote knew what it meant to love. It meant he defended his love's life and honor against endless assaults from windmill dragons and other imagined foes. Don't think too much about what it means to love. Let it happen and it will reveal its true significance to you. (*Famous examples:* Tim Robbins and Susan Sarandon, Michael Douglas and Catherine Zeta-Jones, Roger Vadim and Brigitte Bardot, John Travolta and Kelly Preston, Ellen DeGeneres and Anne Heche.)

Air with water (also, water with air). Two different languages are spoken here. Air lives in the world of the intellect, finding it difficult to discover emotional fulfillment. Water, on the other hand, swims in an emotional sea, finding it impossible to assess life as a series of logical steps. Unless other planetary forces introduce passion or stability, there's little either person can say that won't be misinterpreted. Have you ever visited a country where you don't speak the language? You might not have been able to sit and talk about current events with the locals, but you always managed to find a restaurant and order food with a simple smile and point of the finger. Occasionally you might've even pulled out the guidebook and pointed to the pictures so someone who wasn't able to read the book could still give you directions. If you want this relationship to work, you'll need to think of communication on this level. Avoid subtleties. (*Famous examples:* Michael J. Fox and Tracy Pollan, Donald Trump and Marla Maples, Donald Trump and Ivana Trump, Richie Sambora and Heather Locklear, Kurt Cobain and Courtney Love, Tommy Lee and Heather Locklear, John W. Warner and Elizabeth Taylor.)

The fourth-century B.C. orator Aeschines wrote that young maidens about to marry in ancient Greece traditionally bathed in the river Scamander before their wedding. As they splashed in the waters, they said: "Scamander, accept my virginity." The bride and groom also bathed before the wedding ceremony, hoping that the water nymphs would bless the couple with fertility.

Earth with air (also, air with earth). It can get a bit chilly since air breathes in the intellectual, nonemotional world and earth rumbles in the lower depths of reserved, concealed feelings. Unless other planetary forces impart passion or emotion, the marriage unites two powerful forces who can reshape their environs but can't celebrate the outcome. Even the biggest mansion is as cold as a tomb unless it's filled with happiness. It's the little gestures, like smiles, kisses, and whispers of affection, not just physical togetherness, that add life to love. To keep love alive, be loving. (*Famous examples:* Humphrey Bogart and Lauren Bacall, André Agassi and Steffi Graf, André Agassi and Brooke Shields, Johnny Depp and Vanessa Paradis, Johnny Depp and Kate Moss, Roger Vadim and Jane Fonda, David Arquette and Courteney Cox Arquette, Peter Sellers and Britt Ekland.)

Earth with earth. You both strive for rewards in the material world, so you may not always emerge from your reserved and somewhat rigid selves to encounter emotional highs such as ecstasy or joy. Mountains can be built with this type of ambition, but emotional deserts may surround the summit unless other planetary forces impart passion. "Of all the earthly music," American clergyman Henry Ward Beecher wrote, "that which reaches farthest into heaven is the beating of a truly loving heart." Just remember, you can only hear that beating heart when your head is nestled against your mate's chest. Spend time being tender. Keep the romance thriving with little gestures. They may seem silly, but those moments keep love alive. (*Famous examples:* the Reverend Dr. Martin Luther King and Coretta Scott King Jr., Marilyn Manson and Rose McGowan.)

Earth with water (also, water with earth). Stability and compassion can be either complementary or lopsided. While earth finds it difficult to expose well-concealed emotions, water finds stability as difficult to uncover as the proverbial needle in a haystack. It might seem like a solid relationship: water cuts endlessly mutable and ever-deepening paths through earth. But it's just slow erosion. Unless other planetary forces impart passion and logic, the union could become more codependent than either side willingly admits. Don't confuse "I love sharing my life with you" with "I can't live without you." Feeling like you'd be unable to survive without someone is not a healthy sentiment. In fact, if the feelings of dependency are too strong, it's time to get out of the relationship. With that said, an earth-with-water relationship can work, in cases where water finds stability from earth and earth finds emotional release through water. (*Famous examples:* Daniel Day-Lewis and Isabelle Adjani, Jack Nicholson and Anjelica Huston, Louis Malle and Candice Bergen, Mike Nichols and Diane Sawyer, Larry Fortensky and Elizabeth Taylor, Ringo Starr and Barbara Bach.)

Fire with air (also, air with fire). Enthusiasm and optimism spur each other on in a crazy array of activities when the two of you unite. The encounters between fire's passionate and somewhat illogical nature and air's intellectual and frequently emotionless temperament can lead to either frustration or exhilaration. It all depends on the introduction of a modicum of steadfastness or sensitivity by other planetary factors. The difference between progress and regress is one of desire, not direction. Your happiness in this relationship depends on your desire to go where it's going. (*Famous examples:* Ben Affleck and Gwyneth Paltrow, Brad Pitt and Gwyneth Paltrow, Lukas Haas and Natalie Portman, Roger Vadim and Catherine Deneuve, Brad Pitt and Jennifer Aniston, Woody Allen and Mia Farrow.)

Fire with earth (also, earth with fire). Unless other planetary factors temper fire's enthusiasm and earth's ambition with logic and sensitivity, there's always a chance someone's ego will be bruised. Negotiation and compromise aren't easy if impulsiveness and single-mindedness are allowed to reign over this union. Each of you may instantly know the right answer to any dilemma, and find that you completely disagree. There's a simple unwritten code known as the Marriage Preservation Act (MPA for short). The idea behind the MPA is that sometimes it's best to concede to prevent damage to the relationship. Explain the MPA to your mate. You should both put it to use. As actress Patricia Arquette said of her marriage to actor Nicolas Cage (long before their divorce), "Neither of us entered marriage thinking it wouldn't be a strain. Life has strains in it, and he's the person I want to strain with." (*Famous examples:* Nicolas Cage and Patricia Arquette, Peter Horton and Michelle Pfeiffer, Steven Spielberg and Amy Irving, Ted Turner and Jane Fonda, John F. Kennedy Jr. and Carolyn Bessette Kennedy, Woody Allen and Diane Keaton, Warren Beatty and Diane Keaton.)

Fire with fire. "Some day after we have mastered the winds, the waves, the tides, and gravity we shall harness the energies of love," wrote the Jesuit paleontologist Pierre Teilhard de Chardin. "Then for the second time in the history of the world, man will have discovered fire." You're both endowed with enthusiasm and energy, preferring to move dynamically despite potential danger or remorse. Passions such as impulsiveness, rashness, and drive could cause head-on collisions unless other planetary factors redirect your excessive energy. Pursue common goals. To succeed, you need to work together, not against each other, to assist one another, and always come to your mate's defense against outside attacks. (*Famous examples:* Matthew Broderick and Sarah Jessica Parker, Al Gore and Tipper Gore, Alec Baldwin and Kim Basinger, Antonio Banderas and Melanie Griffith, Don Johnson and Melanie Griffith, Anthony Armstrong-Jones and Princess Margaret Windsor.)

Fire with water (also, water with fire). Passion and emotion may create a steamy sex life but can make the day-to-day matters of real love difficult to manage unless other planetary factors instill logic and stability. Fire's impulsiveness could send water into a monumental geyser of ecstasy or a bottomless pit of self-pity. On the other side of the coin, water's undulating moods could darken fire's eternal flame of optimism. After fire unsuccessfully attempts to rekindle the spark a few times, fire is likely to move. To make this relationship last, don't entwine your lives too tightly. Distance makes both hearts' flames burn longer. There's no better reminder of a person's place in one's life than their obvious absence. (*Famous examples:* Daniel Day-Lewis and Isabelle Adjani, Dennis Quaid and Meg Ryan, Kevin Bacon and Kyra Sedgwick, Arnold Schwarzenegger and Maria Shriver, Eddie Fisher and Elizabeth Taylor, Michael Wilding and Elizabeth Taylor, Steven Spielberg and Kate Capshaw, Steven Tyler and Bebe Buell, Goldie Hawn and Kurt Russell.)

Water with water. You both wear your emotions on your shirtsleeves and sway with the prevailing winds. The slightest perceived shift could send both of you on an upward spiral into clouds of ecstasy or down into the depths of depression unless other planetary forces induce reality. While everyone has emotions, as a couple you sense more and your feelings are deeper. Your sorrows may seem severe, yet they're a small price to pay for the moments of ecstasy you can share. However, no one can ride a roller-coaster forever. You might need time apart now and then. Separate lives will help this relationship last. Anne Morrow Lindbergh, wife of aviation pioneer Charles Lindbergh, wrote: "Him that I love, I wish to be free—even from me." (*Famous examples:* Tom Cruise with Nicole Kidman, Tommy Lee and Pamela Anderson Lee, Nicky Hilton and Elizabeth Taylor, Bruce Willis

and Demi Moore, Todd Rundgren and Bebe Buell, Richard Burton and
Elizabeth Taylor.)

As astrologer might caution Michael J. Fox and Tracy Pollan about their
air-water relationship, citing a difference in the way each person com-
municates. Fox lives in the world of the intellect, while Pollan swims in
an emotional sea. Fortunately, other planetary forces introduce passion,
stability, and communication, which make their relationship viable.

'Tis the Season to Wed

As it says in Ecclesiastes 3:5–6, there's "a time to embrace, and a time to
refrain from embracing; a time to get, and a time to lose; a time to keep,
and a time to cast away." According to
Edward J. Wood in his 1869 book, *The
Wedding Day in All Ages and Countries*: "In
early times in England the date of a marriage was often fixed after due consultation of the aspect of the heavens, which
regulated every affair of importance, and
instances are recorded in which the bride
and groom would not consummate the
marriage until the proper hour has been
fixed by the astrologers."

Although in Western cultures astrology played a much less pivotal role in
wedding date selection than it did and
does in other societies, it has been consulted from time to time to make this
determination. If you're interested in finding the perfect wedding day, in Western
astrological terms, here's what you need
to know.

Based on the daily time for sunrise
and sunset at the wedding's location, the

Until the mid-1800s, brides
and grooms in Brandenburg,
Germany, used to run a race
of sorts on their wedding day
while the guests stood on the
sidelines. According to *The
Golden Bough's* author, Sir James
Frazer: "Two sturdy men took
the bride between them and set
off. The bridegroom gave them a
start and then followed hot-foot.
At the end of the course stood
two or three young married
women, who took from the
bride her maiden's crown and
replaced it with a matron's cap.
If the bridegroom failed to
overtake his bride, he was
much ridiculed."

perfect planetary hours for a wedding ceremony occur when the Sun influences:

Sunday: the first and eighth hours after sunrise, the third and tenth hours after sunset

Monday: the fifth and twelfth hours after sunrise, the seventh hour after sunset

Tuesday: the second and ninth hours after sunrise, the fourth and eleventh hours after sunset

Wednesday: the sixth hour after sunrise, the first and eighth hours after sunset

Thursday: the third and tenth hours after sunrise, the twelfth hour after sunset

Friday: the seventh hour after sunrise, the second and ninth hours after sunset

Saturday: the fourth and eleventh hours after sunrise, the sixth hour after sunset

However, if you're more concerned with determining the best time to consummate the union, you'll need to look to the planet Venus.

Sunday: the second and ninth hours after sunrise, the fourth and eleventh hours after sunset

Monday: the sixth hour after sunrise, the first and eighth hours after sunset

Tuesday: the third and tenth hours after sunrise, the twelfth hour after sunset

Wednesday: the seventh hour after sunrise, the second, fifth, and ninth hours after sunset

Thursday: the fourth and eleventh hours after sunrise, the sixth hour after sunset

Friday: the first and eighth hours after sunrise, the third and tenth hours after sunset

Saturday: the fifth and twelfth hours after sunrise, the seventh hour after sunset

The ancient Irish, Welsh, and Scots believed that marriages should take place when the Moon was in its waxing phase (first or second quarter). According to them, as the Moon grows, it enhances the outcomes of new beginnings and increased the couple's potential for a successful union. The Moon's waning phases (third or fourth quarter) were considered by many to be inauspicious in these matters. As Theseus said in William Shakespeare's *A Midsummer Night's Dream*, the couple would be fated to chant "faint hymns to the cold fruitless Moon."

In the Scottish Highlands, a Tuesday or Thursday during a waxing Moon was considered to be an optimal wedding date. There were also a number of rhymes that helped people remember the best months and days on which to tie the knot. In the British isles, Sunday was a day of rest, so God wouldn't be present to bless a young couple's union. The first three days of the week were considered to be the most auspicious for matrimony:

> *Monday for wealth,*
> *Tuesday for health,*
> *Wednesday the best day of all,*
> *Thursday for losses,*
> *Friday for crosses,*
> *Saturday for no luck at all.*

Each month of the year carried its own omen as well:

> *Married when the year is new, he'll be loving, kind, and true.*
> *When February birds do mate, you wed nor dread your fate.*
> *If you wed when March winds blow, joy and sorrow both you'll know.*
> *Marry in April when you can, joy for maiden and for man.*
> *Marry in the month of May, and you'll surely rue the day.*
> *Marry when June roses grow, over land and sea you'll go.*
> *Those who in July do wed, must labor for their daily bread.*
> *Whoever wed in August be, many a change is sure to see.*
> *Marry in September's shrine, your living will be rich and fine.*
> *If in October you do marry, love will come but riches tarry.*
> *If you wed in bleak November, only joys will come, remember.*
> *When December snows fall fast, marry and true love will last.*

Samhain (November) was regarded as the best month for nuptials. It's no surprise that on Samhain Eve (31 October) most young men and women whiled away the night in the execution of divinations that were said to reveal who would be married to whom within the year. Beltaine (May) was considered the worst month in which to marry, because among the Celts it was a time in which eligible singles danced around the Maypole: a period to begin a handfast or a court-ship, but not a permanent union. Each man had a colored ribbon that matched the hue of a ribbon held by a woman. As they danced around the pole, it became more and more evident who had the matching color. After dinner, the matched couples spent the night together in the forest and greeted the sunrise together. The first day of Bel-taine was also the official day to pub-licly declare a divorce or the end of a handfast that had begun by the first day of Lunasdal (August). Being from good Scottish stock, Great Britain's Queen Victoria was even rumored to have told her numerous children they couldn't wed in May.

In northern Albania, many peasants still adhere to the code of behavior set forth in a fifteenth-century book called the *Kanun of Lek Dukagjin*. According to this ancient text, when the last male head of a family dies, his widow becomes a "sworn virgin." She assumes a traditionally male role as head of the household, and becomes responsible for the defense of her family's name and property until her death. From that day on she also dresses, acts, and is treated like a man whenever she's in public.

The months of Samhain, Beltaine, and Lunasdal were chosen because each correlated to an optimal placement of the Moon for the performance of certain events, based on the observations of Druidic priests. In Western cultures, wedding dates are rarely selected be-cause the Moon or any other planet is posited in an ideal celestial position. June has become the month to perform a wedding in the United States simply because the weather is generally ideal for an outdoor ceremony or reception, flowers are cheaper and easier to acquire, and honeymoons are more easily taken during prime vaca-tion time.

Joining Hands and Tying the Knot

One type of Western wedding that dates back to medieval times is the handfast ceremony. An outdoor affair, this ritual ensured that nature and all of its spirits blessed the newlyweds. The bride and groom faced each other and joined right hand to right hand and left hand to left hand. A ceremonial rope was tied into a knot around their hands, signifying their union. The Celtic Druids frequently called upon the river, lake, or well god to sanctify the union, giving wedding guests pebbles to toss into the water so the resulting ripples could send good tidings to the couple.

There's been more than one account of ancient Irish nuptials that tell of the bride being placed on horseback so she could ride away with her husband, who was on another horse, by her side. Twelve bridesmaids plus the bride's brothers and close male kin had to chase the newlyweds in a hot but jovial pursuit all the way to the groom's house. Upon her arrival the bride's mother-in-law broke an oat cake above the bride's head as a wish for future abundance. In Scotland, the wedding guests used to *broose* (race on horseback) for a prize, which was often the bride's cake, which had been set up on a pole in front of the groom's house.

There's a nineteenth-century account of a couple who were married near a hawthorn tree that stood beside a stream. A procession of musicians played flutes and drums while a young boy followed, bearing a torch made of lit bogwood. The bride and groom walked hand in hand behind this parade, stepping under a canopy that seemed to veil them from view. When they arrived at a bonfire that had been lit near the tree, the canopy was lifted and the couple kissed each other before the assembled party, who waved green branches and shouted in approval.

Retiring to a feast at the bride's family home, the bride was presented with a new dress and her father paid out her dowry in public. The eating, drinking, and dancing continued well into the night. Great care was taken to avoid quarrels because it was an inauspicious sign, affecting the couple's future together. As one Irish nuptial song goes:

It is not day nor yet day,
It is not day nor yet morning;
It is not day nor yet day,
For the Moon is shining brightly.

People increasingly look back to past times for inspiration around such life-changing events, especially if they live in places where more natural settings abound. Whether or not your own wedding will include an indoor or outdoor handfast ceremony; or guests tossing pebbles into a river; or the couple and their wedding party riding away on horseback to the groom's house; or a ceremony held outdoors under a canopy, the small sampling of traditional Western weddings offered above can provide some tasty food for thought.

♥ ♥ ♥

As you can see, love comes in many shapes and forms. Throughout the myriad of cultures that have lived and died over the past millennia, people have looked to the stars and planets to point the way in these complicated waters. In times past, navigators steered their ships through unknown seas, relying on the polestar and the Moon as their only faithful guides. Is it any wonder, then, that men and women looked to those same celestial entities as they embarked on their quest for true love?

CHAPTER SIX

Putting It All Together

THE LOVE LIVES OF MICHAEL J. FOX

AND JOHNNY DEPP

Seldom or never does a marriage develop into an individual relationship smoothly and without crisis. There is no birth of consciousness without pain.

—Carl Jung

*N*ow that we've shown you how people in Chinese, Hindu, Jewish, and Western cultures use astrology to guide their love lives and to direct their choice of marriage partners, you probably want to know how you can combine these traditions to get the most out of this wealth of information.

To show you how the tools we've provided can be developed into a substantial love and marriage profile of your own life, we'll now present two celebrity profiles as examples. There's a fun reason why we picked these two actors: they're born on the same day, two years apart. Just imagine four astrologers (one from each of the traditions we've discussed—Western, Hindu, Chinese, and Judaic) getting together to determine the love potential and marriageability of actors Michael J. Fox and Johnny Depp. That is what you'll find in the following pages. And even though we didn't construct birth charts for their respective mates—Tracy Pollan and Vanessa Paradis—we've used them as examples of how much can be learned by just using a birth date and the tables in this book.

To help you follow along, we've included Fox's and Depp's *bhava-cakra* (house chart) and Western birth charts in this chapter. We've also added key planetary and astrological symbols within the text and provided references back to the previous chapters so you can locate the planets, nodes, and houses for yourself.

The Unstoppable Performer: Michael J. Fox

Actor Michael J. Fox, best known for roles in television's *Spin City* and *Family Ties* and the *Back to the Future* film trilogy, was born on **9 June 1961 at 12:12:00 A.M. Mountain daylight time in Edmonton, Alberta, Canada.** Fox's family relocated a number of times before settling in Vancouver, British Columbia, where he attended Burnaby Central High School. His acting career started when he landed a role in the CBC-TV series *Leo and Me* at the age of fifteen. Enthralled with the profession, Fox dropped out of school to pursue his main obsession. (His other great passion is music.)

Fox moved to Los Angeles when he was eighteen, appearing in a number of TV shows and films including *Palmerstown USA, Letters from Frank, Trapper John, M.D., Lou Grant, Family,* and *Night Court.* He even starred in the Walt Disney feature *Midnight Madness.* Then, in 1982, he got the dream role of teenage capitalist Alex P. Keaton on NBC's *Family Ties.* He met actress Tracy Pollan when she played his first girl-friend on this long-running show. (She was born on 22 June 1960 in Long Island, N.Y.) In 1985, Fox demonstrated how driven he really is, filming the feature *Back to the Future* at night and episodes of *Family Ties* during the day. This didn't deter Pollan, who wed the workaholic actor in 1988.

Married and on a professional hot streak, Fox duplicated the same grueling production schedule in 1989, filming the two *Back to the Future* sequels during another season of *Family Ties.* He managed to see the birth of his first child, Sam Michael Fox, that year as well. He was diagnosed with Parkinson's disease two years later. Despite this, Fox continued to vigorously pursue his professional ambitions. Just before he took on the role of New York's deputy mayor Michael Fla-herty in the TV series *Spin City,* Fox and Pollan relocated to Manhattan, where their twin daughters Aquinnah Kathleen and Schuyler Frances were born in 1995.

Tough production schedules and the endless maintenance of a public persona are not always the best ingredients for a happy relationship. What would astrologers in each of the traditions presented in this book have to say about Fox's prospects for love and marital bliss as well as his selection of a mate?

The Chinese View

The Chinese astrologer would approve of Fox's marriage to Tracy Pollan as well as their 17 July 1988 wedding date. Although their *ming shu* (reckoned fate) signs don't allude to their marriage's true strengths, their birth year *xing* (planets) and lunar month signs highlight a match filled with devotion and mutual success.

Fox was born in a Metal Ox year (1961) (see page 43). He could easily find a heavenly match with an Earth Rooster (1969), if that person was mature enough by the time was he was ready to consider marriage. There could also be a strong attraction and many benefits in the arms of a Water Snake (1953), if he doesn't mind courtship with an older woman. A compassionate match could also be found with a Wood Snake (1965), but Fox would need a good accountant to handle the mutual finances in this situation.

Tracy Pollan was born in a Metal Rat year (1960) (see page 42), which makes her neither perfect nor disastrous for Fox. Believe it or not, Chinese astrologers usually find neutral unions like this to be just as good as an absolute match, if the couple's birth year *xing* and lunar month signs improve their prospects.

In the case of Fox and Pollan, their 1960 and 1961 birth year *xing* pair makes their union of male earth to female earth (see page 18) start out easy and descend into hard work in later years. Devotion and compassion aid them through good times and hardships such as illness or accident.

The couple's lunar month signs are also a positive match. Fox's driven, ambitious personality is only slightly tempered by his birth in 1961's fourth lunar month (see page 63). He can't be pushed, but he can be swayed with logical persuasion. This particular facet also suggests that he's a very lovable and compassionate person who demonstrates his affection freely. A good speaker and a naturally active listener, Fox is supportive of his wife's dreams and ideas, not just his own.

Pollan's birth in the fifth lunar month of 1960 (see page 63) inspires her to travel and to conquer the world. She needs to be kept busy, happy at home, and she must feel truly fulfilled to remain devoted to her husband. She has very high personal values, and rarely tolerates less than the best in life and love.

Her ability to keep up with her husband, coupled with his support-ive nature, further enhances a potentially positive outcome to their relationship. Their wedding day (17 July 1988) was presided over by *sieu* 4 (see page 81), implying that happiness, longevity, honor, riches, and glory would emerge from the union.

The Hindu View

The Hindu astrologer is the only potential doubter in this group. Someone using this tradition might discover too many flaws in the Fox-Pollan match to recommend marriage. Hindu astrology also would've indicated that they should delay their wedding by one day to improve their union's outcome.

The perceived weakness in Fox's choice of a spouse is found in the seventh house (VII) of Fox's *bhavacakra* which is ruled by Gemini (3) (see page 99 and fig. 13, which illustrates Michael J. Fox's *bhava-cakra*). To the Hindu astrologer, this indicates that he's inclined to marry more than once or not at all. This ruling Gemini could be inter-preted as an indication that he's picky and cautious about the subject. Ideally, his mate might be an educator or a writer, or work in the com-munications, publishing, or advertising world, and be born west of his birthplace. Born in Long Island, New York, Pollan's birthplace was east of Fox's. Her acting career doesn't quite place her in one of the fields mentioned above either.

Another perceived weakness is found in Fox himself. The planet Venus (VE) occupies Aries (1) in his *bhavacakra*'s fifth house (V) (see page 124), indicating that he's inclined to appreciate the opposite sex before his twenty-fourth birthday and has a strong potential for romantic happiness. Consequently, he could marry very early or hastily. Impulsiveness, however, would only lead to an inharmonious relationship. Fortunately, Fox and Pollan spent fourteen months together before they tied the knot.

The planet Mars (MA) occupies Cancer (4) in his *bhavacakra's* eighth house (VIII) (see page 136). This means that before he turned thirty, he tended to nurse negative sentiments such as anger and anguish for long periods of time. This placement also suggests that his joint finances might have been disrupted by difficulties with property and legacies. His marriage could've also been potentially harmed by trouble with his spouse's finances before that critical thirtieth birthday diminished Mars's sway on Fox's life. (Remember, this planet's influence dissipates after age thirty.) Normally, the astrologer suggests that someone like Fox should marry someone whose Mars is associated with the same zodiac sign to alleviate potential financial problems or permanently injured feelings.

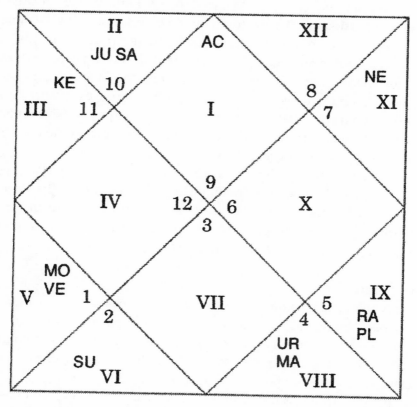

Figure 13. Michael J. Fox's *Bhavacakra*.

Ketu (KE) in his *bhavacakra*'s third house (III) (see page 147) suggests that Fox tends to fulfill his desires easily. Strange as it might
seem, this could ignite into serious bouts of sibling rivalry, which can
ricochet in his mate's direction. It'd be easy for others to celebrate
his success if his achievements didn't highlight their lack of success
by comparison. Since two of his siblings are construction workers, a
younger sister is also an actress, and a late brother was a jockey, there
were probably issues that had to be worked out among them as Fox's
star took off on its meteoric rise. The astrologer may have prescribed
additional mantras and talismans to remedy this problem.

A critical component in this astrological assessment, however,
actually works in the couple's favor. Providing insight into their emotional makeup, their *naksatras* (lunar mansions) suggest it's a favorable match. Fox's Moon was placed in the *naksatra* Asvini at his birth
(see page 152), indicating he's inclined to be very moral, very positive,
and very passionate. Heroes are frequently born under this *naksatra*.
Admired by the general public, a hero's life is privately filled with
many self-doubts and fears that can negatively affect even the most
patient spouse. Since Pollan was born while the Moon was in the
naksatra Rohini, patience isn't necessarily her strongest point. This
placement indicates that she's very critical of other people. This union
can work to the betterment of both people, as he won't settle for less
than the best in himself, and she won't either.

As we mentioned earlier, the Hindu astrologer would've also suggested the couple move their wedding date (17 July 1988). The Moon
was situated in the *naksatra* Magha on that day. This placement isn't
as auspicious as the next day's *naksatra*, Uttaraphalguni, which is best
known for bestowing marital happiness (see page 156).

The Judaic View

Fox and Pollan would get a resounding thumbs-up from the Judaic
astrologer. From this vantage point, the marriage is blessed with a
host of positive planetary influences that complement every strength
and weakness that the couple has. But like the Hindu astrologer, the
Judaic practitioner would've changed their wedding date.

The first strong point occurs in Fox's birth chart's seventh house
(7) (fig. 14 illustrates Michael J. Fox's birth chart), which is ruled by

Cancer (♋) (see page 185). This indicates that he maintains a very close, caring relationship with his wife. It also suggests that he might marry someone who's much younger or who strongly resembles his mother.

However, his ideal wife's youth is overruled because the planet Jupiter (♃) in Aquarius (♒) (see page 216) in his chart suggests that marriage to an older person or marriage later in life may bring him good fortune. On the basis of this, the astrologer would, therefore, advise him to choose a bride who is older than he is. Pollan fits the bill, being born a year before Fox.

Another plus is a result of the planet Venus's (♀) placement in the second house (2) of Fox's chart in Taurus (♉) (see page 204). This

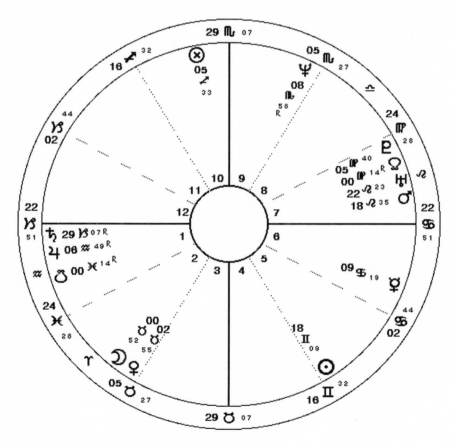

Figure 14. Michael J. Fox's Birth Chart.

location potentially affords the actor a happy domestic life, suggesting that he's inclined to be very affectionate and possess deep, enduring emotions. He may, however, encounter some delays or obstacles during his marriage—but who in this world doesn't encounter some setbacks, even in the arms of the perfect mate?

Together, Fox and Pollan share five planetary conjunctions (see page 217), and this also points to their union's strength and promise. Fox's Sun conjuncts Pollan's Moon, which is a textbook match made in heaven. It is considered by many astrologers to be the most permanent and romantic union (and one of the strongest sexual attractions) that can occur. Fox's Venus conjuncts Pollan's Mars, which also suggests that there's loads of sexual magnetism here.

Pollan's Sun conjuncts Fox's Mercury, instigating a lucrative exchange of ideas and the combined power to execute them. Compatibility in this case is inclined to be extremely intellectual and communicative, and this has the makings of an expansive and productive union.

Pollan's Mercury conjuncts Fox's Mercury, which suggests they can finish thoughts together and they communicate extremely well on exactly the same level. However, perfect communication can be a double-edged sword. At times when they're tired or tense, they have to be twice as careful not to unintentionally spout hurtful words, which will invariably hit home.

It's not surprising that Fox's Mercury conjuncts Pollan's Venus, which implies that art and life potentially become one in this union. This couple tends to communicate deep emotional thoughts and creative interests to each other freely and frequently.

As we mentioned before, the Judaic astrologer would've suggested moving the couple's mid-July wedding date to the next month, Ellul (late August to late September), which is considered by Orthodox Jews to be an optimal time for nuptials. There are a number of days in that month that both the Chinese and Hindu astrologers would've also approved.

The Western View

Another thumbs-up would come from the Western astrologer, who'd agree with the Judaic practitioner's assessment of the couple's many planetary conjunctions, the placements of Venus and Jupiter in Fox's birth chart, plus the positive rulership of Fox's seventh house. There are a few more components that would bolster the Western astrologer's support as well.

In Fox's Western birth chart (fig. 14), the Moon (☽) occupies the second house (2) in Taurus (♉) (see page 295). This suggests Fox is driven by love, marriage, and friendship. It also implies that his financial life is aided by the opposite sex, as he experiences financial gain through women.

From a Celtic perspective, the Moon in the lunar month of the Hawthorn (see page 283) cautions that Fox might find it difficult to establish a relationship because he never stays in one place long enough. He's easily bored as well. Granted, Fox moved a great deal during the first eighteen years of his life, but his film and TV commitments forced him to settle down just long enough for him to get seriously involved with Tracy Pollan. The Moon was in the lunar month of the Oak when Pollan was born, which indicates she sets very high standards for loved ones, rejecting anyone who can't live up to her ideals. It's very hard to become bored with a person like this.

Although Fox's chart indicates he was ready for marriage after his seventeenth birthday, since the planet Saturn (♄) rests in his chart's twelfth house (12) (see page 310), it also offered two cautionary notes. Saturn (♄) in Capricorn (♑) suggests he's very anxious to succeed and ultimately does. He's always needed, however, to be prudent about marriage. An unsatisfactory union would've diminished his achievements on many levels. Luckily, Fox chose wisely, selecting a partner in life whose ideals and ambitions were just as high as his own.

The other cautionary note involves the matter of communication. Since their Suns are represented by the Western elements air and water (see page 315), a practitioner would surmise two different languages are spoken between them. Fox, whose Sun is ruled by air, lives in the world of the intellect, finding it difficult to attain emotional fulfillment. Pollan, on the other hand, swims in an emotional sea ruled by water, finding it impossible to assess life as a series of logical steps. Unless other planetary forces introduce passion or stability, there is little either person can say that won't be misinterpreted. But when you consider some of the more positive influences seen among the planetary conjunctions in their Judaic charts (which would also apply in their Western charts), this singular factor causes little concern.

From a Celtic astrologer's perspective, the couple's choice of wedding date was poor (see page 320). As the old rhyme states: "Those who in July do wed, must labor for their daily bread." September or November would have been a wiser choice, offering riches and joys.

Astrosynthesis: Combining the Interpretations

The big picture we've drawn thus far looks something like this. The Chinese astrologer tells us that Fox's and Pollan's marriage starts out easy and descends into hard work during their later years, but devotion and compassion assist them through good times and bad.

According to the Hindu tradition, Fox is affectionate and supportive of his wife's dreams and ideas, despite his driven personality. Pollan, on the other hand, has very high standards for both herself and Fox on personal and professional levels.

The Judaic practitioner agrees that the couple's marriage will be close and very tender even though it may involve some obstacles or delays. The Hindu astrologer adds that Fox was ready to wed early in life and married for love, not because the arrangement was fiscally or politically acceptable. Although there was the potential for financial or sibling problems before Fox turned thirty, there's nothing to indicate that the couple couldn't handle any family situation that may have come up.

Both the Judaic and Western practitioners note that Fox and Pollan share five planetary conjunctions that potentially stimulate a strong marital relationship. Romance, sexual attraction, and strong communication keep this relationship strong and vibrant. Although Fox's Western chart cautions that his selection of a spouse was critical to his success, he chose wisely, selecting a life partner whose ideals and ambitions are set on a very high level.

The astrological consensus of Fox's marriage to Pollan is that the couple shows a strong ability to work together, achieving mutual goals with devotion and compassion. These are the sorts of qualities that make any marriage admirable.

I Did It My Way: Johnny Depp

Actor Johnny Depp has starred in the TV series *21 Jump Street* and in more than two dozen films, including *Nightmare on Elm Street, Edward Scissorhands, The Ninth Gate,* and *Chocolat.* Depp was born on **9 June 1963 at 08:44:00** A.M. **Central daylight time in Owensboro, Kentucky.** He lives with singer and actress Vanessa Paradis. Just like Michael J. Fox, Depp moved a lot as a child. His family relocated over a dozen times before settling down in Florida. His parents divorced when Depp was fifteen years old. This gave him a personal excuse to enter into a world of rock 'n' roll. Fortunately, his mother noticed that he was enthralled with music and bought him a used electric guitar. Before long, Depp joined a rock band and played in local nightclubs, even though he was still a minor. Like Fox, Depp dropped out of high school, but in his case it was to pursue a music career, which never really ignited.

Depp's big break occurred while he was briefly married to makeup artist Lori Allison. She introduced him to actor Nicolas Cage, who arranged a meeting between Depp and his agent, which yielded Depp's first acting job in the 1984 film *Nightmare on Elm Street.* In 1986, he landed a role in *Platoon,* which still left him enough time to play with his new band, the Rock City Angels. But it was his role as Detective Tom Hanson on the TV series *21 Jump Street,* from 1987 until 1990, that made him into a teen idol overnight.

In hot pursuit of a more serious career, Depp has taken on film projects including *Cry-Baby* (1990), *Edward Scissorhands* (1990), *What's Eating Gilbert Grape?* (1993), *Ed Wood* (1994), *Dead Man* (1995), *Donnie Brasco* (1997), *Fear and Loathing in Las Vegas* (1998), *The Astronaut's Wife* (1999), *Sleepy Hollow* (1999), *The Ninth Gate* (1999), and *Chocolat* (2000). He has turned down the lead roles for *Interview with a Vampire, Legends of the Fall,* and *Speed,* commenting that he didn't want to be stuck in the world of blockbuster films.

In the meantime, his personal life has been spread over the tabloids for all to see: the death of actor River Phoenix of a drug overdose at Depp's nightclub, the Viper Room; his breakup with actress

Winona Ryder after a three-year engagement; a raucous affair with model Kate Moss that led to trashed hotel rooms in New York and London on more than one occasion and a champagne bath in a British boutique hotel. (Incidentally, it takes approximately fifty bottles of bubbly to fill a tub, and their champagne bill came to $1,290.) The French singer-actress Vanessa Paradis has seemingly convinced Depp to settle down since they met, in June 1998 (she was born 22 December 1972 in St.-Maur-des-Fosses, France), and the couple had their first child, a daughter, in 1999.

As was the case with Michael J. Fox, Depp's grueling production schedule tends to overstep the boundaries most people set for marital sanity. He's been hospitalized for exhaustion thanks to his ambition, but it hasn't slowed him down. Although Michael J. Fox and Johnny Depp share the same birthday and similar careers, they've chosen very different mates. Would the Chinese, Hindu, Judaic, and Western astrologers agree that both men have chosen partners that will allow them to experience long-lasting love and true commitment?

The Chinese View

The Chinese astrologer would approve of Depp's relationship with Vanessa Paradis. Although their *ming shu* (reckoned fate) signs don't reveal their union's true strengths, their birth year *xing* (planets) and lunar month signs tell of a match filled with mutual compassion and maturity. Both Depp and Paradis possess the sort of positive traits that serve as strong building blocks for any relationship.

Born in a Water Hare year (1963) (see page 44), Depp might be considered a little dull by his ideal mate, a Fire Ram (1967). But a Wood Ram (1955) would soon discover that he's a positive influence. A Metal Dog (1970) is a strong and beneficial attraction. His sense of morals and ethics benefit from a match with someone born in 1971 (Metal Pig), which, incidentally, is the year of Winona Ryder's birth.

Vanessa Paradis was born in a Water Rat year (1972) (see page 47), which is neither perfect nor disastrous for Depp's Water Hare birth year. As with Fox and Pollan, the Chinese astrologer would find Depp's and Paradis's neutral union to be just as good as an ideal match, if the couple's birth year *xing* (planets) and lunar month signs improve their prospects.

Depp's metal birth year *xing* and Paradis's wood birth year *xing* (see page 23) indicate that this union may get off to a difficult start, but their lives together should improve gradually with age. They must learn to build their relationship on communication, respect, and trust while avoiding the urge to repeatedly put their bond under the microscope.

As with Fox, Depp's fourth lunar birth month (see page 63) suggests he's a very lovable and compassionate person who demonstrates his affections publicly. He's also supportive of his mate's dreams and ideas. He can't be pushed but he can be swayed by logical persuasion.

His traits are complemented by those of Paradis's eleventh lunar month birth. Nothing keeps her down for so long that she'd be unwilling to rise and start from the ground up again. Even when she's weathered the darkest day, she's always able to turn her love light on for her mate. Like a phoenix, she's a symbol of happiness and success. When the going gets tough, neither of them throws in the towel or points a finger in a loved one's direction.

The Hindu View

The placements of Depp's Venus and Mars give some cause for concern just as they did in Fox's case. The Hindu astrologer would also say there's great promise in his relationship with Paradis because stability and compassion are on their side.

The seventh house (VII) in Depp's *bhavacakra* (fig. 15) is ruled by Capricorn (10) (see page 101). This indicates that if he waited until his twenty-seventh birthday, he'd have a chance to attain a stable and long-lasting marriage with someone born south of his birthplace. (None of Depp's celebrity lovers were born south of his Kentucky origins.)

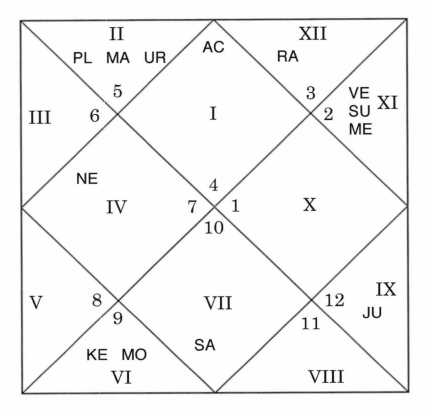

Figure 15. Johnny Depp's *Bhavacakra*.

The planet Venus (VE) occupies Taurus (2) in his *bhavacakra*'s twelfth house (XII) (see page 117), indicating that he tends to have a strong sexual appetite. He's also inclined to be very affectionate and possess deep, enduring emotions. These alleged personality assets might cause more potential problems than benefits, however, since this placement implies that women and romance create some disappointments or delays in his married life or long-term relationship.

The planet Mars (MA) resides in Leo (5) in Depp's *bhavacakra*'s second house (II) (see page 140), hinting that marital and family difficulties stem from financial worries. Although he is capable of being a very aggressive opponent, he has to apply his aptitude as a forgiving friend when money matters involve family, a lover, or a spouse.

In the same respect, Ketu (KE) in his *bhavacakra*'s sixth house (VI) (see page 148) suggests that Depp's inclined to experience difficulties with coworkers, classmates, or employees. The real trouble, however, begins when he carries his job-related frustrations home. In Depp's profession, it's difficult to mentally and emotionally "clock out." It's easier for him to remain in character throughout an entire project. Fortunately, Paradis's life as a singer, model, and actress has given her the wisdom and maturity to understand Depp's arduous business.

Depp's Moon was placed in the *naksatra* Purvasadha at his birth (see page 158), which suggests that he tends to be an outgoing, independent person, and is lucky in love. Few attributes are as attractive as self-assuredness. Since Paradis was born while the Moon was in the *naksatra* Pusya, she's inclined to be a stable, easygoing person who has a successful career and a good family life.

The Judaic View

The strengths would outweigh any weaknesses in Depp's chart in the eyes of the Judaic astrologer, who'd also approve of Depp's relationship with Vanessa Paradis. Here's a person who is capable of the sort of steadfastness and compassion that any woman could appreciate.

Depp's Judaic birth chart reveals Aquarius ($\approx$) as the ruler of his seventh house (7) (fig. 16 illustrates Johnny Depp's Western birth chart) (see page 188). This indicates he's inclined to marry more than once or not marry at all. If he does take that life-altering step again, he'll wed (or simply have a long-term committed relationship with) an unconventional mate and have an equally nonconformist union.

Just like Michael J. Fox, Depp has the planet Venus ($♀$) in Taurus ($♉$), which suggests he's inclined to be very affectionate and possess deep, enduring emotions. But like Fox, he may encounter some delays or disappointments during his marriage. But then again, who doesn't? Because Venus is situated in his chart's eleventh house (11), he potentially experiences fortunate opportunities and encounters artistic lovers. Paradis's Venus resides in Sagittarius, suggesting she's a romantic at heart. She's inclined to conduct a long-distance relationship at some point during her life. (They have homes in Paris and Los Angeles.)

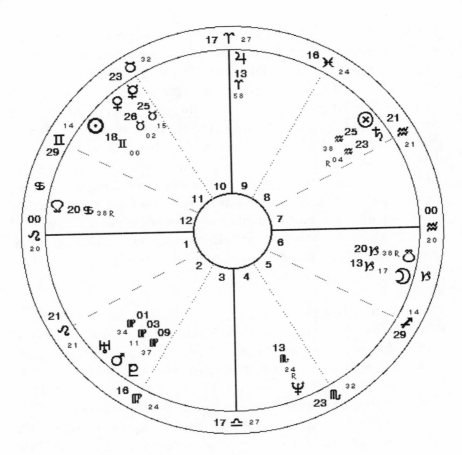

Figure 16. Johnny Depp's Birth Chart.

The planet Jupiter (♃) in Aries (♈) (see page 213) in Depp's birth chart suggests that while he's married, he may experience good fortune and business success. (Depp's first wife, Lori Allison, did introduce him to Nicolas Cage, changing his career from obscure musician to film star in one appointment. The number of roles he's taken on during the past few years has also significantly increased.)

Although this couple doesn't have as many conjunctions between their respective planets as Fox and Pollan, the two connections that exist establish a solid basis for a lasting relationship (see page 217). Depp's Sun and Paradis's Saturn potentially create the foundation for long-term stability. Both of them are very conscious of their responsibilities as a couple and as parents. Duty plays a strong role in their lives. Additionally, Depp's Moon and Paradis's Jupiter instill a strong potential for extreme trust, which is another necessary element in any good relationship.

The Western View

A Western astrologer would completely agree with the Judaic practitioner's positive assessment of this couple's planetary conjunctions, the placements of Venus and Jupiter in Depp's birth chart, and the positive rulership of Depp's seventh house. In addition, the Moon (☽) occupies Capricorn (♑) in his chart's sixth house (6) (see page 296), suggesting that Depp's relationship troubles stem from other people's perception of him. A portion of his relationship troubles also stem from his friendships with (you could even call it dependence upon) women.

From a Celtic perspective, the Moon in the lunar month of the Hawthorn (see page 283) cautions that he might find it difficult to establish a relationship because he never stays in one place long enough. Just like Michael J. Fox, Depp quickly becomes bored. Granted, Depp moved a great deal during the first eighteen years of his life, but his film and TV commitments made him settle in at least two cities for quite some time. It was long enough for him to get seriously involved with Lori Allison, Winona Ryder, Kate Moss, and Vanessa Paradis. Fortunately for him, it's hard to get bored with a person like Paradis, who maintains a certain level of emotional distance, instigating perpetual desire because she'll never allow herself to be completely conquered. Born with the Moon in the lunar month of the Elder, Paradis tends to stay on the shallow side of love's pool, never falling head over heels for anyone. Although she's honest in her relationships, her emotional involvement is never 100 percent. She's just as committed, but her commitment emerges in forms other than emotion.

The planet Saturn (♄) resides in Aquarius (♒) in Depp's chart's seventh house (7) (see page 309), gracing him with something rare and precious. It's quite possible he'll find one real romantic tie that lasts. This placement also suggests that he's ready for marriage after his thirtieth birthday. Once wedded, he might still face some marital difficulties. However, this is not unusual even in strong unions.

Since their Suns are represented by the Western elements air and fire (see page 317), the Western practitioner would surmise that Depp and Paradis are full of enthusiasm and optimism, spurring each other into a dizzying array of activities when they unite. But the encounters between Paradis's fire-based passion and somewhat illogical nature and Depp's air-based intellectual and frequently emotionless temperament can lead to frustration or exhilaration.

Astrosynthesis: Combining the Interpretations

In summary, the combined astrological profile of the relationship between Johnny Depp and Vanessa Paradis looks something like this: the Chinese astrologer sees a union that gets off to a difficult start but improves gradually with age, if they learn to build the relationship on communication, respect, and trust while avoiding the urge to spend too much time analyzing the relationship. Their lunar month signs indicate a powerful, harmonious balance between a supportive, headstrong man and an eternally optimistic and positive woman.

According to the Western astrologer, the elements that rule the couple's Suns suggest that this relationship has its fair share of enthusiasm and optimism. The Judaic astrologer tells us that both people are very conscious of their responsibilities as a couple and as parents. Duty plays a strong role in both of their lives and there's a strong potential for extreme trust.

With a touch of concern and a few prescribed remedies, the Hindu astrologer suggests that Depp entertained thoughts of marriage during his teens but would have been better off waiting until his twenty-seventh birthday to tie the knot. Then he'd have a chance to attain a stable and long-lasting marriage. The Judaic astrologer adds that he'd wed an unconventional mate and have more than one unconventional union. While he's married, he may experience good fortune and business success. The Western astrologer notes that the planet Saturn graces Depp with something rare and precious. It's quite possible he'll find one real romantic tie that lasts. This placement also suggests that he's truly ready for marriage after his thirtieth birthday. Once wedded, however, he might still face some marital difficulties.

The Judaic astrologer suggests Depp's a very affectionate person and possesses deep, enduring emotions. The Hindu astrologer tells us that this affectionate nature causes more troubles than benefits with women, especially when he's involved in a long-term relationship. The Western astrologer agrees, and suggests that he may have romantic troubles that stem from other people's perception of him. It may also emerge from his positive dependence upon women on the job.

Fortunately, the Hindu astrologer also tells us that Paradis has the wisdom to handle the mental and emotional frustrations Depp might bring home with him from the film set since she's been in similar businesses herself. Together, the couple's *naksatras* also point to a union built on overall success. The Judaic astrologer indicates that Depp encounters fortunate opportunities and artistic lovers. (Paradis became a rock star in France when she was fourteen years old.)

The astrological consensus: this match has all the maturity and exuberance that a pair of success-bound people need to maintain a solid, long-lasting union.

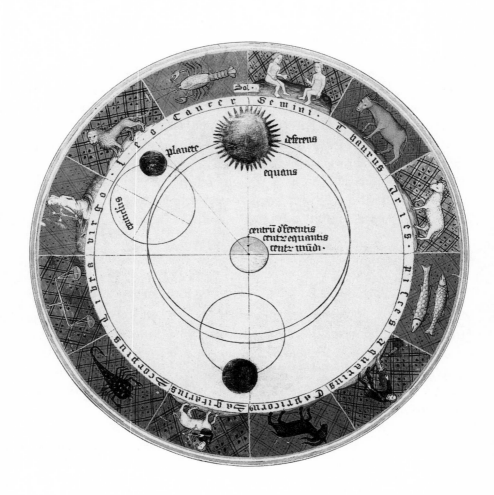

CHAPTER SEVEN

Entwined As One

WHERE TO FIND THE ANSWERS TO YOUR
ROMANCE AND MARRIAGE QUESTIONS

If love is the answer, could you rephrase the question?

—Lily Tomlin

*Y*ou've now had a chance to see what various astrological traditions can tell you about your potential love life and present (or future) relationships. We realize, however, that not everyone has the time or the inclination to seek out and synthesize all the information these four astrological methods offer. So we've designed a simpler way for you to get what you're looking for. This section provides a checklist of likely questions related to romance and marriage, and references to the chapters and sections in this book where you can find the answers.

Question	Chapter	Section	Astrological Tradition Used	Astrological Factor Used
Am I capable of being loved?	2	As the Moon Rises	Chinese	your lunar birth month
Am I destined to get married or have a long-term relationship?	4	Are You Marriage Material?	Judaic	the zodiac sign in your birth chart's seventh house
Am I sexy?	3	Where's the Romance?	Hindu	the planet Venus in your birth chart

Question	Chapter	Section	Astrological Tradition Used	Astrological Factor Used
Are my spouse (or lover) and I really compatible?	4	When Like Minds Fall in Love	Judaic	the Sun, Moon, Mercury, Jupiter, Mars, Saturn, and Venus in your and your mate's charts
Are we soulmates?	4	When Like Minds Fall in Love	Judaic	the Sun, Moon, Mercury, Jupiter, Mars, Saturn, and Venus in your and your mate's charts
Can I keep the romance alive in my marriage (or long-term relationship)?	3	Where's the Romance?	Hindu	the planet Venus in your birth chart
Can I love someone?	2	As the Moon Rises	Chinese	your lunar birth month
Do other people see me as being romantic?	3	Where's the Romance?	Hindu	the planet Venus in your birth chart
How do I fare as a potential spouse (or lover) in someone else's eyes?	3	The Matchmaker	Hindu	the Moon in your birth chart
How do my and my mate's temperaments potentially influence each other?	5	Discovering Your True Essence	Western	the Sun in your birth chart
How does my emotional makeup influence my love life?	5	Under a Celtic Moon	Western	the Moon in your birth chart

Question	Chapter	Section	Astrological Tradition Used	Astrological Factor Used
How does my general relation-ship with the opposite sex color my love life?	5	Under a Celtic Moon	Western	the Moon in your birth chart
How does my lifestyle directly affect my spouse (or lover)?	3	Carnal Knowledge	Hindu	the planet Mars in your birth chart
How does my romantic nature influence my love life?	4	Will You Feel the Earth Move?	Judaic	the planet Venus in your birth chart
How will mar-riage or a long-term relationship influence my life in general?	4	Are You Marriage Material?	Judaic	the zodiac sign in your birth chart's seventh house
What are my general ambitions and drives?	3	Carnal Knowledge	Hindu	the planet Mars in your birth chart
What are my marriage prospects?	3	Will You Ever Marry?	Hindu	your birth chart's seventh house
What aspects of my personality or lifestyle cause concern within my lover or spouse?	3	The Marriage Killer	Hindu	the Moon's South Node (also called Ketu) in your birth chart
What kind of a love life do I have?	5	Under a Celtic Moon	Western (Celtic)	the Moon in your birth chart
What kind of sex drive do I have?	3	Carnal Knowledge	Hindu	the planet Mars in your birth chart

Question	Chapter	Section	Astrological Tradition Used	Astrological Factor Used
What measure of good fortune have I been allotted in relation to my marriage (or long-term relationship)?	4	Are You Lucky in Love?	Judaic	the planet Jupiter in your birth chart
What sort of difficulties or delays do I face in my love life?	5	What Kinds of Difficulties Lie Ahead?	Western	the planet Saturn in your birth chart
What type of marriage will I have?	3	Will You Ever Marry?	Hindu	the zodiac sign in your birth chart's seventh house
What type of spouse (or lover) will I attract?	4	Are You Marriage Material?	Judaic	the zodiac sign in your birth chart's seventh house
What's my compatibility with other types of people?	2	A Match Made in Heaven	Chinese	your birth year
What's the best date for the wedding?	2	Choosing the Most Auspicious Day; As the Moon Rises	Chinese	the Moon's position on your chosen date; your lunar birth month, if you're female
	3	Choosing the Perfect Day	Hindu	the Moon's position on your chosen date
	4	Seizing the Right Day	Judaic	N/A
	5	'Tis the Season to Wed	Western	N/A

Question	Chapter	Section	Astrological Tradition Used	Astrological Factor Used
What's the potential outcome of my relationship with my spouse (or lover)?	2	Destiny's Pillars	Chinese	the birth years of you and your mate
When am I old enough to consider marriage (or a long-term relationship)?	5	What Kinds of Difficulties Lie Ahead?	Western	the planet Saturn in your birth chart
Will I get married more than once?	3	Will You Ever Marry?	Hindu	your birth chart's seventh house

As we've said before, in a complete professional consultation, an astrologer in any discipline employs dozens of calculations, charts, and years of clinical expertise in the interpretation of your and your mate's birth charts. Although we definitely encourage you to seek out a certified practitioner to guide you, we also believe that an educated astrological client is an empowered one, gaining more from a consultation than an ignorant client. Learning how the planets and their interactions influence these very critical facets of your life even on this introductory level serves to improve your comprehension of the astrologer's art.

Celebrity Birth Data

*F*or those of you who want to practice the astrological interpretation outlined in this book, we've provided the birth data for all of the 209 celebrities and public figures mentioned as examples. We've also included the names of people they've been romantically linked with who are also included in this book. The birth information provided here has been rated for accuracy using the Rodden Data Rating System as follows:

AA   birth certificate
A   memory or news report
B   bio/autobiography
C   original source isn't known
DD   data is conflicting or unverified
X   only the date was available
XX   date is in question

Isabelle Adjani
Born: 27 Jun 1955, Gennevilliers, France. Rodden Rating: C. Source: The Internet Movie Database. Romantic attachment: Daniel Day-Lewis.

Ben Affleck
Born: 15 Aug 1972, 02:53:00 A.M. PDT, Berkeley, Calif. Rodden Rating: AA. Source: Astrodatabank. Romantic attachment: Gwyneth Paltrow.

André Agassi

Born: 29 Apr 1970, Las Vegas, Nev. Rodden Rating: C. Source: Biography.com. Romantic attachments: Brooke Shields, Steffi Graf.

Christina Aguilera

Born: 18 Dec 1980, Staten Island, N.Y. Rodden Rating: C. Source: Altocelebs.com.

Woody Allen

Born: 1 Dec 1935, 10:55:00 P.M. EST, Bronx, N.Y. Rodden Rating: AA. Source: *Star*Tech #6*, 1988. Romantic attachments: Mia Farrow, Diane Keaton.

Ursula Andress

Born: 19 Mar 1936, Bern, Switzerland. Rodden Rating: C. Source: The Internet Movie Database. Romantic attachment: John Derek.

Jennifer Aniston

Born: 11 Feb 1969, Sherman Oaks, Calif. Rodden Rating: C. Source: Biography.com. Romantic attachment: Brad Pitt.

Anthony Armstrong-Jones

Born: 7 Mar 1930, London, U.K. Rodden Rating: C. Source: *Chambers Biographical Dictionary*. Romantic attachment: Princess Margaret Windsor.

Courteney Cox Arquette

Born: 15 Jun 1964, Birmingham, Ala. Rodden Rating: C. Source: Biography.com. Romantic attachment: David Arquette.

David Arquette

Born: 8 Sep 1971, Winchester, W.V. Rodden Rating: C. Source: The Internet Movie Database. Romantic attachment: Courteney Cox Arquette.

Patricia Arquette

Born: 8 Apr 1968, Chicago, Ill. Rodden Rating: C. Source: The Internet Movie Database. Romantic attachment: Nicolas Cage.

Lauren Bacall

Born: 16 Sep 1924, 02:00:00 A.M. EDT, New York, N.Y. Rodden Rating: A. Source: *Profiles of Women*, 1979. Romantic attachment: Humphrey Bogart.

Barbara Bach

Born: 27 Aug 1947, New York, N.Y. Rodden Rating: C. Source: The Internet Movie Database. Romantic attachment: Ringo Starr.

Burt Bacharach

Born: 12 May 1929, Kansas City, Mo. Rodden Rating: C. Source: Biography.com. Romantic attachment: Angie Dickinson.

Kevin Bacon

Born: 8 Jul 1958, Philadelphia, Pa. Rodden Rating: C. Source: Biography.com. Romantic attachment: Kyra Sedgwick.

Alec Baldwin

Born: 3 Apr 1958, Amityville, N.Y. Rodden Rating: C. Source: Biography.com. Romantic attachment: Kim Basinger.

Antonio Banderas

Born: 10 Aug 1960, 09:00:00 CET, Malaga, Spain. Rodden Rating: AA. Source: *Data News #64*. Romantic attachment: Melanie Griffith.

Brigitte Bardot

Born: 28 Sep 1934, 01:15:00 P.M. GMD, Paris, France. Rodden Rating: B. Source: *Profiles of Women, 1979*. Romantic attachment: Roger Vadim.

Drew Barrymore

Born: 22 Feb 1975, 11:51:00 A.M. PST, Culver City, Calif. Rodden Rating: AA. Source: Astrodatabank. Romantic attachment: Tom Green.

Kim Basinger

Born: 8 Dec 1953, 12:00:00 P.M. EST, Athens, Ga. Rodden Rating: C. Source: *Current Biography*. Romantic attachment: Alec Baldwin.

Warren Beatty

Born: 30 Mar 1937, 05:30:00 P.M. EST, Richmond, Va. Rodden Rating: AA. Source: *American Book of Charts, 1980*. Romantic attachments: Julie Christie, Annette Bening, Diane Keaton.

Eric Benét

Born: 15 Oct 1966, Milwaukee, Wis. Rodden Rating: C. Source: *Celebrity Birthdays A2Z*. Romantic attachment: Halle Berry.

Annette Bening

Born: 29 May 1958, Topeka, Kans. Rodden Rating: C. Source: Biography.com. Romantic attachment: Warren Beatty.

Richard Benjamin

Born: 22 May 1938, New York, N.Y. Rodden Rating: C. Source: The Internet Movie Database. Romantic attachment: Paula Prentiss.

Candice Bergen
Born: 8 May 1946, 09:52:00 P.M. PST, Los Angeles, Calif. Rodden Rating: AA. Source: *Gauquelin Book of American Charts,* 1982. Romantic attachment: Louis Malle.

Halle Berry
Born: 14 Aug 1966, Cleveland, Ohio. Rodden Rating: C. Source: Biography.com. Romantic attachment: Eric Benét.

Valerie Bertinelli
Born: 23 Apr 1960, Wilmington, Del. Rodden Rating: C. Source: The Internet Movie Database. Romantic attachment: Eddie Van Halen.

Humphrey Bogart
Born: 23 Jan 1899, 01:40:00 P.M. EST, New York, N.Y. Rodden Rating: C. Source: Astropro.com. Romantic attachment: Lauren Bacall.

Lisa Bonet
Born: 16 Nov 1967, San Francisco, Calif. Rodden Rating: C. Source: The Internet Movie Database. Romantic attachment: Lenny Kravitz.

Helena Bonham Carter
Born: 26 May 1966, London, U.K. Rodden Rating: C. Source: The Internet Movie Database. Romantic attachment: Kenneth Branagh.

Sonny Bono
Born: 16 Feb 1935, Detroit, Mich. Rodden Rating: C. Source: The Internet Movie Database. Romantic attachment: Cher.

David Bowie
Born: 8 Jan 1947, 11:50:00 P.M. GMT, Brixton, U.K. Rodden Rating: B. Source: *American Book of Charts,* 1980. Romantic attachment: Iman Abdul Majid.

Patti Boyd
Born: 17 Mar 1945, Somerset, U.K. Rodden Rating: C. Source: The Internet Movie Database. Romantic attachments: George Harrison, Eric Clapton.

Kenneth Branagh
Born: 10 Dec 1960, Belfast, Northern Ireland. Rodden Rating: C. Source: Biography.com. Romantic attachments: Emma Thompson, Helena Bonham Carter.

Benjamin Bratt

Born: 16 Dec 1963, San Francisco, Calif. Rodden Rating: C. Source: Biography.com. Romantic attachment: Julia Roberts.

Matthew Broderick

Born: 21 Mar 1962, New York, N.Y. Rodden Rating: C. Source: The Internet Movie Database. Romantic attachment: Sarah Jessica Parker.

Garth Brooks

Born: 7 Feb 1962, Yukon, Okla. Rodden Rating: C. Source: The Internet Movie Database.

James Brolin

Born: 18 Jul 1941, Los Angeles, Calif. Rodden Rating: C. Source: The Internet Movie Database. Romantic attachment: Barbra Streisand.

Helen Gurley Brown

Born: 18 Feb 1922, 03:00:00 A.M. CST, Green Forest, Ark. Rodden Rating: C. Source: The Internet Movie Database.

Bebe Buell

Born: 14 Jul 1953, Portsmouth, Va. Rodden Rating: C. Source: The Internet Movie Database. Romantic attachments: Steven Tyler, Todd Rundgren.

Barbara Bush

Born: 8 Jun 1925, 07:00:00 P.M. EDT, Rye N.Y. Rodden Rating: A. Source: *The International Astrologer*, vol. XXX, no. 1. Romantic attachment: George H. Bush.

George H. Bush

Born: 12 Jun 1924, 11:45:00 A.M. EDT, Milton, Mass. Rodden Rating: A. Source: *The International Astrologer*, vol. XXX, no. 1. Romantic attachment: Barbara Bush.

George W. Bush

Born: 6 Jul 1946, 07:26:00 A.M. EDT, New Haven, CT; Rodden Rating: AA; Source: *The Mountain Astrologer* #96. Romantic Attachment: Laura Bush.

Laura Bush

Born: 4 Nov. 1946, Midland, Tex. Rodden Rating: C. Source: *The International Astrologer*, vol. XXX, no. 1. Romantic attachment: George W. Bush.

Richard Burton
Born: 10 Nov 1925, 02:30:00 P.M. GMT, Pontrhydfen, U.K. Rodden Rating: C. Source: *AstroCarto*Graphy Book of Maps*, 1989. Romantic attachment: Elizabeth Taylor.

Nicolas Cage
Born: 7 Jan 1964, Long Beach, Calif. Rodden Rating: C. Source: Biography.com. Romantic attachment: Patricia Arquette.

Sir Michael Caine
Born: 14 Mar 1933, 10:00:00 A.M. GMT, London, U.K. Rodden Rating: B. Source: *Star*Tech #2*, 1988. Romantic attachment: Shakira Caine.

Shakira Caine
Born: 23 Feb 1947, Guyana. Rodden Rating: C. Source: The Internet Movie Database. Romantic attachment: Michael Caine.

Kate Capshaw
Born: 3 Nov 1953, Fort Worth, Tex. Rodden Rating: C. Source: Biography.com. Romantic attachment: Steven Spielberg.

Cher
Born: 20 May 1946, 07:31:00 A.M. PST, El Centro, Calif. Rodden Rating: A. Source: *Star*Tech #6*, 1988. Romantic attachment: Sonny Bono.

Amy Chow
Born: 15 May 1978. Rodden Rating: X. Source: Infoplease.com.

Julie Christie
Born: 14 Apr 1941, 10:00:00 A.M. LST, Shillong, India. Rodden Rating: C. Source: *Profiles of Women*, 1979. Romantic attachment: Warren Beatty.

Eric Clapton
Born: 30 Mar 1945, 08:45:00 P.M. GMD, Ripley, U.K. Rodden Rating: DD. Source: *Astrological Association Newsletter #1–2*, 1991. Romantic attachment: Patti Boyd.

Bill Clinton
Born: 19 Aug 1946, 08:51:00 A.M. CST, Hope, Ark, Rodden Rating: A. Source: Astrodatabank. Romantic attachment: Hillary Rodham Clinton.

Hillary Rodham Clinton
Born: 26 Oct 1947, 08:00:00 P.M. CST, Chicago, Ill. Rodden Rating: B. Source: Astrodatabank. Romantic attachment: Bill Clinton.

Kurt Cobain

Born: 20 Feb 1967, 07:20:00 P.M. PST, Aberdeen, Wash. Rodden Rating: C. Source: *Data News #80*. Romantic attachment: Courtney Love.

Sean "Puffy" Combs

Born: 4 Nov 1970, New York, N.Y. Rodden Rating: C. Source: Biography.com. Romantic attachment: Jennifer Lopez.

Tom Cruise

Born: 3 Jul 1962, Syracuse, N.Y. Rodden Rating: C. Source: Biography. com. Romantic attachment: Nicole Kidman.

Macaulay Culkin

Born: 26 Aug 1980, New York, N.Y. Rodden Rating: C. Source: Astronet.com. Romantic attachment: Rachel Miner Culkin.

Rachel Miner Culkin

Born: 19 Jul 1980, Connecticut. Rodden Rating: C. Source: The Internet Movie Database. Romantic attachment: Macaulay Culkin.

Claire Danes

Born: 12 Apr 1979, New York, N.Y. Rodden Rating: C. Source: The Internet Movie Database.

Ray Davies

Born: 23 Jun 1944, 02:00:00 A.M. CEW, London, U.K. Rodden Rating: A. Source: *Astro-Data #3*, 1986. Romantic attachment: Chrissie Hynde.

Daniel Day-Lewis

Born: 20 Apr 1957, London, U.K. Rodden Rating: C. Source: The Internet Movie Database. Romantic attachment: Isabelle Adjani.

Ellen DeGeneres

Born: 26 Jan 1958, Metarie, La. Rodden Rating: C. Source: Astronet.com. Romantic attachment: Anne Heche.

Catherine Deneuve

Born: 22 Oct 1943, 01:35:00 P.M. GMD, Paris, France. Rodden Rating: AA. Source: *New Birth Data Series*, vol. 3, 1984. Romantic attachment: Roger Vadim.

Johnny Depp

Born: 9 Jun 1963, 08:44:00 A.M. CST, Owensboro, Ky. Rodden Rating: A. Source: *Dell Horoscope*. Romantic attachments: Vanessa Paradis, Winona Ryder, Kate Moss.

Bo Derek
Born: 20 Nov 1956, 02:13:00 P.M. PST, Long Beach, Calif. Rodden Rating: AA. Source: *Astro-Data #3*, 1986. Romantic attachments: John Derek.

John Derek
Born: 12 Aug 1926, 01:20:00 P.M. PST, Hollywood, Calif. Rodden Rating: AA. Source: *American Book of Charts*, 1980. Romantic attachments: Ursula Andress, Linda Evans, Bo Derek.

Leonardo DiCaprio
Born: 11 Nov 1974, Hollywood, Calif. Rodden Rating: C. Source: The Internet Movie Database.

Angie Dickinson
Born: 30 Sep 1931, Kulm, N.D. Rodden Rating: C. Source: Biography.com. Romantic attachment: Burt Bacharach.

Michael Douglas
Born: 25 Sep 1944, 10:30:00 A.M. EWT, New Brunswick, N.J. Rodden Rating: AA. Source: *Star*Tech #6*, 1988. Romantic attachment: Catherine Zeta-Jones.

David Duchovny
Born: 7 Aug 1960, New York, N.Y. Rodden Rating: C. Source: Biography.com. Romantic attachment: Téa Leoni.

Britt Ekland
Born: 6 Oct 1942, Stockholm, Sweden. Rodden Rating: C. Source: The Internet Movie Database. Romantic attachment: Peter Sellers.

Linda Evans
Born: 18 Nov 1947, Hartford, Conn. Rodden Rating: C. Source: The Internet Movie Database. Romantic attachment: John Derek.

Mia Farrow
Born: 9 Feb 1945, 11:27:00 A.M. PWT, Los Angeles, Calif. Rodden Rating: AA. Source: *Gauquelin Book of American Charts*, 1982. Romantic attachment: Woody Allen.

Carrie Fisher
Born: 21 Oct 1956, 12:49:00 P.M. PST, Burbank, Calif. Rodden Rating: AA. Source: *Astro-Data #3*, 1986.

Eddie Fisher

Born: 10 Aug 1928, Philadelphia, Pa. Rodden Rating: C. Source: The Internet Movie Database. Romantic attachment: Elizabeth Taylor, Debbie Reynolds.

Calista Flockhart

Born: 11 Nov 1964, Freeport, Ill. Rodden Rating: C. Source: Astronet.com. Romantic attachment: Ben Stiller.

Bridget Fonda

Born: 27 Jan 1964, 03:45:00 A.M. PST, Los Angeles, Calif. Rodden Rating: A. Source: *American Book of Charts*, 1980. Romantic attachment: Dwight Yoakam.

Jane Fonda

Born: 21 Dec 1937, 07:57:00 P.M. EST, New York, N.Y. Rodden Rating: A. Source: *Profiles of Women*, 1979. Romantic attachments: Roger Vadim, Ted Turner.

Harrison Ford

Born: 13 Jul 1942, 11:41:00 A.M. CWT, Chicago, Ill. Rodden Rating: AA. Source: *Astro-Data #3*, 1986. Romantic attachment: Melissa Mathison.

Larry Fortensky

Born: Jan 1952. Rodden Rating: C. Source: *Celebrity Birthdays A2Z*. Romantic attachment: Elizabeth Taylor.

Michael J. Fox

Born: 9 Jun 1961, 00:12:00 A.M. MST, Edmonton, Canada. Rodden Rating: B. Source: Astrodatabank. Romantic attachment: Tracy Pollan.

Mayte Garcia

Born: 12 Nov 1973, Puerto Rico. Rodden Rating: C. Source: *Hundalasiliah!* Romantic attachment: Prince.

Bill Gates

Born: 28 Oct 1955, 10:00:00 P.M. PST, Seattle, Wash. Rodden Rating: C. Source: Astrodatabank.com.

Mikhail Gorbachev

Born: 2 Mar 1931, 12:00:00 P.M. BGT, Privolnoje, U.S.S.R. Rodden Rating: B. Source: *Current Biography*, 1985. Romantic attachment: Raisa Gorbachev.

Raisa Gorbachev
Born: 5 Jan 1932. Rodden Rating: X. Source: *Celebrity Birthdays A2Z*.
Romantic attachment: Mikhail Gorbachev.

Al Gore
Born: 31 Mar 1948, 06:20:00 P.M. EST, Washington, D.C. Rodden Rating: AA. Source: Astrodatabank. Romantic attachment: Tipper Gore.

Tipper Gore
Born: 19 Aug 1948, 02:40:00 A.M. EDT, Washington, D.C. Rodden Rating: A. Source: Astrodatabank. Romantic attachment: Al Gore.

Elliot Gould
Born: 29 Aug 1938, New York, N.Y. Rodden Rating: C. Source: The Internet Movie Database. Romantic attachment: Barbra Streisand.

Steffi Graf
Born: 14 Jun 1969, 04:40:00 A.M. CET, Mannheim, Germany. Rodden Rating: AA. Source: *Data News #16*. Romantic attachment: André Agassi.

Hugh Grant
Born: 9 Sep 1960, London, U.K. Rodden Rating: C. Source: Biography.com. Romantic attachment: Elizabeth Hurley.

Tom Green
Born: 30 Jul 1971, Pembroke, Ontario, Canada. Rodden Rating: C. Source: The Internet Movie Database. Romantic attachment: Drew Barrymore.

Melanie Griffith
Born: 9 Aug 1957, 11:49:00 P.M. EDT, New York, N.Y. Rodden Rating: A. Source: *Data News #64*. Romantic attachments: Antonio Banderas, Don Johnson.

Lukas Haas
Born: 16 Apr 1976, West Hollywood, Calif. Rodden Rating: C. Source: The Internet Movie Database. Romantic attachment: Natalie Portman.

Jerry Hall
Born: 2 Jul 1956, Mesquite, Tex. Rodden Rating: C. Source: The Internet Movie Database. Romantic attachment: Mick Jagger.

Daryl Hannah
Born: 13 Dec 1960, Chicago, Ill. Rodden Rating: C. Source: Astronet.com. Romantic attachment: John F. Kennedy Jr.

Taylor Hanson

Born: 14 Mar 1983, Tulsa, Okla. Rodden Rating: X. Source: Xtreme Musician.com.

Zac Hanson

Born: 22 Oct 1985, Tulsa, Okla. Rodden Rating: C. Source: Xtreme Musician.com.

George Harrison

Born: 25 Feb 1943, 11:42:00 P.M. GDT, Liverpool, U.K. Rodden Rating: A. Source: Astrodatabank. Romantic attachment: Patti Boyd.

Ethan Hawke

Born: 6 Nov 1970, Austin, Tex. Rodden Rating: C. Source: The Internet Movie Database. Romantic attachment: Uma Thurman.

Goldie Hawn

Born: 21 Nov 1945, 09:30:00 A.M. EST, Washington, D.C. Rodden Rating: A. Source: *Profiles of Women,* 1979. Romantic attachment: Kurt Russell.

Salma Hayek

Born: 2 Sep 1966, Coatzacoalcos, Mexico. Rodden Rating: C. Source: Astronet.com. Romantic attachment: Edward Norton.

Anne Heche

Born: 25 May 1969, Aurora, Ohio. Rodden Rating: C. Source: Astronet.com. Romantic attachment: Ellen DeGeneres.

Katharine Hepburn

Born: 12 May 1907, 05:47:00 P.M. EDT, Hartford, Conn. Rodden Rating: C. Source: AdZe MiXXe. Romantic attachment: Spencer Tracy.

Nicky Hilton

Born: 6 Jul 1926. Rodden Rating: X. Source: Dr. Nack's Cultural Calendar. Romantic attachment: Elizabeth Taylor.

Peter Horton

Born: 20 Aug 1953, Bellevue, Wash. Rodden Rating: C. Source: The Internet Movie Database. Romantic attachment: Michelle Pfeiffer.

Elizabeth Hurley

Born: 10 Jun 1965, Hampshire, U.K. Rodden Rating: C. Source: The Internet Movie Database. Romantic attachment: Hugh Grant.

Anjelica Huston
Born: 8 Jul 1951, Los Angeles, Calif. Rodden Rating: C. Source: Biography.com. Romantic attachment: Jack Nicholson.

Chrissie Hynde
Born: 7 Sep 1951, Akron, Ohio. Rodden Rating: C. Source: Biography.com. Romantic attachment: Ray Davies.

Amy Irving
Born: 10 Sep 1953, Palo Alto, Calif. Rodden Rating: C. Source: The Internet Movie Database. Romantic attachment: Steven Spielberg.

Mick Jagger
Born: 26 Jul 1943, Dartford, U.K. Rodden Rating: C. Source: Biography.com. Romantic attachment: Jerry Hall.

Don Johnson
Born: 15 Dec 1949, Flat Creek, Mo. Rodden Rating: C. Source: The Internet Movie Database. Romantic attachment: Melanie Griffith.

Angelina Jolie
Born: 4 Jun 1975, Los Angeles, Calif. Rodden Rating: C. Source: Biography.com. Romantic attachment: Billy Bob Thornton.

Grace Jones
Born: 19 May 1952, Spanishtown, Jamaica. Rodden Rating: C. Source: The Internet Movie Database.

Quincy Jones
Born: 14 Mar 1933, Chicago, Ill. Rodden Rating: C. Source: Biography.com. Romantic attachment: Nastassja Kinski.

Diane Keaton
Born: 5 Jan 1946, 02:53:00 A.M. PST, Los Angeles, Calif. Rodden Rating: C. Source: *Celebrity Birthdays A2Z*. Romantic attachments: Woody Allen, Warren Beatty.

Carolyn Bessette Kennedy
Born: 7 Jan 1966, 08:45:00 A.M. EST, White Plains, N.Y. Rodden Rating: A. Source: Astrodatabank. Romantic attachment: John F. Kennedy Jr.

John F. Kennedy Jr.
Born: 25 Nov 1960, 00:22:00 A.M. EST, Washington, D.C. Rodden Rating:

A. Source: *Astro-Data #3*, 1986. Romantic attachments: Carolyn Bessette Kennedy, Daryl Hannah.

Nicole Kidman
Born: 21 Jun 1967, Honolulu, Hawaii. Rodden Rating: C. Source: Biography.com. Romantic attachment: Tom Cruise.

Coretta Scott King
Born: 27 Apr 1927, Marion, Ala. Rodden Rating: C. Source: Biography.com. Romantic attachment: the Reverend Dr. Martin Luther King Jr.

Reverend Dr. Martin Luther King Jr.
Born: 15 Jan 1929, 11:21:00 A.M. EST, Atlanta, Ga. Rodden Rating: DD. Source: *American Book of Charts*, 1980. Romantic attachment: Coretta Scott King.

Nastassja Kinski
Born: 24 Jan 1960, Berlin, Germany. Rodden Rating: C. Source: The Internet Movie Database. Romantic attachment: Quincy Jones.

Lenny Kravitz
Born: 26 May 1964, New York, N.Y. Rodden Rating: C. Source: Astronet.com. Romantic attachment: Lisa Bonet.

Simon LeBon
Born: 27 Oct 1958. Rodden Rating: X. Source: *Celebrity Birthdays A2Z*. Romantic attachment: Yasmin Parvaneh LeBon.

Yasmin Parvaneh LeBon
Born: 29 Oct 1964. Rodden Rating: X. Source: *Celebrity Birthdays A2Z*. Romantic attachment: Simon LeBon.

Pamela Anderson Lee
Born: 1 Jul 1967, 04:08:00 A.M. PDT, Ladysmith, Canada. Rodden Rating: B. Source: *Data News #60*, 1996. Romantic attachment: Tommy Lee.

Tommy Lee
Born: 13 Oct 1962, Athens, Greece. Rodden Rating: C. Source: *Celebrity Birthdays A2Z*. Romantic attachments: Pamela Anderson Lee, Heather Locklear.

John Lennon
Born: 9 Oct 1940, 06:30:00 P.M. GMD, Liverpool, U.K. Rodden Rating: A. Source: Astropro.com. Romantic attachment: Yoko Ono.

Téa Leoni
Born: 25 Feb 1966, New York, N.Y. Rodden Rating: C. Source: The Internet Movie Database. Romantic attachment: David Duchovny.

Juliette Lewis
Born: 21 Jun 1973, Los Angeles, Calif. Rodden Rating: C. Source: The Internet Movie Database. Romantic attachment: Brad Pitt.

Heather Locklear
Born: 25 Sep 1961, 05:40:00 P.M. PST, Los Angeles, Calif. Rodden Rating: X. Source: *Data News*, 1995. Romantic attachments: Richie Sambora, Tommy Lee.

Jennifer Lopez
Born: 24 Jul 1970, Bronx, N.Y. Rodden Rating: C. Source: Biography.com. Romantic attachment: Sean "Puffy" Combs.

Courtney Love
Born: 9 Jul 1964, 02:08:00 P.M. PDT, San Francisco, Calif. Rodden Rating: C. Source: *Data News #80*. Romantic attachment: Kurt Cobain.

Madonna
Born: 16 Aug 1958, 07:05:00 A.M. EST, Bay City, Mich. Rodden Rating: AA. Source: *Data News #64*. Romantic attachment: Sean Penn.

Iman Abdul Majid
Born: 25 Jul 1955, Mogandishu, Somalia. Rodden Rating: C. Source: The Internet Movie Database. Romantic attachment: David Bowie.

Louis Malle
Born: 30 Oct 1932, Thumeries, France. Rodden Rating: C. Source: Biography.com. Romantic attachment: Candice Bergen.

Marilyn Manson
Born: 5 Jan 1969, Canton, Ohio. Rodden Rating: C. Source: The Internet Movie Database. Romantic attachment: Rose McGowan.

Marla Maples
Born: 27 Oct 1963, Dalton, Ga. Rodden Rating: C. Source: The Internet Movie Database. Romantic attachment: Donald Trump.

Melissa Mathison
Born: 3 Jun 1950, Los Angeles, Calif. Rodden Rating: C. Source: The Internet Movie Database. Romantic attachment: Harrison Ford.

Linda Eastman McCartney

Born: 24 Sep 1941, New York, N.Y. Rodden Rating: C. Source: The Internet Movie Database. Romantic attachment: Sir Paul McCartney.

Sir Paul McCartney

Born: 18 Jun 1942, Liverpool, U.K. Rodden Rating: C. Source: Biography.com. Romantic attachment: Linda Eastman McCartney.

Rose McGowan

Born: 5 Sep 1975, Florence, Italy. Rodden Rating: C. Source: The Internet Movie Database. Romantic attachment: Marilyn Manson.

Bob Moffatt

Born: 8 Mar 1984, Victoria, Canada. Rodden Rating: C. Source: TeenCelebsPlus.com.

Clint Moffatt

Born: 8 Mar 1984, Victoria, Canada. Rodden Rating: C. Source: TeenCelebsPlus.com.

Dave Moffatt

Born: 8 Mar 1984, Victoria, Canada. Rodden Rating: C. Source: TeenCelebsPlus.com.

Demi Moore

Born: 11 Nov 1962, Roswell, N.M. Rodden Rating: C. Source: Biography.com. Romantic attachment: Bruce Willis.

Kate Moss

Born: 16 Jan 1974, Croydon, U.K. Rodden Rating: C. Source: The Internet Movie Database. Romantic attachment: Johnny Depp.

Mike Nichols

Born: 6 Nov 1931, Berlin, Germany. Rodden Rating: C. Source: Biography.com. Romantic attachment: Diane Sawyer.

Jack Nicholson

Born: 22 Apr 1937, 11:00:00 A.M. EDT, Neptune, N.J. Rodden Rating: A. Source: *American Book of Charts*, 1980. Romantic attachment: Anjelica Huston.

Edward Norton

Born: 18 Aug 1969, Boston, Mass. Rodden Rating: C. Source: Biography.com. Romantic attachment: Salma Hayek.

Ashley Olsen
Born: 13 Jun 1986, Sherman Oaks, Calif. Rodden Rating: C. Source: The Internet Movie Database.

Mary-Kate Olsen
Born: 13 Jun 1986, Sherman Oaks, Calif. Rodden Rating: C. Source: The Internet Movie Database.

Athina Onassis Roussel
Born: 28 Jan 1985. Rodden Rating: X. Source: UltimateItalian.com

Yoko Ono
Born: 18 Feb 1933, Tokyo, Japan. Rodden Rating: C. Source: Biography.com. Romantic attachment: John Lennon.

Ozzy Osbourne
Born: 3 Dec 1948, Aston, U.K. Rodden Rating: C. Source: Xtreme Musician.com. Romantic attachment: Sharon Osbourne.

Sharon Osbourne
Born: 1956, England. Rodden Rating: C. Source: GroupieCentral.com. Romantic attachment: Ozzy Osbourne.

Gwyneth Paltrow
Born: 28 Sep 1972, Los Angeles, Calif. Rodden Rating: C. Source: Biography.com. Romantic attachments: Brad Pitt, Ben Affleck.

Vanessa Paradis
Born: 22 Dec 1972, St.-Maur-des-Fossés, France. Rodden Rating: C. Source: The Internet Movie Database. Romantic attachment: Johnny Depp.

Sarah Jessica Parker
Born: 25 Mar 1965, Nelsonville, Ohio. Rodden Rating: C. Source: The Internet Movie Database. Romantic attachment: Matthew Broderick.

Sean Penn
Born: 17 Aug 1960, Burbank, Calif. Rodden Rating: C. Source: Biography. com. Romantic attachment: Madonna.

Michelle Pfeiffer
Born: 29 Apr 1958, 08:11:00 A.M. PDT, Santa Ana, Calif. Rodden Rating: A. Source: *Astro-Data #3*, 1986. Romantic attachment: Peter Horton.

Brad Pitt
Born: 18 Dec 1963, 06:00:00 A.M. CST, Shawnee, Okla. Rodden Rating: C.

Source: The Internet Movie Database. Romantic attachment: Jennifer Aniston, Gwyneth Paltrow, Juliette Lewis.

Tracy Pollan

Born: 22 Jun 1960, Long Island, N.Y. Rodden Rating: C. Source: The Internet Movie Database. Romantic attachment: Michael J. Fox.

Natalie Portman

Born: 9 Jun 1981, Jerusalem, Israel. Rodden Rating: C. Source: The Internet Movie Database. Romantic attachment: Lukas Haas.

Paula Prentiss

Born: 4 Mar 1939, San Antonio, Tex. Rodden Rating: C. Source: The Internet Movie Database. Romantic attachment: Richard Benjamin.

Elvis Presley

Born: 8 Jan 1935, 04:35:00 A.M. CST, Tupelo, Miss. Rodden Rating: AA. Source: *American Book of Charts,* 1980. Romantic attachment: Priscilla Beaulieu Presley.

Priscilla Beaulieu Presley

Born: 24 May 1945, Brooklyn, N.Y. Rodden Rating: C. Source: Biography.com. Romantic attachment: Elvis Presley.

Kelly Preston

Born: 13 Oct 1962, Honolulu, Hawaii. Rodden Rating: C. Source: The Internet Movie Database. Romantic attachment: John Travolta.

Prince

Born: 7 Jun 1958, 06:17:00 P.M. CDT, South Minneapolis, Minn. Rodden Rating: C. Source: *Dell Horoscope* supplement, 1985. Romantic attachments: Vanity, Mayte Garcia.

Dennis Quaid

Born: 9 Apr 1954, Houston, Tex. Rodden Rating: C. Source: Biography.com. Romantic attachment: Meg Ryan.

Debbie Reynolds

Born: 1 Apr 1932, 05:29:00 P.M. MST, El Paso, Tex. Rodden Rating: AA. Source: *Profiles of Women,* 1979. Romantic attachment: Eddie Fisher.

Naya Rivera

Born: 12 Jan 1987. Rodden Rating: X. Source: Daily Almanacs.com.

Tim Robbins
Born: 16 Oct 1958, West Covina, Calif. Rodden Rating: C. Source: *Celebrity Birthdays A2Z*. Romantic attachment: Susan Sarandon.

Julia Roberts
Born: 28 Oct 1967, 12:16:00 A.M., Atlanta, Ga. Rodden Rating: AA. Source: Astrodatabank. Romantic attachment: Benjamin Bratt.

Isabella Rossellini
Born: 18 Jun 1952, Rome, Italy. Rodden Rating: C. Source: The Internet Movie Database.

Todd Rundgren
Born: 22 Jun 1948, Philadelphia, Pa. Rodden Rating: C. Source: The Internet Movie Database. Romantic attachment: Bebe Buell.

Kurt Russell
Born: 17 Mar 1951, 10:42:00 A.M. EST, Springfield, Mass. Rodden Rating: AA. Source: *Gauquelin Book of American Charts*, 1982. Romantic attachment: Goldie Hawn.

Meg Ryan
Born: 19 Nov 1961, Fairfield, Conn. Rodden Rating: C. Source: Biography.com. Romantic attachment: Dennis Quaid.

Winona Ryder
Born: 29 Oct 1971, Winona, Minn. Rodden Rating: C. Source: Biography.com. Romantic attachment: Johnny Depp.

Richie Sambora
Born: 11 Jul 1959, 07:33:00 A.M. EDT, Perth Amboy, N.J. Rodden Rating: X. Source: *Data News*, 1995. Romantic attachment: Heather Locklear.

Susan Sarandon
Born: 4 Oct 1946, New York, N.Y. Rodden Rating: C. Source: Biography.com. Romantic attachment: Tim Robbins.

Diane Sawyer
Born: 22 Dec 1945, Glasgow, Ky. Rodden Rating: C. Source: Biography.com. Romantic attachment: Mike Nichols.

Arnold Schwarzenegger
Born: 30 Jul 1947, 04:10:00 CED, Graz, Austria. Rodden Rating: A. Source: *American Book of Charts*, 1980. Romantic attachment: Maria Shriver.

Kyra Sedgwick
Born: 19 Aug 1965, New York, N.Y. Rodden Rating: C. Source: The Internet Movie Database. Romantic attachment: Kevin Bacon.

Peter Sellers
Born: 8 Sep 1925, Southsea, U.K. Rodden Rating: C. Source: The Internet Movie Database. Romantic attachment: Britt Ekland.

Brooke Shields
Born: 31 May 1965, 01:45:00 P.M. EDT, New York, N.Y. Rodden Rating: B. Source: *American Book of Charts*, 1980. Romantic attachment: André Agassi.

Maria Shriver
Born: 6 Nov 1955, 05:12:00 P.M. CST, Chicago, Ill. Rodden Rating: C. Source: *Profiles of Women*, 1979. Romantic attachment: Arnold Schwarzenegger.

Nicole Brown Simpson
Born: 19 May 1959, West Germany. Rodden Rating: C. Source: *Celebrity Birthdays A2Z*. Romantic attachment: O. J. Simpson.

O. J. Simpson
Born: 9 Jul 1947, 08:08:00 A.M. PST, San Francisco, Calif. Rodden Rating: AA. Source: *Gauquelin Book of American Charts*, 1982. Romantic attachment: Nicole Brown Simpson.

Jada Pinkett Smith
Born: 18 Sep 1971, Baltimore, Md. Rodden Rating: C. Source: Biography.com. Romantic attachment: Will Smith.

Jamie Renée Smith
Born: 10 Apr 1987. Rodden Rating: X. Source: The Internet Movie Database.

Kim Smith
Born: 2 Mar 1983, Houston, Tex. Rodden Rating: C. Source: Kim Smith Unofficial Fan Club.

Will Smith
Born: 25 Sep 1968, Philadelphia, Pa. Rodden Rating: C. Source: Biography.com. Romantic attachment: Jada Pinkett Smith.

Britney Spears
Born: 4 Dec 1981, 12:30:00 A.M. CST, Kentwood, La. Rodden Rating: C. Source: Astrology Path. Romantic attachment: Justin Timberlake.

Steven Spielberg
Born: 18 Dec 1946, 06:16:00 P.M., Cincinnati, Ohio. Rodden Rating: AA. Source: *Money, How to Find It with Astrology*, 1994. Romantic attachments: Kate Capshaw, Amy Irving.

Ringo Starr
Born: 7 Jul 1940, 00:05:00 A.M. GMD, Liverpool, U.K. Rodden Rating: B. Source: *American Book of Charts*, 1980. Romantic attachment: Barbara Bach.

Ben Stiller
Born: 30 Nov 1965, New York, N.Y. Rodden Rating: C. Source: The Internet Movie Database. Romantic attachment: Calista Flockhart.

Michael Stipe
Born: 4 Jan. 1960, Decatur, Ga. Rodden Rating: C. Source: The Internet Movie Database.

Barbra Streisand
Born: 24 Apr 1942, 05:08:00 A.M. EWT, Brooklyn, N.Y. Rodden Rating: A. Source: Astropro.com. Romantic attachments: James Brolin, Elliot Gould.

Elizabeth Taylor
Born: 27 Feb 1932, 02:00:00 A.M. GMT, London, U.K. Rodden Rating: A. Source: *Data News #10*. Romantic attachments: Richard Burton, Nicky Hilton, Eddie Fisher, Larry Fortensky, John W. Warner.

Emma Thompson
Born: 15 Apr 1959, London, U.K. Rodden Rating: C. Source: Biography. com. Romantic attachment: Kenneth Branagh.

Billy Bob Thornton
Born: 4 Aug 1955, Hot Springs, Ark. Rodden Rating: C. Source: Biography.com. Romantic attachment: Angelina Jolie.

Uma Thurman
Born: 29 Apr 1970, Boston, Mass. Rodden Rating: C. Source: Biography. com. Romantic attachment: Ethan Hawke.

Justin Timberlake
Born: 31 Jan 1981, 02:34:00 A.M. EST, Memphis, Tenn. Rodden Rating: C. Source: Astrology Path. Romantic attachment: Britney Spears.

Spencer Tracy
Born: 5 Apr 1900, 01:57:00 A.M. CST, Milwaukee, Wis. Rodden Rating: C. Source: AdZe MiXXe. Romantic attachment: Katharine Hepburn.

John Travolta
Born: 18 Feb 1954, 02:53:00 P.M. EST, Englewood, N.J. Rodden Rating: AA. Source: *Gauquelin Book of American Charts,* 1982. Romantic attachment: Kelly Preston.

Donald Trump
Born: 14 Jun 1946, 09:51:00 A.M. EDT, Queens, N.Y. Rodden Rating: A. Source: Astrodatabank. Romantic attachments: Ivana Trump, Marla Maples.

Ivana Trump
Born: 20 Feb 1949, Czechoslovakia. Rodden Rating: C. Source: Biography.com. Romantic attachment: Donald Trump.

Ted Turner
Born: 19 Nov 1938, 08:50:00 A.M. EST, Cincinnati, Ohio. Rodden Rating: AA. Source: *Gauquelin Book of American Charts,* 1982. Romantic attachment: Jane Fonda.

Liv Tyler
Born: 1 Jul 1977, Portland, Maine. Rodden Rating: C. Source: The Internet Movie Database.

Steven Tyler
Born: 26 Mar 1948, Yonkers, N.Y. Rodden Rating: C. Source: The Internet Movie Database. Romantic attachment: Bebe Buell.

Roger Vadim
Born: 26 Jan 1928, Paris, France. Rodden Rating: C. Source: *Today's Astrologer,* March 2000. Romantic attachment: Jane Fonda, Catherine Deneuve, Brigitte Bardot.

Eddie Van Halen
Born: 26 Jan 1955, Nijmegen, The Netherlands. Rodden Rating: C. Source: The Internet Movie Database. Romantic attachment: Valerie Bertinelli.

Vanity
Born: 4 Jan 1959, Niagara Falls, Canada. Rodden Rating: C. Source: The Internet Movie Database. Romantic attachment: Prince.

John W. Warner
Born: 18 Feb 1927, Washington, D.C. Rodden Rating: C. Source: Biography.com. Romantic attachment: Elizabeth Taylor.

Bruce Willis
Born: 19 Mar 1955, Idar-Oberstein, Germany. Rodden Rating: C. Source: Biography.com. Romantic attachment: Demi Moore.

Prince Charles Windsor
Born: 14 Nov 1948, 09:14:00 P.M. GMT, London, U.K. Rodden Rating: A. Source: *American Book of Charts*, 1980. Romantic attachment: Princess Diana Spencer Windsor.

Prince Henry Windsor
Born: 15 Sep 1984, London, U.K. Rodden Rating: C. Source: Royal.gov.uk

Princess Margaret Windsor
Born: 21 Aug 1930, Glamis, Scotland. Rodden Rating: C. Source: Biography.com. Romantic attachment: Anthony Armstrong-Jones.

Princess Diana Spencer Windsor
Born: 1 Jul 1961, 07:45:00 P.M. GMD, Sandringham, U.K. Rodden Rating: C. Source: Biography.com. Romantic attachment: Prince Charles Windsor.

Prince William Windsor
Born: 21 Jun 1982, 09:08:00 P.M. GMT, London, U.K. Rodden Rating: C. Source: FamousPeople.com

Oprah Winfrey
Born: 29 Jan 1954, 07:51:00 P.M. CST, Kosciusko, Miss. Rodden Rating: A. Source: ACT Online, 31 Jan 2000.

Evan Rachel Wood
Born: 7 Sep 1987, Raleigh, North Carolina. Rodden Rating: C. Source: The Internet Movie Database.

Dwight Yoakam

Born: 23 Oct 1956, 02:41:00 A.M. EST, Pikeville, Ky. Rodden Rating: C. Source: The Internet Movie Database. Romantic attachment: Bridget Fonda.

Catherine Zeta-Jones

Born: 25 Sep 1969, Swansea, U.K. Rodden Rating: C. Source: Biography. com. Romantic attachment: Michael Douglas.

Select Bibliography

Ashmand, J. M., trans. *Ptolemy's Tetrabiblos or Quadrapartite Being Four Books of the Influence of the Stars.* Chicago: The Aries Press, 1936.

Butler, Alan. *Tung Jen's Chinese Astrology.* Chippenham: Quantum, 1996.

Cornu, Philippe. *Tibetan Astrology.* Translated by Hamish Gregor. London: Shambala, 1997.

Doré, Henry. *Researches into Chinese Superstitions.* Vols. 1–5. Translated by M. Kennelly. Shanghai: T'usewei Printing Press, 1914–1918.

Dreyer, Ronnie Gale. *Vedic Astrology: A Guide to the Fundamentals of Jyotish.* York Beach: Samuel Weiser, 1997.

Dubin, Lois Sherr. *The History of Beads: From 30,000 B.C. to the Present.* New York: Harry N. Abrams, 1987; 1995.

Frazer, Sir James George. *The Golden Bough: A Study in Magic and Religion.* 3rd ed. Vols. I, II, III, IV, VI, IX, X, XI. London: Macmillan and Co., 1923–1926.

Fu, Shen. *Six Records of a Floating Life.* Translated by Leonard Pratt. Edited by Chiang Su-Hui. New York: Viking Press, 1983.

Gall, Timothy L., ed. *Worldmark Encyclopedia of Cultures and Daily Life.* Vol. 3. Detroit: Gale Research, 1998.

George, Ted. "Determining the Proper Age for Marriage." *Today's Astrologer* 59, no. 8.

Gröning, Karl. *Body Decoration: A World Survey of Body Art.* New York: The Vendome Press, 1998.

Hamilton, Lady Augusta. *Marriage Rites, Customs, and Ceremonies of All Nations of the Universe.* London: Chapple and Son, 1822.

Huon de Kermadec, Jean-Michael. *The Way to Chinese Astrology: The Four Pillars of Destiny.* Translated by N. Derek Poulsen. London: Unwin Books, 1983.

Hutchinson, H. N. *Marriage Customs in Many Lands.* London: Seeley and Co., 1897.

MacKay, Charles. *Extraordinary Popular Delusions and the Madness of Crowds.* London: Richard Bentley, 1841.

Sachau, Dr. Edward C. *Alberuni's India: An Account of the Religion, Philosophy, Literature, Geography, Chronology, Astronomy, Customs, Laws, and Astrology of India About A.D. 1030.* London: Kegan Paul, Trench, Trübner & Co., 1910.

Tsao, Hsueh-Chin and Chan Tsao. Translated by Florence and Isabel McHugh. *Dream of the Red Chamber: Hung Lou Meng: A Chinese Novel of the Early Ching Period.* Westport: Greenwood Publishing Group, 1975.

Wood, Edward J. *The Wedding Day in All Ages and Countries.* New York: Harper, 1869.

Index

Page numbers in boldface refer to celebrity birth data.

About the Authors

Anistatia Miller, ISAR CAP, RMAFA, is an astrologer who specializes in comparing and utilizing various forms of Eastern and Western astrology. She is a certified astrological professional of the International Society for Astrological Research and a research member of the American Federation of Astrologers. She teaches on-going classes in Chinese astrology at the Astrology Center of America.

Miller and her husband, Jared Brown, write the "Fusion Astrology" column for *Hamptons Magazine* and "In the Stars" for *Gotham Magazine*. And they told their love-at-first-sight story on an episode of WTN's *Best Places to Kiss*.

They have written articles on modern iconography for *Silicon Alley Reporter, Icon: Thoughtstyle Magazine, Adobe Magazine, Wine Spectator, Publish,* and *FoodArts*. They have also written more than a dozen books on subjects ranging from corporate trademarks and symbology in modern graphic design to the history of martinis.

Since 1992, they have lived in New York twice, Vancouver, San Francisco, and Boise. They currently live in Manhattan with their two nameless cats.